Linguistic Perspectives on
Second Language Acquisition

THE CAMBRIDGE APPLIED LINGUISTICS SERIES

Series editors: Michael H. Long and Jack C. Richards

This new series presents the findings of recent work in applied linguistics which are of direct relevance to language teaching and learning and of particular interest to applied linguists, researchers, language teachers, and teacher trainers.

Linguistic Perspectives on Second Language Acquisition

Edited by

Susan M. Gass

Michigan State University

Jacquelyn Schachter

University of Southern California

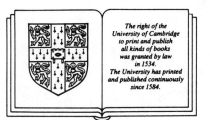

The right of the
University of Cambridge
to print and publish
all kinds of books
was granted by law
in 1534.
The University has printed
and published continuously
since 1584.

Cambridge University Press

Cambridge
New York   Port Chester
Melbourne   Sydney

Published by the Press Syndicate of the University of Cambridge
The Pitt Building, Trumpington Street, Cambridge CB2 1RP
40 West 20th Street, New York NY 10011, USA
10 Stamford Road, Oakleigh, Melbourne 3166, Australia

First published 1989
Second printing 1990

Printed in the United States of America

Library of Congress Cataloging-in-Publication Data

Linguistic perspectives on second language acquisition / edited by
Susan M. Gass, Jacquelyn Schachter.
p.   cm. – (The Cambridge applied linguistics series)
Includes index.
ISBN 0-521-37170-8 hardback.   ISBN 0-521-37811-7 paperback.
1. Second language acquisition.   2. Applied linguistics.
I. Gass, Susan M.   II. Schachter, Jacquelyn.   III. Series.
P118.2.L55   1989
418'.007 – dc19
                                                        89-451
                                                        CIP

British Library Cataloguing in Publication Data

Linguistic perspectives on second language
acquisition. – (The Cambridge applied
linguistics series)
1. Foreign language skills.   Acquisition
I. Gass, Susan M.   II. Jacquelyn Schachter
401.'9

ISBN 0-521-37170-8 hardback
ISBN 0-521-37811-7 paperback

Contents

Contributors

Josh Ard, University of Michigan, Ann Arbor
Robert Bley-Vroman, The University of Hawaii at Manoa
Suzanne Flynn, Massachusetts Institute of Technology, Cambridge
Susan M. Gass, Michigan State University, East Lansing
Kevin R. Gregg, St. Andrew's University, Osaka, Japan
Wesley Hudson, University of Southern California, Los Angeles
Juana M. Liceras, University of Ottawa
Jane Lowenstein Mairs, University of Texas at Austin
William Rutherford, University of Southern California, Los Angeles
Jacquelyn Schachter, University of Southern California, Los Angeles
Lydia White, McGill University, Montreal
Helmut Zobl, Carleton University, Ottawa

Series editors' preface

The Cambridge Applied Linguistics Series (CALS) seeks to publish theoretically motivated, data-based work in applied linguistics, especially work which succeeds in relating research and practice. *Linguistic Perspectives on Second Language Acquisition*, edited by Susan M. Gass and Jacquelyn Schachter, meets these specifications. It is a collection of original papers dealing with linguistically motivated studies of second language development, where implications can be drawn for the foreign and second language classroom.

The relationship between theoretical and applied linguistics has been both productive and stormy, nowhere more so than in language teaching. As might be expected, most useful collaboration has occurred when it has been recognized that insights about language and languages can inform us about part of what is to be taught, but that language is just one term in the equation, one element in a *psycho*-linguistic process. Who is to learn and how the learning takes place are equally important.

Allowing language analysis to determine teaching practice is to reduce applied linguistics to linguistics applied. Exporters of ideas, like everything else, need importers, too, however, and while some linguists have been guilty of assuming their findings were all that teachers needed to know, some applied linguists have been guilty of believing them. There is still a grain of truth to the saying, "When linguists sneeze, language teachers catch cold."

The growing maturity of applied linguistics as an interdisciplinary but autonomous field is reflected in the present volume. Drs. Gass and Schachter have assembled a fine collecton of papers written by leaders in the field. They provide a coherent introduction to the scope, methodology, findings, and implications of an important body of second language acquisition research – work that is not only of considerable relevance to language teaching, but which also contributes to developments in linguistic theory.

Michael H. Long
Jack C. Richards

Introduction

Susan M. Gass
Jacquelyn Schachter

Theories of how second languages are learned have been approached from a variety of perspectives: sociolinguistic, educational, neurolinguistic, psycholinguistic, linguistic. Each of these approaches brings to second language studies its goals, its data collection methods, and its analytic tools. Because of this diversity, it is often difficult for researchers from different traditions to communicate with one another or to fully appreciate the significance of the questions being addressed.

The purpose of this book is to elucidate these issues from a linguistic point of view, focusing in particular on the potential relationship between second language acquisition and linguistic theory. Thus, the papers represent a range of views on this relationship and describe a variety of linguistic theories. However, they all agree on the importance of grounding second language acquisition research within a theoretical framework that will illuminate the nature of language.

There are many ways of characterizing the relationship between a theory of language and a theory of second language acquisition. In the ideal situation, this relationship is, or should be, bidirectional. The theory will guide and constrain the hypotheses that the researcher is willing to entertain and test in considering both the course of language development and the ultimate knowledge to be attained. Conversely, particular language acquisition studies will provide empirical evidence for or against specific theoretical models. We hope that this book will clarify and hence shed light on these issues.

Linguistic theory and first language acquisition

In the field of first language acquisition, most linguists would agree that this notion of bidirectionality is, at least in principle, well-established. The issue of learnability, for example, has long been among the interests of grammatical theorists, whose goal has been to characterize adult grammatical competence, especially when considering the underdeterminate input available to the child and the limited amount of time it takes to reach adult competence. The notion of bidirectionality has

1

assumed even greater significance in recent theoretical developments within generative grammar (see work within the Chomskyan Government and Binding Model [e.g., Chomsky 1981, 1986], as well as Bresnan's [1978] work in lexical-functional grammar). Here the main idea is that learnability is one of the criteria for evaluating particular grammar models. In a complementary vein, language acquisition theorists have, both in their consideration of the input available to the child and in their hypothesized mechanisms for progressing from one developmental stage to another, leaned heavily on theory-specific conceptualizations of what it is the child must know innately (the initial state) and what it is the child must accomplish (the adult grammar), and thus the paths the child has to take to reach such knowledge (see Brown and Hanlon 1970; Braine 1971; Gleitman, Gleitman, and Shipley 1972; Culicover and Wexler 1977; Wexler and Culicover 1980; Hornstein and Lightfoot, 1981; Otsu 1981; Roeper 1982; Berwick and Weinberg, 1984; Hyams 1986). Tavakolian (1981, p. vii) clearly states the relationship between linguistic theory and child language acquisition.

Linguistic theory provides a general framework within which data from child language can fruitfully be analyzed. Theoretical considerations can unify otherwise disparate and seemingly unrelated data from language-acquisition studies to provide a uniform account of children's linguistic knowledge. Conversely, theories of language acquisition constrain proposals about adult grammars by requiring that adult grammars be learnable within a relatively short period of time, that theories of adult language be consistent with what is known about children's acquisition of language, and that the acquisition process not depend on impossible learning procedures.

As we shall point out, many of the same claims can be made for second language acquisition research.

The development of second language acquisition research

The claim that second language acquisition research should be guided by theoretical models and that it should address theoretical linguistic issues is not as well attested or accepted. Much work in second language acquisition has dealt with linguistic concepts in a more or less haphazard fashion, without a firm theoretical basis. One reason for this state of affairs comes from within the field itself. The initial impetus for studies of second language learning came from contrastive analysis, a well-established field with its own traditions and interests, and the emergence of error analysis, a discipline which developed in reaction to the unsubstantiated claims made by proponents of contrastive analysis regarding the sources of learner difficulty in second language learning. During the 1970s it became apparent that the study of second language acquisition was a viable topic of study in and of itself; its justification no longer came from the concerns of language pedagogy, as had been the case within the framework of contrastive analysis and error analysis. Instead, its justification came from the insights that it provided about the nature of the process of acquisition (see Perdue 1982; Ellis 1985; Sharwood Smith 1985).

Another reason for the reluctance to see the relevance of second language acquisition research as a source of illumination in the resolution of theoretical concerns comes from outside the field, and it arises from a basic misunderstanding of what second language acquisition researchers do. Second language acquisition is concerned with: (1) what is acquired of a second language; (2) what is not acquired of a second language; (3) the mechanisms which bring that knowledge (or lack thereof) about; and ultimately (4) explanations for this process in terms of both its successes and failures. Earlier work in the field of second language acquisition focused on acquisition from a pedagogical perspective, in the sense that the goals of research were ultimately to refine our knowledge about classroom practices. With such a focus, at least in the United States, second language acquisition (SLA) and English as a Second Language (ESL) were often considered to be one and the same discipline. But currently, most scholars engaged in second language acquisition research view the field as an autonomous discipline with its own set of questions and issues and its own research agenda and goals.

With regard to the pedagogical focus of second language acquisition, Pankhurst and Sharwood Smith (1985: editorial) state:

Such an endeavour is undoubtedly useful, but has led to a diminution of the more fundamental goal of understanding how a second language is acquired, of understanding how the language acquisition skills interact with other cognitive skills in the unique situation where the learner already has the advantage (or disadvantage) of a relative degree of conceptual maturity, and a fully implemented realization of Universal Grammar in his first language.

As is apparent from the chapters in this volume, the goals of linguistic-oriented second language acquisition research are not pedagogical; they do not directly impinge on questions of language pedagogy, language teaching methodology, or classroom behavioral studies. This lack of focus on pedagogical concerns does not come from the belief that these concerns are uninteresting or without value; instead, it stems from the belief that sound pedagogical practice must be anchored in in-depth knowledge of the capabilities of second language learners and the processes and strategies that they need for language learning to take place.

Linguistic theory and second language acquisition

Second language research has developed into an independent nonapplied discipline (see Sharwood Smith 1985), focusing on the sources of the learner's hypotheses about the target language, the paths the learner takes to reach ultimate proficiency, and the characterization of the knowledge underlying that ultimate proficiency. Thus, it comes as no surprise to find that in recent years there has been a surge of interest in the ways in which particular approaches to linguistic theory inform us about how second languages are learned. This is seen in work by Adjemian (1983), Bley-Vroman (in press), Felix (1985), Flynn (1983, 1987), Gass (1979, 1986), Hilles (1986), Rutherford (1983), Schachter (1988), van Buren and Sharwood Smith (1985), White (1985a, b), and Zobl (1986a, b). The guiding assumptions are exactly those of first language acquisition research – a theory of language acquisition must be constrained by knowledge of what a grammar consists of, and a grammar of a language must be something that humans are capable of constructing, given the general characteristics of the information available to the learner.

Granted, these beliefs must be justified by data that are of interest and relevance both to those involved in theory development as well as to those involved in discovering and characterizing the process of second language acquisition itself. While it is impossible to know what findings future research might produce, it *is* possible to characterize existing positions and to point out some of the areas of recent and/or current focus.

There are presently two major perspectives from which to view the relationship between theories of language and theories of second language acquisition: One involves claims regarding the impact of a theory of language on the development of a theory of second language learning, and the other involves claims regarding the use of second language data to test or develop a theory of language.

The first perspective, involving the impact of a linguistic theory on an acquisition theory, essentially contends that an adequate model of second language acquisition is quite impossible without a coherent theory of language, as Chomsky (1981) has argued in the case of first language acquisition research. We illustrate this position with a discussion of Universal Grammar (UG), since it is the theory most commonly applied to second language data. The fundamental claim of the first position is that characterizing the process of language acquisition is impossible without knowing what language consists of (see Chapter 1). So many of the abstract and complex properties of language cannot be determined from a mere inspection of utterances or surface sentences. The problem for acquisition is this: How do learners come to incorporate this abstract knowledge given that they are only exposed to surface structures? As regards child language acquisition, this problem is solved if one takes the position that these abstract principles are innate, not learned. Thus, it is assumed that children come into the world equipped with the principles necessary for language learning. The raw data to which they are exposed serve to establish the language specifics of a given abstract principle. In Chomsky's words:

UG is taken to be the set of properties, conditions or whatever that constitute the initial state of the language learner, hence the basis on which knowledge of language develops.

For second language learners, the situation of learnability is similar, but not identical. It is clear that the evidence learners have from the input is insufficient for the appropriate determination of second language grammars. And yet there must be some explanation of why second language learners do come up with grammars that are more complex than the data they receive would warrant. It is here that researchers using the UG paradigm appeal to an explanation similar to that which has been proposed for child language acquisition: Second language learners have access to universal principles – either indirectly, through the facts of their native language, or directly, in much the same way as do child first language learners. Thus, a theory of second language acquisition must elucidate the interaction between innate linguistic principles and input so as to explain how a learner can arrive at a grammar of the target language (see, for example, the work of Flynn 1983; Liceras 1983; White 1985a, b).

A weaker version of the first position would be that linguistic theory, or a particular linguistic model, while not essential for characterizing the process of second language acquisition, provides indirect insight into the nature of the knowledge of the second language. This indirect insight may serve as only a basis of comparison between the knowledge of the language eventually gained by the first, as opposed to the second, language learner. Bley-Vroman (in press) and Schachter (1988) are among the advocates of this position.

The second perspective, involving the relation between linguistic theory and second language acquisition data, argues that linguistic theory, because it is a theory of natural language, must be tested against second language data to be validated. Thus, any theory of language would be false if it failed to account for second language data. The underlying assumption is that a comprehensive theory of language must account for all language systems that involve human processing mechanisms. The strong position (as seen in the work of Gass 1979; Gass and Ard 1980; Eckman, Moravcsik, and Wirth, 1983) is that second language data can and should be used as evidence for distinguishing between linguistic theories, which, of course, attributes the power of falsification to second language data.

A more moderate position is that a coherent theory of language would be enhanced by evidence from second language data, although the theory itself is not intended to account for anything other than the facts of primary language acquisition and as a result cannot be falsified by second language data. Enhancement can be of many sorts. For example, second language data may shed light on the way native languages are organized (cf. Ritchie 1978; Kellerman 1979, 1983, 1987; Broselow 1988). In this vein, Kellerman has argued that the organizational structure an individual imposes on the native language is one of the factors that determines those aspects of the native language which can be transferred in a second language situation, and that knowledge of such organizational structure can only be determined from the study of second language learner strategies. Thus, by considering which aspects of one's native language are transferred in which language learning situations and which are not, one can gain insight into the ways humans organize language. Similarly, Broselow (1988), using phonological data from second language learners, contends that errors which can be argued to stem from the transfer of native language rules or principles "provide evidence for particular analyses of the native language grammar, evidence that may not be available from the study of the native language alone" (p. 295).

In another example, investigations of the ways learners handle conflicting and competing language data and the generalizations they then make can also shed light on language theory. An important difference between first and second language acquisition from the point of view of linguistic theory is that in second language acquisition, learners are confronted with the dynamic interplay of two (or more) linguistic systems. In fact, a central question of second language acquisition is concerned with the ways in which conflicting language information is ultimately resolved (see Bates et al. 1982; Gass 1986, 1987; Harrington 1987; McDonald 1987).

We expect that as the field of second language acquisition research develops, it will eventually become clear to all that the relationship between linguistic theory construction and second language acquisition research development is a symbiotic one and mutually beneficial. We believe that the authors of the articles in this volume have made significant contributions toward elucidating the benefits to be achieved.

References

Adjemian, C. 1983. The transferability of lexical properties. In *Language Transfer in Language Learning,* S. Gass and L. Selinker, eds. Rowley, Mass.: Newbury House.

Bates, E., S. McNew, B. MacWhinney, A. Devescovi, and S. Smith. 1982. Functional constraints on sentence processing: a cross-linguistic study. *Cognition* 11: 245–99.

Berwick, R., and A. Weinberg. 1984. *The Grammatical Basis of Linguistic Performance: Language Acquisition and Use.* Cambridge, Mass.: MIT Press.

Bley-Vroman, R. In press. The logical problem of foreign language learning. *Linguistic Analysis.*

Braine, M.D.S. 1971. On two types of models of the internalization of grammars. In *The Ontogenesis of Grammar: A Theoretical Symposium,* D. I. Slobin, ed. New York: Academic Press.

Bresnan, J. W. 1978. A realistic transformational grammar. In *Linguistic Theory and Psychological Reality,* M. Halle, J. Bresnan, and G. Miller, eds. Cambridge, Mass.: MIT Press.

Broselow, E. 1988. Metrical phonology and the acquisition of a second language. In *Linguistic Theory in Second Language Acquisition,* S. Flynn and W. O'Neil, eds. Dordrecht, The Netherlands: Kluwer.

Brown, R., and C. Hanlon. 1970. Derivational complexity and order of acquisition in child speech. In *Cognition and the Development of Language,* J. R. Hayes, ed. New York: Wiley.

Chomsky, N., 1981. *Lectures on Government and Binding.* Dordrecht, The Netherlands: Foris.

    1986. *Knowledge of Language: Its Nature, Origin, and Use.* New York: Praeger.

Culicover, P., and K. Wexler. 1977. Some syntactic implications of a theory of language learnability. In *Formal Syntax,* P. Culicover, T. Wasow, and A. Akmajian, eds. New York: Academic Press.

Eckman, F., E. Moravcsik, and J. Wirth. 1983. On interlanguages and language universals. Paper presented at Linguistic Society of America, Minneapolis, Minn.

Ellis, R. 1985. *Understanding Second Language Acquisition.* Oxford: Oxford University Press.

Felix, S. 1985. More evidence on competing cognitive systems. *Second Language Research* 1(1): 47–72.

Flynn, S. 1983. A study of the effects of principal branching direction in second language acquisition: the generalization of a parameter of Universal Grammar from first to second language acquisition. Ph.D. dissertation, Cornell University.

    1987. Contrast and construction in a parameter setting model of L2. *Language Learning* 37(1): 19–62.

Gass, S. 1979. Language transfer and universal grammatical relations. *Language Learning* 29(2): 327–44.

    1986. An interactionist approach to L2 sentence interpretation. *Studies in Second Language Acquisition* 8(1): 19–37.

    1987. The resolution of conflicts among competing systems: a bidirectional perspective. *Applied Psycholinguistics* 8(4): 329–50.

Gass, S., and J. Ard. 1980. L2 data: their relevance for language universals. *TESOL Quarterly* 14(4): 443–52.

Gleitman, L. R., H. Gleitman, and E. K. F. Shipley. 1972. The emergence of the child as grammarian. *Cognition* 1: 137–64.

Harrington, M. 1987. Processing transfer: language-specific processing strategies as a source of interlanguage variation. *Applied Psycholinguistics* 8(4): 351–78.

Hilles, S. 1986. Interlanguage and the pro-drop parameter. *Second Language Research* 2(1): 33–52.

Hornstein N., and D. Lightfoot, eds. 1981. *Explanations in Linguistics: The Logical Problem of Language Acquisition*. London: Longman.

Hyams, N. 1986. *Language Acquisition and the Theory of Parameters*. Dordrecht, The Netherlands: Reidel.

Kellerman, E. 1979. Transfer and non-transfer: where we are now. *Studies in Second Language Acquisition* 2(1): 37–57.

    1983. Now you see it, now you don't. In *Language Transfer in Language Learning*, S. Gass and L. Selinker, eds. Rowley, Mass.: Newbury House.

    1987. Aspects of transferability in second language acquisition. Ph.D. dissertation, Katholieke Universiteit of Nijmegen, The Netherlands.

Liceras, J. 1983. Markedness, contrastive analysis and the acquisition of Spanish syntax by English speakers. Ph.D. dissertation, University of Toronto.

McDonald, J. 1987. Sentence interpretation in bilingual speakers of English and Dutch. *Applied Psycholinguistics* 8(4): 379–413.

Otsu, Y. 1981. Universal Grammar and syntactic development in children: toward a theory of syntactic development. Ph.D. dissertation, Massachusetts Institute of Technology.

Pankhurst, J., and M. Sharwood Smith. 1985. Editorial. *Second Language Research* 1(1).

Perdue, C. 1982. *Second Language Acquisition by Adult Immigrants: A Field Manual*. Strasbourg: European Science Foundation.

Ritchie, W. 1978. The right roof constraint in adult-acquired language. In *Second Language Acquisition Research: Issues and Implications*, W. Ritchie, ed. New York: Academic Press.

Roeper, T. 1982. The role of universals in the acquisition of gerunds. In *Language Acquisition: The State of the Art*, L. Gleitman and E. Wanner, eds. Cambridge: Cambridge University Press.

Rutherford, W. 1983. Language typology and language transfer. In *Language Transfer in Language Learning*, S. Gass and L. Selinker, eds. Rowley, Mass.: Newbury House.

Schachter, J. 1988. Second language acquisition and its relationship to Universal Grammar. *Applied Linguistics* 9(3): 219–35.

Sharwood Smith, M. 1985. Preface. *Applied Linguistics* 6(3): 211–13.

Tavakolian, S. 1981. *Language Acquisition and Linguistic Theory*. Cambridge, Mass.: MIT Press.

van Buren, P., and M. Sharwood Smith. 1985. The acquisition of preposition stranding by second language learners and parametric variation. *Second Language Research* 1(1): 18–46.

Wexler, K., and P. Culicover. 1980. *Formal Principles of Language Acquisition*. Cambridge, Mass.: MIT Press.

White, L. 1985a. The acquisition of parameterized grammars: subjacency in second language acquisition. *Second Language Research* 1(1): 1–17.

    1985b. The "pro-drop" parameter in adult second language acquisition. *Language Learning* 35(1): 47–62.

Zobl, H. 1986a. A functional approach to the attainability of typological targets in L2 acquisition. *Second Language Research* 2(1): 16–32.

1986b. Word order typology, lexical government and the prediction of multiple, graded effects in L2 word order. *Language Learning* 36(2): 159–84.

PART I:
THEORIES OF ACQUISITION

The two chapters in this section deal with the relationship of second language acquisition to a theory of language. The first chapter, by Kevin Gregg, is concerned with general issues of that relationship, whereas the chapter by Robert Bley-Vroman takes a specific theory of language (Universal Grammar [UG]) and examines it within the context of second language learning.

Gregg's chapter looks at traditional concepts in the second language literature. Specifically, he points out that we must have a clear idea of the domain of inquiry of second language acquisition before attempting to construct a theory of it. He argues from a Chomskyan perspective that in characterizing second language knowledge, as in characterizing primary language knowledge, it is necessary to differentiate between competence and performance. Competence is the knowledge that we have about our language, knowledge which goes beyond what we produce, to include the recognition of ambiguities, ungrammatical utterances, and so forth. Thus, while as native speakers of English we know that a sentence such as "I saw the man that you met yesterday" is grammatical and are freely able to produce it, we also know that a sentence such as "I saw the man that you met him yesterday" is not standard English. Information about grammatical and ungrammatical sentences is included in what is called grammatical competence. Performance, on the other hand, refers to what we actually produce, or our linguistic behavior, and can be more closely aligned to ability. While one's performance in a second language clearly depends on one's knowledge of the second language, these two aspects of language are not identical.

Gregg claims that the domain of inquiry of second language acquisition research is to characterize the linguistic competence of second language learners. This being the case, he argues that such concepts as variability in L2 (second language) performance are beyond the scope of a theory of linguistic competence. Thus, to account for the acquisition of linguistic competence, one needs a theory of language, for we cannot understand the acquisition of something without an understanding of what that something is.

Gregg further takes the position that linguistic knowledge (i.e., grammar) is autonomous. That is, it is not a special instance of other kinds of knowledge. He argues against the opposite position, which is that language form cannot be studied independently of its function in discourse. While he contends that language form can and should be examined in terms of form alone, he also argues that grammar is not monolithic. Rather, it is a "module" that interacts with other modules, such as conceptual knowledge, pragmatic knowledge, and perception, and is governed by human processing constraints. The result of this interaction is *language*. Hence, the position that views grammar as interrelated with other areas and the position that finds form and function can be studied independently both view language as a result of interacting factors. The difference is the level at which that interaction takes place.

In sum, Gregg argues that we need a formal theory of language in order to deal with second language acquisition; we further need a theory whose formalisms are well established instead of terms or concepts that can be better described as ad hoc conventions adopted at a particular time to account for a specific set of data, which in his view do not provide an explanation. While Gregg views a formal theory of grammar as essential for understanding a theory of second language acquisition, he also points out that such a theory is not an end in itself but only a means of studying one aspect of language.

Bley-Vroman argues against the notion that adult second language learners have access to Universal Grammar. While acknowledging that the logical problem for adults in learning a second language (in his terms, *foreign* language) is the same as for children learning a first language, he also points out that there are differences in the two situations. The logical problem in both cases is explaining how, on the basis of limited data, learners of both (first and second languages) can arrive at grammars of a language. That is, there are many possible sentences in a language which a learner never hears. How do learners determine whether these sentences are not heard due to chance or are not heard because they are in fact ungrammatical sentences of that language? The sentences or utterances to which one is exposed comprise the positive evidence on which learners base a grammar. Negative evidence, on the other hand, is that information provided to a learner that an utterance or sentence is ungrammatical or is in some way deviant. Within a Universal Grammar framework, negative evidence is considered to be of little theoretical value. However, it is argued that a lack of negative evidence would make the task of learning impossible. It is then claimed that there is a language learning system (known as the language acquisition device [LAD]) that constrains the possible grammars. This system is comprised of principles of Universal Grammar.

Bley-Vroman argues against the position that adult and child language learning are fundamentally the same and rejects the notion that adults have access to principles of Universal Grammar. This is what he calls the *Fundamental Difference Hypothesis*.

He notes ten areas – including lack of success, variation in goals, indeterminate intuitions, significance of instruction, the role of negative evidence, and the role of affect – where adult second language learning is unlike child language learning, and where it shows greater similarity to general adult problem solving.

If adults do not have access to UG, what do they have access to in learning an L2? Bley-Vroman proposes that some universal principles are indeed available through a native language. Thus, learners come to the task of learning a second language with a set of assumptions about the nature of language. Clearly, some of these assumptions are correct *because* they are universal, while others are erroneously inferred as universal. Besides the significant role which Bley-Vroman attributes to the native language as a device through which universals can be inferred, he also emphasizes the problem-solving capability of adults, an ability young children do not have.

1 Second language acquisition theory: the case for a generative perspective

Kevin R. Gregg

The ultimate goal of second language acquisition research is the development of a theory of second language acquisition. I think there is fairly widespread agreement that no such theory exists;[1] beyond that rather minimal point, the consensus starts to dissolve. Once we get to questions about the likely nature of the theory we are seeking, we find all kinds of differences of opinion. What would a second language acquisition (SLA) theory look like if it existed? What would it explain? What kind of evidence would be legitimate to use in support of it? There has been disappointingly little said in explicit answer to these questions, and the field of second language acquisition research is the poorer for this lack of attention to what are, after all, fundamental questions. In what follows, I want to show how thinking about questions of this sort can help to straighten out some unfortunate and unnecessary confusions in the literature.

More specifically, I propose to take a closer look at the two key words in the term *second language acquisition*: *language* and *acquisition*. I will suggest how a particular approach to the study of the former could help us gain a more precise understanding of the latter. More specifically still, I will try to show that a linguistic theory of the kind perhaps currently best exemplified by Chomskyan generative grammar[2] could give us insights into SLA not available from other linguistic theories.

I am grateful to Lynn Eubank and Bruce W. Hawkins for comments on and criticisms of earlier versions of this paper. Some of the contents of this paper started as part of a presentation on theory construction in second language acquisition at the 1986 TESOL Summer Institute at the University of Hawaii; I would like to express my thanks to Michael H. Long for his kindness in inviting me to join him in that presentation.
1 Krashen (e.g., 1982, 1985) is evidently one exception to this consensus, but there are good reasons to believe that he is overly sanguine as to the status of his proposals (for detailed discussion see, *inter alia*, McLaughlin 1978, 1989; Gregg 1984, 1989; Spolsky 1985). Long (1985:11), in a rare and most welcome discussion of the problem of SLA theory construction, comments on the proliferation of " 'theories', 'models', 'perspectives', 'metaphors', 'hypotheses' and 'theoretical claims' in the SLA literature," noting that these terms "are generally used in free variation."
2 Please note the phrasing here; I am not making any claims about the superiority of Government-Binding Theory over other variants of generative grammar (e.g., Lexical-Functional Grammar). I am simply claiming – and this claim will be more than

15

Acquisition and theories of acquisition

I will start with the "A" of SLA: acquisition. Like so many other terms in the field, *acquisition* is in many ways infelicitous. It is important to remember – and surprisingly easy to forget – that when we talk about acquisition in SLA research, we are not talking about acquisition in the sense that one acquires polo ponies, Lladró figurines, or CBS, but rather in the sense that one acquires vicious habits, a taste for Brie, or a potbelly. We are talking, that is, about some sort of change in the organism resulting from its interaction with the environment. The change can be of greater or lesser permanence – the acquirer of a potbelly can, I fervently hope, *disacquire* it – but the use of the term does presuppose a minimum degree of stability. Thus one does not normally speak of the acquisition of a bloody nose or of bad breath.

I stress this point because I feel there is a great deal of unconscious, and not so harmless, reification of *acquisition* in the literature, especially in combination with an equally dangerous reification of *language* – in short, what Chomsky characterizes as the "incorrect metaphysical assumptions" that "among the things in the world there are languages or dialects, and that individuals come to acquire them" (in Paikeday 1985:49). It is necessary to separate the commonsense idea of language – which, like many commonsense ideas, serves us quite well in everyday life – from the idea of language as an object of scientific inquiry. The commonsense idea not only involves a degree of reification, it also contains, as Chomsky says, a

normative-teleological element that is eliminated from scientific approaches. ...Consider the way we describe a child or a foreigner learning English.... We do not, for example, say that the person has a perfect knowledge of some language L, similar to English but still different from it. What we say is that the child or foreigner has a "partial knowledge of English," or is "on his or her way" toward acquiring knowledge of English.... Whether or not a coherent account can be given of this aspect of the commonsense terminology, it does not seem to be one that has any role in an eventual science of language. (1986:16)[3]

In any case, if we are to arrive at a reasonable theory of second language acquisition (rather than simply doing SLA research), there are certain criteria we will have to meet above and beyond the normal criteria set for scientific theories in general. Atkinson (1982) addresses this problem in first language acquisition, and I think it is worth trying to extend

enough to tax my argumentative abilities – that the *kind* of theory represented by Government-Binding is a superior kind.
3 White (1982:2) makes this point explicitly in reference to first language acquisition: "I shall argue that the child's grammar must be seen as 'optimal' at all stages, that his or her grammar is correct for the data, as he or she perceives it."

his analysis to SLA theory as well. As Atkinson points out, for any acquisition theory we first need to identify a specific domain of inquiry (D); that is, we must identify what it is that we think is being acquired.

Once a domain is established, we then examine at least one subject on at least two occasions (t_1 and t_2) and the differences between t_1 and t_2 in D will be determined. If D is at all complex, we are going to need some sort of theory (T) of D to account for the content of D at t_1 and t_2 – ideally the same theory for each t. If D is going to represent anything like an actual language, then presumably we will want something like a linguistic theory, or rather a series of such theories T_1, $T_2 \ldots T_n$, for times t_1, $t_2 \ldots t_n$.

Atkinson sets other conditions for a successful acquisition theory (e.g., that the specific sequence of T_1, T_2, T_3, etc., rather than T_1, T_3, T_2, be explicable, or that a plausible mechanism be provided to explain the movement from one stage to another), but I am going to restrict myself to the problems of D and T, the domain of inquiry and the explanatory theory used in investigating that domain.

Behavior, ability, knowledge

Shapere (1977:533) makes a useful distinction between what he calls "domain problems" ("those problems which are concerned with the clarification of the domain itself") and "theoretical problems" ("problems calling for a 'deeper' account of the domain"; "answers to [the latter] are called 'theories' "). Depending on how one defines a domain, there may very well be important differences in, say, what will count as evidence for one's theory. This kind of difference can at times be simply a matter of the theoretician's specific goals, but domain problems can also be empirical ones. Before Copernicus, for example, astronomers did not feel any need to account for the behavior of comets, since comets were assumed to be sublunary phenomena and hence fell into the domain of meteorology (see Laudan 1977).

SLA researchers find themselves facing domain problems as well as theoretical problems. There is general agreement that SLA theory should be concerned with the acquisition of a second language. But what is it that is acquired when one has acquired a language?

If, for instance, like Searle (1969:17), one believes that "a theory of language is a part of a theory of action," then presumably one will claim that it is rules of behavior that are acquired. This position, which confuses language with speech, sometimes appears in the SLA literature, although usually implicitly rather than explicitly. One explicit example, however, is Tarone, who endorses the Observer's Paradox of Labov (1969) and extends it to interlanguage: "[T]he aim of (applied) linguistic research is to describe the way people talk when they are not being systematically observed" (1979:181).

The trouble with this concept of language is that it fails to distinguish between competence and performance. As has often been pointed out, acquisition of a language involves more than the acquisition of rules for the production of utterances. It involves the acquisition of knowledge, including knowledge that will never find expression in output: knowledge of ambiguity, anaphoric relations, possible versus impossible interpretations of sentences, possible versus impossible sentences, and so forth. Of course, some of our linguistic knowledge is not, strictly speaking, acquired; it is innate. It is this knowledge, acquired or innate, that I believe should be viewed as the domain of SLA theory. I am *not* saying that we should not study the linguistic behavior of learners – only that such behavior should not be made the goal of acquisition theory.

But even if we agree that we are interested in the acquisition of knowledge rather than behavior, we must be careful about the use of the term *knowledge*. There are two different distinctions that need to be made: the traditional distinction between knowing how and knowing that;[4] and the more recent (and controversial) distinction, introduced by Chomsky, between knowing that and *cognizing*.

To take the know/cognize distinction first, Chomsky (1975) introduced the nonce word *cognize* (in effect, "know") in order to clarify the distinction he has long made between the unconscious knowledge one has of one's language and the knowledge (knowledge that) traditionally conceived of as justified true belief. That is, one can say that I know that blue is the color of the sky because: (1) I believe it is the color of the sky, (2) it is in fact the color of the sky, and (3) my belief is justified, as can be demonstrated by my successful use of the word *blue* when referring to the color of the sky. On the other hand, my knowledge that *grue* type predicates (an object is *grue* if it is examined at time *t* and is green, or if it is not so examined and is blue [see Goodman 1983]) do not exist cannot be called justified true belief, since it is not a belief in the first place.[5]

Consider, for example, the following sentences:

1. John promised Mary to wash the dishes.
2. Max didn't lose his temper, but he could have done.

I *know* that these two sentences both are and are not grammatical. That is, as far as I am concerned they are both impossible sentences; I could

4 Sharwood Smith (1986) equates knowing how with performance, although he does not explicitly equate knowing that with competence. In any case, I am not making such an equation.
5 The traditional idea of knowledge as justified true belief has in any case been challenged (Gettier 1963), but the know/cognize distinction is still worth keeping in mind.

never produce them, except either as citation forms or as performance errors. Yet I also know that many (most?) English speakers find (1) perfectly acceptable, and that (2) is perfectly acceptable among many (most?) British English speakers. In other words, I have a justified true belief that the two sentences are grammatical (for other people), and I also *cognize* that they are not grammatical (for me). I want to stress that my *knowledge that* is basically accidental, and incidental to any interest as a researcher. I should also point out that I could make use of this *knowledge that* in the manner of a Krashenian Monitor user, producing utterances of these two types without ever *acquiring* them.[6] And to the extent that I did produce such sentences, I would be producing distorted data about my actual competence.

This brings us to the other distinction between kinds of knowledge – between knowledge that and knowledge how, or between knowledge and ability. This is an intuitively appealing, but not necessarily simple, distinction and one that is often clouded over in practice. For instance, I know the rules of chess; in that sense I may be said to know how to play, although anyone who watched me would be likely to dispute that claim. In other words, my ability to play chess is next to nil. But my knowledge of the rules of chess is pretty much the same as Bobby Fischer's. Thus, although in everyday usage I might say that I know how to play chess, strictly speaking (at least in terms of the distinction I am making here) I only know that, and barely know how. My knowledge of chess is not enough to lead to the actual performance of a real chess game, and yet the knowledge I have is essential for the playing of a game of chess.

Similarly, humans have knowledge of language quite apart from their ability to use that knowledge. As Chomsky (1975:23) says, "[I]t does not seem ... quite accurate to take 'knowledge of English' to be a capacity or ability, though it enters into the capacity or ability exercised in language use. In principle, one might have the cognitive structure that we call 'knowledge of English,' fully developed, with no capacity to use this structure." All kinds of different physical or emotional problems might render someone incapable of producing or comprehending speech or writing, without altering the content of that person's knowledge in the least. To use the analogy made by Kean (1981), if someone were to glue the pages of your dictionary together, you would not be able to look up the meaning of *passacaglia*, but the information would still be there. Our linguistic ability rests primarily, but not exclusively (as we shall see later) on our linguistic knowledge; but it is not identical to that knowledge.

---

6 If I understand Comrie (1984a) correctly, as far as Sentence (1) goes I am in the mortifying position of having become fossilized in the use of my native language!

Competence

The question thus becomes one of choosing between ability and knowledge as the domain of SLA theory. First language acquisition theory (see, e.g., Wexler and Culicover 1980; Pinker 1984; Berwick 1985) has generally taken the acquisition of knowledge as its domain; the term generally employed for one's linguistic knowledge (innate and acquired) is *competence*. In SLA research, too, the term "competence" is frequently used, but unfortunately the distinction between ability and knowledge has all too often been blurred, with a concomitant loss of clarity and coherence.[7]

Take, for instance, the so-called Variable Competence Model (Tarone 1984; Ellis 1985). Researchers working within this framework address themselves to the question of variability in the output of L2 learners, not so much the variability among learners but instead the variability within the output of any single learner, depending on the task or situation. Ellis (1989) correctly notes that from a generative perspective such variability would be treated as a performance question. He then goes on, however, to contrast that perspective with a sociolinguistic one, "which emphasizes the *systematic* way in which learner behaviour is influenced by context. In other words, variability is now seen to be an integral feature of competence" (emphasis in original). Here we have two confusions: performance ("learner behaviour") is argued to be a feature of competence (knowledge), and systematicity is evidently seen as a sufficient condition for qualifying something as being part of competence. Having merged performance and competence, it is easy to go on to claim that the learner's competence is heterogeneous. But this misuses the term "competence"; "heterogeneous competence" is simply a contradiction in terms.[8]

Tarone (1984) uses the term "capability continuum" to refer to her SLA paradigm, explicitly avoiding the use of "competence." So far so good, but what is capability? "The learner's IL [interlanguage] capability is that which underlies, or guides, the regular language behavior of the second language learner.... [It] is made up of a continuum of styles" (1984:13). But this, if it is not simply a category error (a capability is not made up of styles), tells us nothing about what that capability and those styles consist of. And to claim that the capability continuum paradigm "maintains the same distinction between underlying IL capability and IL behavior that [the generative paradigm] maintains between competence and performance" (1984:14) is to discard the essential distinc-

7 Sharwood Smith has probably done the most to try to clarify the concepts of competence and performance as they relate to SLA (see especially 1981, 1986).
8 We must distinguish heterogeneous competence from multiple competences; I will argue for the latter further on.

tion between performance and competence in exchange for little beyond terminological confusion.

A glance at some of the IL data that led to this confusion may give us an idea of just what went wrong. For instance, Tarone cites data from Schmidt (1980) to the effect that L2 learners of English performed systematically differently, according to task, with regard to gapped sentences of the form, *Mary is eating an apple and Sue a pear.* Such sentences never appeared in free oral production; they were successfully imitated 11 percent of the time; they were produced in sentence-combining writing tasks 25% of the time; and 50 percent of the subjects accepted such sentences as grammatical. Tarone asks how we are to account for this "continuum"; her answer is that there is a continuum of styles underlying the continuum of data and adds, "[T]hat portion of the continuum which underlies a particular instance of regular learner performance is determined primarily by the degree of attention which the learner pays to language form in that instance" (1984:14). Whatever this might mean, we certainly have not replaced the "homogeneous competence paradigm" – that is, the performance/competence distinction – with a more "constrained" (p. 17) paradigm. If there is a continuum of styles, and no principled limit to their number, then we have made the acquisition of a grammar by a learner immensely more difficult.

Tarone (1984:15) herself gives an indication of just how difficult when she says, "The various styles of the IL may be described and related to one another in terms of a set of underlying variable and categorical rules." A variable rule, according to Labov (1972), is a rule whose output varies according to context. The question is, how is one to *acquire* a variable rule? Tarone acknowledges the problem and backs off from her statement about rules by saying, "The 'rules' referred to here in [the capability continuum paradigm] are perhaps better viewed as 'regularities' in the sense that they describe patterns in observed behavior which are regular, and do not make claims about 'what the learner is doing' because he 'knows' a form is 'right' " (1984:22, fn. 10). *But to say this is to admit that the capability continuum paradigm explains nothing whatever.* Variable rules are descriptive rules, expressing statistical generalizations about a given speech community. Since Tarone explicitly (and properly) rejects the concept of IL speakers as a speech community (1984:22), it is not at all clear to me why she wants to make use of variable rules in the first place. But in any case, they will not be of use in explaining acquisition since such rules cannot, by their very nature, be acquired.[9]

9 Ellis (1985) also discusses variable rules, but does not commit himself to them. Bialystok and Sharwood Smith (1985) criticize the use of variable rules, but mainly because they believe it blurs over the distinction they want to make between diachronic and synchronic variability. I find this objection of limited relevance.

I suggest that instead of asking Tarone's question – how are we to account for the variability in such data as Schmidt's? – we ask another: Do we need to account for such variability? Look again at those data; when is the last time you said something like "Mary ate an apple and Sue a pear"? Yet you know the sentence is grammatical. So in our case we would have a continuum ranging from something near 0 percent to something very near 100 percent, with the imitation and sentence-combining figures somewhere in between. Is it necessary to explain this continuum within an *acquisition* theory? I know why I do not produce utterances like "Mary ate an apple and Sue a pear"; I do not produce them because I think they sound incredibly affected, and I have enough problems of that sort already. On the other hand, if I were to score less than perfect on the elicited imitation task, as I imagine would be the case, I might appeal to some sort of processing model in which one keeps propositional content in memory but discards specific structural information. But I would not try to account for these different results with an acquisition theory. In other words, I would flatly reject Tarone's claim that "the phenomenon of systematic variability in the utterances produced by second language learners as they attempt to communicate in the target language" is a "phenomenon which must be accounted for by any theory of second language acquisition" (p. 3).

It is not that the data on variability are necessarily uninteresting or unworthy of study. But if we are careful to establish the domain of a theory of second language acquisition so that it is confined to the acquisition of linquistic competence, then we will not be compelled to account for those data on variability as far as that theory is concerned; and by ignoring them we can avoid the conceptual contradictions and confusions exemplified in such terms as "heterogeneous competence" or "capability continuum."

A competence theory, as Pylyshyn (1973:24) says, "differs from a performance theory in two principal respects: its goal is to characterize mental representations rather than observed behavior, and it is based primarily on a somewhat different class of evidence." The evidence Pylyshyn refers to is the intuitions of the competent subject – in our case, the language learner. "The term 'intuition' is used here because it traditionally suggests a knowledge which is not mediated by rational processes, is self-justifying, and is accompanied by strong conviction" (1973:30).[10]

Of course, as Pylyshyn also says, in the typical case of a competence theory (such as generative grammatical theory), the subject whose in-

---

10 Notice that Pylyshyn (1973) says "intuition," not "introspection." Later he makes this distinction explicit: "[T]he empirical world with which [linguistics and mathematics] deal is a world of mental structures which are explored via the intuitions (not introspections) of experimenter-subjects" (p. 31).

tuitions are being examined is at the same time the investigator. In the case of an acquisition theory, however, we are going to have to be more indirect in our approach. And as Ellis (1989) correctly reminds us, it is by no means clear what the best method is for determining what an L2 learner's intuitions are.[11] But no one said it would be easy. In first language acquisition theory it is even harder to get intuition data from subjects, but that has not kept theorists of competence acquisition from maintaining that "grammatical rules themselves seem to be the natural domain for an acquisition theory" (Pinker 1984:22) or from devising methods for inferring the presence of such rules among such subjects' mental representations. If we take the concept of competence seriously, we will have to recognize the primacy of intuitions; how we go about determining those intuitions is another matter, about which we cannot afford to be dogmatic.

I have been restricting my discussion of competence to grammatical competence. But this is not the only kind of competence that a language learner makes use of. Chomsky himself suggests the existence of a separate "pragmatic competence" that "underlies the ability to use [grammatical competence] along with the conceptual system to achieve certain ends" (1980:59). And the SLA literature overflows with references to "communicative competence." In principle, there is nothing whatever improper about investigating the acquisition of such competences. But most discussions of "communicative competence" in the SLA literature ("pragmatic competence" is less often mentioned) suffer from the earlier mentioned confounding of competence with ability.[12]

A competence-based approach to cognition "claims that underlying

---

11 Lightbown (1984) thinks that grammaticality judgment tests and comprehension tests are the most appropriate for research within a competence framework, and specifically that they are superior to elicited imitation or free production tasks. This is not, however, a foregone conclusion. Working within a Chomskyan framework, Hilles (1986), for example, on the basis of an analysis of data from Cancino, Rosansky, and Schumann (1978) – including spontaneous speech data – draws conclusions about the effect of the pro-drop parameter on SLA.

Nor do I share Lightbown's confidence that such tests "assur[e] the researcher that the relevant linguistic structure has been the basis for judgement or comprehension because the sentence has been removed from any non-linguistic context which might affect its interpretation" (1984:242). Things should only be so clear-cut. Carden (1973), for instance, while studying the interpretation of negative sentences containing quantifiers, had to reject the responses of 4 out of 48 native-speaker informants because they considered tag questions ungrammatical! Carden was lucky to have been told the reason for rejection; it is not always so easy.

12 In a thoughtful discussion of this problem, Canale and Swain (1980) endorse the claim that grammatical competence is included in communicative competence, since they wish to preclude the possibility that grammatical competence is not essential for communicative competence. But this confuses, once again, language with communication. In fact, grammatical competence is not essential for communication, if that communication is not linguistic.

all cognitive activity is a more perfect system than that displayed by the record of behavior itself" – this, of course, is the standard competence/performance distinction – "and furthermore that this system can be adequately characterized by a set of formal logical rules; indeed, that to understand cognition at all in the scientific sense *is* to describe it in terms of such a formal system" (Pylyshyn 1973:31). When, for instance, Pinker talks about children acquiring grammatical rules, he is talking about precisely such a formal system. The problem is that we have as yet no such formal system to characterize pragmatic or communicative competence. Once again, I am not suggesting that investigations into the pragmatics of second language use are misguided, incoherent, beside the point, or anything like that. I *am* saying that in comparison with an attempt to construct a theory of acquisition in the domain of grammar, any attempt to construct a theory of acquisition in the domain of pragmatics or communication is going to be handicapped by the lack of a well-articulated formal characterization of the domain. As Wexler and Culicover (1980:596, n. 10) state: "If a sufficiently precise theory of what is achieved does not exist, we cannot evaluate (or even do a reasonable job of creating) a theory of the learning of the achievement." In the area of grammatical competence we do have such theories, and to this area I now want to turn. It is time to look at the "L" of SLA.

Language and linguistic theory

Having fixed our domain as the acquisition of linguistic competence, we now need a linguistic theory to account for that competence, as opposed to its acquisition. (Let me remind the reader that I am ignoring the whole problem of the actual mechanism that governs the process of acquiring linguistic competence.) On the one hand, it is fruitless to want an overall theory of language at this point, since none exists; what we refer to as "language" in everyday speech (or even, often enough, in technical literature) is far too general and all-encompassing a phenomenon to likely be amenable to description by a single theory. On the other hand, we do want something more than a bunch of mini-theories – of negation, of dative movement, of vowel reduction, and so forth – to account for the various phenomena found in a language. These would get us no further than the so-called set of laws type of theory (see Long 1985), if "theory" is in fact the correct word.

What we need, minimally, is a theory of grammar. Moreover, we will need a grammatical theory that sees linguistic competence as both *autonomous* and *modular*. These two terms, as Newmeyer (1983) points out, indicate the two defining characteristics of a generative grammar of the sort proposed by Chomsky. Since I began by arguing for a Chomskyan perspective, it is no accident that I should now argue for autonomy and modularity. But of course these terms require some explanation, and equally, of course, my claim requires some justification.

By *autonomy* I mean that grammatical competence – one's knowledge ("cognition") of the syntax, phonology, and (within certain limits) semantics of a language – is a separate mental system. Its "primitive terms are not artifacts of a system that encompasses both human language and other human facilities or abilities" (Newmeyer 1983:2). Thus, grammatical knowledge is not simply a special case of more general knowledge. By *modularity* I mean that grammar, while autonomous, is not isolated from other mental systems, nor is it monolithic and undifferentiated. Instead, what we call "language" in everyday usage is the result of the interaction of grammar with other mental systems – conceptual knowledge, pragmatic knowledge, perception, etc. – each of which constitutes a *module*.[13] Let us look at these two ideas in turn in greater detail.

Autonomy

One consequence of an autonomy position is that it denies the reducibility of grammar to something else. Reductionist explanations attempt to show that phenomenon X is nothing more than a special case of phenomenon Y, and that X is thus explained if Y is explained. Kuhn suggests that "as a science develops, it employs in explanations an ever increasing number of irreducibly distinct forms" (1977a:30). If this is indeed the case, the popularity of reductionism among second language acquisition researchers may be an index of the progress we have made.[14]

Perhaps the best example of a reductionist explanation of language acquisition is Skinner (1957), who sees the acquisition of language as nothing more than a special case of operant conditioning, in principle no different from learning to tie one's shoelaces or to avoid touching burning objects. The day is long past when anyone in language acquisition research took Skinner seriously, but other reductionist positions are still quite highly regarded. Those who appeal to Piagetian theories, for instance, usually claim, even if only implicitly, that language acquisition is simply a special case of general cognitive development, and that there is one human cognitive system that is uniform and omnicompetent in all cognitive domains.

But probably the most common anti-autonomy positions are those

13 The idea of modularity, which in some ways goes back to the "faculty psychology" of Gall, was revived (and, needless to say, revised) by Chomsky and by Jerry A. Fodor (for a detailed discussion, see Fodor 1983).

14 See Fodor (1978) for a discussion of the problem of reduction in psychological explanation.

which view language primarily as a form of communication. I am think-ing of what are variously called *discourse-based* or *discourse-functional* approaches, or what Long and Sato (1984) characterize as *function to form* approaches, and what I am tempted to refer to simply as *holistic* approaches. The basic line goes something like this: You can't under-stand a sentence / talk about language / study language acquisition / construct a grammar, etc., etc., in a vacuum / apart from its sociolin-guistic setting / except as a communicative process / while ignoring function, etc., etc. Foley and Van Valin, for instance, insist that "lan-guage must be studied in relation to its role in human communication" and that "one cannot understand form independent of function" (1948:7,9). Givón (1985), attacking Chomsky's idea of autonomy, ar-gues that a biologist, for example, would never dream of ignoring the function of a given structure while concentrating solely on its form. (And yet just such an emphasis on form over function contributed greatly to the development of Darwinian theory; see Kuhn 1977b.) In SLA, Ruth-erford considers one of the "very serious flaws" of the "product-oriented approach" to have been "the assumption that language form could be studied independent of language function" (1984:130).[15]

At first this sort of argument may sound plausible. But in fact language does not have to be studied in relation to its role in communication any more than digestion has to be studied in relation to its role in human socialization. For example, one might wish to explain my stomachache while in Japan by appealing to the peer-group bonding process in Jap-anese society and its requirement that one join one's fellows in consuming vast quantities of whiskey, but I would expect something rather different from a physiologist.

And (*pace* Foley and Van Valin 1984) one *can* understand form in-dependent of function; however, function is not enough to explain form. When Kumpf (1984:132), for instance, asserts that "any grammatical form appears to fill a function in the discourse: it is the discourse context which creates the conditions under which the forms appear, and in order to explain the forms, it is necessary to refer to this context," she is making a claim that is much too strong to be tenable.[16] What, for instance, is the discourse function of grammatical gender, or third person singular -*s*, or vowel harmony?

The holistic position rests on a failure (or rather a refusal) to separate

15 Rutherford is being rather inconsistent here, since he goes on to report – favora-bly, so far as I can tell – on research conducted within the framework of Govern-ment-Binding Theory, which makes a point of investigating form independent of function.

16 She is also, it is worth noting, confusing competence and performance. Context may explain the *appearance* of a form, but not its existence.

form from function, grammar from communication. Sperber and Wilson
(1986:173–74) put the point forcefully:

[A] language...is a grammar-governed representational system.... [T]he
property of being a grammar-governed representational system and the property of being used for communication are not systematically linked. They are
found together in the odd case of human natural languages, just as the property of being an olfactory organ and the property of being a prehensile organ, though not systematically linked in nature, happen to be found together
in the odd case of the elephant's trunk.... [I]t is as strange for humans to
conclude that the essential purpose of language is for communication as it
would be for elephants to conclude that the essential purpose of noses is for
picking things up.

We cannot escape from grammar; no matter how hard we try to
subsume it under some other category like "communication" or "discourse function," it just won't go away. Consider the following
sentences:

3a. Who did you believe that the woman met in town?
 b. *Who did you see the woman that met in town?

(from Lightfoot 1982)

4a. *The man who I saw the dog that bit fell down.
 b. ?The man who I saw the dog that bit him fell down.

(from Newmeyer 1983)

It might appear at first that the difference in acceptability between the
(a) and (b) sentences in each pair could be attributed to processing
difficulties; that is, instead of a grammatical rule blocking (3b) or (4a),
there is a discourse-related problem of interpretation. Thus, by inserting
the resumptive pronoun in (4b) the sentence becomes communicatively
more acceptable, making it (closer to) a grammatical sentence. However,
if this were the case, Sentence (5) should be more acceptable than (3b):

5. *Who did you see the woman that met him in town?

Yet (3b) and (5) are equally unacceptable, which suggests, in this case
at least, that something other than a discourse-based explanation is
necessary.

Obviously, "mere" grammar is not all there is to language; if it were,
phrases like "Void Where Prohibited" would cause a lot more trouble
than they do. But grammar is essential, and it cannot be reduced away
to communication or discourse function. Of course, many linguists
interested in functional explanations recognize this (e.g., Comrie 1984b;
Kuno 1987). The problem in SLA is that too many researchers have
tended to take the holistic position as a truism, without noticing the
dangers lurking therein.

There is one more problem with the holistic approach to second language acquisition, and it is a big one: *Functional theories cannot explain the acquisition of competence.* Knowing what the liver does may explain why I have a liver (or at least why I should be grateful to have one); it does not explain how I came to have one. By the same token, knowing what functions are served by, say, topicalization may explain why English has devices for topicalizing; it does not say anything about how I came to acquire those devices. As Foley and Van Valin (1984:20–21), themselves functional theorists, point out, "none of the functional theories of UG [Universal Grammar] thus far proposed are primarily concerned with explaining language acquisition, and accordingly they are not psychological theories." But if we are to take as the domain of our theory the *acquisition* of *competence* – that is, the change over time in the mental state of the learner – then our acquisition theory is by definition a psychological one. And if that is the case, it would seem that no discourse-based linguistic theory, no matter how interesting, plausible, or cogent, could be expected to have a direct role to play in the construction of our acquisition theory.[17]

Modularity

Thus, it seems we cannot deny the existence of an autonomous grammatical component to language. On the other hand, we do not want to claim that grammar includes everything there is in language any more than we would want to claim that digestion includes such things as neurotic dispositions to overeat. There will be all kinds of occasions when we will definitely know ("cognize"), for example, that such and such a sentence is impossible, but will not want to account for the impossibility by positing a grammatical rule. Center-embedded relative clauses, to take a frequently cited example, are extremely hard to understand or produce:

6. The cheese the rat the cat the boy petted killed ate stank.

Here, unlike the case of Sentences (3) and (4), it seems intuitively plausible to posit some sort of processing constraint, especially since center-embedded relative clauses are not always impossible, and since a grammatical rule limiting the number of possible embeddings would be an undesirable complication of the grammar.

---

17 Long and Sato (1984:276) touch on this problem in their discussion of "collaborative discourse": "That the collaborative/scaffolding phenomenon exists is undeniable. What is still highly controversial is its role, if any, in language acquisition." But whereas they take an agnostic position, and even then only with one type of discourse "strategy," I am making a much broader, negative claim.

Or, to take an example suggested by Lightfoot (1982), consider the following sentences:

7a. John must study every day.
  b. John must study every day, and so must Mary.

The first sentence is ambiguous in two ways: Either John is obliged to study or else it is highly likely that he does. But (7b), where two identically ambiguous sentences are conjoined, is not ambiguous in four ways; a reading where John is obliged to study while Mary no doubt does so is not possible. This seems to be a general fact about ambiguous sentences, and indeed this so-called do-so test is often used to check for ambiguity (see Zwicky and Sadock 1975). The question is: How do we account for this general fact? One possible solution would be to add some sort of statement of the do-so test to the grammar. This would appear to be extremely difficult, however, especially since the test does not always work. Thus it might be necessary to add the do-so information to the grammar at each point (lexical item or syntactic construction) where it is pertinent. But even if we could work out a rule limiting ambiguous readings, it would be a complicated rule, to say the least.

Lightfoot (1982) suggests a modular way out. He notes that the same sort of phenomenon occurs in visual perception: When two identical Necker cubes (a Necker cube is a cube drawn only in outline and that can be seen only from above and diagonally) are placed side by side, it is virtually impossible to see them as being differently oriented one from the other. He suggests that the same perceptual strategy applies to interpreting ambiguous sentences as to seeing the Necker cubes; the grammar can be allowed to generate "crossed" interpretations, and these interpretations will be blocked by an extragrammatical principle.

There are two good reasons to prefer the modular solution. First of all, the perceptual rule already has independent support (i.e., in the field of perception), which suggests that it is not an ad hoc solution. More important, a grammatical do-so rule would complicate the grammar just as a rule that counts embeddings would; if our goal is to account for acquisition, we need to keep our rules as simple as possible and still have them consistent with the facts, since these rules must be learnable. The idea of modularity is a way of doing this: The complexity of language can (it is hoped) be explained as the outcome of interactions between various combinations of comparatively simple systems.

What's in it for us?

So far I have tried to show that an SLA theory should be concerned (centrally, at least) with the acquisition of linguistic competence, and that in order to talk about linguistic competence we need a linguistic theory that makes use of the concepts of autonomy and modularity. Thus, I am claiming that a generative theory of grammar is a necessary component of a theory of second language acquisition. I now want to show how such a theory is not only necessary, but also useful, even to those of us whose primary concern is not generative linguistic theory or the acquisition of competence.

First of all, it adds rigor to SLA theory. Generative grammar is a formal theory, and its formality is one of its major strengths.[18] Remember that it is, in Pylyshyn's words, "a set of formal logical rules" that characterizes a cognitive system (including grammar), or indeed any physical system. And since we want to characterize the competence acquired by a second language learner (as well as the process of acquiring that competence), we will need formalisms. No one, I trust, would think of talking about interlanguage phonology without using phonetic symbols and formal phonological rules: why should so many people be so anxious to talk about interlanguage syntax without syntactic rules? Clearly, there are still areas of linguistic competence that have so far resisted characterization by a system of formal rules, and in these areas we must make do for the time being with description and explanation at a less precise level, but that in no way alters the fact that the ideal competence theory will be a formal one. Formalisms, in short, are Good Things.

This seems to be quite a minority view in the second language acquisition field. Far too many holists, implicitly or explicitly, seem to share the horror of "forbidding formalisms" expressed by Givón (1985:83). Indeed, among a large number of discourse researchers there seems to be no need felt for a theory of any sort, and in fact the lack of one seems to be regarded as a plus. But in the absence of any formal rules and in the absence of research guided by a commitment to devising such rules, all we can hope for is informal description. And that, by and large, is all we get in the discourse-analysis type of SLA research; to read a typical piece of SLA "discourse analysis" is to be reminded of Bernard Shaw's parody of "technical analysis" in music criticism.[19]

---

18 Formality, however, is not enough to distinguish generative grammar from all other grammatical theories; Montague grammar, for instance, is also a formal theory. However, Montague grammar, unlike generative grammar, is not concerned with the problem of acquisition.

19 Analyzing Hamlet's famous soliloquy in the manner of a "technical analyst," Shaw writes: "Shakespeare, dispensing with the customary exordium, announces his subject at once in the infinitive, in which mood it is presently repeated after a short connecting passage in which, brief as it is, we recognize the alternative and negative forms on which so much of the significance of repetition depends. Here we reach a colon; and a pointed pository phrase, in which the accent falls decisively on the relative pronoun, brings us to the first full stop" (quoted by Edward Rothstein in the *New York Review of Books* 29:5 [1 April 1982], p. 31).

Actually, in the absence of a formal theory, we get not only informal description, but also a proliferation of terminology, either produced ad hoc ("creative construction," Krashen's "output filter" [1985], Tarone's "capability continuum," the various "competences," etc.; my favorite invention is "semantic clout") or imported unthinkingly from other disciplines; added to this are a lot of flow charts and diagrams.[20] In the absence of a theory we run the risk of getting mired in sterile taxonomies that, however plausible or locally useful, are not constrained by any principle. Schachter (1984), for instance, basing herself partly on a classification proposed by Long (1981),[21] proposes the following two response types, among others, along with examples of each:

clarification requests
child: Read to me a book.
adult: What?
child: Read a book to me.

"recognized failures" to understand
NNS: Um in Harvard, what you study?
NS: What?
NNS: What you es study?

In each case, the response type is exemplified by the utterance of "What?" Now, the presence of what looks like the same item in two different categories is not necessarily a problem. If we had a way of making principled distinctions among response types – in other words, a theory of conversational responses – we might be able to justify the separation of "what" from "what." But we don't, and so we can't.

A similar problem besets research that makes use of such concepts as "language typology" and "typological universal" (see Greenberg 1978). Take, for example, the finding of Schachter and Rutherford (1979; Rutherford 1983) that sentences like (8) through (10) reflect the *topic-comment* organization of the native languages of the learners who wrote them (Mandarin, Mandarin, and Japanese, respectively):

8. These ways almost can classify two types.
   [i.e., can be classified into two types]
9. A man choose a wife is a man's business.

20 See Schumann (1984) for some samples of different SLA "models" taken from the literature. Schumann seems to think that the distinctions between the models are essentially aesthetic, and that there really is no fact of the matter involved; I think there is. "The fictionalist view of theories," as Harré (1972:81) says, "... is particularly common when there is some kind of crisis in a science where the current theories are many, and there seems to be no way of resolving the issue between them." My point is that there is a way of resolving the issue.

21 Her use of Long's classification may not be warranted, since she is talking about negative input, whereas Long's terms pertain to forms of interaction, which he explicitly distinguishes from input. This may, of course, be simply one more terminological problem.

10. In my country, hasn't army, navy and air force.

(from Rutherford 1983)

As far as I can tell, this is a genuine insight. But what can it tell us about acquisition? Unfortunately, given the undeveloped state of the construct *topic*, not a great deal. Rutherford (1983) follows Li and Thompson's (1976) idea of *topic prominence* and *subject prominence*, distinguishing Mandarin (topic prominent), English (subject prominent), and Japanese (topic and subject prominent).[22] But as Li himself points out (1976), there is no agreed upon definition of topic to guide our categorizations. Thus, there is no theory of topic-comment grammar available to account for, say, a Mandarin-speaking learner's competence at t_n, and hence no way to account for, or even adequately describe, the change from topic-comment grammar to subject-predicate. Unless and until we have such a theory, the facts unearthed by Schachter and Rutherford about the output of Mandarin, Korean, and Japanese learners will remain resistant to assimilation into a theory of second language acquisition.

Greenbergian universals, like Labovian variable rules, are basically statistical in nature: They state that phenomenon X occurs with frequency Y among the languages of the world.[23] But typological generalizations are either uninteresting (no language has labiovelar stops) or interesting only in the questions they raise, not in the answers they provide. Thus, when Gass and Ard (1984:33) ask, "[W]hat can we expect the influence of language universals to be on the acquisition process...?", my answer is, "Probably none." What the learner has to work with is input (definitely), plus (hypothetically) her acquired and innate competence. A learner might gain some knowledge of these universals (she could read Greenberg, for instance), but that knowledge certainly is not innate and is not provided in the input.[24]

---

22 Li and Thompson (1976) make a four-way classification of languages: topic prominent, subject prominent, topic and subject prominent, neither. Evidently, either this classification is not mutually exclusive, in that topic-and-subject-prominent languages share the characteristics of topic-prominent languages and of subject-prominent languages, or else Li and Thompson are not being consistent, since in one place they classify Japanese as a topic-and-subject-prominent language (p. 460) while later citing it as an example of a topic-prominent language (p. 467).

23 A distinction is usually made between absolute and statistical universals, but the distinction is quantitative, not qualitative. If we find one language that violates an absolute universal, the universal becomes statistical; if we find enough languages that violate a statistical universal, it loses its universal status. Eckman, who has done the most interesting work on SLA and universals, claims that "a communication system [sic] that did not have at least two color terms [or had only agentive passives or violated some other absolute universal – KRG] would not be a human language" (1984:79). But such a claim – although probably true – is an unjustified extension of an inductive generalization about languages into a statement of a necessary condition on membership in the category *language*.

24 Kellerman's "psychotypology" concept (1979, 1983) is immune to this kind of

It is worth keeping in mind that when we discarded the Contrastive Analysis Hypothesis, we also discarded the theoretical construct, namely the behavioristic account of habit formation, that it employed to explain the acquisition (or nonacquisition) of second language structures. An unreconstructed contrastivist, confronted with Sentences (8) through (10), would explain the "errors" by appealing to topic-comment habits formed in the native language, and would explain the ultimate acquisition of the correct subject-predicate forms by claiming that the learner had formed new habits. We are all so prone to dismiss this explanation as inadequate (which, of course, it is) that we tend to overlook the fact that at least it was an attempt at an explanation. If we explain these data now by simply appealing to a difference in typology between language A and language B, we have in one sense taken a step backward, since all we have to justify this explanation is the commonsense plausibility of the idea that difference means difficulty. The popularity of contrastive analysis rested largely on precisely this commonsense plausibility, but contrastive analysis also tried to underwrite that plausibility theoretically. In the absence of a theoretical explanation for the acquisition of typological distinctions, we have no particular reason, other than common sense, to believe that acquisition across typological boundaries should be different from acquisition within the same type.

Here is where a generative grammar comes in. By formulating precise formal rules for the generating of sentences, it is possible (in principle at least) to describe what it is that is acquired by a learner of a specific language, and what it is that must be "cognized" by any human by virtue of knowledge that is innate. Given this kind of information, we are in a position to make fairly precise predictions about SLA where the second language in some respect differs from (or is the same as) the native language.

Take, for example, the problem of pronoun anaphora, as illustrated by the following sentences (the subscripts indicate *he* and *John* refer to the same person):

11a. John$_i$ thought he$_i$ would win.
   b. *He$_i$ thought John$_i$ would win.

To deal with this problem, Reinhart (1983) developed the idea of *c-command*, a relation between two nodes in a tree. Reinhart claims that an antecedent must c-command its anaphor. Now, if this is a fact about all languages (not by virtue of its appearing as a rule in every language, but conversely because it is part of Universal Grammar), one might wish to claim that second language learners, regardless of the second or first

criticism since, as his term suggests, the typological relationships between two languages are in fact individual learners' mental representations, not statistical generalizations across languages.

language, would not make errors that violate this rule. And indeed, Gundel and Tarone (1983), using an earlier formulation of the c-command condition, found no violations in their data, although in other areas where there is variation from language to language there seemed to be native language influence.

Notice that the concept of c-command is not even conceivable outside a specific kind of linguistic theory, and is validated in part by its applicability within that theory to other problems. For instance, the existence of a c-command rule presupposes phrase structure rules; more specifically, it also turns out to be of importance within Government-Binding Theory in accounts of movement. By ignoring function and by calling upon a theory capable of making precise, detailed structural descriptions, we have found a possible explanation for a phenomenon that cannot be described, let alone explained, in functional or typological terms.[25]

The same centrality of formal theory to explanation can be seen in recent work done on parameter setting in SLA. Since examples of SLA research in this framework appear in this volume I need not give a detailed account of this kind of research (Rutherford 1984 and 1986 are convenient surveys).[26] I must point out, however, that when White, for instance, talks about the "pro-drop parameter" (1985), she means something much more specific than that in Spanish a pronoun subject can be deleted. Whether White is correct about the acquisition of English by Spanish speakers, she cannot be accused of using an ad hoc term. The pro-drop parameter is part of a larger and well-motivated theory, and stands or falls with that theory. And this is right, for what we want in an SLA theory is not simply rigor − although God knows we want that − but explanatory power, and it is just that ability to appeal to a related, well-developed theory that allows us to explain phenomena in the domain of SLA.

Thus, a linguistic perspective of the type I have suggested here can add both clarity and explanatory power to the research being carried

25 And make no mistake, this *is* an explanation. One may well wonder why on earth the c-command constraint on anaphora obtains for every natural language − that is to say why on earth it is part of Universal Grammar (if in fact it is, which of course is another question), and I would be the last one to try to dissuade anyone from investigating this question. But an *acquisition* theory is not committed to explaining why what is acquired exists, only *that* it exists, and how it is acquired.

26 Nor am I interested in the actual accuracy of the findings reported therein. Kellerman (1985), for instance, offers specific methodological criticisms of Mazurkewich (1984). Again, Flynn's work in the area of principal branching direction (e.g., 1984) may be problematic in that she relies a great deal on the work of Lust (e.g., 1983), and Lust's findings have been called into question (e.g., O'Grady, Suzuki-Wei, and Cho 1986). These criticisms, whether right or wrong, do not bear on my point.

out in SLA. Beyond that, by relating SLA research to first language acquisition theory and linguistic theory, such a perspective can give our field something else it could do with: a sense of direction. Although there is a great deal of SLA research going on, what is much harder to find is a research *program*. In SLA research in general, there has been little sense of an overall guiding purpose beyond the general one of finding out things.

Finally, looking at second language acquisition from the perspective of generative grammar would help clarify the division of labor in the field. As White makes amply clear (e.g., 1984), and as I suggested in the discussion of competence, grammar is not coterminous with language, and a perfect theory of grammatical competence by itself will no more tell us all we need to know about SLA than a perfect grammatical competence by itself will enable us to talk about the weather. For instance, Japanese is a pro-drop language, and knowing that, when speaking Japanese I drop pronouns left and right – including at times when a native speaker would not. That is to say, as I do not yet know the discourse restraints (at least) on pronoun-dropping in Japanese, my "communicative competence" is not up to native standards.

SLA researchers need to know about communicative competence, not as it is usually discussed in the literature, but as competence. We need to know about pragmatic competence, if in fact there is any meaningful difference between communicative competence and pragmatic competence. One way to help us find out about them is to find out more clearly what they are not. Anyone who is truly interested in developing a theory of the acquisition of communicative competence in a second language could only be grateful for a fully developed theory of the acquisition of grammatical competence.

And of course I have said nothing at all about the acquisition process itself, either in the sense of processing input or in the sense of the mechanisms involved in moving a learner along from T_1 to T_2. Research in either of these areas would be complemented and enhanced by the more accurate knowledge of a learner's competence that would hopefully be gained through the insights of generative theory.[27]

27 Having gone and used the word "process," I had better say something about the "process/product" distinction, for every mention of which if I had a dollar I would be only slightly less rich than if those dollars represented mentions of "communicative competence." It has become a part of the orthodox position to pooh-pooh product and push process. If by "product" one means "output data" – and this does seem to be the common interpretation – well and good. But if it means competence – which, after all, is the real product of acquisition, output being a by-product – then I must defy the pooh-poohers and insist that we must study the product if we wish to make sense of the process. As Chomsky (1982:69) once said, "It is absolutely suicidal for a field to define itself...as dealing only with

In short, we don't want a thousand graduate students all looking for parameters any more than we (should have) wanted them all doing morpheme studies or contrastive analyses. Second language acquisition research, just like its object of inquiry, is modular, or should be. We cannot expect much progress to be made either through reductive hobbyhorse riding or through a nonprincipled eclecticism that is simply an excuse for avoiding method; but if we take a good hard look at the one piece of the language puzzle that has acquired something like a recognizable shape, we should be in a better position to start putting the whole puzzle together.

References

Atkinson, M. 1982. *Explanations in the Study of Child Language Development.* Cambridge Studies in Linguistics, Vol. 35. Cambridge: Cambridge University Press.

Berwick, R. C. 1985. *The Acquisition of Syntactic Knowledge.* Cambridge, Mass.: MIT Press.

Bialystok, E., and M. Sharwood Smith. 1985. Interlanguage is not a state of mind. *Applied Linguistics* 6: 101–17.

Canale, M., and M. Swain. 1980. Theoretical bases of communicative approaches to second language teaching and testing. *Applied Linguistics* 1: 1–47.

Cancino, H., E. J. Rosansky, and J. H. Schumann. 1978. The acquisition of English negatives and interrogatives by native Spanish speakers. In *Second Language Acquisition: A Book of Readings*, E. Hatch, ed. Rowley, Mass.: Newbury House.

Carden, G. 1973. *English Quantifiers: Logical Structure and Linguistic Variation.* New York: Academic Press.

Chomsky, N. 1975. *Reflections on Language.* New York: Pantheon.
   1980. *Rules and Representations.* New York: Columbia University Press.
   1982. *On the Generative Enterprise.* Dordrecht, The Netherlands: Foris.
   1986. *Knowledge of Language: Its Nature, Origin, and Use.* New York: Praeger.

Comrie, B. 1984a. Why linguists need language acquirers. In *Language Universals and Second Language Acquisition*, W. E. Rutherford, ed. Amsterdam: John Benjamins.
   1984b. Form and function in explaining language universals. In *Explanations for Language Universals*, B. Butterworth, B. Comrie, and Ö. Dahl, eds. The Hague: Mouton.

Eckman, F. R. 1984. Universals, typologies, and interlanguage. In *Language Universals and Second Language Acquisition*, W. E. Rutherford, ed. Amsterdam: John Benjamins.

processes but not with the structures that might enter into them, or to deal with the observed stages of growth and development, but not with the systems that underlie them."

Ellis, R. 1985. *Understanding Second Language Acquisition*. Oxford: Oxford University Press.

1989. Variability and the Natural Order Hypothesis. In *Responses to Krashen*, R. Barasch, ed. New York: Harper & Row.

Flynn, S. 1984. A universal in L2 acquisition based on a PBD typology. In *Universals of Second Language Acquisition*, F. R. Eckman, L. H. Bell, and D. Nelson, eds. Rowley, Mass.: Newbury House.

Fodor, J. A. 1978. Computation and reduction. In *Representations: Philosophical Essays on the Foundations of Cognitive Science*, by J. A. Fodor. Brighton, U.K.: Harvester Press. [Originally published in *Perception and Cognition*, W. Savage, ed. Minnesota Studies in the Philosophy of Science, Vol. 9. Minneapolis: University of Minnesota Press.]

1983. *The Modularity of Mind*. Cambridge, Mass.: MIT Press.

Foley, W. A., and R. D. Van Valin, Jr. 1984. *Functional Syntax and Universal Grammar*. Cambridge Studies in Linguistics, Vol. 38. Cambridge: Cambridge University Press.

Gass, S., and J. Ard. 1984. Second language acquisition and the ontology of language universals. In *Language Universals and Second Language Acquisition*, W. E. Rutherford, ed. Amsterdam: John Benjamins.

Gettier, E. L. 1963. Is justified true belief knowledge? *Analysis* 23: 121–23.

Givón, T. 1985. Language, function and typology. *Journal of Literary Semantics* 14: 83–97.

Goodman, N. 1983. *Fact, Fiction and Forecast*. 4th ed. Cambridge, Mass.: Harvard University Press.

Greenberg, J. H., ed. 1978. *Universals of Human Language*. Stanford: Stanford University Press.

Gregg, K. R. 1984. Krashen's Monitor and Occam's Razor. *Applied Linguistics* 5:79–100.

1989. Krashen's theory, acquisition theory, and theory. In *Responses to Krashen*, R. Barasch, ed. New York: Harper & Row.

Gundel, J. K., and E. E. Tarone. 1983. Language transfer and the acquisition of pronominal anaphora. In *Language Transfer in Language Learning*, S. M. Gass and L. Selinker, eds. Rowley, Mass.: Newbury House.

Harré, R. 1972. *The Philosophies of Science*. Oxford: Oxford University Press.

Hilles, S. 1986. Interlanguage and the pro-drop parameter. *Second Language Research* 2: 33–52.

Kean, M.-L. 1981. Explanation in neurolinguistics. In *Explanation in Linguistics*, N. Hornstein and D. Lightfoot, eds. New York: Longman.

Kellerman, E. 1979. Transfer and non-transfer: where we are now. *Studies in Second Language Acquisition* 2: 37–57.

1983. Now you see it, now you don't. In *Language Transfer in Language Learning*, S. M. Gass and L. Selinker, eds. Rowley, Mass.: Newbury House.

1985. Dative alternation and the analysis of data: a reply to Mazurkewich. *Language Learning* 35: 91–101.

Krashen, S. D. 1982. *Principles and Practice in Second Language Acquisition*. Oxford: Pergamon Press.

1985. *The Input Hypothesis: Issues and Implications*. London: Longman.

Kuhn, T. S. 1977a. Concepts of cause in the development of physics. In *The Essential Tension*, by T. S. Kuhn. Chicago: University of Chicago Press.

[Originally published as Les notions de causalité dans le développement de la physique, *Etudes d'épistémologie génétique* 25 (1971): 7–18]

1977b. The relations between history and the history of science. In *The Essential Tension*, by T. S. Kuhn. Chicago: University of Chicago Press. [Originally published in *Daedalus* 100 (1971): 271–304]

Kumpf, L. 1984. Temporal systems and universality in interlanguage: a case study. In *Universals of Second Language Acquisition*, F. R. Eckman, L. H. Bell, and D. Nelson, eds. Rowley, Mass.: Newbury House.

Kuno, S. 1987. *Functional Syntax*. Chicago: University of Chicago Press.

Labov, W. 1969. The study of language in its social context. *Studium Generale* 23: 30–87.

1972. *Sociolinguistic Patterns*. Philadelphia: University of Pennsylvania Press.

Laudan, L. 1977. *Progress and Its Problems: Towards a Theory of Scientific Growth*. Berkeley: University of California Press.

Li, C. N. 1976. Introduction. In *Subject and Topic*, C. N. Li, ed. New York: Academic Press.

Li, C. N., and S. A. Thompson. 1976. Subject and topic: a new typology of language. In *Subject and Topic*, C. N. Li, ed. New York: Academic Press.

Lightbown, P. M. 1984. The relationship between theory and method in second-language-acquisition research. In *Interlanguage*, A. Davies, C. Criper, and A.P.R. Howatt, eds. Edinburgh: Edinburgh University Press.

Lightfoot, D. 1982. *The Language Lottery: Toward a Biology of Grammars*. Cambridge, Mass.: MIT Press.

Long, M. H. 1981. Input, interaction, and second-language acquisition. In *Native Language and Foreign Language Acquisition*, H. Winitz, ed. New York: New York Academy of Sciences. New York Academy of Sciences *Annals* 379: 259–78]

1985. Theory construction in second language acquisition. Paper presented at the Second Language Research Forum, University of California at Los Angeles, February 1985.

Long, M. H., and C. J. Sato. 1984. Methodological issues in interlanguage studies: an interactionist perspective. In *Interlanguage*, A. Davies, C. Criper, and A.P.R. Howatt, eds. Edinburgh: Edinburgh University Press.

Lust, B. 1983. On the notion "principal branching direction": a parameter of Universal Grammar. In *Studies in Generative Grammar and Language Acquisition*, Y. Otsu, H. van Riemsdijk, K. Inoue, A. Kamio, and N. Kawasaki, eds. Tokyo: International Christian University.

Mazurkewich, I. 1984. The acquisition of the dative alternation by second language learners and linguistic theory. *Language Learning* 34: 91–109.

McLaughlin, B. 1978. The Monitor model: some methodological considerations. *Language Learning* 28: 309–32.

1989. The input hypothesis and second-language theory. In *Responses to Krashen*, R. Barasch, ed. New York: Harper & Row.

Newmeyer, F. J. 1983. *Grammatical Theory: Its Limits and Possibilities*. Chicago: University of Chicago Press.

O'Grady, W., Y. Suzuki-Wei, and S. W. Cho. 1986. Directionality preferences in the interpretation of anaphora: data from Korean and Japanese. *Journal of Child Language* 13: 409–20.

Paikeday, T. M., ed. 1985. *The Native Speaker Is Dead!* Toronto: Paikeday Publishing.

Pinker, S. 1984. *Language Learnability and Language Development*. Cambridge, Mass.: Harvard University Press.

Pylyshyn, Z. W. 1973. The role of competence theories in cognitive psychology. *Journal of Psycholinguistic Research* 2: 21–50.

Reinhart, T. 1983. *Anaphora and Semantic Interpretation*. Chicago: University of Chicago Press.

Rutherford, W. E. 1983. Language typology and language transfer. In *Language Transfer in Language Learning*, S. M. Gass and L. Selinker, eds. Rowley, Mass.: Newbury House.

1984. Description and explanation in interlanguage syntax: state of the art. *Language Learning* 34: 127–55.

1986. Grammatical theory and L2 acquisition: a brief overview. *Second Language Research* 2: 1–15.

Schachter, J. 1984. A universal input condition. In *Language Universals and Second Language Acquisition*, W. E. Rutherford, ed. Amsterdam: John Benjamins.

Schachter, J., and W. E. Rutherford. 1979. Discourse function and language transfer. *Working Papers in Bilingualism* 19: 1–12.

Schmidt, M. 1980. Coordinate structures and language universals in interlanguage. *Language Learning* 30: 397–416.

Schumann, J. H. 1984. Art and science in second language acquisition research. In *An Epistemology for the Language Sciences*, A. Z. Guiora, ed. Ann Arbor: University of Michigan Press.

Searle, J. 1969. *Speech Acts*. Cambridge: Cambridge University Press.

Shapere, D. 1977. Scientific theories and their domains. In *The Structure of Scientific Theories*, F. Suppe, ed. Urbana: University of Illinois Press.

Sharwood Smith, M. 1981. The competence/performance distinction in the theory of second language acquisition and the "pedagogical grammar hypothesis." Paper presented at the Contrastive Linguistics Conference, Boszkowo, Poland, December 1981.

1986. Comprehension versus acquisition: two ways of processing input. *Applied Linguistics* 7: 239–56.

Skinner, B. F. 1957. *Verbal Behavior*. New York: Appleton-Century-Crofts.

Sperber, D., and D. Wilson. 1986. *Relevance: Communication and Cognition*. London: Blackwell.

Spolsky, B. 1985. Formulating a theory of second language learning. *Studies in Second Language Acquisition* 7: 269–88.

Tarone, E. 1979. Interlanguage as chameleon. *Language Learning* 29: 181–91.

1984. On the variability of interlanguage systems. In *Universals of Second Language Acquisition*, F. R. Eckman, L. H. Bell, and D. Nelson, eds. Rowley, Mass.: Newbury House.

Wexler, K., and P. W. Culicover. 1980. *Formal Principles of Language Acquisition*. Cambridge, Mass.: MIT Press.

White, L. 1982. *Grammatical Theory and Language Acquisition*. Publications in Language Sciences, Vol. 8. Dordrecht, The Netherlands: Foris.

1984. Universal Grammar as a source of explanation in second language acquisition. In *Current Approaches to Second Language Acquisition: Proceedings of the 1984 University of Wisconsin-Milwaukee Linguistics Symposium*, B. Wheatley, A. Hastings, F. R. Eckman, L. Bell, G. Krukar, and R. Rutkowski, eds. Bloomington: Indiana University Linguistics Club.

1985. The "pro-drop" parameter in adult second language acquisition. *Language Learning* 35:47–62.

Zwicky, A. M., and J. M. Sadock. 1975. Ambiguity tests and how to fail them. In *Syntax and Semantics*, J. P. Kimball, ed. Vol. 4. New York: Academic Press.

2 *What is the logical problem of foreign language learning?*

Robert Bley-Vroman

The linguistic data to which children are exposed appear to be insufficient to determine, by themselves, the linguistic knowledge that children eventually attain. The gap between available experience and attained competence forms what has been called the logical problem of language acquisition. The approach to a solution, which has been followed in linguistic theory over the past two decades, is to suggest that the gap is bridged by an innate Universal Grammar: a system of knowledge of what a human language can be and innate domain-specific procedures for arriving at a grammar. The classic statement is that of Chomsky:

A consideration of the character of the grammar that is acquired, the degenerate quality and narrowly limited extent of the available data, the striking uniformity of the resulting grammars, and their independence of intelligence, motivation and emotional state, over wide ranges of variation, leave little hope that much of the structure of language can be learned by an organism initially uninformed as to its general character. (Chomsky 1965:58)

Adults may also learn foreign languages. Abstractly, the logical problem of adult foreign language learning is the same as for childhood language learning: explaining how acquisition takes place, given the limitations of the data. But the problem is also different, in important ways. Foreign language learning differs in degree of success, in the character and uniformity of the resulting systems, in its susceptibility to factors such as motivation, and in the previous state of the organism: The learner already has a knowledge of one language and a powerful system of general abstract problem-solving skills. Within what general framework is the logical problem of foreign language learning to be addressed? And specifically, what is the role of the domain-specific learning system, including principles of Universal Grammar? Does this *language acquisition device* continue to function in adults?

One obvious possibility is that the innate system that guides child acquisition no longer operates in adult foreign language learning (or, more weakly, that its operation is partial and imperfect). This would

Lynn Eubank, Susan F. Schmerling, and C. L. Baker provided helpful comments on an earlier version of this paper.

easily explain why foreign language learning is often a difficult and ultimately unsuccessful task. (This view is often associated with Lenneberg's Critical Period Hypothesis. Lenneberg himself, however, seems to have considered foreign language learning only a tangential issue, and as not so much providing evidence for his hypothesis as complicating the question [Lenneberg 1967: 176].)

The initial plausibility and explanatory power of this view are so clear that one might expect it to be widely held among scholars of foreign language learning. Despite its evident appeal, however, it is by no means the dominant position in current second language acquisition research. Among many scholars, a consensus has developed during the last decade that the same fundamental process controls both the child's learning of a first language and the adult's learning of a foreign language.[1]

In this essay, I explore and defend the proposition that child language development and foreign language learning are in fact fundamentally different. The domain-specific acquisition system does not have the role in addressing the logical problem of foreign language learning that it has in child learning.

My strategy will be as follows. In the next section I discuss the fundamental large-scale characteristics of adult foreign language learning as a phenomenon. Viewed macroscopically, adult foreign language learning resembles general adult problem solving and not child language development. The burden of proof ought then to fall on proponents of the view that child and adult language learning are fundamentally the same – that is, that things are not as they seem to be. I then (in "The logical problem") outline a view of foreign language learning in which first language knowledge fills the role which Universal Grammar has in child language acquisition, and in which general problem-solving principles fill the role of the language-specific learning procedures of children. The following section ("Alternate explanations") describes some of the major alternative approaches to explaining the obvious differences between the two kinds of language learning. There are difficulties – both empirical, and especially conceptual – with most views that claim fundamental sameness. Finally, I discuss the importance and logical status of current work in parameter setting and Universal Grammar.

A word about terminology. In current scholarship, a distinction is often made between foreign language acquisition and second language acquisition. Foreign language learning takes place when the language to be learned is not the native language of the society: for example, learning English as a foreign language in Japan. Second language learning takes

---

1 One version of this view is clearly crystallized in the textbook *Language Two* (Dulay, Burt, and Krashen 1982), which has now figured in the basic training of a generation of second language acquisition researchers.

place in a country where the language is spoken: for example, learning English as a second language in the United States. This difference in setting is of very great practical importance to teachers. The term "second language" is often also used for the phenomenon in general. "Second" is an unfortunate term both in that it suggests that third (and fourth, etc.) languages are not included, and also in that it departs from ordinary nontechnical usage, where "foreign" is the common general term. For the purposes of this essay, the setting ("second" or "foreign") is not crucial. I will usually use "foreign." In one particular perspective on second/foreign language acquisition – the Monitor Model of Krashen (see especially 1981) – a distinction is also made between "learning" and "acquisition," where the term "learning" refers to the conscious learning of explicit rules, and "acquisition" is used for the unconscious internalization of knowledge. Conscious memorization of grammar rules is held – correctly – not to be the same thing as developing real language competence. While not denying the importance of the distinction, I will use the terms interchangeably, preferring the less technical term "learning": hence, "foreign language learning" rather than "second language acquisition." "Development" is sometimes used to describe child language acquisition, because it connotes internally driven growth. The juxtaposition of "adult foreign language learning" and "child language development" best fits, considering the terms' connotations, the view to be argued here.

The fundamental character of foreign language learning

In this section I briefly discuss nine fundamental characteristics of adult foreign language learning. These are all relatively apparent, large-scale characteristics, and few are controversial. Scholarly research has in general confirmed commonsense observation. It will be useful to compare in each case foreign language learning with child language development on the one hand and with general adult skill acquisition and problem solving on the other. The picture that emerges is that, at least in its gross features, adult foreign language learning is much more like general adult learning than it is like child language development.

Lack of success

The lack of general guaranteed success is the most striking characteristic of adult foreign language learning. Normal children inevitably achieve perfect mastery of the language; adult foreign language learners do not.

Lack of inevitable perfect mastery is, of course, a characteristic of general adult learning in fields for which no domain-specific cognitive facility is thought to exist, especially in areas of substantial complexity. Not everyone with an opportunity to learn chess will become a world-class chess player; not everyone who is exposed to geometry becomes skilled at geometry proofs; careful schooling and years of experience do not guarantee that one will be a competent auto mechanic. Any model which entails uniform success – as child first language acquisition models must – is a failure as a model of adult language learning. Lack of guaranteed success in adult foreign language learning would, of course, follow from a theory which holds that this learning is controlled by general human cognitive learning capacities rather than by the same domain-specific module which guarantees child success in first language acquisition. Frequent lack of success in adults, against uniform success in children, is a serious obstacle to the view that the same process underlies child and adult language acquisition.

General failure

Not only is success in adult foreign language learning not guaranteed, but complete success is extremely rare, or perhaps even nonexistent, especially as regards "accent" and the ability to make subtle grammaticality judgments (on this last, see under "Evidence for Universal Grammar"). Indeed, in his influential "Interlanguage" paper, Selinker (1972) even suggested that the rare cases of apparent complete success could perhaps be regarded as peripheral to the enterprise of second language acquisition theory. The rare successes may have the same "pathological" status for adult acquisition as the rare failures in first language acquisition are considered to have.[2] One has the impression of ineluctable success on the one hand, and ineluctable failure on the other. For a theory which holds that adult foreign language acquisition and child first language development are fundamentally different, this follows naturally. Language is not merely difficult to learn with only general cognitive strategies, it is virtually impossible. This is one important reason for attributing an innate domain-specific language faculty to children.

2 There is some debate among workers in second language acquisition about the frequency of perfect success. Selinker (1972) hazarded 5 percent. See Seliger (1978) for a more generous estimate. The research in the scholarly literature is complicated by the question of who one counts and what one means by success, or potential success. I believe that virtually no normal adult learner achieves perfect success, if what one means thereby is development of native-speaker competence, even though some may have a performance difficult to distinguish from that of native speakers.

Later I will consider how the Fundamental Difference Hypothesis can accommodate the fact that adults do even as well as they do.

Variation in success, course, and strategy

Among adults, there is substantial variation in degree of success, even when age, exposure, instruction, and so forth are held constant. Adults not only generally do not succeed, they also fail in different degrees. This fact is so evident that it has never been thought necessary to demonstrate it by formal academic study. Instead, the assumption of variation in attainment has formed the basis of a whole tradition in second language acquisition scholarship: the attempt to correlate something else with this wide variation in success. It also forms the basis of the TOEFL (Test of English as a Foreign Language) and Michigan Test industries. Again, the similarity to general adult skill acquisition is striking, as is the difference from child language development, where there is no such variation. The lack of variation among first language learners requires that the child language acquisition theory "must be embedded in a theory of Universal Grammar that allows only one grammar ... to be compatible with the sorts of sentences children hear" (Pinker 1984:5). Clearly, a formal model of adult foreign language learning must allow many different "grammars" to be arrived at.

In foreign language acquisition, different learners also "follow different paths," as Meisel, Clahsen, and Pienemann (1981) put it in their study of the stages of learning German syntax in adult *Gastarbeiter* (foreign workers in Germany). There is a good deal of intersubject variation in second language *acquisition order* studies (see especially Rosansky 1976). There is also variation in what one might call *learning strategies* – from large-scale differences like the distinction between "avoiding" and "guessing" suggested by Madden, Bailey, Eisenstein, and Anderson (1978) to something as specific as the use of poetry memorization or of a particular mnemonic trick in vocabulary learning. The same is true among adults learning to play bridge or do phonology problems.[3]

Again, substantial variation among learners – variation in degree of attainment, in course of learning, and in strategies of learning – is exactly what one expects to find in general adult skill acquisition.

3 "Different paths" have also been claimed to exist among children in first language performance. The variation appears, on the face of it, to be much less dramatic than among adult learners. The situation is complicated by the fact that it is always difficult to know, especially in the case of young children, whether we are faced with actual differences in the course or "methods" of language development, or merely with different responses to the exigencies of communication using an incompletely developed grammar or with differing enjoyment of certain sorts of verbal play – which may or may not actually "feed" language development.

Variation in goals

There is not only variation in degree of attainment, there is also variation in what one might call type of attainment. For example, some adult learners seem to develop "pidginized" systems that have rudimentary grammatical devices but seem nonetheless to be quite successful in fulfilling the communicative needs of the speaker (see Schumann 1976, 1978; Meisel, Clahsen, and Pienemann 1981, esp. 121). Others seem concerned about grammatical correctness, even though fluency may suffer. Some develop just enough foreign language competence as is necessary to wait on tables or to lecture in philosophy; others may become skilled at cocktail party story telling. Some have good pronunciation but primitive grammar. Some lay great importance on vocabulary size. Some work at passing for a native speaker; others seem proud of their foreignness (the "Charles Boyer phenomenon"). Instruction that is consonant with student goals is more successful.[4]

This variation in aims follows naturally from the hypothesis that adult foreign language acquisition is a type of general problem solving. Cognitive models of general problem solving involve setting goals. It is to be expected that different people will view the problem to be solved in different ways and will set different goals in a given domain. A keyboard student may want to be able to play popular songs by ear at parties, or to play harpsichord continuo with colleagues in the math department; a friend of mine once had as a primary goal of performance to be able to eventually play the Promenade from Mussorgsky's *Pictures at an Exhibition* – and that was all. Different goals require setting different subgoals, involving perhaps different learning strategies. All of this is commonplace in general human problem solving. Children, on the other hand, driven by the inexorable operation of the domain-specific language faculty, do not have the luxury of setting their own individual goals. For children, the "goal" – if one can even speak of it as such – is predetermined by the language faculty and not under learner control.

Fossilization

It has long been noted that foreign language learners reach a certain stage of learning – a stage short of success – and that learners then permanently stabilize at this stage. Development ceases, and even serious

---

4 The fact of such variation, and its central importance to second language acquisition, is not only universally accepted by all scholars of adult language learning, it is even the basis of a whole pedagogical theory of curriculum design: the so-called needs-based, specific purpose, and communicative syllabi (see especially Van Ek 1975; Munby 1978). The journal *English for Special Purposes* is dedicated to this tradition.

conscious efforts to change are often fruitless. Brief changes are sometimes observed, but they do not "take": The learner backslides to the stable state. Selinker (1972) called this phenomenon *fossilization*. Fossilization often seems to be observed in learners who have achieved a level of competence that ensures communicative success, even though the grammar may be very unlike that of a native. Fossilized learners are the despair of language teachers: Nothing seems to have an effect. Sometimes in a classroom drill with abundant opportunity for conscious monitoring, a change is observed. But minutes later during the break, all the old forms reappear – completely unaffected. In children, of course, there is no fossilization (short of success). Stages are inevitably passed through; the system remains plastic until success is achieved.

Indeterminate intuitions

In a substantial number of cases, even very advanced non-native speakers seem to lack clear grammaticality judgments. The unclear character of non-native intuitions has even prompted some scholars to suggest that a third class of grammaticality judgments – *indeterminate* – is needed in the description of learner language (Schachter, Tyson, and Diffley 1976). This suggests that the knowledge underlying non-native speaker performance may be incomplete (in the technical sense) and thus may be a different sort of formal object from the systems thought to underlie native speaker performance. A non-native system may, for example, be in part a relatively heterogeneous collection of strategies for achieving communicative goals: A system of rules generating all and only the sentences of a language may even be absent. Despite the early conjecture that "an 'interlanguage' may be linguistically described using as data the observable output resulting from a speaker's attempt to produce a foreign norm" (Selinker 1969:71), no systematic grammar has yet been produced for any substantial portion of any learner's language (see Bley-Vroman 1983 for discussion). Such fundamental differences between the knowledge systems produced in first and foreign language acquisition suggest that the same cognitive learning system does not give rise to them both.

Importance of instruction

Children clearly do not require organized formal lessons to learn a language. "While it is debatable exactly how much deliberate shaping the average child receives, no one would claim that deliberate feedback and control over the child's linguistic experience is necessary" (Moulton and Robinson 1981:245). On the other hand, a whole industry is built on the consensus that instruction matters in foreign language learning.

One must, to be fair, use caution in this argument. Does formal instruction really make a difference in foreign language learning? Might not mere exposure to native-speaker input be equally effective? Experimental tests of the general efficacy of instruction are difficult to carry out. Uncontrolled variables abound; individual variation will often swamp the data; the Hawthorne effect (subjects conscious of being studied are predisposed to perform better) may interfere; not all instruction is expected to be equally successful, and some may actually impede success. In spite of the difficulties, such studies as exist seem to show that instruction does aid foreign language learning (Krashen and Seliger 1975; Long 1983). Also, the survival of the industry amid selective economic pressures suggests that it has some utility.

Much the same may be said of the importance of practice. Systematic, organized, controlled drill is believed to be important by many teachers and learners (though certainly not by all). It plays no obvious role in child language acquisition. Of course, practice of this sort is well-known to have an important function in adult skill acquisition, where it is held to be the mechanism whereby controlled processing becomes automatized. It is another instance where foreign language learning more closely resembles general adult learning. To be fair, it must be said that this evidence, especially as it depends on the evaluation of belief data, must be interpreted cautiously.

Despite these difficulties, it does seem prudent to take such evidence seriously to the extent that it does not conflict with such experimental evidence as exists and does not contradict common sense.

Negative evidence

Child language acquisition seems not to use – and surely does not rely upon – any consistent source of negative evidence. Indeed, all serious attempts to construct formal first language learning theories assume that negative evidence is not used and that success is possible nonetheless (Wexler and Culicover 1980; Pinker 1984). Even attempts made outside the tradition of generative grammar make this assumption (e.g., Moulton and Robinson 1981, Chapter 6).

Among teachers and learners of foreign languages there is general agreement that negative evidence is at least sometimes useful, and sometimes, though not always, necessary. Experimental evidence is inconclusive, but suggests that correction in particular may be helpful (Cohen and Robbins 1976). As shown by theoretical work, some of the errors made by foreign language learners suggest that they hold hypotheses requiring negative evidence for disconfirmation (Bley-Vroman 1986). Despite the lack of very convincing empirical evidence, even scholars who argue for the essential similarity of first and foreign language acquisition are forced to cautiously conclude that the unclear findings of empirical studies on the efficacy of correction "do not mean that correction plays no role in language learning" and that one may expect that research will "uncover specific situations in which error correction may be effective" (Dulay, Burt, and Krashen 1982:36).

Role of affective factors

Success in child language development seems unaffected by personality, socialization, motivation, attitude, or the like. This is consistent with the view that the process is controlled by the development of an innate domain-specific faculty, and it contrasts strongly with the case of general adult skill acquisition, which is highly susceptible to such "affective factors."[5]

There is a universal consensus among second language acquisition researchers, as well as among language teachers and students, that such factors are essential in foreign language learning. Since the early 1970s, beginning with the work of Gardner and Lambert (1972), numerous empirical studies have shown significant correlations between affective factors and proficiency. The situation is, to be sure, very complicated: Affect itself is complex and hard to measure; different groups and different situations show different sorts of córrelations; explanations are in short supply. Still, the central role of affect in foreign language learning is absolutely indisputable.

The logical problem of foreign language learning

These general characteristics of foreign language learning tend to lead to the conclusions that the domain-specific language acquisition system of children ceases to operate in adults, and in addition, that adult foreign language acquisition resembles general adult learning in fields for which no domain-specific learning system is believed to exist. Let us tentatively assume, therefore, that the same language acquisition system which guides children is not available to adults. The assumption that the acquisition system no longer functions easily predicts failure. Nevertheless, although few adults, if any, are completely successful, and many fail miserably, there are many who achieve very high levels of proficiency, given enough time, input, and effort, and given the right attitude, motivation, and learning environment. The logical problem of foreign lan-

---

5 Here and throughout, I use *affect* loosely to refer to a whole range of loosely associated factors. This is not to deny the correctness of the distinctions among them; it is just that the distinctions are not relevant to the argument.

guage acquisition then becomes that of explaining the quite high level of competence that is clearly possible in some cases, while permitting the wide range of variation that is also observed.

Language remains an abstract formal system of great complexity – one which is, furthermore, underdetermined by the data of experience. On the face of it, the contention that the language acquisition faculty does not effectively exist in adults could be understood to suggest that the adult learner should abandon all hope of any degree of success. This would be the correct conclusion were it not for the fact that the adult possesses other knowledge and faculties which are absent in the infant. And these may, in part, take some of the explanatory ·burden usually assumed by the language acquisition device. Most obvious of these other faculties is that the adult already has knowledge of at least one language. My specific proposal here is that the function of the innate domain-specific acquisition system is filled in adults (though indirectly and imperfectly) by this native language knowledge and by a general abstract problem-solving system. I shall call this proposal the Fundamental Difference Hypothesis.[6]

The Fundamental Difference Hypothesis

The Fundamental Difference Hypothesis, articulated here in its strongest version, is thus much more than the observation that there are differences between child and adult language acquisition; it is a specific hypothesis about just wherein those differences reside. In particular, it asserts that the nature of the difference is *internal, linguistic,* and *qualitative*:

Internal: It is caused by differences in the internal cognitive state of adults versus children, not by some external factor or factors (insufficient input, for example).

Linguistic: It is caused by a change in the language faculty specifically, not by some general change in learning ability.

Qualitative, not quantitative: The difference is not merely quantitative; the domain-specific acquisition system is not just attenuated, it is unavailable. Period.[7]

To be more precise, let us say that the child learner possesses a language acquisition system that contains the following two sub-components:

6 This proposal is explored in much greater detail in Bley-Vroman (in press), especially the relationship of the Fundamental Difference Hypothesis to technical questions of current linguistic theory.

7 One obvious way of revising the Fundamental Difference Hypothesis is by modifying the claim that the difference is absolutely qualitative. We retain the strong claim unless clear disconfirming evidence arrives. The section "Evidence for Universal Grammar" discusses some possible forms such evidence might take. See also Footnote 9.

A. A definition of possible grammar: a Universal Grammar
B. A way of arriving at a grammar based on available data: a Learning Procedure (or set of procedures)

Workers in the formal theory of language acquisition have generally assumed such a framework with these components, at least since Chomsky (1965). Let us say that function A is filled by a system that we shall call *Universal Grammar*, and that function B is filled by what we shall call a system of *Learning Procedures*.[8]

Thus, the picture of the difference between child language development and foreign language learning as advocated here is the following:

Child language development	*Adult foreign language learning*
A. Universal Grammar	A. Native language knowledge
B. Domain-specific learning procedures	B. General problem-solving systems

The role of the native language

By the adult's knowledge of a language, I do not mean simply the set of well-formed sentences, but also the full range of subtle intuitions native speakers possess. A great deal of information about the general character of language – about language universals – is implicit in a single language precisely because universals are universal. This is most evidently true in the broad architectural features of language. The learner will have reason to expect that the language to be learned will be capable of generating an infinite number of sentences; a language of finite cardinality will not be expected. The learner will expect that the foreign language will have a syntax, a semantics, a lexicon which recognizes parts of speech, a morphology which provides systematic ways of modifying the shapes of words, a phonology which provides a finite set of phonemes, and syllables, feet, phonological phrases, etc. Universals of this sort are available to the foreign language learner merely by observing

8 There have been differences in terminology, emphasis, and specific proposal. Chomsky, in *Aspects of the Theory of Syntax*, proposed that a formal evaluation metric would fill function B, allowing the learner to "select from the store of potential grammars a specific one that is appropriate to the data available to him" (Chomsky 1965:13). A different approach to B is, for example, that of Pinker (1984), who suggests a system of many highly specific learning procedures that construct and revise a grammar (within the constraints provided by Universal Grammar) bit by bit, as data become available. Also, there is clearly a potential trade-off relationship between A and B: Tight constraints on possible grammars (A) may carry some of the burden of choosing a grammar that would otherwise fall on B. Despite the numerous possible variations, something like a distinction between A and B seems justified. The term "Universal Grammar" is sometimes used to comprise both A and B. This is especially appropriate within evaluation metric theories, where the procedure for selecting a grammar is so closely related to the formal properties of rules. I shall use the term in the more restricted sense.

(not necessarily consciously) the most obvious large-scale characteristics of the native language – no deep analyses are necessary – and by making the very conservative assumption that the foreign language is not an utterly different sort of thing from the native language.

In syntax, the learner might also expect to find principles of constituent structure and of recursive embedding with no intrinsic limit. There will be grammatical functions, and these will not always correspond to semantic roles. There may be something like relative clauses, sentential complements to verbs, and the like also assumed. There will be Booleanlike connectors, quantifiers, pronouns, anaphors, "understood" elements of various kinds. There will be devices for giving orders, making requests, asking yes-no and *wh*-questions. There will be devices for focus, for backgrounding.

Thus, even supposing that the original scheme of Universal Grammar is no longer available, the foreign language learner can, in a sense, reconstruct much of it by observing the native language. The foreign language learner does not therefore come to language as "an organism initially uninformed as to its general character" (Chomsky 1965:58).

In some regards, the foreign language learners may even know more than children equipped with a general Universal Grammar. They will know that there will likely be words for the sun, the moon, for mother, father, for body parts, colors, directions; and that there will probably be styles, registers, and regional and social dialects.

This information the foreign language learner has is, of course, not complete. The speaker of a language with little inflectional morphology and heavily dependent on word order to convey grammatical function may initially be surprised by many of the characteristics of a language less dependent on rigid configuration. The phonemic use of tone will not be expected by speakers of a non-tone language. The speakers of a language with obligatory overt subjects may initially be baffled by a null-subject language.

On the other hand, foreign language learners may also be said to know too much. They may presume that certain features of the native language are universal; they may not only expect that the language to be learned will have some relatively small set of phonemes but that it will have exactly the same set as the native language, that the language to be learned will have an analogous politeness system, that noun phrases with numerals may omit plural marking, and so forth.

The adult foreign language learner constructs, therefore, a kind of surrogate for Universal Grammar from knowledge of the native language. The native language must be sifted: That which is likely to be universal must be separated from that which is an accidental property of the native language. Different learners may be expected to approach this task differently, and not all can be expected to come up with the same surrogate, and not all will be equally successful. The process of learning a foreign language may itself have an effect on this sifting, as the learner gradually realizes what of the native language seems to transfer well. And learners of third and fourth languages may be presumed to have a richer source of information and to stand a better chance of building an adequate surrogate Universal Grammar. In an interesting and ingenious series of studies, Kellerman (1977) showed that adult learners had ideas of what, in their native languages, was universal (and hence transferable to the language to be learned) and what was specific to the native language (and hence probably would not transfer well).

In summary, for what success is achieved in foreign language learning, the knowledge of the native language can assume much of the burden taken in child first language development by the assumption of an innate Universal Grammar. The foreign language learner is not a Martian, nor a hypothetical blank-slate infant. But because the indirect knowledge of Universal Grammar (UG) possible through the native language is incomplete and accidental, and since it also depends on the individual learner's ability to construct a UG-surrogate, one can expect some partial success, little chance of perfect success, and some considerable individual variation. This, of course, is exactly what is found.[9]

The nature of the general problem-solving cognitive system

One of the motivations for attributing a domain-specific language acquisition device to children is that language is a complicated abstract formal system, and young children seem not to have the general cognitive capacity to deal with such systems.[10] Adults, however, clearly do have that capacity, which is sometimes thought to arise around the age of puberty with the onset of what Piaget calls the stage of "formal operations" (Inhelder and Piaget 1958). This general human formal problem-

---

9 Although it seems to me that the view is quite plausible that both components of the domain-specific acquisition device have ceased to function in adults, there are other reasonable possibilities. One potentially interesting one is that the principles which define possible language may still be around, but that the means of constructing a particular grammar given the data of experience may not be. Thus A is still functioning, but B is not. Shuldberg (1986) has developed a model of L2 acquisition which seems to make this assumption. Though this alternative view is conceptually coherent, I do not pursue it here. The empirical issue is essentially whether there are characteristics of learner language which prove a knowledge of possible language above that which can be obtained as a by-product of the native language. As of now, there is no clear evidence of such characteristics. If such evidence should turn up, a somewhat less radical view of the Fundamental Difference Hypothesis than that proposed here may be justified.

10 Felix (1981) makes this point very convincingly.

solving capacity is immensely powerful, and it can be expected to shoulder a substantial explanatory burden. But its very powerful generality will limit its efficiency in the very specific case of language.[11]

A consideration of the precise nature of an adequate model of general adult cognitive problem solving as it functions in foreign language learning would take us too far afield. Some of its characteristics, however, are apparent. It must, for example, be goal-oriented. It must have ways of utilizing feedback and instruction. There must be some way of understanding explanations. A variety of mechanisms must clearly be available, including distributional analysis, analogy, and hypothesis formation and testing. The indeterminate intuitions of adult learners suggest something vaguely probabilistic and non-monotonic. There ought to be some way to move from controlled to automatic processing.

Work in cognitive science over the past decade or so has in general tended toward the development of very rich models of cognition with properties of just the sort that seem required. I have in mind particularly work in general problem solving, in schema theory, production systems, and the like. Representative work would include that of Newell and Simon (1972), Sacerdoti (1977), McDermott and Doyle (1980), and – my favorite candidate – Anderson (1983). There is, therefore, every reason to be optimistic that human cognitive systems will be found to have the correct properties.

In summary, the two substantial advantages which adults possess – previous knowledge of a language and a general cognitive ability to deal with abstract formal systems – are able approximately, but not perfectly, to compensate for the loss in adults of the child's knowledge of Universal Grammar and of a Learning Procedure designed specifically to construct grammars.

Alternative explanations

The proposal advanced here to explain the substantial obvious differences between child language development and adult foreign language learning is that in adults the language acquisition device ceases to operate, and that knowledge of first language and general problem solving serve as imperfect substitutes. This is not the only possibility, nor is it

11 One way to view this aspect of the problem is from the perspective of mathematical linguistics. Because general human cognition must be able to deal with such a wide variety of systems (not just the human languages), it clearly runs the danger of trying to pick out the language from much too large a set. If that set is really much too large (as, for example, the set of recursively enumerable languages), then Gold's (1967) theorems would apply, and the impossibility of foreign language learning without negative evidence would follow.

the dominant explanation in the field of second language acquisition research. Among the attempts which have been made, one can distinguish several general lines of approach.

1. First language development is controlled by an innate language acquisition system that no longer operates in adults. Adult language learning resembles general adult learning. This is the explanation advocated in this essay: The *Fundamental Difference Hypothesis* developed here is a radical version of this position.
2. Knowledge of an existing language interferes with the acquisition of a subsequent language: the *L1 Interference Hypothesis*.
3. There is something missing in the input to adults, so that adults do not get enough input or do not get the right kind: the *Input Hypothesis*.
4. Children have a crucial something, such as a personality state, attitude, degree of motivation, way of interacting, stage of ego development or socialization, or the like, which adults do not have: the *Affect or Socialization Hypothesis*.
5. Adults have a developed general problem-solving cognitive system that competes with their language acquisition system: the *Competing Cognitive Systems Hypothesis*.

This is quite a mixed bag of explanations. Some attribute the fact that adults often fail where children always succeed to a lack in adults (as the Input Hypothesis, the Affect Hypothesis, the Fundamental Difference Hypothesis); others attribute it to something extra in adults that gets in their way (as the Interference Hypothesis or the Competing Cognitive Systems Hypothesis). It is fair to say that among professional second language acquisition researchers, the Input Hypothesis (often buttressed by affect) has been most influential.

In the following sections, each major alternative to the first approach is discussed briefly and generally. The intent is not to review the often substantial body of published research dealing with each perspective but to show the conceptual strengths and weaknesses of each approach.

Interference

The idea that interference from the first language is the major obstacle to adult foreign language learning was dominant in (at least American) applied linguistics from the 1940s through the late 1960s. Here is a classic statement of the position:

The basic problems [of foreign language learning] arise not out of any essential difficulty in the features of the new language themselves, but primarily out of the special "set" created by the first language habits. (Charles C. Fries, in his foreword to Robert Lado's contrastive analysis textbook [1957:v])

The clear advantage to this explanation is that it relies on a very obvious and uncontroversial difference between adults and children. Children do not know a language yet, while adults do. Other explanations rely on differences which are much more nebulous and difficult to specify. Nevertheless, there are both empirical and theoretical reasons to doubt the adequacy of the Interference Hypothesis.

Note at the outset that the Interference Hypothesis, by itself, does not explain why children should differ from adults in their ability to learn a second language, and does not explain why a third language should often seem to be less difficult than a second. In the Interference Hypothesis, it is previous knowledge of a language, not some factor related to age, which impedes foreign language learning. In addition, no really adequate psychological mechanism was available to proponents of this hypothesis. The suggestion that interference is caused by proactive inhibition in habit formation relies on a view of language knowledge (of patterns as habits) that is now universally rejected.[12] Indeed, it is not really clear why previous knowledge of one language ought not to make learning subsequent languages easier rather than harder.

There is also an important empirical difficulty. It is now known that a substantial number of adult learners' errors are not attributable to interference. Many researchers have argued that interference accounts for perhaps 5–25 percent of grammatical errors.[13] Of course, the percentages themselves are not terribly important; they will depend greatly on what and how you decide to count, as well as on the (often difficult to make) attribution of error to cause. The important point is that many errors are clearly not the result of interference, no matter how one counts.

Input

Many adults trying to learn a foreign language, especially in a country where the language is not spoken and in a course that meets just a few hours a week for a year or two, obviously are exposed to much less language input than the average child. Often this difference is compounded by the fact that teachers may not themselves speak the language well and may content themselves with giving imperfect grammar lessons and quizzes. Also – and more speculatively – much of the language children hear directed at them deals with the "here and now."[14] Such

12 Actually, it has been pointed out that even within habit formation theory, there were reasons to reject proactive inhibition, since the relevant animal studies which provided the basis for the notion normally dealt with cases where an old set of habitual responses is extinguished and replaced by a new set. First languages are not extinguished when second languages are learned (Selinker 1969).
13 The most influential early study is that of Dulay and Burt (1973). Dulay, Burt, and Krashen (1982:102–8) provide a summary of the research of the 1970s.
14 As Newport, Gleitman, and Gleitman (1977) point out, this facet of adult–child interaction probably derives simply from the fact that the topics adults and children want to talk about are quite limited; that is, the immediate purpose of the use of concrete referents is not to facilitate language acquisition.

input may thus be more easily comprehended than much of the language addressed to adults. (Presumably, if the learner hasn't any idea of what an utterance is about, that input is of little value in acquisition.) Thus, the concentration of usable material in the input may be denser for a child than for an adult. A general deficiency of input may well explain many cases of adult foreign language errors.

However, what of the variation noticed among adults who have superficially equivalent input? And what of the cases where adults fail to attain native-speaker competence even after decades of residence among native speakers – a situation extremely common among adult immigrants and workers in foreign countries? Here the total amount of comprehensible input to which the adult learner is exposed must surely equal or even exceed the three-year-old child's.[15] And what of the observed inverse correlation of ultimate success with age? The response of the Input Hypothesis to these evident difficulties is to propose a more subtle definition of "exposed to input."

In its most clearly articulated form, for example that cautiously argued by Krashen (1982), the Input Hypothesis posits a learner-internal "filter" that prevents the input to which the learner is exposed from getting into the language acquisition device (LAD): "[I]t [the filter hypothesis] claims that no real change in the language acquisition device occurs at puberty. The LAD does not shut off, nor does it even 'degenerate.' Rather, the necessary input may be kept out" (Krashen 1982:216). Children either do not have such a filter, or it is relatively weak. The filter strengthens (or arises) around the age of puberty, and once strengthened, it may stay strong indefinitely. Hence the correlation of age with degree of success.

By positing the filter, the Input Hypothesis changes from an appealingly concrete explanation to one based on difficult-to-specify internal states of mind. What is this filter exactly? How can one tell whether it is strong or weak (apart from noticing how successful language learning is)? Most crucially, what specific characteristic does the filter have (What is its "bandwidth"?) that cuts out particular aspects of the input? And how does the lack of just these particular input characteristics account for acquisition failure? It makes little sense to think that the hypothetical filter would eliminate, say, every third sentence to which the learner is exposed and that this could explain failure. Krashen (1982), borrowing terminology from Stevick (1976), speaks of the input in some cases "striking deeper" (Krashen 1982:212). We are now sliding from theory into metaphor.

---

15 We put aside here cases where an immigrant lives in a socially isolated community, consorts only with colinguists, reads only native-language papers, watches only native-language television. The failure of such learners is no problem for even the most primitive input hypothesis.

In order to evaluate the input-cum-filter proposal, it will be necessary for its proponents to tell us much more exactly what the filter is, how it arises or is strengthened, and how its operation on the input can result in failure of the LAD (which is presumed still to operate and which, after all, is an extremely powerful engine: well-designed to be resistant to degenerate data and input deficiencies). This last and most essential step will also require some specification of the theory of the LAD (or at least of its crucial vulnerable aspects). Adherents of the Input Hypothesis have not yet addressed this question.[16] The Input Hypothesis still lacks any specified acquisition model.

Affect

As noted earlier, adult language learning seems to be much influenced by such factors as motivation, attitude, socialization, self-image, ego, and so forth. The effects are complicated and often confusing, but they are there. Child language development is not influenced by these factors, although general adult learning undeniably is. I have taken this as evidence that child first language development and adult foreign language learning are fundamentally different.

However, affect can be built into a version of the L1 = L2 perspective and has been used in attempts to explain differences in success. This requires a denial of the (apparently) obvious, that child language development is not crucially influenced by affective factors. Given the universal success of children, these crucial affective factors, whatever they are, must be invariably present in childhood. The difficulty with this approach is that it is not clear how to specify these crucial affective factors and how to identify them with the factors seen to influence adult language learning. For example, Heyde (1983) shows a correlation between proficiency and self-esteem in adult learners. Do all children have equal (and perfect) self-esteem? Naiman, Frohlich, Stern, and Todesco (1978), in a general study of what makes a good language learner, report an apparent lack of self-confidence among less successful second language learners. Do all children have equal (and perfect) self-confidence? There is a real danger here that concepts like self-esteem (etc.) may end up being defined as "self-esteem (etc.) in whatever sense children all may be said to have it and use it for language development." Although efforts have so far failed to define exactly what these crucial factors are which

---

16 The best efforts to specify how input might "strike deeper" in some cases – and thus account for differential success – really depend on the implicit assumption that adult language learning is governed by the same principles that control general adult nondomain-specific skill acquisition. Stevick (1976) relies heavily on the results of psychological research on general adult learning and the principles of memory. This is, of course, consistent with the position advocated here.

all children have and which adults do not always have, one should not perhaps give up entirely. Young children are, after all, very different from adults in many respects.

However, even if one could spot some consistent affective difference, it would still be necessary to present a theory of language acquisition in which such a difference could be expected to influence language acquisition in the observed ways. This requirement is analogous to that which filter theorists must meet in showing just what the filter is and how it would work in a general theory of language acquisition. As it stands, the Affect Hypothesis amounts to saying that children have a certain *je ne sais quoi*, absent in adults, which is crucial to language acquisition, *je ne sais comment*.

In many foreign language learning studies that purport to zero in on the affective factors, it seems just as likely that the affective variable is the result of proficiency rather than the cause. If this is true, then one might truly conclude that if a child should (for some mysterious reason) fail to acquire its native language, it would have, say, a poor self-image – be anxious, withdrawn, unwilling to speak. But now the explanation is backward. For example, in the Naiman, Frohlich, Stern, and Todesco (1978) study cited earlier, it was found that learners of French who enthusiastically raise their hands in class to volunteer also tend to do well on proficiency tests. The poorer performers do not like to be called on and are embarrassed when required to speak French. This is not really surprising: It follows from the reasonable assumption that people by and large like to do what they are good at, and they feel better about themselves if they succeed;[17] it probably tells us little about what the crucial affective factors are and how they work.

Affect may be conceived of as influencing acquisition more or less directly, or it may be combined in an interesting way with the filter hypothesis. It is claimed, by Krashen and others working in that framework, that affective states influence the strength of the filter. Thus, the effect of affect is indirect, via the filter. Again, at this stage of their development, the ideas here are still too nebulous to bear scrutiny.

Competing cognitive systems

Felix has suggested that adults do not suffer from some lack, but rather from an excess. Adult general problem solving gets in the way of a still functioning language acquisition system (Felix 1982, 1985). The story proceeds as follows. We know that language is a complex and abstract

17 This law is not absolute: Some people seem not to depend so much on overt success for a positive self-image; some people like to do things which they are not good at. This variation may explain why the observed correlations in the French study are only modest (r is about .3 to .4).

formal system. We know that children of age two cannot in general deal with abstract formal systems (compare Piaget's stage of concrete operations). Since young children can develop language, we can argue that a Language-Specific Cognitive System (LSC) allows the child to come up with the formal properties of language, even though formal systems in general are beyond the child. In young children, this LSC is the only cognitive module capable of dealing with language. (The LSC is the language acquisition device of other terminology.) So far we are on familiar ground.

Around puberty, humans develop a general ability to deal with abstract formal systems. Felix identifies this development with the onset of Piaget's stage of formal operations. This newly available general formal ability Felix calls the Problem-Solving Cognitive System (PSC). Now the adolescent has two ways to approach the processing of language data: either through the LSC or the PSC. That is, the Problem-Solving Cognitive System begins to *compete* with the Language-Specific Cognitive System in the analysis of language data. However, the PSC, unlike the LSC, is not particularly well-equipped to deal with language acquisition. (All the standard arguments about general problem solving being unable to account for language acquisition apply here.) In addition, the PSC is *insuppressible*, so that even though it is not particularly good at language learning, it will necessarily be used. Thus, adults fail to acquire languages. Variation in success may perhaps be attributed to variation in the degree to which the PSC wins the struggle. A strong PSC ought to inhibit natural language acquisition; a weak PSC ought to facilitate it.

This explanation has the advantage in that it attributes the decline in adult language learning ability to a relatively specific, locatable development – the rise of formal operations. There are, however, several difficulties with the proposal. First, it seems to suggest that good general problem solvers should be poor language learners, and vice versa. This has never been shown, and there is no reason to think that it is true. Going by this theory, the very worst language learners should be professional linguists, with their strong tendency to approach language analytically. While many linguists are not skilled polyglots, they are certainly not the very worst language learners, as the theory apparently would predict. One may try to get around this by claiming that those successful learners who are also skilled systematic problem solvers are not *really* applying problem solving to (internal, subconscious) language acquisition, even though it looks like they are. But now the concept of the PSC is driven inside, and we have no way of knowing the degree to which it is operating except by observing the degree of learner success.

A related problem involves motivation. Felix notes that the LSC is apparently not affected by motivation, attitude, and so forth since all children succeed regardless. Attitude and motivation do, of course, affect general adult problem solving. Here is the difficulty: If learners fail because of the strong competition from the PSC, and if low motivation and bad attitude can suppress the PSC (as we know they can), then the learners with the poorest attitudes and least motivation ought to be the most successful language learners.[18]

In both these cases, the Competing Cognitive Systems Hypothesis makes predictions that run opposite to the apparent truth. The basic difficulty is that adult foreign language acquisition seems to be favored by exactly those attributes which favor successful adult cognitive problem solving in general. The competition model predicts that anything favoring problem solving should prevent adult language learning.

A third difficulty is the timing of the system. Some mid-adolescents, on moving to a foreign country, seem to acquire the language extremely well (Asher and Garcia 1969; Seliger, Krashen, and Ladefoged 1975). The obvious explanation for these successes within the framework of competing cognitive systems would have to be a delayed development of formal operations. No one would suggest that this is the reason. From the perspective adopted by the Fundamental Difference Hypothesis, the decline of the LAD is not a consequence of the rise of formal operations, but an independent development. The decline clearly does not take place at puberty, but some years later, perhaps toward the end of the teens. We might therefore expect that the early teens, where both formal operations and the LAD are available, would be an especially good time for foreign language learning. This would be in accord with the evidence cited by Snow (1983).

A final difficulty is conceptual. It is highly unlikely that an existing cognitive system, designed perfectly for a specific task, should then be somehow blocked by a later arising system, ill-suited for that task. It is not impossible that such a situation should arise in evolution, but it seems unlikely. Humans possess a good system for depth perception; this they have at a very young age, long before formal operations. After the onset of formal operations, humans do not then cease to use the old system for depth perception and instead rely on formal geometrical analysis (and bumbling about). Rather, humans regularly use general problem solving for just those cases in which no specific cognitive module provides an adequate solution. General problem solving will ordinarily be observed to supplement domain-specific systems, not to supplant them. If the LSC did cease to operate, as argued by the Fundamental

18 Felix, of course, recognizes this problem. He suggests a sort of loop or bleed-across, where some of the input that makes its way past an affective filter into the PSC might then also feed the LSC. In this way, the affective filter on the PSC might indirectly affect the LSC. To the extent to which modifications of this sort are necessary, the model loses much of its appeal.

Difference Hypothesis, then it would be natural for the PSC to take over. If the LSC did continue to be available and in good shape, it is difficult to see why it would not process linguistic data as it is designed to.

Evidence for Universal Grammar in adult foreign language learning

Up to this point, I have considered only very general characteristics of adult foreign language learning that seem to favor the Fundamental Difference Hypothesis (the nine points listed earlier in this chapter), and I have shown how major alternative approaches encounter difficulties. But since the Fundamental Difference Hypothesis makes specific claims about the nature of the difference (see "The logical problem of foreign language learning"), it also yields definite predictions about the sort of linguistic knowledge adults can be expected to attain or fail to attain, and about the course of acquisition.

Recently, several lines of research have begun to bring evidence that in principle bears on the Fundamental Difference Hypothesis. I will mention three such lines here, which I formulate as three important research questions. There are others, but these three seem particularly promising. All are closely related and are informed by Chomsky's recent views on the nature of Universal Grammar and language acquisition (e.g., 1981a, b).

1. Are learners' languages constrained by Universal Grammar (UG)? If adults do not have direct access to UG, then in principle interlanguages need not be "natural languages." This is not to say that an interlanguage can be just anything. After all, the learner does have data about the foreign language and at least an imperfect surrogate UG based on already known languages. Still, especially in the case of relatively abstract properties of a language, learners might come up with "impossible" principles. For example, English reflexives must be *locally bound*, where "locally" means approximately that a reflexive pronoun and its antecedent must be arguments of the same predicate. (In the typical case, they must be, respectively, subjects and objects of the same verb.) Thus, *John shaved himself* is grammatical, since *John* and *himself* are both arguments of *shave*. But **John told Mary to shave himself* is ungrammatical, since *John* is an argument of *told* while *himself* is an argument of *shave*. Other languages also have bound anaphors like reflexives, but some variation is possible in the definition of "local." Korean, for example, has a "reflexive" (*caki*) that can be bound by an antecedent anywhere so long as it is in the same sentence. Thus, the Korean equiv-

alents of both of the examples are grammatical. Universal Grammar allows other definitions of locality that languages can use. Wexler and Manzini's (1987) theory of Universal Grammar allows about half a dozen possible locality definitions – values of their Governing Category Parameter. Will a speaker of Korean learning English have trouble arriving at the correct locality definition for anaphoric binding? Will the student's initial hypotheses proceed from a view of language colored by the knowledge of Korean? And – crucially – will a Korean's guesses be constrained to just those possibilities countenanced by Universal Grammar? Or will certain "unnatural possibilities" also be entertained? Finer and Broselow (1986), in a small-scale (six-subject) pilot study, investigated Korean intuitions about English reflexives and personal pronouns. The subjects' hypotheses about English reflexive binding seemed to be Korean-influenced. In some cases, the learners seemed to be quite confused about binding possibilities, not operating consistently according to any known UG-permitted definition of locality. (This is my interpretation, not Finer and Broselow's.) However, Finer and Broselow emphasize that there is a clear *trend* toward using a locality definition which, while not exactly Korean and not exactly English, is indeed one of the possibilities countenanced by Universal Grammar. The results are thus ambiguous. While the shadowy hand of UG does seem to be pushing learners in one direction (a finding obviously uncomfortable to the Fundamental Difference Hypothesis), learners do not seem to be constrained consistently by the "laws" of UG. Only additional studies along these lines, more subtle methodology, clearer statements of the principles of UG, and refined theories of the place of UG in foreign language learning will eventually clarify the picture.

2. Do adults have access to UG-generated knowledge? In many cases, knowledge which native speakers demonstrably have about what is and what is not a possible sentence of the language cannot be derived in any obvious way from the data of experience. What, for example, led a native speaker of English to realize that *What guns did the police arrest the men who were carrying?* is ungrammatical? (The sentence fronts *what guns* from object position after *carrying*; if it were grammatical the sentence would mean *The police arrested the men who were carrying what guns?*) Knowledge of the ungrammaticality of sentences such as these is thought to derive by the interaction of the principle of Universal Grammar with the specific principles of English. In this case, Universal Grammar constrains the English *wh*-movement so as not to apply across a relative clause boundary. The Universal principle is called Subjacency. In any language with *wh*-movement, movement must be constrained by Subjacency. Of course, if a language does not have *wh*-movement at all – and many languages do not – then the constraining effects of UG on *wh*-movement will not be evident in that language. Do native speakers

of a language without *wh*-movement, when learning a language with
wh-movement as adults, know that *wh*-movement cannot cross relative
clause boundaries? If they do, this is *prima facie* evidence that Universal
Grammar continues to operate in adult language learning. Here, too,
the results are ambiguous. For example, Bley-Vroman, Felix, and Ioup
(1988) studied the intuitions of native speakers of Korean (which does
not have *wh*-movement) in English. While subjects did perform significantly better than chance would have predicted, they did not all show
the sort of consistent lawful behavior which one would expect if UG
were clearly operating. While conceding that the results were somewhat
equivocal, the authors concluded that UG (or something very like it)
must be operating. (See Schachter, this volume, for a closely related
study.) But they were puzzled that the results were not stronger. Other
scholars have also done work with the same general logic and with the
same general results. The work of White (see, for example, this volume)
is particularly well-reasoned. In one earlier study, White gives a judicious
evaluation of one typical set of results. The majority of her subjects, she
says, "do not give the impression of floundering around in the way that
might be expected if unconstrained hypothesis testing was the means by
which the L2 learner establishes the bounding nodes for subjacency in
L2. However, 40 per cent do give the impression of indecisiveness, and
whilst this might be explicable in a number of ways, one cannot exclude
the possibility that some L2 learners do not have access to UG any more
... so that *ad hoc* behaviour results"(White 1985a:12). One must agree
with White that "this whole issue has to be extensively pursued with
more varied testing" (White 1985a:12).

3. Do properties "cluster" in adult-learned languages? Certain properties in languages tend to go together. For example, languages which
may optionally omit pronoun subjects (Spanish is an example) also allow
free inversion of subject and object, do not have pleonastic "dummy"
subjects, and share a variety of other properties. Such languages are
often called *pro-drop* (pronoun dropping) or *null subject*. English, unlike
Spanish, has none of these properties. It has been conjectured that such
clusters of properties are controlled by Universal Grammar. Essentially,
the child learner "notices" a triggering property in the input and then
deduces that all the other correlated properties must also be present. In
the terminology of current generative grammar, the learner is said to
"set a parameter of UG," of which the correlated properties are "deductive consequences." (See Chomsky [1981b] for discussion. White
[1985b] provides a good summary of the logic as applied to second
language acquisition.) Do learners' languages show such clusterings?
Does the acquisition of the "trigger" push over the deductive dominoes?
White's(1985b)study of the pro-drop parameter is an excellent example;
it seems not to show clear clustering in foreign language acquisition.

Hilles's (1986) longitudinal study, also of the acquisition of pro-drop, seems to show both clustering and a triggering effect (the presence/absence of pleonastics). (But Hilles studied a subject who was but twelve years old.) Our investigation of these questions is just beginning.

The possibility of exploring such specific questions gives current research in second language acquisition its brisk air of excitement and promise. The fact that the results are often difficult to interpret is not surprising and should not discourage. The arguments from linguistic theory to particular predictions are often intricate chains of inference. Experimental tests themselves are fraught with uncertainty: What is the real relationship between a learner's internal grammar and performance on a grammaticality judgment test, or on a repetition task, or in free production? One weak link in the chain is often the initial linguistic theory of Universal Grammar. The theory of parameters, especially, is just in its infancy. We can expect both theories and experimental techniques to be sharpened.

Conclusion

Linguistic theory and cognitive psychology have made great strides in recent years. On the horizon we can now see the possibility of explaining some of the mysteries of child language development. It is precisely this progress which now enables the mysteries of adult foreign language learning to be investigated from a new perspective. In particular, we can now ask from a new perspective whether the adult is guided by the language faculty in the same way that a child is. And we know just what sort of evidence is relevant. It is possible that the Fundamental Difference Hypothesis, at least as articulated here in its radical form, may turn out to be false. Surely it will emerge as overly crude. But we can be certain that the debate will enrich our understanding.

References

Anderson, J. R. 1983. *The Architecture of Cognition*. Cognitive Science Series, Vol. 5. Cambridge, Mass.: Harvard University Press.

Asher, J., and G. Garcia. 1969. The optimal age to learn a foreign language. *Modern Language Journal* 38: 334–41.

Bley-Vroman, R. 1983. The comparative fallacy in interlanguage studies: the case of systematicity. *Language Learning* 33: 1–17.

1986. Hypothesis testing in second language acquisition theory. *Language Learning* 36: 353–76.

In press. The logical problem of foreign language learning. *Linguistic Analysis*.

Bley-Vroman, R., S. Felix, and G. Ioup. 1988. The accessibility of Universal Grammar in adult language learning. *Second Language Research* 4: 1–32.

Chomsky, N. 1965. *Aspects of the Theory of Syntax.* Cambridge, Mass.: MIT Press.

1981a. Principles and parameters in syntactic theory. In *Explanation in Linguistics: The Logical Problem of Language Acquisition*, N. Hornstein and D. Lightfoot, eds. London: Longman.

1981b. *Lectures on Government and Binding: The Pisa Lectures.* Dordrecht, The Netherlands: Foris.

Cohen, A. D., and M. Robbins. 1976. Toward assessing interlanguage performance: the relationship between selected errors, learners' characteristics, and learners' explanations. *Language Learning* 26: 45–66.

Dulay, H., and M. K. Burt. 1973. Should we teach children syntax? *Language Learning* 23: 245–58.

Dulay, H., M. Burt, and S. Krashen. 1982. *Language Two.* Oxford: Oxford University Press.

Felix, S. 1981. On the (in)applicability of Piagetian thought to language learning. *Studies in Second Language Acquisition* 3:201–20.

1982. *Psycholinguistische Aspekte des Zweitsprachenerwerbs.* Tübingen: Günter Narr.

1985. More evidence on competing cognitive systems. *Second Language Research* 1: 47–72. (Contains an English-language summary of theory of Felix [1982])

Finer, D., and E. Broselow. 1986. Second language acquisition of reflexive binding. In *Proceedings of NELS 16.* Amherst: University of Massachusetts.

Gardner, R., and W. Lambert. 1972. *Attitudes and Motivation in Second Language Learning.* Rowley, Mass.: Newbury House.

Gold, E. M. 1967. Language identification in the limit. *Information and Control.* 16: 447–74.

Heyde, A. 1983. Self-esteem and the acquisition of French. In *Second Language Acquisition Studies*, K. M. Bailey, M. Long, and S. Peck, eds., 175–87. Rowley, Mass.: Newbury House.

Hilles, S. 1986. Interlanguage and the pro-drop parameter. *Second Language Research* 2:33–52.

Inhelder, B., and J. Piaget. 1958. *The Growth of Logical Thinking from Childhood to Adolescence.* New York: Basic Books.

Kellerman, E. 1977. Toward a characterisation of the strategy of transfer. *Interlanguage Studies Bulletin* 2: 59–92.

Krashen, S. 1981. *Second Language Acquisition and Second Language Learning.* London: Pergamon Press.

1982. Accounting for child-adult differences in second language rate and attainment. In *Child-Adult Differences in Second Language Acquisition*, S. Krashen, R. Scarcella, and M. Long, eds., 202–26. Rowley, Mass.: Newbury House.

Krashen, S., and H. Seliger. 1975. The essential contributions of formal instruction in adult second language learning. *TESOL Quarterly* 9: 173–83.

Lado, R. 1957. *Linguistics Across Cultures.* Ann Arbor: University of Michigan Press.

Lenneberg, E. 1967. *Biological Foundations of Language.* New York: Wiley.

Long, M. 1983. Does second language instruction make a difference? A review of the research. *TESOL Quarterly* 17: 359–82.

Madden, C., N. Bailey, M. Eisenstein, and L. Anderson. 1978. Beyond statistics in second language acquisition research. In *Second Language Acquisition Research: Issues and Implications*, W. Ritchie, ed., 109–25. New York: Academic Press.

McDermott, D., and J. Doyle. 1980. Non-monotonic logic I. *Artificial Intelligence* 13: 41–72.

Meisel, J. M., H. Clahsen, and M. Pienemann. 1981. On determining developmental stages in natural second language acquisition. *Studies in Second Language Acquisition* 3: 109–35.

Moulton, J., and G. Robinson. 1981. *The Organization of Language*. Cambridge: Cambridge University Press.

Munby, J. 1978. *Communicative Syllabus Design*. Cambridge: Cambridge University Press.

Naiman, N., M. Frohlich, D. Stern, and A. Todesco. 1978. *The Good Language Learner*. Toronto: Ontario Institute for Studies in Education.

Newell, A., and H. Simon. 1972. *Human Problem Solving*. Englewood Cliffs, N.J.: Prentice-Hall.

Newport, E. L., L. R. Gleitman, and H. Gleitman. 1977. Mother, I'd rather do it myself: some effects and non-effects of maternal speech style. In *Talking to Children: Language Input and Acquisition*, C. E. Snow and C. A. Ferguson, eds. Cambridge: Cambridge University Press.

Pinker, S. 1984. *Language Learnability and Language Development*. Cambridge, Mass.: Harvard University Press.

Rosansky, E. 1976. Methods and morphemes in second language acquisition. *Language Learning* 26: 409–25.

Sacerdoti, E. D. 1977. *A Structure for Plans and Behavior*. New York: Elsevier.

Schachter, J., A. F. Tyson, and F. J. Diffley. 1976. Learner intuitions of grammaticality. *Language Learning* 26: 67–76.

Schumann, J. 1976. Social distance as a factor in second language acquisition. *Language Learning* 26: 135–43.

1978. *The Pidginization Process*. Rowley, Mass.: Newbury House.

Seliger, H. 1978. Implications of a multiple critical periods hypothesis for second language learning. In *Second Language Acquisition Research: Issues and Implications*, W. Ritchie, ed., 11–19. New York: Academic Press.

Seliger, H., S. Krashen, and P. Ladefoged. 1975. Maturational constraints in the acquisition of second language accent. *Language Sciences* 36: 20–22. [Reprinted in *Child-Adult Differences in Second Language Acquisition*, S. Krashen, R. Scarcella, and M. Long, eds. Rowley, Mass.: Newbury House]

Selinker, L. 1969. Language transfer. *General Linguistics* 9: 67–92.

1972. Interlanguage. *IRAL* 10: 209–31.

Shuldberg, K. 1986. Syntactic and Semantic Issues in Second Language Acquisition. Ph.D. dissertation, University of Texas at Austin.

Snow, C. 1983. Age differences in second language acquisition: research findings and folk psychology. In *Second Language Acquisition Studies*, K. M. Bailey, M. Long, and S. Peck, eds., 141–50. Rowley, Mass.: Newbury House.

Stevick, E. 1976. *Memory, Meaning, and Method*. Rowley, Mass.: Newbury House.

Van Ek, J. A. 1975. *The Threshold Level*. Cambridge: Cambridge University Press.

Wexler, K., and P. W. Culicover. 1980. *Formal Principles of Language Acquisition*. Cambridge, Mass.: MIT Press.

Wexler, K., and R. Manzini. 1987. Parameters and learnability in binding theory. In *Parameter Setting*, T. Roeper and E. Williams, eds. Dordrecht, The Netherlands: Reidel.

White, L. 1985a. The acquisition of parameterized grammars: subjacency in second language acquisition. *Second Language Research* 1: 1–17.

1985b. The "pro-drop" parameter in adult second language acquisition. *Language Learning* 35: 47–62.

PART II:
SYNTAX

All of the chapters in this section are concerned with the acquisition of the syntactic component of a grammar and all assume the Government-Binding Theory of language outlined in Chomsky (1981, 1986), van Riemsdijk and Williams (1986), and elsewhere. Furthermore, they all, to some extent, focus on the logical problem of foreign language learning (Bley-Vroman), that is, how the adult second language learner who attains reasonable proficiency in the target language does so on the basis of impoverished input – thus necessitating another knowledge source and/or set of learning procedures to be posited, which will, together with the input, suffice to explain the attained proficiency.

The claim that the input to the learner is impoverished needs to be amplified somewhat since it is crucial to the argumentation underlying the work of those espousing a Universal Grammar approach to language acquisition. Let us consider two different kinds of input problems. In the first case, the learner will doubtless hear two phrases: *thanks a lot* and *thanks anyway*. The learner's task is to figure out on which occasions each is appropriate and whether or not they are interchangeable. Although the distinction between these two phrases is not necessarily an easy one, the learner will have information from the input indicating that each phrase does occur and that guides in the appropriate use of each phrase. The second case, however, is more complicated. Suppose the learner has figured out how to make *wh*-questions from simple sentences and is working on making them from more complex sentences. The learner can produce such sentences as *Who came?*, *What did the boy do?*, and *Where did the ball come from?*, and notices that *wh*-questions involve movement of the *wh*-word to the beginning of the sentence (unless it is already there) and inversion of subject and auxiliary verb. Thus, he or she might formulate a rule such as: Move a *wh*-word to the beginning of the sentence and invert subject and auxiliary. This works for many simple sentences and for many complex ones as well, for example: *Who do you think Sam hit?* and *What did he say killed the rabbit?*. But this rule will also allow the learner to produce such sentences as *What did Susan visit the store that had in stock?* and *What did the police detective recognize the man that had sold?*. Such sentences do *not* occur in the input from native speakers, and as any native speaker knows, they are ungrammatical. The simple, logical, "move *wh-*" rule stated earlier is insufficient. The only way the learner could learn that the starred sentences are ungrammatical would be for these sentences to occur in the input and be identified as ungrammatical (which we know does not happen) or for the learner to produce them and get sufficient corrective feedback so that she or he can figure out what the appropriate constraints are – and we do not find convincing evidence of this either. The logical conclusion is that if the learner has knowledge that the starred sentences are ungrammatical, this knowledge must *not* be derived by the learner from the input but instead is determined by the learner's *innate language faculty*.

The four authors in this section assume, then, that child first language learners are equipped with certain innate knowledge, called Universal Grammar (or UG), in the form of a set of universal substantive *principles* (which prevent them from producing sentences such as the starred sentences given earlier and many, many others). In addition, associated with some of these principles are *parameters* – strictly defined possibilities of variation across languages. Each parameter is associated with a cluster of linguistic properties. The values of the parameters are set by interaction with the input to which the learner is exposed, thus allowing the learner to arrive at the core grammar of the target language.

Given these assumptions, interesting questions can then be posed about the case of adult second language learning. Are the principles and parameters of UG available in their entirety to adult language learners? Can the parameter match/mismatch between native and target languages account for the influence of the native language on the acquisition of the target? Is there an implicational hierarchy in the acquisition of the set of properties associated with a particular parameter? Are there certain types of failures to fully acquire second languages that involve principles other than those of UG – in other words, are there learning principles that do not fully operate in the adult language learner? These are the questions addressed in this section.

In addressing one aspect of the first question, Schachter considers a case in which a proposed universal, Subjacency, does not appear at the level of surface structure in one language (Korean), and exhibits itself in more restricted ways in some languages (Chinese and Indonesian) than it does in English. Given that Subjacency is assumed to be innate and to have psychological reality for speakers of all languages, and given that it is never explicitly taught in language classes, Schachter questions whether evidence for its universality can be found in proficient speakers of English whose native languages are Korean, Chinese, or Indonesian. She suggests that if these subjects show evidence of Subjacency in their English grammaticality judgments, then this would provide convincing evidence of the psychological reality of this principle and would also indicate that all humans have access to the principles of UG, even as adults. It would also provide an explanation for the fact that second language speakers do not ever seem to violate linguistic universals. What she finds is a rather more complicated picture, in which a distinct minority of proficient non-native English speakers appear to have access to the Subjacency principle, whereas most do not. These results are problematic, she argues, both for those who claim the principles of UG are available in their entirety to adult second language learners as well as to those who claim that only those principles available in the learner's first language are available in the adult second language learning case.

Both Liceras and Flynn investigate situations in which a parameter of an individual's native language differs from a parameter of the individual's target language – forcing a "resetting" of that first parameter, which necessarily influences a cluster of linguistic properties.

Liceras chooses Spanish as the target language and the pro-drop parameter (involving null subjects, verb-subject inversion, and apparent *that*-trace violations) as the variables to be studied. She suggests that there may be an implicational hierarchy among the pro-drop properties such that if *that*-trace has been acquired, subject-verb inversions and null subjects must have been acquired at an earlier stage in the learner's target language development.

She also explores the possibility that one setting of a parameter may be considered to be the unmarked setting, the other setting being the marked one, and argues that if the target language setting of the parameter is the unmarked one, learners of that target language may begin with that unmarked setting rather than their (marked) native language setting. This in effect would mean that adult second language learners have access to all possible parameter settings, not just the ones instantiated in their native languages.

Flynn continues her earlier exploration of the head-initial/head-final parameter, extending it to the investigation of the acquisition of bound variables in English restrictive relative clauses by adult native speakers of Japanese and Spanish. Of special interest in this study is that in both English and Spanish the head-position setting is the same (head-initial), whereas in Japanese the head-position setting is different (head-final). Thus Flynn can observe the differences in behavior between subjects whose native language head-position setting coincides with that of English and subjects whose native language head-position setting differs from that of English.

Her main question is: Are learners' hypotheses about restrictive relative clauses in English constrained by the head-direction parameter? And her results indicate significant differences in patterns of acquisition between Spanish and Japanese speakers, which, she argues, provide important corroboration for a parameter-setting model of UG as well as evidence for the psychological reality of the head-direction parameter in a theory of grammar.

In the last essay in this section, White tackles a complicating factor that has not been raised as an issue by the first three authors. She assumes, as do the others, that the principles of UG are innate and that they place limitations on the types of grammars that learners develop, thus facilitating the acquisition of the correct grammar. She points out, in addition, that recent proposals within learnability theory argue for learning principles, independent of UG, which further facilitate the acquisition process. One of these proposed principles is the *Subset* Principle, which is said to order the child's hypotheses in such a way that the child will not start off with overinclusive grammars that would require negative evidence for disconfirmation.

Assuming that the principles of UG and the learning principles are distinct, which White does, one can then investigate whether certain types of failure among second language learners to arrive at nativelike grammars may be attributed either to the impossibility of access to UG or to the failure of operation of one or more of the learning principles. White suggests that the latter is the case, and that the Subset Principle no longer operates effectively in second language acquisition. This failure, she suggests, is linked to certain cases of mother tongue influence and also to fossilization.

References

Chomsky, N. 1981. *Lectures on Government and Binding*. Dordrecht, The Netherlands: Foris.

1986. *Barriers*. Cambridge, Mass.: MIT Press.

van Riemsdijk, H., and E. Williams. 1986. *Introduction to the Theory of Grammar*. Cambridge, Mass.: MIT Press.

3 *Testing a proposed universal*

Jacquelyn Schachter

Background

About 20 years ago, the fledgling field of second language acquisition research received considerable impetus from the suggestion by S. P. Corder, that although there may be differences in such factors as previous knowledge, motivation, and so forth, the processes of child first and adult second language acquisition may very well be the same. "Let us say," he argued, that "given motivation, it is inevitable that a human being will learn a second language if he is exposed to the language data" (1967:166).

More recently, the question of how the process of second language acquisition is best accounted for has been reformulated by several linguists interested in exploring the implications of the currently evolving linguistic theory known as Universal Grammar (UG). As is well known, UG is viewed as a theory designed to account in part for an adult's mature grammatical competence. It is also a theory consistent with what are known to be the general facts of child first language acquisition. Grammatical theory, according to UG proponents, is developed in the context of this remarkable feat of children and is meant to be a partial explanation of it. If one were convinced that the claims of Corder and many others who have followed this line of thinking are correct, that the processes of second language acquisition are essentially those of first language acquisition, then it would seem reasonable that the next step would be to explore, within the UG framework, the possibilities of finding further similarities in first and second language acquisition, and, even better, explanations for them.

White, in a 1985 article, points out that adults as well as children are faced with what is known as the logical problem of language acquisition, that is, that the input they are exposed to is degenerate, finite, and underdeterminate, and that neither first nor second language learners have available to them from the data the same kinds of crucial information that linguists have, the information that certain strings are grammatical and others are not. She states:

[I]f interlanguage grammars are natural languages as many have argued...
then it is possible that the range of options available to the second language
learner is constrained by Universal Grammar in ways similar to what happens in first language acquisition. (1985:3–4)

I shall not attempt a complete characterization of Universal Grammar
here (see Chomsky 1981a, b), except to say that it is conceived of by
its proponents as a linguistic theory consisting of relatively autonomous
modules, each characterized by a small number of nonviolable universal
principles of a quite abstract sort that account to a large extent for the
similarities across all languages. Associated with some of these principles
are sets of parameters that define possible variations across languages,
the setting of each parameter being determined on the basis of experience
with the input. These principles and parameters are said to constitute
the human language endowment, the initial state which determines,
together with the input from a specific language, the grammar of an
individual, "i.e., the mentally (ultimately physically) represented system
that constitutes the state of knowledge attained by a given individual"
(Chomsky 1981a:33).

In the case of first language acquisition, the child is said to bring to
the language acquisition task this innately specified system, the components of which sharply restrict the kinds of hypotheses the child will
consider for a given set of empirical data, and which, together with the
input, will determine the grammar of a specific language. This system
of linguistic principles, together with an as yet not well-specified set of
domain-specific learning procedures, is said to constitute the language
faculty, a faculty largely independent of, but interacting with, other
cognitive systems or modules.

In the case of postpuberty second language learning, there are currently
three positions on the question of the reactivation of the language faculty.

1. The first position is that as long as the language faculty has been
activated normally in the course of first language acquisition, it can be
reaccessed and reactivated in the course of acquiring a second language,
and that the learner's knowledge of the first language and greater cognitive development will have no serious effects on the process itself or
on the hypotheses the learner is capable of constructing or does construct
(see Krashen 1981, 1985).

2. The second position also assumes that UG can be and is reactivated.
However, advocates of this second position claim that the first language
parameter settings have an impact on the acquisition of the second
language in that the learner will assume that the settings of the first
language are appropriate for the second language as well, unless positive
evidence from the input indicates otherwise. In this view, language transfer errors arise because the L2 (second language) learner assumes the
L1 (first language) parameter setting still holds; in cases in which the

appropriate setting for the second language is less marked, transfer errors may occur that will never be eradicated (see Flynn 1983 and this volume, White 1985 and this volume).

With both of these positions, then, learners have access to all principles and possible parameter settings; they differ only in their account of what constitutes the default parameter setting.

3. The third position constitutes a direct challenge to the notion that UG in its entirety is available to the language learner after the critical period for first language acquisition. Its advocates propose that an individual retains only that portion of UG that is instantiated in the individual's first language, and that access to those principles defining possible rule systems may no longer be available, nor may the other possible parameter settings not instantiated in the first language. According to this view, the adult second language learner would have available for acquisition of the target language only the principles and parameter settings instantiated in the first language (see Bley-Vroman, this volume, and Schachter 1988 for some discussion).

Positions 1 and 2 are, clearly, variants of the same general position, since both assume that the learner has available both the principles and parameters of UG, differing only in their account of how the parameters get set (or reset). Position 3, in contrast, challenges the assumption that UG in its entirety is still available, asserting that there will be certain principles and many parameter settings not available to the adult second language learner – that is, all those not instantiated in the learner's native language. As Bley-Vroman (this volume) points out, the contrast in consequences is clear: If adult language learners use the same cognitive module as child language acquirers, then adults will have access to the principles of Universal Grammar in their totality, and acquired foreign language competence will reflect these principles in the same way that native language competence does, even though the principles themselves cannot be derived from the input directly (Positions 1 and 2). If, on the other hand, adults do not demonstrate such competence, then one can only conclude that adult learners do *not* have access to Universal Grammar in the same way that a child does (Position 3). And, as he further points out, the evidence ought not, in principle, be difficult to obtain. One need "merely" ascertain whether non-native speakers who have learned a language as adults share native-speaker intuitions on the relevant structures. If they do, then we can say they have access to UG. If they do not, then their knowledge of UG must be restricted to that which is instantiated in their native language.

In this article I want to focus on the *contrast* between Position 3 and Positions 1 and 2, ignoring the question of how parameters get set, and aim directly at the underlying question: Do postpuberty second language learners have access to the principles of UG?

The choice of a principle

Not all principles are appropriate candidates for such testing since not all principles are accessible to surface level analysis. One principle amenable to testing is that of Subjacency, which has been formulated as a constraint on movement rules at the S-structure level (but see Huang 1982). The principle itself is that no constituent can be moved over more than a single bounding category,[1] bounding categories for English being noun phrase (NP) and subject (S). This allows one to account for the difference in grammaticality between the sentences in (1) as well as in many other cases.

1a. What did Sue destroy?
     What [$_s$ did Sue destroy t]²
1b. *What did Sue destroy a book about?
     *What [$_s$ did Sue destroy [NP a book about t]]

In 1a, the *wh*-word must cross only one bounding category (S) in order to get into the complementizer position (COMP),[3] but in 1b it must cross two bounding categories (NP and S) and is thus ungrammatical.

If one ignores the question of what counts as a bounding category, which is relevant only to the question of parameterization, language can vary in two ways with respect to Subjacency.

a. type of extraction: *wh*-word, relative pronoun, topic
b. domain of extraction: sentential subject, relative clause, noun phrase complement, embedded question

That is, Subjacency is claimed to be incorporated in the grammar of all languages, but evidence for it will vary from language to language depending on what can be extracted in a language or what constructions there can be extraction from. These are the kinds of variability between languages which I wish to consider here, since they allow for a direct test of the existence of the proposed Subjacency principle as a psychological knowledge-state in speakers of second languages.

Indonesian (according to F. Müller-Gotama, personal communication) is a language in which Subjacency appears to operate somewhat as it does in English, at least with regard to *wh*-movement. It allows *wh*-movement, but with one significant difference. The *wh*-word must

---

1 A bounding category can be viewed as a barrier to extraction of a constituent from an embedded clause. In English, bounding categories are said to be S and NP (see van Riemsdijk and Williams 1986).
2 The symbol t marks the site from which a *wh*-word was extracted; it is called a *trace*.
3 Following Bresnan (1970, 1972) and van Riemsdijk and Williams (1986), I am assuming that the initial position of a clause is characterized by a complementizer position (COMP) introduced by the following rules: S'→COMP S, S→NP AUX VP.

be promoted to subject in its own clause before being moved to the beginning of the sentence.[4] If the principle of Subjacency is available for adult second language learning, according to all three positions laid out earlier, native speakers of Indonesian who are proficient in English should have no trouble identifying Subjacency violations in English that involve *wh*-movement of subjects. Whether or not the possibility of moving *wh*-subjects will extend to the movement of *wh*-objects is unclear. (As will be seen, all the test sentences involving Subjacency violations are ones in which *wh*-objects have been moved.)

Note, however, that if a language does not make use of movement rules of the type that are constrained by Subjacency (i.e., clause-external movement), then it will show no evidence of Subjacency at the level of S-structure. A number of languages exist, for example, which do not form *wh*-questions by moving the *wh*-word to the front of the sentence, thus obviating the need for the Subjacency principle to apply to *wh*-question formation. Korean and Chinese are languages of this type. Korean, furthermore (according to M. Saito, personal communication), is tightly constrained in that it does not allow other types of extraction that show evidence of Subjacency at the level of S-structure. Chinese (see Huang 1982) is somewhat less constrained in that while it does not allow *wh*-word extraction, it does allow relative pronoun extraction from certain constructions (complex noun phrases and sentential subjects but not embedded questions) and topic extraction; it thus shows limited evidence of Subjacency at the level of S-structure.

The question of the psychological status of universals such as Subjacency in the minds of individual speakers of languages that show more severely restricted surface Subjacency effects than English immediately arises. If Subjacency is part of the latent knowledge of native speakers of Korean, then it would be valuable to find demonstrable evidence provided by speakers of Korean that could validate this. And if it is true, as Huang (1982) claims, that Subjacency obtains in Chinese as it does in English, although some of its effects are vacuous, then it would be valuable to find demonstrable evidence provided by speakers of that language that could validate it, in the vacuous cases as well as in the occurring (nonvacuous) ones. Yet grammatical judgments on *wh*-movement in those languages cannot provide us with such evidence because those languages do not have *wh*-movement.

Speakers of these languages do, however, learn, or at least become proficient communicating in, second languages that exhibit the configurations necessary to determine evidence of Subjacency in a wider range of constructions than those exhibited in the native language. Speakers

---

4 How the Subjacency principle interacts with relative pronoun extraction and topic extraction in Indonesian is not yet clear.

of Korean and Chinese can and do learn to communicate in English, and English does have a *wh*-fronting rule together with the Subjacency constraint on its applicability. If Subjacency exists as a constraint in the psychological knowledge-state of these individuals, it might be detectable through their English grammaticality judgments.

This issue of the latent status of universal principles such as Subjacency is of critical concern to the field of second language acquisition, in particular to the debate as to whether and to what extent UG is reactivated in the case of postpuberty second language acquisition. If native speakers of a language that does not exhibit evidence of Subjacency (e.g., Korean) or evidence regarding a particular type of extraction or extraction from a particular domain (e.g., Chinese and Indonesian) become proficient speakers of languages that do exhibit Subjacency in these areas, then testing these speakers for evidence of Subjacency in the second language becomes a critical test of the three positions stated earlier. Those who espouse Positions 1 and 2 must claim that speakers of Korean and Chinese have latent knowledge of this abstract principle (since it is a universal and part of UG) and can make use of it in all cases where it is required in the second language. Those who hold Position 3 must argue that when Subjacency is not instantiated in the first language (e.g., Korean), it is no longer available for constraining extraction in the second language. Much less clear is the relationship between Position 3 and the case of a speaker of a language in which some, but not all, of the possible effects of Subjacency are in evidence (e.g., Chinese and Indonesian, each for different reasons). One reasonable hypothesis is that since the principle is partially instantiated in the first language, it may be available for all possible extractions in the second language; alternatively, it may be available only for those extractions instantiated in the first language.

The hypotheses

The experiment described later in this section was designed to test for the presence of Subjacency in the psychological knowledge-state of three types of proficient speakers of English: (1) native speakers of English (to be used as controls); (2) proficient Korean speakers of English (whose native language shows no evidence of Subjacency); and (3) proficient Chinese and Indonesian speakers of English (whose native languages show some evidence of Subjacency but are more limited than is English, as Chinese allows no *wh*-movement and Indonesian allows it but only for subjects). A set of grammaticality judgment tests was constructed in English involving structures that can be used to test for Subjacency.

Thus, this experiment was designed to test for knowledge of two interrelated sets of phenomena in English:

1. Knowledge of four syntactic constructions out of which *wh*-movement is impossible in English – sentential subjects (SS), relative clauses (RC), noun phrase complements (NC), embedded questions (EQ).
2. Knowledge of Subjacency violations of these constructions.

The research hypothesis can then be stated as follows:

Hypothesis 1a: For each of the four constructions, subjects who demonstrate knowledge of that construction (i.e., pass the syntax tests) will exhibit evidence of Subjacency in their judgments of *wh*-movement out of that construction (i.e., pass the Subjacency tests).

It is possible that non-natives, even very proficient ones, would not have acquired such complex constructions as SS, RC, NC, and EQ, and if that were the case, they would not have the requisite knowledge to pass the Subjacency tests.

Thus, a corollary to this hypothesis is:

Hypothesis 1b: For each construction in question, subjects who fail the syntax test will also fail the Subjacency test.

The results of the syntax test together with the Subjacency test thus form a two-by-two contingency table:

		Syntax Test	
		Pass	*Fail*
Subjacency	Pass	A	B
test	Fail	C	D

If these two hypotheses are correct, the subjects should, for each construction, tend to fall either in the A cell and exhibit knowledge of both the syntax test and the Subjacency test or in the D cell and exhibit lack of knowledge of both the syntax test and the Subjacency test. And if the test itself is an appropriate one, the native speaker controls should tend to fall in the A cell.

The tests

Constructions

There are four syntactic construction tests, each consisting of six grammatical sentences. The constructions are as follows: sentential subjects (SS), relative clauses (RC), noun phrase complements (NC), and embedded questions (EQ), each of which is in italics in the following sentences.

SS: *That oil prices will rise again this year* is nearly certain.
RC: The theory *we discussed yesterday* will be on the exam next week.
NC: There is a good possibility *that we can obtain the information elsewhere*.
EQ: The dorm manager asked me *who I wanted to have as a roommate*.

The criterion for passing each of the construction tests was for the subject to judge five of the six sentences as grammatical. Thus, a subject who passed the SS test would have had to judge as grammatical at least five of the six grammatical sentences containing SS, and so on for each construction.

Subjacency violations

There were also four Subjacency tests, based on violations involving the previously mentioned four constructions (enclosed in brackets in the following sentences)

SS: *Which party did [for Sam to join t]^5 shock his parents?
RC: *What did Susan visit the store [that had t in stock]?
NC: *Who did the police have evidence [that the mayor murdered t]?
EQ: *Who did the Senator ask the President [where he would send t]?

The criterion for passing each of the Subjacency tests was for the subject to correctly judge five of the six sentences ungrammatical. Thus, a subject who passed the SS Subjacency test would have had to judge as ungrammatical five of the six ungrammatical sentences containing an impossible extraction from sentential subjects, and so on for each construction.

The test thus consists of a total of eight subtests, each designed to probe for a separate linguistic property: the SS test, the RC test, the NC test, the EQ test, the *SS test, the *RC test, the *NC test, the *EQ test. It also allows one to probe for the relationship (if any) between knowledge of SS and *SS, RC and *RC, NC and *NC, EQ and *EQ.

The subjects

The grammaticality judgments were elicited from 20 Chinese, 21 Korean, and 20 Indonesian subjects, as well as 19 native-speaker controls. All were students in sections of an introductory linguistics course at the University of Southern California (USC) or in freshman English courses required of all undergraduates. The non-native subjects were all highly proficient speakers of English who had either: (a) taken the USC English placement exam required of almost all non-natives and been exempted from any ESL requirement, or (b) who had in fact been required to take an advanced ESL course but had completed all such requirements in a semester prior to the one in which the Subjacency tests were administered. The 11 subjects (9 Chinese, 2 Korean) who were not required to

---

5 The brackets and traces are inserted here to indicate the construction constituting a barrier to extraction of the *wh*-word and the original position of the moved constituents, respectively. No such brackets or traces appeared in the test instrument.

take the USC placement test had all completed high school in the United States. All non-native subjects had begun the process of acquisition of English at age 12 or later. The general characteristics of their backgrounds are listed in Table 3.1.

The administration

The 48 test sentences were randomized and counterbalanced[6] and were administered at one sitting in each class. Preceding the test, the teachers discussed grammaticality judgments and how they were used in linguistic study, the differences between prescriptive judgments and those based on "feel," and so forth. The directions at the beginning of the test gave a few examples of grammatical and ungrammatical sentences together with discussions of them. Subjects were given approximately 25 minutes to complete the test, and all did so.

The results

Preliminary analysis

As a preliminary step in the analysis of the results, a generalized linear model regression procedure was used to test for the possibility that the attribute variables of the non-native subjects might have had a biasing effect on test scores. Two separate regression procedures were carried out, one with scores on the set of grammatical sentences as the dependent variable and the other with scores on the ungrammatical sentences as the dependent variable. The attribute variables are: (1) age of first exposure to English, (2) number of years of English study, (3) months of residence in the United States, (4) attendance in an American Language Institute course, (5) age, and (6) language background. With the scores on the set of grammatical sentences as the dependent variable, the results were nonsignificant $(F(6,41) = 0.93, p = 0.48)$,[7] as they were with the scores on the set of ungrammatical sentences as the dependent variable $(F(6,41) = 1.28, p = 0.29)$.

These results demonstrate the relative homogeneity of the subjects in

---

6 Included in the study, in addition to the sentences described in the text and listed in the appendix, were a set of nine grammatical *wh*-questions involving varying degrees of *wh*-movement, and a set of nine ungrammatical strings involving extraposition to the right to balance the *wh*-movement to the left. It would not therefore be possible for a subject to infer that all declaratives were grammatical and all questions ungrammatical.

7 Subject sample size was reduced to 48 for this analysis since not all subjects answered all questions regarding their backgrounds.

TABLE 3.1. LANGUAGE BACKGROUND OF SUBJECTS

Language	Age at first exposure (mean)	No. of years of study (mean)	Months in U.S. (mean)	Age at test time (mean)
Indonesian	13.1	6.8	27.6	20.7
Chinese	13.9	5.6	48.5	21
Korean	15.2	6.6	37.3	21.8

terms of the effects of their exposure to English, and show that no single language group performed significantly better than the other groups on the total set of grammatical sentences and on the total set of ungrammatical sentences.

Testing the model

Remember that the hypothesis was that, for each construction, subjects who passed the syntax test would also pass the Subjacency test for that construction. Hypothesis 1a predicts that if subjects have knowledge of the constructions in question, they will also have knowledge of the Subjacency violations involving them (and will thus fall in the A cell); Hypothesis 1b predicts that if subjects do not have knowledge of the constructions in question they will, correspondingly, have no knowledge of what constitutes Subjacency violations involving them (and will thus fall in the D cell). Any non-native subject who falls in either the A cell or the D cell will behave according to Hypothesis 1 (a and b). Any non-native subject who falls into the B cell (having knowledge of Subjacency violations involving a certain construction but not having knowledge of the construction itself) or the C cell (having knowledge of the syntactic construction but not the Subjacency violations involving it) will constitute evidence against Hypothesis 1 (a and b). If the test itself is an appropriate one, the native speakers should tend to fall in the A cell.

The native speakers perform as expected in three of the four constructions, as Table 3.2 indicates. They pass both the syntax and Subjacency tests for the constructions tested; thus they overwhelmingly fall into the A cell. Sign tests (comparing the combined A and D cells with the combined B and C cells) indicate a p of .01 or better for SS and RC, a p of .032 for EQ, and a p of .32 for NC[8] (cf. Champion 1970).

The non-natives, however, perform quite differently, as Table 3.3 indicates. Note first that the non-natives generally can recognize the

---

8 I am not sure why native speakers performed relatively poorly on the NC test. It has been brought to my attention, however, that Chomsky (1986) has argued that extractions of the type I am testing are in fact grammatical. It appears that seven of these subjects would agree with his judgments.

TABLE 3.2. NATIVE RESULTS

SS		RC		NC		EQ	
15	3	17	1	10	1	14	2
1	0	0	1	7	1	3	0

Note: Subjects in cell A satisfy Hypothesis 1a; those in cell D satisfy Hypothesis 1b.

constructions in question, as exhibited by the fact that approximately three quarters of them, by passing the syntax tests, fall into cells A or C. In other words, most subjects, if given grammatical sentences containing the constructions in question, judge those sentences to be grammatical.

However, only about one third of the subjects exhibit knowledge of both a construction and a Subjacency violation involving it, thus falling into cell A. These are the subjects whose behavior is in accordance with Hypothesis 1a.

A smaller number of subjects demonstrate that they neither have knowledge of the construction in question nor of Subjacency violations involving it. These are the subjects whose behavior is in accord with Hypothesis 1b, and one must conclude that these subjects are not as advanced in their knowledge of English as the other subjects are.

By combining cells A and D, we see that in the Indonesian group, for sentential subjects 8 of 20 subjects behave as predicted, for relative clauses 10 of 20 do so, for noun phrase complements 9 of 20, and for embedded questions 13 of 20. Among the Chinese group, for SS 8 of 20 subjects behave as predicted, for RC 14 of 20, for NC 11 of 20, and for EQ 9 of 20. The Korean group is the least proficient, with few falling in cell A and many falling in cell D. When the A and D cells are combined, 12 of 21 Korean students behave according to Hypothesis 1 (a and b) for SS, 13 of 21 for RC, 6 of 21 for NC, and 8 of 21 for EQ. Sign tests are not significant for all non-native groups for all constructions (cf. Champion 1970).

It is clear that Hypothesis 1 is substantiated by English native-speaker behavior. The test therefore is an effective test of the theoretical prediction that adult native speakers of English know the principle of Subjacency. They know both the constructions and the constraints on extraction from them and have access to that knowledge. It is equally clear that the behaviors of the three non-native groups fail to substantiate Hypothesis 1; only about one third of the non-native subjects behave as the native controls do, exhibiting knowledge of both a construction and the Subjacency violations involving it. More commonly, non-native subjects exhibit knowledge of a syntactic construction *without* corresponding knowledge of the Subjacency constraint involving it (i.e., will

TABLE 3.3. NON-NATIVE RESULTS

	SS		RC		NC		EQ	
Indonesian	6	1	6	1	8	0	8	1
	11	2	9	4	11	1	6	5
Chinese	7	5	10	0	11	0	7	2
	7	1	6	4	9	0	9	2
Korean	3	2	5	0	2	0	3	0
	7	9	8	8	15	4	13	5

Note: Subjects in cell A satisfy Hypothesis 1a; those in cell D satisfy Hypothesis 1b.

fall into cell C), indicating that the subjects have acquired these constructions without accessing UG. In other words, for a number of non-native subjects the knowledge of a syntactic construction does not automatically mean knowledge of the Subjacency constraint applicable to that construction. The pattern that is repeated again and again is that although most non-natives are able to recognize a grammatical construction, as evidenced by the fact that the majority pass the syntax test (those in cells A or C), less than half of those who pass have the further ability to detect Subjacency violations of that construction.

Given that English native-speaker behavior substantiates Hypothesis 1, that group can then be viewed as a template against which to measure non-native performance. The following question can be posed: Does proficient non-native behavior differ significantly from native behavior regarding *wh*-extraction out of a variety of constructions in English? To answer this question, the four sets of scores were collapsed into one 2×2 matrix for each group (see Table 3.3) and a chi-square analysis was performed.

Viewing the native speaker totals as the expected totals, and the non-native speaker totals as the observed, one can test the hypothesis, posited by Positions 1 and 2, that there is no significant difference between expected and observed totals for each non-native group. This hypothesis must be rejected for each group, as the results in Table 3.4 indicate.

Note also that the existence of Subjacency effects at the level of S-structure in one's native language may have some small effect on the results. Korean is the one native language with no evidence of Subjacency; Chinese and Indonesian show limited evidence. The Korean group, correspondingly, has fewer subjects who show knowledge of Subjacency effects in English and thus deviates most from native-speaker norms, although not to the extent that it is possible to claim they differ significantly from the other non-native groups. Perhaps more sophisticated statistical analysis could isolate this effect.

TABLE 3.4. COMPARISONS OF NATIVES WITH NON-NATIVES

Native		Indonesian[a]		Chinese[b]		Korean[c]	
56	7	28	3	31	8	13	2
11	2	37	12	33	8	43	26

[a]$DF = 3, \chi^2 = 237.196, p < .001.$
[b]$DF = 3, \chi^2 = 116.688, p < .001.$
[c]$DF = 3, \chi^2 = 614.297, p < .001.$

Conclusions

These results constitute a major difficulty for advocates of Positions 1 and 2, that is, those who believe that all the principles of UG are available and accessible to postpuberty language learners. If Positions 1 and 2 were correct, the subjects would have performed well on determining Subjacency violations for the constructions they knew in English. Yet many subjects did not do so, passing the syntax test but failing the Subjacency test for the same construction. It would appear that for those subjects falling in cell C, the notion of their having access to a fully formed UG is an inappropriate one. They constitute the major challenge to acceptance of Positions 1 and 2.

The results offer partial confirmation for holders of Position 3, but not total support. This position, that adult learners have available and accessible only the specific instantiation of UG exhibited in one's native language, is certainly well-supported by the Korean data. Korean shows no evidence of Subjacency and, correspondingly, extremely few Korean subjects fall into cell A (or B), even though they are proficient speakers of English and have acquired the constructions in question. The Indonesian and Chinese results present a more blurred picture: Each language has evidence of Subjacency, and Indonesian even has *wh*-movement (of subject only). Yet while both groups performed better as a whole than did the Koreans, a number of subjects in each group failed to reach criterion on recognizing Subjacency violations for constructions they knew. It would appear that these subjects had difficulty either in generalizing their knowledge to new cases, or in accessing their knowledge reliably. Which of these possibilities holds is not clear.

The notion that innate linguistic principles of UG are available to adult language learners has been an appealing one both from a theoretical perspective and from a data-driven one, since learners do not appear to violate universals in production. Yet close scrutiny of the judgments of 61 non-native subjects who are proficient in a language (other than the native one) that shows the effects of one such principle does not substantiate this notion. These data constitute a serious challenge to Positions 1 and 2 and indicate directions in which further exploration will be useful. One obvious task is to attempt to replicate this test with other subjects from these and other language backgrounds, paying particular attention to methodology, since the hypotheses themselves are very rich, and the methods of experimentation extremely limited.

Finally, the question of what it means to learn a second language must be more clearly defined, since the non-native speakers tested here, according to commonsense notions of language learning, have been successful at it.

Appendix

Set of test questions for Subjacency experiment

Included are:*

1. 24 Subjacency violations involving *wh*-movement
2. 24 grammatical declaratives involving *wh*-islands

1. Subjacency violations.
   (The following ungrammatical sentences have traces (*t*) inserted to indicate the extraction site. No such traces were inserted on the tests.)
   A. *Violates Subjacency – sentential subject.*
      1. *Which party did for Sam to join *t* shock his parents?
      2. *What did that he got *t* on his first midterm please Tom?
      3. *Who did that his sister went out with *t* upset Frank?
      4. *Who was for a student to disagree with *t* impossible in his country?
      5. *What was that a serious discussion of *t* could occur in class surprising?
      6. *Which medals is for great athletes to earn *t* easy?
   B. *Violates Subjacency – noun complement.*
      1. *Who did the police have evidence that the mayor murdered *t*?
      2. *What did they have to accept the idea that they couldn't operate *t* by themselves?
      3. *Which paper did the professor refuse to believe the claim that someone had stolen *t*?
      4. *Which city was the news that the Nazis had captured *t* a blow to French pride?
      5. *What does the fact that you didn't send *t* prove your lack of interest?
      6. *Who does the claim that the Malvinas Islands are owned by *t* annoy the Argentinians?
   C. *Violates Subjacency – relative clause.*
      1. *Which problem did Bill find a principle which solves *t*?
      2. *What did Susan visit the store that had *t* in stock?
      3. *Who did the news reporters surround the cabinet officer that had criticized *t*?
      4. *What did the police detective recognize the man that had sold *t*?

*See Footnote 6.

    5. Who has the administration really improved the restaurant that serves *t*?

    6. *Which surgeon does he feel sorry for the patients that chose *t*?

D. *Violates Subjacency – embedded question.*

    1. *Who did the police wonder who saw *t*?

    2. *Who did the senator ask the President where he would send *t*?

    3. *What don't they know why Sue tolerates *t*?

    4. *What did John wonder who would break *t*?

    5. *Which books did Mary ask Hank where he bought *t*?

    6. *Which test don't you know who failed *t*?

2. 24 grammatical declaratives.

A. *Sentential subjects.*

    1. That oil prices will rise again this year is nearly certain.

    2. That Leslie decided to attend college three thousand miles from home meant a financial burden for her parents.

    3. To discover that he has cancer should come as no surprise to a cigarette smoker.

    4. To live next door to a superpower is painful.

    5. Discovering that they owed $5000 in back taxes was an unpleasant surprise.

    6. Not being able to get the books he needed during the first week of class annoyed Sam.

B. *Noun complements.*

    1. There is a good possibility that we can obtain the information elsewhere.

    2. The fact that we settled the dispute was surprising to all of us.

    3. Bill complained about the fact that the company promoted Hank over him.

    4. The fact that the Quebec government uses French upsets some Canadians.

    5. The judge rejected the evidence that the student committed the crime.

    6. The idea that he was going to die soon passed through the prisoner's mind.

C. *Relative clauses.*

    1. The professor that gave the most interesting lectures just left for Harvard.

    2. Vicki doesn't like desserts that have cream in them.

    3. I want to know the answer to the problem that Tom discussed with Mary.

    4. The theory we discussed yesterday will be on the exam next week.

    5. Dr. Aston was the professor I received the most encouragement from.

    6. The population of the world that we live in is increasing dramatically.

D. *Embedded questions.*

    1. The police didn't discover who the murderer was.

    2. Many Americans don't even know who the Vice President of the U.S. is.

    3. We still don't know what the answer is to question number six.

    4. I can't remember what I ate three days ago.

5. My host asked me which dessert I preferred.
6. The dorm manager asked me who I wanted to have as a roommate.

References

Bresnan, J. W. 1970. On complementizers: toward a syntactic theory of complement types. *Foundations of Language* 6: 297–321.

1972. Theory of complementation in English syntax. Ph.D. dissertation, MIT. (New York: Garland, 1979.)

Champion, D. J. 1970. *Basic Statistics for Social Research.* Scranton, Pa.: Chandler.

Chomsky, N. 1981a. Principles and parameters in syntactic theory. In *Explanation in Linguistics*, N. Hornstein and D. Lightfoot, eds. London: Longman.

1981b. *Lectures on Government and Binding.* Dordrecht, The Netherlands: Foris.

1986. *Barriers.* Cambridge, Mass.: MIT Press.

Corder, S. P. 1967. The significance of learners' errors. *International Review of Applied Linguistics* 5(4): 161–70.

Flynn, S. 1983. Differences between first and second language acquisition: setting the parameters of universal grammar. In *Acquisition of Symbolic Skills*, D. R. Rogers and J. A. Sloboda, eds. New York: Plenum Press.

Huang, C.-T. J. 1982. Move wh in a language without wh movement. *The Linguistic Review* 1 (4).

Krashen, S. 1981. *Second Language Acquisition and Second Language Learning.* Oxford: Pergamon Press.

1985. *The Input Hypothesis: Issues and Implications.* New York: Longman.

Schachter, J. 1988. Second language acquisition and its relationship to universal grammar. *Applied Linguistics* 9(3): 219–35.

van Riemsdijk, H. C., and E. Williams. 1986. *Introduction to the Theory of Grammar.* Cambridge, Mass.: MIT Press.

White, L. 1985. Island effects in second language acquisition. Paper delivered at the MIT Conference on Second Language Acquisition, Fall, 1985.

4 The role of the head-initial/head-final parameter in the acquisition of English relative clauses by adult Spanish and Japanese speakers

Suzanne Flynn

One of the most widely investigated structures in adult second language (L2) research is restrictive relative clauses. One reason for this is that though they are the principal structural devices used by languages of the world for encoding recursion, they can vary considerably in terms of their distribution and syntactic forms. For example, languages can differ with respect to the noun phrase (NP) positions that can be relativized, with respect to the nature of the complementizer used, and with respect to their use of resumptive pronouns. At a more abstract level, these structures differ configurationally across languages. Following from the head-direction parameter (defined more fully later), relative clauses can be head-initial as in English, they can be head-final as in Japanese (Kuno 1973), or they may be medially headed as in Hindi (Comrie 1981). Because of these properties, relative clauses provide a unique and an important domain of investigation of L2 learning. By systematically varying both the first language (L1) of adult learners and the target L2 to be learned, we can isolate in what ways and at which levels knowledge of the L1 may "mediate" the L2 acquisition process. At the same time, we can isolate ways in which principles independent of L1 knowledge determine patterns of acquisition (see Gass and Ard 1980; Tarallo and Myhill 1983 for related discussions).

Traditionally, L2 studies within this domain have focused on differences between the L1 and the L2 in terms of their distributional and surface structure syntactic properties. For example, Gass and Ard (1980) investigated differences between the L1 and the L2 in terms of NP positions relativizable. Gass (1979), Ioup and Kruse (1977), and Myhill

The author wishes to thank the editors of this book, as well as Bill Ritchie, Katya Chvany, Wayne O'Neil, and Jack Carroll for their helpful comments and suggestions in editing and revising this paper.

A version of this paper was originally presented at the Winter 1985 Linguistic Society of America meeting, Seattle, Washington. An extended set of these results are reported in Flynn (1989).

89

(1981) considered differences between the L1 and the L2 in terms of deletion of the relativizer. Differences between languages in terms of their use of resumptive pronouns were considered in the work of Ioup and Kruse (1977), Gass (1979), Tarallo and Myhill (1983), and Hyltenstam (1981).

Few studies, however, have focused on differences among relative clauses in terms of their abstract structural configurations. Exceptional in this regard is the work of Schachter (1974) and Tarallo and Myhill (1983). While relative clauses were not the principal focus in either of these investigations, results in both studies suggest that differences between the L1 and the L2 in the configurational structures of these complex sentences may significantly determine observed L2 patterns of acquisition. For example, Schachter found in results from an elicited composition task in English that Arabic and Farsi speakers produced more relative clause structures than did Japanese and Chinese speakers. She suggested that these differences were due to the match/mismatch between the L1 and the L2 in branching direction (head direction) of these complex sentences. Speakers from languages that did not match English in branching direction progressed more slowly in acquisition than those speakers from languages that matched English in branching direction. As a result, the speakers in the former case were less likely to use sentence structures that instantiated the branching direction configuration, as they did not yet control the structures to the degree that speakers from languages that matched the L2 branching direction did. Relative clauses in Arabic and Farsi, as in English, are right-branching (head-initial); relative clauses in Chinese and Japanese are left-branching (head-final).

In the Tarallo and Myhill study, differences in results are reported between learners of left-branching languages and learners of right-branching languages in terms of their *acceptance* of *unacceptable* resumptive pronouns in various grammatical positions in target relative clause structures. "RPs [resumptive pronouns] were accepted more often in positions other than subject in right-branching languages (Portuguese and German), while in left-branching languages (Chinese and Japanese) direct objects were not favorable for RPs" (1983:71). Tarallo and Myhill tentatively suggest two possible reasons for these findings, both of which have to do with learners' expectations and abilities to deal with structural configurations in the target L2 that follow from a match or mismatch in the branching directions of the learners' L2s and English.

The purpose of this chapter is to build upon the results of this earlier work by focusing solely on the role of the head-direction parameter in adult L2 acquisition of restrictive relative clauses by adult Spanish and Japanese speakers. By narrowing the focus in this way, we can systematically control the relevant variables for such a study at the level appropriate to the questions asked. Specifically, does a match or a mismatch in the head direction of the L1 and the L2 significantly determine L2 patterns of learning for relative clauses? In other words, are learners' hypotheses about restrictive relative clauses constrained by the head-direction parameter?

In this study, two groups of adult learners – Spanish and Japanese – at three levels of English proficiency were tested on their elicited production of English restrictive relative clauses. Results indicate, as suggested in the Schachter and the Tarallo and Myhill studies, significant differences in patterns of acquisition between the Spanish and Japanese speakers. At the same time, these results replicate earlier reported findings with respect to the role of the head-direction parameter in the acquisition of adjunct adverbial clauses in English (see summary in Flynn 1987). Taken together, I argue that these results provide important corroboration for a parameter-setting model of Universal Grammar (UG). Specifically, these results provide important new converging evidence for the psychological reality of the head-direction parameter in a theory of grammars, and for the validity of claims made with respect to a complex set of deductive consequences associated with the choice of a particular value for a parameter. At the same time the results provide important new evidence for the development of the parameter-setting model for L2 acquisition proposed by Flynn (1983, 1987).

Parameter-setting model within a Universal Grammar framework

In this chapter I assume the familiar Universal Grammar parameter-setting model of language and language acquisition proposed by Chomsky (1980, 1981, 1982, 1986). This model is argued to account for both the diversity of languages and for the rapid and uniform development of language among children on the basis of a fixed set of principles. As such, it is both a theory of the properties of grammars and a theory of the biological endowment for language with which all individuals are uniformly and uniquely endowed. As a theory of a domain-specific faculty of human cognition, UG "provides a sensory system for the preliminary analysis of linguistic data and a schematism that determines quite narrowly a certain class of grammars" (Chomsky 1975:12). Essentially, the mediation of UG in language learning restricts the infinite number of false leads that could be provided by random induction from unguided experience of surface structure data (Lust 1986).

As a theory of grammars, UG attempts to provide "a system of principles, conditions, and rules that are elements or properties of all human languages, not merely by accident, but by necessity" (Chomsky 1975:29). The rules and principles specified by UG should rule out an infinite set of grammars that do not conform to these fundamental properties. Universal Grammar specifies those aspects of rules and principles that are uniformly attained in language but underdetermined by evidence. In addition, a number of these principles are associated with certain parameters. Parameters specify dimensions of structural variation across all languages; their values are fixed by the experience gained in the language learning process. Setting the parameters in one way or another will have a set of deductive consequences for the rest of the grammar. One such parameter is the head-initial/head-final parameter of X-bar theory for phrase structure rules (Stowell 1981). Languages, in general, can be shown to differ with respect to the placement of a head – for example, a *noun* in a noun phrase construction or a verb in a *verb* phrase construction – in relation to its complements. In English, complements follow their heads, so that we have *noun-complement*, *verb-complement*, and other structures; in Japanese, complements precede their heads, yielding *complement-noun, complement-verb* type structures. Setting the parameter in one way yields English and Spanish; setting the parameter in another way yields Japanese.

The grammar of a particular language can be regarded as a specification of these UG values. The overall system of rules, principles, and parameters is UG.

Universal Grammar and L2 acquisition

As is well known, UG as a theory of acquisition characterizes L1 learning but does not make explicit predictions about L2 acquisition. However, if principles of UG do in fact characterize a language faculty that is biologically determined and that is necessary for the acquisition of an L1, then it seems quite reasonable to assume that principles of UG also play a role in L2 acquisition. Operating on just this assumption, I have attempted to construct a model of L2 learning that is consistent with a UG formulation of language and language learning. That is, one that accounts for L2 acquisition in terms of principles and parameters isolated in the L1 acquisition process (for example, see Flynn and Espinal 1985, Flynn 1987).

In this parameter-setting model, it is argued that L2 learners use principles of syntactic organization isolated in L1 acquisition in the construction of the L2 grammar. Where principles involve parameters, L2 learners from early stages of acquisition recognize a match or a mismatch in the values of these parameters between the L1 and the L2. In the cases in which the L1 and the L2 values differ, L2 acquisition is disrupted as learners must and do assign new values to cohere with the L2 grammar. In the case in which they match, L2 acquisition is facilitated as learners do not need to assign a new value to this parameter. They can, instead, rely upon the L1 value in guiding their construction of English.

There are two important features of this model for L2 learning. First, it claims that both L1 and L2 learners are guided by the same set of structural principles in their construction of the target grammars. This aspect of the proposed model allows us to account for similarities between L1 and L2 acquisition that have been observed in the literature – a component of L2 learning captured by the Creative Construction Model of Dulay and Burt (1974). In addition, within this model, the L1 experience is important to the extent that it determines whether or not assigning a new value for a structural parameter of language is necessary. That is, a match or mismatch in the values of parameters associated with principles of UG determine whether or not L2 learners must assign a new value to a particular parameter for coherence with the L2. This aspect of the model allows us to account for the role of the L1 experience in L2 acquisition – an aspect of L2 learning captured by traditional contrastive analysis models of L2 acquisition (Fries 1957; Lado 1957).

Previous studies

Original empirical evidence in support of this model derives from several studies that investigated the role of the head-direction parameter in adult L2 acquisition of English grammatical anaphora in adverbial adjunct clauses (see summary in Flynn and Espinal 1985, Flynn 1987). Adult speakers of Spanish and Japanese[1] were tested in their elicited production and comprehension of sentences such as those in (1) and (2).

1a. The boss informed the owner when the worker entered the office.
 b. The man answered the boss when he installed the television.
2a. When the actor finished the book, the woman called the professor.
 b. When he delivered the message, the actor questioned the lawyer.

The two groups tested differed in terms of the match/mismatch in head direction of their native language to English, which is a head-initial language (see Sentence 3). Spanish is head-initial, as shown in Sentence 4; Japanese is head-final, as shown in Sentence 5.

English
3. [The child [who is eating rice]] is crying.

Spanish
4. [El niño [que come arroz]] llora.
   "The child who eats rice cries."

---

1 Chinese speakers learning English were also tested with these sentence structures. See summary of results in Flynn and Espinal (1985) and Flynn (1989).

Japanese
5. [[Gohan-o-tabete-iru] ko-ga] naite-imasu.
   "Rice-object eating is child-subject crying is."

Consistent with findings isolated in extensive cross-linguistic L1 acquisition studies (English: C. S. Chomsky 1969; Solan 1977, 1978, 1983; Tavakolian, 1977; Goodluck 1978, 1981; Lust 1981, 1986; Lust et al. 1986; Japanese: Lust et al. 1982; Chinese: Lust and Chien 1984; Sinhalese: Lust, de Abrew, and Gair, in preparation), results from these L2 studies indicated that adult L2 learners are constrained in their early hypotheses about grammatical anaphora by the head-direction parameter, regardless of the match/mismatch in head direction between the L1 and the L2. At the same time, these results indicated significant differences in acquisition patterns between the case in which the L1 and L2 matched in head direction (Spanish speakers) and the case in which they did not (Japanese speakers). Specifically, acquisition of these sentence structures was significantly disrupted for the Japanese speakers, as they had to assign a new value to the head-direction parameter in order that it cohere with English. In contrast, acquisition was significantly facilitated for the Spanish speakers, as they did not need to assign a new value to the parameter under discussion but could rely upon the head-direction configuration established by the L1 setting in working out the grammar of the new target language, English (see Flynn 1987 for an extended discussion of these results).

Head direction parameter in the acquisition of restricted relative clauses

Given these results, a number of interesting predictions follow. For example, if, as hypothesized, parameters within a theory of grammar isolate those dimensions of language variation that are significant in possible grammars of a language, and if the choice of a value for the parameter in question provides multiple deductive consequences for grammar construction, and if sensitivity to the head-direction configuration is one such parameter, then one would expect to see as a possible deductive consequence its effects across several different types of constructions that involve head-complement configurations. Previous results have already demonstrated one deductive consequence that follows from the setting of the head-direction parameter in the development of grammars, namely its role in the acquisition of grammatical anaphora (see summary in Flynn 1987).

In this chapter I have extended the original work conducted with adult L2 learners of English to an investigation of the role of the head-direction parameter in the acquisition of restrictive relative clauses (RRCs) in English. RRCs, in contrast to the original sentence structures tested (exemplified in Sentences 1 and 2), involve bound variables and the embedding of a subordinate clause within a noun phrase rather than a sentence or an inflection phrase, as with adverbial clauses. If the head-direction principle is a general principle of structural organization for possible grammars and characterizes acquisition in general, then we would expect that in a test with the identical two groups of ESL learners investigated in earlier studies, significant differences would emerge between the case in which the L1 and L2 match in head direction (Spanish speakers learning English) and the case in which they do not (Japanese speakers learning English).

Experimental design

In this study, the same two groups of adult Spanish and Japanese speakers were tested in their elicited production of four types of RRCs.

In the elicited imitation task, a learner is presented with batteries of randomized stimulus sentences. The experimenter says, one at a time, a sentence from these batteries to the learner, who is then asked to repeat each sentence as presented.

One issue that has been raised recently is that the oral presentation of individual experimental sentences may introduce some uncontrolled variability in the experimental design (Eubank 1989), resulting in an unspecified bias that may seriously affect the results.

In response to this claim, three points need to be made. First, in this study as well as in others (see Flynn 1987) that used the elicited imitation task, several controls were instituted in order to eliminate or substantially reduce the chance occurrence of unwarranted variation:

a. Only one experimenter administered all of the experimental sentences to all of the students.
b. The experimenter was trained so that all sentences were delivered to all students with natural, unmarked English prosody.
c. Throughout testing, all taping sessions were subject to periodic review by independent observers to make sure that the oral presentation was kept constant for all sentence types and for all language groups tested.
d. Three instantiations of each sentence type tested were given in the randomized sentence batteries so that no particular item or particular sequence of test items could significantly affect the results.

Second, the elicited imitation task is a standardized validated experimental task used in language acquisition studies (see Gallimore and Tharp 1981; Flynn 1986, 1987; Lust, Chien, and Flynn 1987 for an extended discussion of this issue). Its administration in the present study was wholly consistent with accepted standards.

Third, assuming that such bias were possible, what kind of bias might it be? It could not be an order bias since the order within sentence batteries was randomized. In addition, presentation of these batteries was randomized across all students tested. It could not be a random bias since a random bias would not have a systematic effect on some language groups and not others. Such a bias would more likely minimize real effects rather than create them. As will be discussed later in this chapter and as demonstrated with earlier work (e.g., Flynn 1987), real effects are indeed observed. Thus, if there is a bias, it has to be a systematic one, but no real cause for such a bias has been proposed.

In summary, the methodology used with this experimental task was standardized across all language groups and across all sentence structures evaluated. The notion that uncontrolled methodological problems created the results is unsubstantiated, as no viable account of how such a bias could actually affect the observed data has been proposed.

Here are some sample stimulus sentences given in the test.

Stimulus Sentences
S/S
6. The student who called the gentleman answered the policeman.

S/O
7. The policeman who the student called greeted the businessman.

O/S
8. The boss introduced the gentleman who questioned the lawyer.

O/O
9. The diplomat questioned the gentleman who the student called.

Sentences such as those in (6) involved subject/subject (S/S) relatives, sentences in (7) involved subject/object (S/O) relatives, sentences in (8) involved object/subject (O/S) relatives, and sentences in (9) involved object/object (O/O) relatives.[2]

As in previous studies, two control measures, designed to ensure comparability in English as a Second Language (ESL) competence between the two groups tested, were utilized. First, before testing began, all speakers were administered a standardized ESL test, the Placement Test (University of Michigan).[3] Based on the results of this test, speakers were

2 The first grammatical position refers to the grammatical function of the relativized noun phrase (NP) in the main clause. The second grammatical position refers to the grammatical function of the NP in the subordinate clause.
3 Another issue to be dealt with is the possibility that there is a mismatch between the requirements of the placement test used for all students and the requirements of the experimental test used in this study. In other words, the results of the experimental test are not valid because the same task was not used to place the students.
   First, this issue can be raised for any study that does not use exactly the same testing procedures used by an independent placement test. For example, the same

TABLE 4.1. ENGLISH AS A SECOND LANGUAGE PROFICIENCY LEVEL PLACEMENT
SCORES (SCORE RANGE 0–50)

Group	Low		Mid		High		Overall	
	n	*M*	*n*	*M*	*n*	*M*	*n*	*M*
Spanish	16	18	21	31	14	42	51	30
Japanese	7	20	25	31	21	42	53	31
Overall	23	19	46	31	35	42	104	31

Note: Means are rounded off to the nearest whole number.

placed into one of three levels of ESL ability. The results are shown in
Table 4.1.

Second, a measure of baseline syntactic competence was established
for the two groups of learners. This was necessary in order to ensure
that production of the experimental sentences was specifically due to
the factor of head direction and not due to some general sentence processing difference between the two language groups. The control provided by the ESL proficiency test allowed a grouping of the speakers
into only three proficiency levels, and did not necessarily ensure a more
precise comparability among speakers within each level or across levels,
which the covariate could provide. Moreover, because the covariate
control was administered orally, it more precisely controlled for any
differences that might exist between the two groups in terms of, for
example, listening comprehension abilities.

To measure this, an assessment of the number correct on imitation
of simple juxtaposed sentences (10–11) was used and treated as a covariate in the statistical design (see Keppel 1973; Kerlinger and Pedhazur
1973 for an extended discussion of this design). The sentences exem-

criticism can be raised when using a grammaticality judgment task, a picture identification task, or a translation task to classify students for a comprehension test.

Second, the standardized placement procedures used in this study and others
(Flynn 1987) are no less precise than a common alternative form of classification –
general groupings based simply upon membership in a beginning ESL or foreign
language (FL) class. In fact, it can be argued that the test used in this study could
only be more precise.

Third, it is unrealistic and in many cases uninformative to require that strictly
equivalent tasks be used for placement and testing.

Fourth, as discussed later in this chapter, an additional placement control was
employed in this study – a covariate control. This measure involved an *oral assessment* of a speaker's abilities to imitate stimulus items that involved two juxtaposed
sentences. This assessment, which tested performance on a task quite similar to that
investigated here, served as a further measure of a speaker's assignment to a particular level and further guaranteed equivalence within levels.

In summary, the claim that the mismatch between the requirements of the placement methods and the actual experimental test invalidates the results is not
supported.

plified in (10) involved two juxtaposed clauses and redundancy in the *subject*. The sentences in (11) similarly involved two juxtaposed clauses; however, instead of redundancy in the *subject*, these sentences involved redundancy in the *verb phrase*.

SVO; SVO
10. *The man* discussed the article; *the man studied the notebook*.

SVO; SVO
11. The mayor *dropped the letter*; the diplomat *dropped the letter*.

Knowledge of the lexical item used in the stimulus sentences was also controlled, as each learner was first taught all the words used in the sentences before the testing began.

Specific hypotheses tested

From the general hypotheses formulated concerning the role of the head-direction parameter in adult L2 acquisition of RRCs, the following set of predictions was generated for this study:

1. Imitation of the sentences in (6–9) should be significantly facilitated for the Spanish speakers but disrupted for the Japanese speakers, even when the two groups are equalized in basic ESL level as measured by the standardized test and controlled for by use of the covariate.

We would expect this because these RRC sentences all involve embedding, which in turn represents some form of head-complementation structure. Since the Spanish speakers' L1 head direction is initial, the head-complement organization of English follows their L1. This structural configuration should be available to these learners to consult in the development of the L2 grammar. On the other hand, the L1 for the Japanese speakers is head-final. As a result, these speakers must revise principles of head complementation when learning English. That is, Japanese speakers must assign a new value to the head-direction parameter when acquiring English. Thus, the Japanese speakers' acquisition of these sentences, as for adverbial clauses, should be significantly hindered by their need to assign a new value to this principle of organization for acquisition of this particular L2.

2. Errors made by the Spanish and Japanese speakers should differ qualitatively. Japanese learners should show difficulty with head-complement relations in this complex sentence formation (RRCs). Spanish speakers should show less difficulty with this aspect of these structures.

3. In addition, the nature of these errors should correspond to those made in imitation of the adverbial adjunct clauses reported in earlier studies (e.g., Flynn 1987). Evidence of this nature would strongly suggest that learners' hypotheses about these two types of head-complement

TABLE 4.2. LEVEL MEANS FOR NUMBER CORRECT (SCORE RANGE 0–3)

Language group	SS	SO	OS	OO	Overall
Spanish					
Low	.63	.69	.38	.75	.61
	(.69)[a]	(.75)	(.44)	(.81)	(.67)
Mid	2.19	1.33	1.00	1.76	1.57
	(2.05)	(1.19)	(.86)	(1.62)	(1.43)
High	2.57	1.93	1.50	2.20	2.05
	(2.21)	(1.57)	(1.14)	(1.86)	(1.70)
Overall	1.80	1.32	.96	1.51	1.40
	(1.65)	(1.17)	(.81)	(1.43)	(1.27)
Japanese					
Low	.14	.00	.29	.14	.14
	(.59)	(.45)	(.74)	(.59)	(.59)
Mid	.64	.16	.20	.12	.28
	(.80)	(.33)	(.37)	(.29)	(.45)
High	1.28	.48	.90	.67	.83
	(1.27)	(.46)	(.89)	(.65)	(.82)
Overall	.69	.21	.46	.31	.41
	(.89)	(.41)	(.67)	(.51)	(.62)

[a] Adjusted means due to the partialling out of the covariate factor are in parentheses. *F*-tests were computed on these means.

structures are constrained by the same principle, namely the head-direction parameter. Moreover, we might expect that the patterns of errors observed for the Japanese speakers correspond to those isolated at early stages of acquisition for children learning English.

Results

The results confirm my predictions. First, there were important overall differences between the Spanish and Japanese speakers in their production of each of the relative clause structures tested. These results hold even though these speakers were all equalized in ESL ability.

Results summarized in Tables 4.2 to 4.5 show that the Spanish speakers were significantly more successful at imitating the sentence types tested than the Japanese speakers $(F (1,97) = 25.91, p = .0001)$. The means for successful imitation for each group are shown in Table 4.2.[4]

Thus, the first prediction, facilitation in production of English embedding under an NP by ESL learners with a head-initial language and

4 For the Spanish speakers there is an interaction of relative clause type that I will not pursue in this paper. I will thus summarize results for the four types of relative clause structures.

TABLE 4.3. LEXICAL ERRORS: % OF ERRORS (% OF RESPONSES)

Language group	Spanish	Japanese
Low	23 (18)	3 (2)
Mid	31 (15)	11 (10)
High	47 (15)	23 (17)
Overall	34 (16)	12 (10)

TABLE 4.4. ONE-CLAUSE REPETITIONS: % OF ERRORS (% OF RESPONSES)

Language group	Spanish	Japanese
Low	30 (24)	83 (79)
Mid	31 (14)	45 (41)
High	20 (7)	23 (18)
Overall	28 (15)	43 (37)

disruption of this production by ESL learners with a head-final language was, in general, confirmed.

The second prediction was also confirmed. Analysis of the errors showed a qualitative difference in the nature of the errors made by the two groups. At the same time, the errors made by the two groups of speakers corresponded to those made in their repetition of the adverbial subordinate clauses (see Flynn 1987), thus confirming the third prediction.

First of all, the errors that differentiated the two groups of ESL learners and accounted for the exceptional difficulty in the Japanese group were not lexical errors. In spite of the fact that the lexicons of Spanish and English are more similar than those for English and Japanese, a greater number of lexical errors were made by Spanish speakers than by Japanese speakers. This is shown in Table 4.3. An example of this error is shown in (12).

12. *Example of lexical error*:
    Stimulus: The policeman questioned the man who carried the baby.
    Response: The *gentleman* questioned the man who carried the baby.

In addition, errors that differentiated between the two sets of learners and accounted for the lower success rate of the Japanese speakers were primarily structural. For example, there are significantly more one-clause repetitions for the Japanese speakers than for the Spanish speakers. This is shown in Table 4.4 and exemplified in (13).

13. *Examples*:
    Stimulus: The policeman questioned the man who carried the baby.
    Response: (a) The policeman questioned the man.   or   (b) Who carried the baby.

TABLE 4.5. CONVERSION TO COORDINATION: % OF TWO-CLAUSE ERRORS

Language group	Spanish	Japanese
Low	20	29
Mid	6	13
High	3	9
Overall	10	17

Moreover, of the two-clause structural errors, there was a greater conversion of these sentence structures to coordinate sentence structures for the Japanese speakers at the intermediate and advanced levels (where control of the two-clause structure is evident) than for the Spanish speakers. This is shown in Table 4.5. Examples of this error are shown in (14).

14. *Examples*:
   Stimulus: The policeman questioned the man who carried the baby.
   Response: (a) The policeman questioned the man and the policeman carried the baby.   or   (b) The policeman questioned the man and carried the baby.

A closer examination of the types of coordinate conversions made by the Japanese speakers indicate that they all involved redundancy in the *subject*. For example, these learners all converted these RRCs to either sentences in which the redundancy had been reduced, as in (14a), or to coordinate sentence structures in which *subject* reduction is allowed, as in (14b). This redundancy reduction is all in a forward direction and coheres with what young children learning English will do in early acquisition of English syntax (see discussion in Lust, Chien, and Flynn 1987). Significantly, the patterns exemplified by the Japanese speakers correspond to English developmental patterns. Moreover, these patterns suggest that these two groups of speakers are attempting to work out the properties of English and are not simply translating from their L1s. If they were simply matching the L1 to the L2, we would have expected patterns to have matched Japanese L1 acquisition for these structures. That is, we would have expected these L2 learners to convert these sentences to coordinate sentence structures in which redundancy reduction goes backward (see discussion in Lust and Mangione 1983).

Other forms of errors also confirm a qualitative difference in the nature of the imitation between the speakers of head-initial languages and head-final languages. The examples of imitation shown in (15) and (16) indicate that the Japanese speakers had particular difficulty establishing a head-complement and a head-anaphor relation, which is required by the relative.

Examples of other errors:

Stimulus: The policeman questioned the man who carried the baby.

15. Japanese response: Who question the man who question the baby.
16. Spanish response: The policeman questioning the man who carried the baby.

Consider the Japanese response in (15): "Who question the man who question the baby." This reflects a structure that is not a head-complement structure but instead suggests, for example, a series of juxtaposed questions. On the other hand, the Spanish response shown in (16) still involves a head-complement structure, "the man who carried the baby," but errs by misrepresenting the tense of the main clause.

Conclusions and discussions

As hypothesized, these results indicate significant differences between the Spanish and Japanese speakers in terms of their patterns of acquisition of RRCs in English. These differences emerge in spite of the fact that the two groups were equivalent at ESL proficiency as measured by a standardized ESL placement test and controlled for more extensively through the use of a covariate factor. The differential set of results emerged in two general ways: significant differences in terms of mean number correct and significant differences in terms of the patterns of errors made in imitation of the structures. In terms of number correct, the Spanish speakers significantly outperformed the Japanese speakers in their imitation of these structures. With respect to patterns of errors, the Spanish speakers indicated no significant structural difficulty with the head-complement configuration instantiated. For example, the principal error category for the Spanish speakers (both overall and at the mid and high levels) was lexical and not structural. At the low level, however, structural and not lexical errors accounted for the highest error category (this will be discussed in more detail later). In contrast, the results for the Japanese speakers indicated significant structural difficulty with these complex sentences; they made significantly more one-clause errors on these structures than did the Spanish speakers at all levels and frequently converted the main-subordinate (head-complement) structure to a coordinate sentence that involved redundancy or deletion of redundancy in the *subject* position, as children learning English as their L1 often do (Lust 1981).

These findings suggest several conclusions. First, they suggest that differences in patterns of mean number correct and errors reported in this chapter can be explained in terms of differences between the head direction of the L1 and the L2. Spanish is head-initial, as is English. Japanese, in contrast, is head-final. Given the controls placed on the study and the use of the covariate factor (imitation of juxtaposed clauses), the results can be explained by the difference in head direction between the two groups tested. In addition, the nature of the errors made by the two groups also supports this conclusion. In spite of all the possible errors that could have been made on these sentences, for example, problems with word order or repeated insertion of resumptive pronouns,[5] the principal error categories for the Japanese speakers were one-clause repetitions and conversions to coordinate sentences. Somewhat paradoxically, while these results suggest difficulty in maintaining the head-complement configuration in repetitions of the sentence structures, at the same time they suggest that these speakers were sensitive to the head-complement structure of these sentences. That is, the errors made by the Japanese speakers on the sentence structures tested suggested that these speakers had isolated the head-complement configuration as the principal structural property to be established for the new grammar. Their errors indicate a computation of the head-complement structure of these sentences and a subsequent transformation of the sentences to either a simpler syntactic paraphrase of this original head-complement relation, as in the conversion to coordination errors,[6] or a repetition of either the head or complement, as in the repetitions of one clause.

Second, given that these results characterize both acquisition of adverbial adjunct clauses and RRCs, they suggest that adult L2 learners' hypotheses about head-complement structures are constrained by the same principle of structural organization – the head-direction parameter. While the complement in both the adjunct adverbial studies (Flynn 1983, 1987) and the study reported in this chapter were sentential,[7] the nature of the head differed in each. In the first study, a main clause constituted the head, and in this study an NP was the head. Yet, in spite of this difference, the same patterns of mean number correct and errors emerged in both studies.

Third, these results provide additional support for the head-complement parameter in a theory of grammar and for its role in acquisition. Findings reported here indicate that this parameter specifies a dimension of structural variation across languages that must be determined in the construction of a specific grammar. If this were not the case, how else would we explain, for example, the fact that the Japanese speakers fail in repetition at just those points where a head and a complement are instantiated configurationally? In addition, how would we

---

5 In contrast to many other studies of L2 acquisition of relative clauses (Hyltenstam 1981; Tarallo and Myhill 1983), in this study the Japanese and the Spanish speakers (and the Chinese speakers [Flynn 1989]) never inserted a resumptive pronoun in the relative clauses in their repetitions of these sentence structures.
6 See supporting arguments in Flynn (1987) that the repetition of only one clause was structure-dependent. That is, speakers did not repeat only the first clause mentioned or the last clause mentioned.
7 Further study demands investigation of the acquisition of head-complement structures, such as prepositional phrases or adjective phrases, that do not necessarily involve a sentential complement.

explain that for the Spanish speakers, at the earliest stages of acquisition (the low group), one-clause repetitions account for the principal error category? While the percentage of these errors for the Spanish speakers is lower than those for the Japanese at this stage and overall, the errors suggest that the Spanish speakers at initial stages are seeking to establish the head-complement configuration of English. The Spanish speakers do not assume, as would be dictated by traditional contrastive analysis models of L2 learning, that the L1 matches the L2. As in my argument earlier, if the head-complement configuration of English were not essential for the construction of the L2 grammar by both groups of learners, then we might have predicted very different categories of errors to emerge – namely ones that suggested a very different property of language as essential for acquisition, as, for example, word order.

Fourth, the results provide important new evidence for the parameter-setting model of L2 acquisition proposed in Flynn (1981, 1983, 1987). As discussed earlier in this chapter, within this model L2 learners are argued to use principles of syntactic organization isolated in L1 acquisition in the construction of the L2 grammar. If principles involve parameters, L2 learners at early stages recognize a match or a mismatch in the values of the parameters between the L1 and the L2. When the L1 and the L2 match in the parameter, acquisition is facilitated; when the L1 and the L2 do not match, acquisition is disrupted, as learners must assign a new value to the parameter in acquisition. Overall, results reported here indicate significant facilitation by the Spanish speakers and significant disruption by the Japanese speakers in terms of their acquisition of restricted relative clauses. Moreover, results for the Spanish speakers beyond the low level indicate no significant difficulty with the head-direction configuration of these sentences. In contrast, while there is a decrease in the number of structural errors made by the Japanese speakers across levels, they continue, as in previous studies, to have difficulty with the head-complement configuration.[8]

Fifth and finally, the results provide important corroborating evidence for a general theory of parameter-setting. Those reported here suggest that the same dimensions of structural variation in grammars isolated in L1 acquisition must be established by adult L2 learners in the construction of the new target L2 grammar. That is to say, in

8 In previous studies, I made the argument that at the high levels, Japanese (and Chinese) speakers had established the head direction of English as head-initial. This is most evident in studies that involved testing structures that did not involve anaphora (as generally defined) but simply the manipulation of a head-final versus a head-initial sentence structure. Such a conclusion is difficult to make with the sentence structures tested in this study, as they involve both a bound variable and only head-initial structures. Continued study demands both an investigation of structures that do not involve anaphora and structures that can be both head-final and head-initial (cf. Footnote 7).

spite of all that adult language learners already "know" about language and in spite of their overall advanced state of cognition, those same abstract properties of languages hypothesized as essential in the development of theories of grammar and demonstrated as essential in the acquisition of an L1 must also be established for the construction of the new L2.

In addition, one central claim of the parameter-setting model of acquisition is that once a parameter is set, a set of complex deductive consequences follow from this setting. In earlier reported studies with adjunct adverbial clauses (e.g., Flynn 1981; Flynn and Espinal 1985; Flynn 1987), one deductive consequence was that L2 learners would calibrate their hypotheses about the direction of the new target language. That is, if a language is head-initial, forward anaphora would be productively licensed. If a language is head-final, backward anaphora would be licensed for production.

In this study, another type of deductive consequence, argued to follow from the setting of the head-direction parameter as either head-initial or head-final, was explored, namely that L2 learners would generalize over different types of syntactic heads and be constrained by a general principle of syntactic organization, the head-direction parameter. The results reported here with respect to NP heads and their complements, along with those reported earlier with respect to sentential heads and their complements (Flynn 1987), strongly suggest that adult L2 learners do this. While additional empirical support is needed (cf. Footnote 6), these results strongly indicate that adult L2 learners are not only capable of shifting L1 hypotheses with respect to a particular parametric value but are also capable of reinterpreting each of the deductive consequences associated with this parameter in terms of the relevant language-specific facts for the L2 (see related discussion in Lust 1988).

In summary, these results replicate earlier findings with respect to the head-direction parameter. Namely, this study specifies a significant dimension of structural variation across languages that must be established in order to construct the grammar of the target L2. Moreover, the findings here confirm earlier studies (Schachter 1974; Tarallo and Myhill 1983) with respect to the role the difference in head direction plays between the L1 and the L2.

References

Chomsky, C. S. 1969. *The Acquisition of Syntax in Children 5 to 10.* Cambridge, Mass.: MIT Press.

Chomsky, N. 1975. *Reflections on Language.* New York: Pantheon.

1980. *Rules and Representations.* New York: Columbia University Press.

1981. *Lectures on Government and Binding: The Pisa Lectures.* Dordrecht, The Netherlands: Foris.

1982. *Some Concepts and Consequences of the Theory of Government and Binding.* Cambridge, Mass.: MIT Press.

1986. *Knowledge of Language: Its Nature, Origin, and Use.* New York: Praeger.

Comrie, B. 1981. *Language Universals and Linguistic Typology.* Chicago: University of Chicago Press.

Dulay, H., and M. Burt. 1974. A new perspective on the creative construction process in child second language acquisition. *Language Learning* 24:253–78.

Eubank, L. 1989. Parameters in L2 learning: Flynn revisited. *Second Language Research* 5:1.

Flynn, S. 1981. The effects of first language branching direction on the acquisition of second language. In *Cornell Working Papers in Linguistics,* W. Harbert and J. Herschensohn, eds. Ithaca, N.Y.: Cornell University.

1983. A study of the effects of principal branching direction in second language acquisition: the generalization of a parameter of universal grammar from first to second language acquisition. Ph.D. dissertation, Cornell University.

1986. Comprehension vs. production: differences in underlying competences. *Studies in Second Language Acquisition* 8:17–46.

1987. *A Parameter-Setting Model of L2 Acquisition: Experimental Studies in Anaphora.* Dordrecht, The Netherlands: Reidel.

1989. Spanish, Japanese and Chinese acquisition of English relative clauses: new evidence for the head-direction parameter. In *Bilingualism Across Life Spans,* L. Obler and K. Hyltenstam, eds. Cambridge: Cambridge University Press.

Flynn, S., and I. Espinal. 1985. The head-initial/head-final parameter in adult Chinese L2 acquisition of English. *Second Language Research* 1:93–117.

Fries, C. 1957. Foreword. In *Linguistics Across Cultures,* R. Lado. Ann Arbor: University of Michigan Press.

Gallimore, R., and R. Tharp. 1981. The interpretation of elicited sentence imitation in a standardized context. *Language Learning* 31(2): 369–92.

Gass, S. 1979. Language transfer and universal grammatical relations. *Language Learning* 29:327–44.

Gass, S., and J. Ard. 1980. L2 data: their relevance for language universals. *TESOL Quarterly* 14:443–52.

Goodluck, H. 1978. *Linguistic Principles in Children's Grammar of Complement Interpretation.* Unpublished Ph.D. dissertation, Amherst: University of Massachusetts.

1981. Children's grammar of complement subject interpretation. In *Language Acquisition and Linguistic Theory,* S. Tavakolian, ed. Cambridge, Mass.: MIT Press.

Hyltenstam, K. 1981. The use of typological markedness as predictors in second language acquisition. Unpublished ms.

Ioup, G., and A. Kruse. 1977. Interference versus structural complexity as a predictor of second language relative clause acquisition. In *Proceedings of* the *Second Language Research Forum*, C. Henning, ed. Los Angeles: University of California at Los Angeles.

Keppel, G. 1973. *Design and Analysis: A Researcher's Handbook*. Englewood Cliffs, N.J.: Prentice-Hall.

Kerlinger, F., and E. Pedhazur. 1973. *Multiple Regression in Behavioral Research*. New York: Holt, Rinehart and Winston.

Kuno, S. 1973. *The Structure of the Japanese Language*. Cambridge, Mass.: MIT Press.

Lado, R. 1957. *Linguistics Across Cultures*. Ann Arbor: University of Michigan Press.

Lust, B. 1981. Constraint on anaphora in child language: a prediction for a universal. In *Language Acquisition and Linguistic Theory*, S. Tavakolian, ed. Cambridge, Mass.: MIT Press.

    1986. Introduction. In *Studies in the Acquisition of Anaphora*, B. Lust, ed. Vol. 1. *Defining the Constraints*. Dordrecht, The Netherlands: Reidel.

    1988. Universal Grammar in second language acquisition: promises and problems in critically relating theory and empirical studies. In *Linguistic Theory in Second Language Acquisition*, S. Flynn and W. O'Neil, eds. Dordrecht, The Netherlands: Reidel.

Lust, B., and Y.-C. Chien. 1984. The structure of coordination in first language acquisition of Mandarin Chinese: evidence for a universal. *Cognition* 7: 49–83.

Lust, B., Y.-C. Chien, and S. Flynn. 1987. What children know: methods for the study of first language acquisition. In *Studies in the Acquisition of Anaphora*, B. Lust, ed. Vol. 2. *Applying the Constraints*. Dordrecht, The Netherlands: Reidel.

Lust, B., K. de Abrew, and J. Gair. In preparation. On the acquisition of Sinhalese anaphora.

Lust, B., and L. Mangione. 1983. The principal branching direction parameter constraint in first language acquisition of anaphora. In *Proceedings of the 13th Annual Meeting of the Northeastern Linguistic Society*. Amherst: University of Massachusetts.

Lust, B., L. Solan, S. Flynn, C. Cross, and E. Schuetz. 1986. A comparison of constraints on the acquisition of null and pronominal anaphora. In *Studies in the Acquisition of Anaphora*, B. Lust, ed. Vol. 1. *Defining the Constraints*. Dordrecht, The Netherlands: Reidel.

Lust, B., T. Wakayama, H. Hiraide, N. Snyder, and M. Bergmann. 1982. Comparative studies on the first language acquisition of Japanese and English: language universal and language specific constraints. Paper presented at the XIIIth International Congress of Linguistics, Tokyo, Japan.

Myhill, J. 1981. The acquisition of complex sentences: a crosslinguistic study. *Studies in Second Language Acquisition* 4: 2–19.

Schachter, J. 1974. An error in error analysis. *Language Learning* 24: 205–14.

Solan, L. 1977. On the interpretation of missing complement NPs. In *Occasional Papers*, H. Goodluck and L. Solan, eds., Amherst: University of Massachusetts.

    1978. Anaphora in child language. Unpublished Ph.D. dissertation, University of Massachusetts.

    1983. *Pronominal References: Child Language and the Theory of Grammar*. Dordrecht, The Netherlands: Reidel.

Stowell, T. 1981. Origins of phrase structure. Ph.D. dissertation, Massachusetts Institute of Technology.

Tarallo, F., and J. Myhill. 1983. Interference and natural language processing in second language acquisition. *Language Learning* 33: 55–76.

Tavakolian, S. 1977. Structural principles in the acquisition of complex sentences. Unpublished Ph.D. dissertation, University of Massachusetts.

5 On some properties of the "pro-drop" parameter: looking for missing subjects in non-native Spanish

Juana M. Liceras

Introduction

The parameterized model of acquisition proposed by Chomsky (1981, 1982) has served as the theoretical framework for a number of studies in the field of second language acquisition, of which Flynn (1987), Phinney (1987), and White (1988) are some recent examples. One of the aims of this research is to find out whether the acquisition device that operates in first language (L1) acquisition continues to operate in the case of second language (L2) acquisition. If that were the case, both L1 and L2 learners would be supposed to set a number of parameters according to the options permitted by Universal Grammar (UG). The question then is whether L2 learners start with their L1 setting of a given parameter and eventually reset it to the L2 option or whether the L1 setting does not play a role in the acquisition process. In other words, we face the traditional problem of the role of the mother tongue in L2 acquisition, but in parameterized terms.

Closely linked to this parametric view of acquisition is the theory of markedness (Chomsky 1981, 1986), which differentiates *core* from *peripheral* grammar. Core grammar is the grammar that is determined by fixing the parameters of UG in one of the permitted ways. Peripheral grammar is the set of marked elements and constructions that are outside of core grammar, but still constitute what is actually represented in the mind of an individual. According to the theory of markedness, learners project the core grammar of their language on the basis to the principles and parameters of UG. Peripheral aspects are exceptions of the settings of core grammar or idiosyncratic features of the language.[1] The periph-

The testing of this study was done with the cooperation of the Department of Modern Languages of the University of Ottawa. I should like to express my gratitude to Louise Fortier for her help in the experimental tasks. I am also grateful to the teachers in the Department, and to all the students who participated.

1 As Hyams (1987) points out, the traditional identification of core (unmarked) and periphery (marked) does not seem to be appropriate. While exceptions and relaxations of the core settings will be marked, not all idiosyncratic features should be marked. In fact, nonparameterized aspects of language may also present hierarchies of difficulty that are not accounted for by the theory of markedness.

eral aspects of grammar, mainly the marked ones, should emerge late in the development of the non-native grammar and should be more difficult to acquire. The existence of a marked option implies that L2 learners may start with the unmarked one regardless of their L1.

An important ramification of the parametric view of acquisition is the question of the relationship between fixing a given parameter and learning nonparameterized aspects of grammar. Williams (1987) points out that "the parametrized model can account for only part of the complete story of language acquisition, and in fact the setting of parameters itself might be contingent on development that is not 'parametric' in nature" (1987:xiv). Even though Williams is referring to L1 acquisition, the question may also apply to L2 acquisition in a very specific way. As I have suggested elsewhere (Liceras 1988), the fixing of a property of a parameter may be triggered by structural properties of the language in question.

The purpose of this chapter is to investigate the setting of the pronoun-dropping (pro-drop) parameter by English and French speakers learning Spanish as a foreign language in order to further elucidate the relationship between parameterized and nonparameterized aspects of grammar. I suggest that: (a) The acquisition in Spanish of three properties associated with pro-drop (null subjects, verb-subject inversion, and apparent *that-t* violations) may be related in that acquiring the first property is a condition for acquiring the other two. (Although pro-drop can refer both to the whole parameter and to the lack of subjects, I use the term *pro-drop* for the parameter, and *null subjects* for the specific property.) However, specific structural properties of Spanish, as well as the complexity of certain syntactic mechanisms, play an important role in the acquisition of inversion and *that-t* effects. (b) The L2 acquisition data in this study favor the hypothesis which states that Spanish represents the unmarked option of the parameter. (c) L2 learners do not necessarily start with the L1 setting of the parameter if the L2 option is the unmarked one. (d) There may be an implicational hierarchy relating the three properties of the pro-drop parameter so that if *that-t* has been acquired, inversion and *pro-drop* will have been acquired too. However, acquisition of inversion does not imply that *that-t* will have been acquired too. The hierarchy would then be as follows: *pro- drop* > inversion > *that-t*. This is also a hierarchy of difficulty, with *that-t* being the most difficult grammatical concept to acquire.

The pro-drop parameter

According to Chomsky (1981), Jaeggli (1982), and Rizzi (1982), the pro-drop parameter differentiates, for instance, Spanish and Italian from English and French with respect to the following properties.

First, Spanish, unlike English or French, can have missing subjects, as shown in (1) and (2).

1. [*pro*] Salieron a las ocho.
   *Left at eight.
   "They left at eight."
2. [*Pro*] Llovió mucho ayer.
   *Rained a lot yesterday.
   "It rained a lot yesterday."

Pro is the empty category which has to have an overt counterpart in English or French.

Second, Spanish can have free subject-verb inversion, as in:

3. [*pro*] Han llegado mis estudiantes.
   *Have arrived my students.
   "My students have arrived."

Third, Spanish can have apparent violations of the so-called *that-t* filter. The *that-t* filter accounts for the fact that extraction of a *wh*-phrase from the subject position next to a lexically filled COMP (the phrase structure category present in the underlying structure of sentences) is excluded in English, as indicated in (4):

4. ¿Quién$_i$ has dicho [*pro*] que t_i va a venir?
   *Who did you say that is going to come?
   "Who did you say is going to come?"

In these sentences, *t* represents the trace left by the *wh*-phrase that has been fronted; *i* is the index that indicates that both the trace (t_i) and the *wh*-phrase (quién$_i$/who$_i$) have the same reference. *Que* ("that") has to be placed before the *t* left by *quién* ("Who") when *wh*-movement applies.

Fourth, Spanish can have long *wh*-movement (movement across at least one clause boundary) as shown in:

5. Ese hombre$_i$ que [*pro*] me pregunto a quién t_i habrá visto.
   *"That man$_i$ that I wonder whom he$_i$ may have seen."

The subject of the embedded clause (*ese hombre*) can be relativized in Spanish.

There is no agreement in the literature with respect to whether the Spanish parameter setting is the unmarked one. Hyams (1986) argues that Spanish and Italian represent the unmarked option on the basis that children learning English as their first language drop subject pronouns until expletives *it* and *there* as well as lexical material in AUX (auxiliary) are incorporated in their grammar.[2] According to Hyams, children do not need negative evidence to assume that missing pronouns are not

---

2 In Hyams's (1983, 1986) analysis, the presence of *pro* in the AGR node excludes the presence of lexical material (such as modals) in the AUX node, and vice versa.

possible in English, because expletives and modals (lexical material in AUX) act as a trigger to fix the parameter setting so that English is *not* a pro-drop language. The opposite would occur in the case of children learning Spanish: They would continue to produce missing pronouns because neither expletives nor modals are encountered in Spanish.

The traditional "non-negative evidence" hypothesis (Baker 1979) predicts that the initial assumption in UG would be to avoid null subjects, the rationale being that if the child overgeneralizes there is no way to correct the overgeneralization, because only positive data are available. Corrections or direct information about ungrammaticality, if available, do not play any role in acquisition.[3] Under this assumption, children who are native speakers of English would always avoid null subjects. In contrast, native speakers of Spanish would first avoid null subjects and then reset the parameter to pro-drop when they encounter sentences with a missing subject. Unlike English-speaking children, Spanish-speaking ones have to change the initial parameter setting. However, if the initial setting posited by UG were null subject, it would be impossible to determine how many overt subject pronouns the English-speaking child would have to encounter in the native language to reset the parameter to non-pro-drop.

It is not clear to me that the non-negative evidence hypothesis is a valid one in the case of L2 acquisition in a classroom setting. Thus, the question of the initial setting might not apply as straightforwardly as in the case of L1 acquisition. First of all, L2 learners of Spanish will encounter null subjects in their very first contact with the language.[4] Second, most of the students will be specifically told that in Spanish subject pronouns are only used for emphatic purposes or to avoid ambiguity. I will argue that, even if it were the marked option, the pro-drop parameter setting would be extremely easy to set in L2 acquisition, as illustrated in (1) above. However, that may not apply to all the properties, illustrated in (1)–(5), associated with this parameter. In fact, the question of which of those properties are actually part of the parameter is also controversial.

There is agreement in the literature with respect to (1) and (2), but Chao (1981) and Safir (1982) have argued that inversion and *that-t* effects – which follow from inversion in their analysis – are not integral to the parameter.

---

3 The Subset Principle (Berwick 1985; Wexler and Manzini 1987) states that when two settings of a parameter give two different languages, L1 and L2, and if L1 is a subset of L2, then the default (or initial, or unmarked) setting should be the one giving the smaller language – L1.
4 Classroom drilling, at least in our program, does not include subject pronouns at all.

L2 acquisition of pro-drop

The acquisition of the pro-drop parameter has been studied by White (1985, 1986), Hilles (1986), Phinney (1987), and Liceras (1988). The different approaches and methodologies of those studies make it difficult to compare the results. Nonetheless, I am going to discuss some interesting coincidences and discrepancies in order to formulate the specific goals of the present chapter.

Phinney (1987) and Liceras (1988) have investigated the acquisition of Spanish (a pro-drop language) by speakers of a non-pro-drop one. White (1985, 1986), Hilles (1986), and Phinney (1987) have investigated the resetting of the pro-drop option to non-pro-drop in the case when subjects were native speakers of Spanish learning English. White used a group of native speakers of French learning English as a control. Her subjects were adults learning English in a classroom setting who had to complete a grammaticality judgment and a question-formation task. Phinney's subjects were also adults in a classroom setting whose written compositions were analyzed. Hilles's subject was a 12-year-old whose spontaneous speech had been elicited over a 10-month period. All three researchers found missing pronouns in the early stages of the acquisition process, which might be interpreted as evidence for the unmarked status of the pro-drop option, with direct access to UG and no role for the L1, or as evidence of the influence of L1. However, the fact that White's French-speaking subjects seldom failed to identify missing pronouns seems to favor the transfer hypothesis, which, as has been proposed in the literature (Adjemian and Liceras 1984; Liceras 1985; White 1985, 1986; Phinney 1987), is perfectly compatible with the UG hypothesis; thus, there may be a role for L1 as well as for principles of UG in L2 acquisition.

There is no agreement between White and Phinney as to the interpretation of the results. Both believe resetting the parameter from Spanish to English is difficult. However, White argues that, according to the logic of markedness, going from L1 (marked setting) to L2 (unmarked) requires negative evidence. Thus, missing pronouns will not be definitely eradicated until negative evidence is available.[5] Phinney, on the other hand, interprets the results as a confirmation of the unmarked status of the Spanish option: Spanish speakers learning English have to reset the L1 (unmarked) to the L2 (marked), and therefore more positive evidence is needed. To support her conclusion, Phinney compares those results

5 In Liceras (1983, 1986) it is suggested that marked constructions in L1 would not cause interference because the amount of evidence needed to fix the parameter in the L1 makes speakers aware of the marked status of the construction.

with the ones provided by her English-speaking subjects. She found that they used null subjects very regularly and found no evidence at all of overuse of pronominal pronouns in the compositions.

In the case of English speakers learning Spanish, Liceras (1988) found that pro-drop was well established both at the acceptance and at the production level. Neither Phinney (1987) nor Liceras (1988) found any instance of lexical expletives in the Spanish L2, which indicates that expletives are not transferred into the Spanish interlanguage. This, together with the fact that her Spanish subjects omitted significantly more expletives than referential pronouns, is interpreted by Phinney as evidence for the unmarked status of Spanish as opposed to English.[6] White (1987), on the contrary, believes that those results prove that expletives are not the trigger for grammar change, as Hyams (1983) and Hilles (1986) argue, but instead an aspect of the parameter that undergoes later revision when acquiring English. In the case of French and English speakers learning Spanish, it seems to be the first aspect to be reset, which confirms the hierarchy of difficulty predicted by Phinney.[7]

White (1985) studying acquisition of English and Liceras (1988) studying acquisition of Spanish tested other properties attributed to the pro-drop parameter besides the presence of missing pronouns. In both studies, it was found that verb-subject inversion and *that-t* effects did not have the same status as null subjects in the respective interlanguages. White's subjects did not accept verb-subject as a possible word order and very seldom detected *that-t* violations. Liceras found that, unlike pro-drop, the properties of inversion and *that-t* were far from being acquired with nativelike proficiency by her French and English learners of Spanish. It is suggested that, instead of being related to the pro-drop parameter, inversion may be triggered by such structural properties of Spanish as the need to have the preposition *a* before direct objects (referring to people) and *that-t* may be related to the acquisition of restrictive relativization.[8]

The above discussion can be summarized as follows:

---

6 Phinney suggests that this difference between pleonastic and nonpleonastic *pro* may be an indication of the correctness of Suñer's (1982) analysis. Suñer considers that sentences such as (2) in the text have Ø (no category whatsoever) rather than *pro* in the underlying structure.

7 Phinney (1987) argues that the parametric model of acquisition provides an explanation for the intuitive sense that some languages are "easier." It also allows for greater accuracy than traditional analyses in predicting directionality of difficulty. According to her, and with respect to pro-drop, going from Spanish (L1 – unmarked) to English (L2 – marked) should be difficult. On the other hand, going from English (L1 – marked) to Spanish (L2 – unmarked) should be easier.

8 Spanish direct objects (referring to people) are always marked with the preposition *a*, as shown. Thus, an inverted subject will easily be interpreted as such and not as

1. Resetting the pro-drop parameter from English or French to Spanish is not difficult with respect to null subjects. Pleonastic *pro* (lack of expletives) will be incorporated in the learners' grammar at the very early stages. No transfer from English or French should be expected. Depending on the analysis, this may provide evidence for the marked or the unmarked status of the L1 (Spanish in the present study).
2. Verb-subject inversion and *that-t* effects do not seem to have the same status as pro-drop in the interlanguage grammars analyzed by White (1985) and Liceras (1988). In the case of inversion, Liceras found that her French- and English-speaking subjects produced and accepted inversion in Spanish when an ambiguous interpretation (subject as direct object) was not possible. She also found that her advanced learners did not have nativelike competence with respect to the stylistic conventions that govern the use of inversion in Spanish. For instance, unlike her control group, the French- and English-speaking subjects did not show any preference for inversion with ergative verbs.[9]
3. Given the fact that both English and French are non-pro-drop languages, no differences between these two speech groups should be found with respect to the various properties of the parameter. White (1985) found that in her study French speakers were more successful than Spanish speakers in the identification of *that-t* errors. She states that the fact that French is not a pro-drop language may have helped her subjects. If the interlanguage of the French- and English-speaking subjects in the present study is different with respect to *that-t* effects, it should be due to transfer of the specific realization of *that-t* in both languages.
4. If learning the specific behavior of *that-t* effects in English is related to learning to avoid the complementizer in subordinate clauses, we should not find any difference in the acceptance of both constructions in this study. If there are differences between our French- and our English-speaking group, they should be due to the facts discussed in 3.

The study

In order to investigate the setting of pro-drop in Spanish, four different groups of French and English speakers learning Spanish in a classroom setting were tested on various constructions.

> a direct object. (1) Telefoneó *a* María. (He/she phoned Maria.) (2) Telefoneó María. (Maria phoned.) Empty complementizers are not possible in Spanish relativization, and they are very rare in subordinate clauses. In fact, *Te ruego (que) vengas* ("I beg you to come") is one of the stylistic exceptions where *que* can be avoided. In Adjemian and Liceras (1984) it was found that it is much easier for learners to identify empty complementizers in subordinate clauses than in relative constructions.

9 Burzio (1981) and Chomsky (1982) propose that the noun phrase that occurs with ergative verbs is generated in postverbal position in the case of (1), but not in the case of the nonergative verb in (2). (1)[*pro*]$_i$ han llegado los estudiantes$_i$. (2) [*e*]$_i$ han telefoneado los estudiantes$_i$. According to this analysis, there should be a clear preference for inversion in the case of ergative verbs.

Subjects

The subjects were 32 French and 30 English speakers learning Spanish at the University of Ottawa (Canada); 5 Spanish speakers who were graduate students at the same university acted as control. The subjects were in four different levels of Spanish proficiency, as determined by the Ottawa placement test for Spanish. Level I (beginners) consisted of six English speakers and eight French speakers who had been studying Spanish for seven months at the time of the testing. In Level II (intermediate), there were five English speakers and seven French speakers. There were 14 English speakers and 15 French speakers in Level III (advanced). Level IV (high advanced) consisted of five English speakers and two French speakers. As the University of Ottawa is a bilingual institution, students may be equally fluent in both English and French. To ensure that they were correctly classified, we only chose those whose native, dominant, and most frequently used language was either English or French. When there was no co-occurrence among these three requirements, the subjects were not included in the study (see Appendix 1). The number of years taking Spanish while staying in a Spanish-speaking country was also taken into consideration when deciding whether to include or exclude students in and from Levels III and IV, so that all subjects had learned Spanish in a classroom setting.

The task

Subjects were asked to respond to a written grammaticality judgment task consisting of 17 items (see Appendix 2). Each item contained one or two instances of missing pronouns, overt pleonastic and nonpleonastic pronouns, verb-subject inversion, *that-t* sentences, and subordinate sentences with empty or lexicalized complementizer. Subjects were asked to correct the sentences that had grammatical mistakes. They were also asked to identify those sentences that were unnatural or rarely used. This was done because of the optionality involved in whether to use null pronouns and inversion in Spanish. We asked subjects to translate all sentences into their native language in order to be able to discard those items not given the appropriate interpretation. This grammaticality judgment task was chosen because it allows one to tap the specific linguistic knowledge that is related to the properties of the pro-drop parameter, and it has previously given useful insights into the learners' linguistic system (Liceras 1983, 1986, 1988).

The various aspects of the realization of pro-drop in Spanish that were tested can be grouped as follows:

1. Overt realization of pleonastic *pro* in "existential" and "atmospheric" sentences, as in (5) and (13), respectively. Existential sentences

are those that refer to the actual existence (presence) of someone or something. They are constructed with *there + be* in English and with impersonal *haber* ("to have") in Spanish. Atmospheric sentences are those whose verbs refer to atmospheric phenomena, such as *to rain, to snow, to be windy*, and so forth. Neither existential *haber* nor "weather" verbs can have a lexical subject in Spanish when the verbs are used as such. Chomsky (1982) proposes that the *pro* (the empty category) that accounts for the fact that those verbs are third person singular is a pleonastic *pro* – namely, it does not have an actual reference in the world.

5. **Ello* hay un reloj muy grande en la clase.
   "It there is a clock very big in the classroom."
13. **Ello* hace mucho frío en Canadá.
   "It is very cold in Canada."

Object pronoun *lo* was used in items (4) and (10) instead of the subject pronoun *ello* because it is the equivalent of the English object pronoun *it* and had been found in the compositions of beginning students.

4. **Lo* lleuve mucho en primavera.
   "It rains a lot in spring."
10. **Lo* había muchos estudiantes en esta clase.
   "It there were many students in this classroom."

Subjects were supposed to reject the overt pleonastic pronouns in all four items.

2. Pleonastic *pro* in "existential" and "atmospheric" sentences, such as those in (6) and (12), which represent the correct version of the sentences in (1).

6. Sí, [*pro*] hay dos libros de español para principiantes.
   "Yes, there are two books of Spanish for beginners."
12. [*pro*] dicen que [*pro*] va a nevar.
   "They say it is going to snow."

Subjects were supposed to accept those sentences as grammatical.

3. An instance of *pro* with an arbitrary reference as the only possible option in Spanish, as in (8) and (12).

8. [*pro*] creo que [*pro*] llaman a la puerta.
   "I think that they are knocking at the door."
12. [*pro*] dicen que [*pro*] va a nevar.

The use of the overt subject pronoun *ellos* ("they") would necessarily imply the existence of a specific reference.

4. Cases of *pro* (items 2, 8, and 16) with specific reference. These items include declarative sentences, where the use of *pro* versus *yo* ("I") is optional and inversion would not be the preferred option if *yo* were present.

2. [*pro*]creo _____Ana estudia filosofía en Harvard.
   "I think Ann studies philosophy at Harvard."
8. [*pro*] creo que [*pro*] llaman a la puerta.
15. [*pro*] creo _____[*pro*] sacaré una A + español.
   "I think I will get an A + in Spanish."

Subjects in the study are supposed to accept *pro* in all three cases and to write *que* ("that") in Sentence 2 and 15. Items (3) and (14) include interrogative sentences, as shown.

3. *¿Quién$_i$ dices [*pro*] _____[t_i] estudia espáñol contigo?
   "Who do you say is studying Spanish with you?"
14. ¿Quién$_i$ has dicho [*pro*] que [t_i] va a llamar?
   "Who have you said that is going to call?"

Sentence 3 is ungrammatical because *que* ("that") is missing, which is not the case in Sentence 14. Subjects in the study are supposed to accept *pro* in both cases and write *que* in (3), as indicated.

   5. Overt realization of pleonastic *pro* with a specific reference, as occurs in (1) and (16).

1. Pedro es mejor de lo que *él* parece.
   "Pedro is better than he looks."
16. Los ví que *ellos* venían a buscarte.
   "Them I saw that they were coming to get you."

As *el* in (1) does not necessarily refer to Pedro, *pro* is preferred to avoid ambiguity. *Ellos* cannot occur in (16) if *los* is also present. Subjects in the study are supposed to choose either *los* or *ellos*.

   6. Inversion with ergative (items 7 and 17) and nonergative (items 9 and 11) verbs, which was supposed to be accepted by all subjects.

7. Ya [*pro*]$_i$ han salido los profesores$_i$.
   "Already have left the professors."
17. [*pro*]$_i$ llegaron muchos estudiantes$_i$...
   "arrived many students"
9. [*e*]$_i$ telefonearon mis padres$_i$...
   "phoned my parents"
11. Ya [*e*]$_i$ han llamado mis hermanos$_i$.
   "already have phoned my brothers."

The sentence that would be the most suitable candidate for nonacceptance of inversion would be (9) because the verb in it is not ergative and there is no adverb in sentence initial position. [*e*] is the empty category originated by inversion.

   7. Cases where the so-called *that-t* filter applies (3) and where it is apparently violated (14).

3. *¿Quién$_i$ dices *t* estudia español contigo?
   "Who do you say is studying Spanish with you?"

14. ¿Quién, has dicho *que t,* va a llamar?
  "Who did you say that is going to phone?"

Subjects are supposed to accept (14) but not (3).

8. Missing complementizers, which were included to find out whether learners relate these cases to those in (7).

2. [*pro*] creo _____ Ana estudia filosofía en Harvard.
  "I think Ann is studying philosophy at Harvard."
15. [*pro*] creo _____[*pro*] sacaré una A + en español.
  "I think I will get an A + in Spanish."

Results

PRO-DROP

Pleonastic *pro* was accepted by all subjects. The results summarized in Table 5.1 indicate that while a few subjects did not reject overt pleonastic *pro ello* and *lo*, acceptance of *ello* and *lo* is very low, indicating that pleonastic *pro* is easily incorporated into the interlanguage. These results confirm previous findings. Phinney (1987) and Liceras (1988) did not find any instance of pleonastic *pro* in written compositions. Liceras's advanced learners did not accept any lexicalized expletive in the grammaticality judgment task. The present study shows a very low acceptance of overt pleonastic *pro*, and then only in the early stages of acquisition. In fact, the French-speaking subjects who accepted *lo* may simply not know what to do with that Spanish clitic. English-speaking subjects may be transferring lexical item "it" regardless of its function in English, since "it" cannot occur in subject position in the English equivalents of (4) and (10).

The acceptance of third person plural null subjects with arbitrary reference is almost total. Only one Level I French speaker wrote *alguien llama* ("someone is knocking") in (8) and two Level III English-speaking subjects wrote *se-llama* (8) and *se-dice* (12). This is interesting, because in Liceras (1988) subjects seemed to have problems concerning the arbitrary reference of the impersonal *se*-constructions. Here, the *se*-constructions may have been preferred by these two subjects because these constructions are totally unambiguous with respect to arbitrary or specific reference.

In the case of *pro* with a specific reference, there was only one Level I English-speaking subject who put *yo* instead of *pro* as the subject of *sacaré* in Sentence 15. All the others accepted *pro* in (2), (8), and (15).

The interrogative sentences in (3) and (14) were difficult to interpret. Subjects changed the sentences to produce cases where both verbs had *quién* as subject, as in (6), or crossed out *dices*, leaving only one verb, as in (7).

TABLE 5.1. OVERT REALIZATION OF PLEONASTIC PRO

	French group				English group			
Item	I (n = 8)	II (n = 7)	III (n = 15)	IV (n = 2)	I (n = 6)	II (n = 5)	III (n = 14)	IV (n = 5)
5	—	—	—	—	1 (16%)	1 (20%)	1 (7%)	—
13	—	—	—	—	1 (16%)	—	1 (7%)	—
4	—	—	—	—	2 (33%)	1 (20%)	1 (7%)	—
10	2 (25%)	—	2 (13%)	—	1 (16%)	1 (20%)	1 (7%)	—
Total	2 (6%)	—	2 (3%)	—	5 (20%)	3 (15%)	4 (7%)	—

Note: The blanks indicate that none of the subjects produced a lexical pronoun that would correspond to English *it* or French *il*, nor any lexical item that would function as the subject of the verbs in those sentences.

6. ¿Quién dice̶(que) estudia español contigo?
  "Who says that is studying Spanish with you?"
7. ¿Quién di̶c̶es estudia español contigo?
  "Who is studying Spanish with you?"

Table 5.2 shows the percentage of subjects who used these strategies to interpret the sentences.

Strategy A refers to the change of person as shown in (6), and strategy B to the crossing out of *dices* in (7). Strategy B was more used in the case of (3) because of the missing complementizer. It is interesting that Level IV students did not use strategies A and B, although not all of them produced the correct results, as is shown in Table 5.6.

Table 5.3 shows the percentage of lexical subject pronouns that were rejected. Rejection increases with level of proficiency and, as expected, is higher in the case of (16). French-speaking subjects show improvement in achieving nativelike competence with respect to the ambiguity produced by *él* in (1). The object *los* and the subject pronoun *ellos* would not occur together in the French and English equivalents of (16). However, not all subjects in the study assume that that is also the case in Spanish.

SUBJECT-VERB INVERSION

Table 5.4 shows the percentage of subjects who accepted inversion,[10] and Table 5.5 shows the percentage of subjects who changed the sentences to subject-verb word order. Both inversion and noninversion are grammatically correct, but usage favors inversion in all cases in Table 5.4, which the results of the control group confirm. The nativelike choice would be to accept inversion in all four items. The rest of the subjects interpreted the noun phrase as a direct object or did not interpret the sentences at all. There is a significant difference between the acceptance of ergative and nonergative verbs, a difference which is more obvious in the early stages of acquisition. These results do not coincide with those in Liceras (1988), where no clear-cut distinction between ergatives and nonergatives was found in the grammaticality judgment task. However, they support the results obtained by Liceras (1988) in the composition task. The fact that subjects used inversion with intransitive verbs when no ambiguity was possible (for instance, interpreting the

10 Inversion is a more complicated phenomenon than it looks when the properties of the pro-drop parameter are listed in the literature. Torrego (1984) maintains that in addition to free subject inversion, Spanish has an obligatory inversion rule that applies when a *wh*-phrase of a certain kind or its trace appears in COMP prior to logical form in finite clauses, as illustrated in (1) and (2): (1) ¿Qué querían esos dos? ("What did those two want?") *¿Qué esos dos querían? (2) ¿Con quién vendrá Juan hoy? ("With whom will Juan come today?") *¿Con quién Juan vendrá hoy? The examples are taken from Torrego (1984). She also discusses the relationship between adverb placement and inversion.

TABLE 5.2. *PRO* WITH SPECIFIC REFERENCE IN *THAT-T* CONSTRUCTIONS

Item	French group				English group				Control group
	I (n = 8)	II (n = 7)	III (n = 15)	IV (n = 2)	I (n = 6)	II (n = 5)	III (n = 14)	IV (n = 5)	(n = 5)
3 A	3 (37%)	1 (14%)	1 (6%)	—	5 (83%)	2 (40%)	3 (21%)	—	—
B	1 (12%)	2 (28%)	1 (6%)	—	1 (16%)	—	1 (7%)	—	1 (20%)
14 A	—	4 (57%)	6 (40%)	—	—	2 (40%)	5 (35%)	—	—
B	—	—	—	—	—	—	—	—	—
Total	4 (25%)	7 (50%)	8 (26%)	—	6 (50%)	4 (40%)	9 (32%)	—	1 (10%)

TABLE 5.3. LEXICALIZED SUBJECT PRONOUNS

Item	French group				English group				Control group
	I (n = 8)	II (n = 7)	III (n = 15)	IV (n = 2)	I (n = 6)	II (n = 5)	III (n = 14)	IV (n = 5)	(n = 5)
1	—	2 (28%)	8 (53%)	2 (100%)	1 (33%)	2 (40%)	3 (21%)	2 (40%)	5 (100%)
16	4 (50%)	5 (71%)	12 (80%)	2 (100%)	—	2 (40%)	10 (71%)	4 (80%)	5 (100%)

TABLE 5.4. ACCEPTANCE OF SUBJECT-VERB INVERSION

| | French group | | | | English group | | | | Control group |
Item	I (n = 8)	II (n = 7)	III (n = 15)	IV (n = 2)	I (n = 6)	II (n = 5)	III (n = 14)	IV (n = 5)	(n = 5)
7	4 (50%)	7 (100%)	15 (100%)	2 (100%)	3 (50%)	3 (60%)	14 (100%)	5 (100%)	5 (100%)
17	5 (62%)	6 (85%)	13 (86%)	2 (100%)	5 (83%)	5 (100%)	14 (100%)	5 (100%)	5 (100%)
Total	9 (56%)	13 (92%)	28 (93%)	4 (100%)	8 (66%)	8 (80%)	28 (100%)	10 (100%)	10 (100%)
9	2 (25%)	1 (14%)	9 (60%)	1 (50%)	—	—	3 (21%)	2 (40%)	5 (100%)
11	1 (12%)	1 (14%)	8 (53%)	2 (100%)	1 (16%)	—	5 (35%)	3 (60%)	5 (100%)
Total	3 (18%)	2 (14%)	17(56%)	3 (75%)	1 (8%)	—	8 (28%)	5 (50%)	10 (100%)

TABLE 5.5. FRONTING OF INVERTED SUBJECT

| | French group | | | | English group | | | | Control group |
Item	I (n = 8)	II (n = 7)	III (n = 15)	IV (n = 2)	I (n = 6)	II (n = 5)	III (n = 14)	IV (n = 5)	(n = 5)
7	1 (12%)	—	—	—	1 (16%)	1 (20%)	—	—	—
17	1 (12%)	—	2 (6%)	—	1 (16%)	—	1 (7%)	—	—
Total	2 (12%)	—	2 (6%)	—	2 (16%)	1 (10%)	1 (3%)	—	—
9	—	—	1 (6%)	—	—	—	2 (14%)	—	—
11	1 (12%)	—	—	—	1 (16%)	—	1 (7%)	—	—
Total	1 (6%)	—	1 (3%)	—	1 (8%)	—	1 (3%)	—	—

subject noun phrase as a direct object) is perfectly compatible with the results in the present study, because there is no possible ambiguity in (7) and (17). However, the noun phrases in (9) and (11) can be interpreted as subjects by those learners who either have not mastered the verb morphology or have not internalized the *a* marking of Spanish direct objects (as referring to people). This seems to indicate that acquisition of inversion is not only related to verb inflection but, as suggested in Liceras (1988), may be triggered by the *a* marking of Spanish direct objects. There are a few more instances of verb fronting in the case of ergative verbs. The reason for this may be that it was easier to interpret those sentences and to provide a "correct" alternative.

The difference between the French- and the English-speaking group may be due to the similarities between French and Spanish with respect to verb inflection, which may favor the correct interpretation of sentences with inversion.

The control group accepted all inversions. This was not the case in Liceras's (1988) study, where the Spanish-speaking subjects showed a clear preference for inversion in the case of ergative verbs. Given that not all the verbs were the same in both studies, and that most native speakers would accept all inversions in the present study – which is exactly what the control group did – it can be concluded that more than the ergative/nonergative distinction is necessary to account for inversion in native-speaker Spanish. These studies show that native and non-native judgments do not coincide, and that the ergative/nonergative dichotomy is far from being powerful enough to explain the stylistic choices made by Spanish speakers in the case of verb-subject inversion.

THAT-T EFFECTS

The percentages in Table 5.6 refer to the number of subjects who inserted *que* in (3) and gave the sentence the expected interpretation. Except for subjects in Level IV, there is no clear-cut pattern of improvement in the case of the French-speaking or the English-speaking group. Level I French subjects did better than the other levels in the case of (3), while Level I English subjects did very poorly. Some similarities between French and Spanish may help French speakers in understanding the Spanish sentence. Also, English and French differ with respect to *that-t* effects. For French speakers it is natural to insert a complementizer, while English-speaking subjects tend not to do it in the early stages of acquisition. Sentence 3, with a missing complementizer, does not create more problems than (14) for Level I French learners and Level IV English learners. On the other hand, some subjects in Levels II, III, and IV in French, in Levels II and III in English, as well as the control group, had problems interpreting Sentence 3, where the complementizer *que* is missing. A possible explanation is that Level I French learners do not have any problem

TABLE 5.6. ACCEPTANCE OF THAT-T

| | French group | | | | English group | | | | Control group |
| | I (n = 8) | II (n = 7) | III (n = 15) | IV (n = 2) | I (n = 6) | II (n = 5) | III (n = 14) | IV (n = 5) | (n = 5) |
Item									
3	5 (62%)	1 (14%)	1 (6%)	1 (50%)	—	2 (40%)	5 (35%)	4 (80%)	2 (40%)
14	3 (37%)	3 (42%)	7 (46%)	2 (100%)	1 (16%)	4 (80%)	7 (50%)	3 (60%)	4 (80%)
Total	8 (50%)	4 (28%)	8 (26%)	3 (75%)	1 (8%)	6 (60%)	12 (42%)	7 (70%)	6 (60%)

with the vocabulary in Sentence 3 (those lexical items are constantly used in the classroom), while they may have problems with Sentence 14. Subjects in Levels II and III have been exposed to a larger number of verb forms and uses of *que*, which may confuse them as they may be paying more attention to the structure than to the actual meaning of the sentences. Level IV English learners have a better command of verb inflection and subordination. This should also be the case for Level IV French learners and, of course, for the control group. In fact, the control group may simply be puzzled by the missing complementizer. The fact that there were only two subjects in Level IV French makes it difficult to determine whether the result is simply due to chance.

Unlike sentences with *that-t* effects, those with a missing complementizer were easily interpreted and corrected. Table 5.7 shows systematic improvement with level. The French-speaking subjects did slightly better than the English-speaking subjects, which was expected because of the differences between the two languages. Both groups did better in the case of (2), explainable by the fact that there is an overt subject, *Ana*, between the matrix and the subordinate verb. The missing subject, as well as the future tense morphology of the subordinate verb in (15), led some subjects to interpret *sacaré* as an infinitive.

Discussion

I chose to analyze the status of three properties of pro-drop in the interlanguage of four different levels of French and English speakers in order to investigate: (a) the process of setting this parameter with respect to each property; and (b) the differences between the two groups. The results confirm that resetting the pro-drop parameter from English and French to Spanish is not difficult with respect to null subjects. Pleonastic *pro* is incorporated in the learners' grammar at the very early stages. A few English-speaking subjects accepted *ello* and *lo*, and a few French subjects accepted *lo*. Acceptance of *ello* may indicate that some subjects do not distinguish between pleonastic and nonpleonastic *pro* with respect to the obligatoriness of the former. However, as in the case of Phinney (1987) and Liceras (1988), the overall results further justify the need to differentiate between both constructions. The rejection of overt subject pronouns increases regularly toward the target norm in the case of the French-speaking group. The English-speaking group shows less consistency, which may reflect their difficulty in mastering the morphology of Spanish verbs.

There was no pattern related to ambiguity, referentiality, and so forth in the acceptance of null subjects with a specific reference, because all study participants accepted all instances. This indicates that there was

TABLE 5-7. INSERTION OF MISSING COMPLEMENTIZER QUE

	French group				English group				Control group
Item	I (n = 8)	II (n = 7)	III (n = 15)	IV (n = 2)	I (n = 6)	II (n = 5)	III (n = 14)	IV (n = 5)		(n = 5)
2	7 (78%)	7 (100%)	15 (100%)	2 (100%)	3 (50%)	4 (80%)	14 (100%)	5 (100%)		4 (80%)
15	4 (50%)	5 (71%)	14 (93%)	2 (100%)	3 (50%)	2 (40%)	10 (71%)	4 (80%)		4 (80%)
Total	11 (68%)	12 (85%)	29 (96%)	4 (100%)	6 (50%)	6 (60%)	24 (85%)	9 (90%)		8 (80%)

no interference at all from either English or French. The overall results for null subjects seem to provide evidence for the unmarked status of Spanish with respect to this property and support the analyses which consider the non-pro-drop parameter setting as the marked option.

The acceptance of verb-subject inversion is very high with ergative verbs but not with transitive verbs in the case of both the French- and the English-speaking group. However, the data show that non-native speakers assign objective case to the postverbal noun phrase more than they reject inversion, which reinforces the suggestion that acquiring verb-subject inversion is related to internalizing the *a* marking of Spanish direct objects (referring to people) and is probably independent of the pro-drop parameter.

French speakers performed better than the English speakers both in acquiring pro-drop and in acquiring inversion. I have suggested that this difference stems from the fact that English – unlike French – does not have verb inflection. The similarity of the lexical items in French and Spanish should also contribute to the French speakers' more accurate interpretation of the sentences.

The results obtained from the *that-t* sentences indicate that many subjects do not interpret the sentences as expected, neither when the complementizer is missing nor when it is present. Adding a subject pronoun in (3) and (14), as has been done in (8) and (9), might have avoided this problem.

8. ¿Quién dices TU estudia español contigo?
9. ¿Quién has dicho TU que va a llamar?

Learners could have concentrated on the absence of *que* in the case of (3) and would have been more successful at interpreting (14). The fact that native subjects also had problems interpreting (3) (one subject also changed Sentence 14) indicates that these sentences demonstrate a complex construction (extraction from an embedded clause). There is no doubt that in the case of (3) the lack of *que* confuses the control group and those French and English speakers who have mastered Spanish verb morphology. The type of construction in the case of (14) must be what causes confusion, because there is no *que* missing. Further confirmation that it is the type of construction that is problematic comes from the results of testing subjects with declarative sentences with missing complementizers. The results in Table 5.7 indicate that these constructions are easier for both the French- and the English-speaking groups, which seems to confirm that acquisition of the obligatory use of *que* in declarative sentences does not imply acquisition of *that-t* in Spanish. They also indicate that there is more than null subjects and verb inflection involved in the interpretation of *that-t* constructions.

The results suggest that the three properties attributed to the pro-drop parameter do not have the same status in the interlanguage. This confirms previous findings by White (1985, 1986) and Liceras (1988). Nonetheless, this is not evidence against the possible relationship among the three properties in the grammar. What the results suggest is that acquisition of inversion and *that-t* effects cannot take place without acquiring pro-drop and verb inflection, which is a necessary but not sufficient condition.

Conclusion

The parameterized model used in this study has allowed the investigation of very specific aspects of the acquisition of Spanish as a foreign language. The results indicate that most Spanish L2 learners do not start with the L1 setting in the case of null subjects. Namely, the English non-pro-drop option is seldom transferred into the interlanguage. In my opinion, these results provide evidence for the unmarked status of the pro-drop option. Verb-subject inversion and *that-t* effects do not have the same status as pro-drop in the interlanguage grammar. However, the reasons for this different status may not necessarily be of a parametric nature. That is, the results indicate that nonparameterized aspects of grammar, such as the Spanish *a* marking of direct objects (referring to persons) and extraction from an embedded clause, may contribute to the difficulty of inversion and *that-t*, respectively. If this is the case, the three properties could still be related in that even though the parametric aspect may be set, its actual realization in a given construction will be conditioned to the acquisition of other aspects of the grammar. The differences between the French- and the English-speaking groups also indicate that language distance plays a role in the interpretation of sentences, but may not necessarily influence the resetting of the parameter itself.

Appendix 1

PROYECTO: EL ESPAÑOL NO NATIVO
(Project: non-native Spanish)
Departamento de Lenguas Modernas
(Department of Modern Languages)
Universidad de Ottawa
1987

CUESTIONARIO (Questionnaire)

Nombre y apellido (First and last name):
Sección (Section):
Fecha (Date):

Por favor, conteste las siguientes preguntas:
(Please, answer the following questions)

1. ¿Cuál es su lengua materna?
   (What is your mother tongue?)
2. ¿En qué partes de Canadá o del mundo vivió usted hasta los 18 años?
   (In which parts of Canada or the world did you live till you were 18 years old?)
3. ¿Qué lengua utiliza con más frecuencia?
   (Which language do you use most frequently?)
4. ¿En qué lengua se siente más cómodo a todos los niveles?
   (Which language do you feel most comfortable with at all levels?)
5. ¿Cuánto tiempo lleva estudiando español?
   (How long have you been studying Spanish?)
6. ¿Qué otras lenguas habla, escribe y/o comprende, y a qué nivel?
   (What other language/s do you speak, write and/or understand, and at which level?)
7. ¿En qué programa está inscrito?
   (In which program are you registered?)
8. ¿Cómo piensa utilizar su conocimiento de español en el futuro?
   (How are you going to use your knowledge of Spanish in the future?)
9. ¿Va a seguir estudiando español en esta universidad?
   (Are you going to continue taking Spanish at this university?)

Appendix 2[*]

EL ESPAÑOL NO NATIVO
(**Non-native Spanish**)
Juicios de gramaticalidad
(Grammaticality judgments)
1987

Nombre (Name):
Sección (Section):
Fecha (Date):

Corrija las oraciones que tengan errores gramaticales. Si hay alguna que considera correcta pero no le parece natural o no le suena bien, indíquelo también. Traduzca las oraciones a su lengua materna.

Corrigez les phrases qui contiennent des erreurs de grammaire. Si vous considérez que certaines sont correctes, mais qu'elles ne vous paraissent pas naturelles ou qu'elles ne sonnent pas bien, indiquez-le également. Traduisez les phrases dans votre langue maternelle.

---

[*]We provide here the English translations of the sentences in the test, as well as an indication (the asterisks) of which sentences are ungrammatical. Neither the asterisks nor the English translations appeared in the test.

Correct the sentences that have grammatical mistakes. If you think that some sentences are correct but unnatural or rarely used, please indicate that too. Translate the sentences into your native language.

1. Pedro es mejor de lo que él parece.
   Pedro is better than he looks.
2. *Creo Ana estudia filosofía en Harvard.
   [I] think Ana studies philosophy at Harvard.
3. ¿Quién dices estudia español contigo?
   Who do [you] say is studying Spanish with you?
4. *Lo llueve mucho en primavera.
   It rains a lot in spring.
5. *Ello hay un reloj muy grande en la clase.
   It there is a clock very big in the classroom.
6. Sí, hay dos libros de español para principiantes.
   Yes, there are two books of Spanish for beginners.
7. Ya han salido los profesores.
   Already have left the professors.
8. Creo que llaman a la puerta.
   [I] think that [they] are knocking at the door.
9. Telefonearon mis padres para preguntármelo.
   Phoned my parents to ask me about it.
10. *Lo había muchos estudiantes en esta clase.
    It there were many students in this classroom.
11. Ya han llamados mis hermanos.
    Already have phoned my brothers.
12. Dicen que va a nevar.
    [They] say that [it] is going to snow.
13. *Ello hace mucho frío en Canadá.
    It is very cold in Canada.
14. ¿Quién has dicho que va a llamar?
    Who have you said that is going to phone?
15. *Creo sacaré una A+ en español.
    [I] think [I] will get an A+ in Spanish.
16. *Los ví que ellos venían a buscarte.
    Them [I] saw that they were coming to get you.
17. Llegaron muchos estudiantes a principios de septiembre.
    Arrived many students at the beginning of September.

References

Adjemian, C., and J. Liceras. 1984. Accounting for adult acquisition of relative clauses: Universal Grammar, L1 and structuring the intake. In *Universals of Second Language Acquisition*, F. Eckman, L. Bell, and D. Nelson, eds. Rowley, Mass.: Newbury House.

Baker, C. L. 1979. Syntactic theory and the projection problem. *Linguistic Inquiry* 10: 533–82.

Berwick, R. 1985. *The Acquisition of Syntactic Knowledge*. Cambridge, Mass.: MIT Press.

Burzio, L. 1981. Intransitive verbs and Italian auxiliaries. Ph.D. dissertation, Massachusetts Institute of Technology.

Chao, W. 1981. PRO drop languages and non-obligatory control. *University of Massachusetts Occasional Papers in Linguistics* 7: 46–74.

Chomsky, N. 1981. *Lectures on Government and Binding.* Dordrecht, The Netherlands: Foris.

1982. *Some Concepts and Consequences of the Theory of Government and Binding.* Cambridge, Mass.: MIT Press.

1986. *Knowledge of Language: Its Nature, Origin, and Use.* New York: Praeger.

Flynn, S. 1987. *A Parameter-Setting Model of L2 Acquisition: Experimental Studies in Anaphora.* Dordrecht, The Netherlands: Reidel.

Hilles, S. 1986. Interlanguage and the pro-drop parameter. *Second Language Research* 2: 33–52.

Hyams, N. 1983. The acquisition of parametrized grammars. Ph.D. dissertation, City University of New York.

1986. *Language Acquisition and the Theory of Parameters.* Dordrecht, The Netherlands: Reidel.

1987. The effects of core and peripheral grammar on grammatical development in children. Ms. UCLA.

Jaeggli, O. 1982. *Topics in Romance Syntax.* Dordrecht, The Netherlands: Foris.

Liceras, J. M. 1983. Markedness, contrastive analysis and the acquisition of Spanish syntax by English speakers. Ph.D. dissertation, University of Toronto.

1985. The role of intake in the determination of learners' competence. In *Input in second language acquisition*, S. Gass and C. Madden, eds. Rowley, Mass.: Newbury House.

1986. *Linguistic Theory and Second Language Acquisition: The Spanish Nonnative Grammar of English Speakers.* Tübingen: Gunter Narr.

1988. Syntax and stylistics: more on the "pro-drop" parameter. In *Learnability and second languages*, J. Pankhurst, M. Sharwood-Smith, and P. van Buren, eds. Dordrecht, The Netherlands: Reidel.

Phinney, M. 1987. The pro-drop parameter in second language acquisition. In *Parameter Setting*, T. Roeper and E. Williams, eds. Dordrecht, The Netherlands: Reidel.

Rizzi, L. 1982. *Issues in Italian Syntax.* Dordrecht, The Netherlands: Foris.

Safir, K. 1982. Syntactic chains and the definiteness effect. Ph.D. dissertation, MIT.

Suñer, M. 1982. On null subjects. *Linguistic Analysis*, 9: 55–78.

Torrego, E. 1984. On inversion in Spanish and some of its effects. *Linguistic Inquiry* 15: 103–29.

Wexler, K., and R. Manzini. 1987. Parameters and learnability in binding theory. In *Parameter Setting*, T. Roeper and E. Williams, eds. Dordrecht, The Netherlands: Reidel.

White, L. 1985. The "pro-drop" parameter in adult second language acquisition. *Language Learning* 35: 47–62.

1986. Implications of parametric variation for adult second language acquisition: an investigation of the pro-drop parameter. In *Experimental Ap-*

proaches to Second Language Acquisition, V. Cook, ed. London: Pergamon Press.

1988. Island effects in second language acquisition. In *Linguistic Theory in Second Language Acquisition*, S. Flynn and W. O'Neil, eds. Dordrecht, The Netherlands: Reidel.

Williams, E. 1987. Introduction. In *Parameter Setting*, T. Roeper and E. Williams, eds. Dordrecht, The Netherlands: Reidel.

6 The adjacency condition on case assignment: do L2 learners observe the Subset Principle?

Lydia White

Since its inception, generative grammar has had two main aims. One is to devise grammars which characterize the ideal speaker-hearer's competence, the underlying system of rules which has been internalized. In other words, the grammars that linguists propose are assumed to have psychological reality. The second aim, which has taken precedence over the first one in recent years, is to provide not only a description of what it is that native speakers unconsciously know about their language but at the same time to explain how they come by this knowledge, to answer the so-called logical problem of language acquisition. Many properties of human languages are extremely complex and subtle, and it is argued that language learners discover such complexities by means of innate linguistic structure, or Universal Grammar (UG).

This innate language component is largely motivated by arguments concerning the poverty of the stimulus. Certain shortcomings in the input, including the lack of negative evidence or information about ungrammaticality, apparently make it impossible for the child to project the adult grammar from the input alone (Baker and McCarthy 1981; Hornstein and Lightfoot 1981). This projection problem can be overcome if the child is predisposed to deal with language input in quite restricted ways, with UG providing limitations on possible grammars. The language learner constructs a particular grammar, or a series of grammars, on the basis of UG interacting with the input data, the language that he or she hears. Thus the grammars of learners can be seen as their attempts to organize the data, to formulate a theory of the language which may change at various points in the acquisition process until the learner arrives at the correct grammar for the target language.

Universal Grammar places limitations on the types of grammars that learners hypothesize. In current Government-Binding Theory (Chomsky

This research was supported by grant no. 410-84-0211 from the Social Sciences and Humanities Research Council of Canada, for which I am grateful. I should like to thank staff and students at all schools and colleges that participated in the testing described here. Many thanks are due to Naomi Holobow for her collaboration in the FSL testing and analyses. I should also like to thank Bill Rutherford and an anonymous reviewer for their comments, and Kevin Gregg for related discussions.

134

1981, 1986), UG contains principles and parameters which between them specify a restricted range of possible core grammars. In addition, recent proposals within learnability theory concentrate on limiting the order in which learners entertain hypotheses in an attempt to ensure that learners do not start off with overinclusive grammars that would require negative evidence for disconfirmation. To this end, a learning principle, known as the Subset Principle, has been proposed (Berwick 1985). Manzini and Wexler (1987) and Wexler and Manzini (1987) argue that the Subset Principle is distinct from UG, although interacting with it.

A number of recent papers have pointed out that second language (L2) learners are also faced with a projection problem (Zobl 1983; Cook 1985; White 1985; Bley-Vroman, this volume). Second language learners, like first language (L1) learners, acquire a system on the basis of impoverished data. Any learner who attains reasonable success in the L2 will end up with very complex and subtle knowledge that was underdetermined by the input. This does not mean that the solution to the projection problem is necessarily identical in both situations, but it suggests that one should consider whether L2 learners have at their disposal the kinds of principles assumed to be available in L1 acquisition.

If principles of UG and principles of learning are distinct, one can investigate whether certain types of failure to arrive at nativelike grammars may be attributed to the fact that one or other of these sets of principles is no longer available. There are those who maintain that UG itself is no longer available to L2 learners (e.g., Clahsen and Muysken 1986; Schachter 1988; Bley-Vroman, this volume). An alternative possibility is that L2 learners cannot make use of the same learning principles as L1 learners. In this chapter, I shall suggest that the Subset Principle, a learning principle, no longer operates effectively in L2 acquisition and that the failure of the Subset Principle is linked to certain cases of mother tongue influence and also fossilization.

The adjacency condition on case assignment

According to recent developments in linguistic theory, principles of UG are subject to parametric variation, in that there are certain limited options associated with various principles. The idea is that a particular parameter is responsible for a number of properties within a language. If the language has a parameter "set" in a particular way, a certain range of consequences results. Another language might have the parameter set differently, with different consequences. A limited number of parameters, or options, will account for considerable diversity in the world's languages. In L1 acquisition, data from the language being learned are assumed to trigger the appropriate parameter setting for that language, with the full range of consequences which it entails.

An example is provided by the adjacency condition on case assignment (Chomsky 1981, 1986; Stowell 1981). Various properties of grammar are the consequences of case theory, which states that all lexical noun phrases must receive abstract case from a case assigner, such as a verb or preposition. One property of the complements of verbs in configurational languages (languages with rich hierarchical structure) is that they are ordered, with the direct object closest to the verb, followed by prepositional complements and adjuncts. Stowell (1981) argues that there is no need for this ordering to be specifically stated, either in phrase structure rules or within the lexicon. Instead, order follows from a requirement that a noun phrase receiving case must be next to its case assigner. This is the adjacency condition, and it explains why nothing can intervene between a verb and its direct object in English, as can be seen in (1):

1. a.   Mary ate her dinner quickly.
   b.* Mary ate quickly her dinner.
   c.   John drank some coffee yesterday.
   d.* John drank yesterday some coffee.
   e.   Mary put the book on the table.
   f.* Mary put on the table the book.

In English, adjacency is very strictly observed.[1] However, this is not the case in all languages. In nonconfigurational languages, complements can be freely ordered. Stowell suggests that this is because case is not assigned structurally but is inherent; verbs subcategorize for complements that are already morphologically marked for specific cases. Since these noun phrases do not get their case assigned by the verb, the adjacency requirement is irrelevant.

There are also some configurational languages, such as French and Italian, that allow certain constituents to intervene between the verb and the direct object, leading to apparent adjacency violations. In French, both (2a) and (2b) are grammatical:

---

1 There are two situations in English where strict adjacency appears to be violated. One concerns *heavy NP shift* in sentences where the direct object is moved to the right for reasons of focus, as in *Mary ate quickly the dinner which John had prepared for her*. Movement of this kind is only allowed when the direct object is a long or complex phrase, or when it is indefinite. As in the case of any other movement, a trace will be left in the original position of the direct object, thus maintaining adjacency with the verb. The other situation concerns the double object construction, as in *John gave Mary a book*, where the second NP (the direct object) is not directly adjacent to the verb. Stowell (1981) argues that in English, the verb and the indirect object together form a complex verb, which is adjacent to the direct object and gives it case. I shall not discuss these cases further.

2. a. Marie a mangé le dîner rapidement.
   b. Marie a mangé rapidement le dîner.

However, constituents are not free to intervene. Both (3a) and (3b) are ungrammatical:

3. a. *Jean a bu hier du café.
   b. *Marie a placé sur la table le livre.

In these languages, there is not a rich morphological case system, and case is assigned structurally by the verb rather than being inherent. What, then, allows violations of the adjacency condition? Stowell claims that violations are only possible when a manner adjunct (adverb or prepositional phrase) intervenes between verb and object, as in (2b), and proposes that there is a level at which such adjuncts can be ignored for the purposes of case assignment. Other adjuncts, such as the temporal expression in (3a), cannot intervene, nor can subcategorized phrases such as the locative prepositional phrase in (3b).[2]

These facts suggest that the adjacency condition is subject to parametric variation: Some languages, such as English, require strict adjacency, in contrast to French, which allows sentences that violate adjacency as well as sentences that observe it. Chomsky (1986) treats the adjacency condition as being parameterized; Stowell (1981) argues that the parameter has to do with the level at which case assignment takes place, and that other phenomena can be explained on the assumption that some languages assign case at a different level than others. For ease of exposition, I shall adopt Chomsky's assumption that there is a parameter with values [+strict adjacency] and [−strict adjacency], without taking a stand on whether or not this is in fact a reflex of other properties of grammar.

Adjacency and the Subset Principle

Assuming that UG allows for the above-mentioned kind of variation in the adjacency condition on case assignment, and that this variation is expressed in terms of a parameter with two values, a potential learnability problem arises as the L1 learner tries to determine whether the input suggests a language that observes the adjacency condition or one

2 Expressions of frequency are able to occur between verb and object, like manner adjuncts. The special behavior of manner adjuncts seems at present to be a descriptive generalization for which there is no obvious theoretical explanation. Stowell suggests that temporals may be independently excluded from the intervening position because they are not subcategorized and hence may not appear in $\bar{V}$. However, any attempt to exclude nonsubcategorized material from $\bar{V}$ should apply equally to manner adjuncts.

that violates it. A child faced with data like those in (4) might mistakenly assume that adverb placement is free in English:

4. a. Mary ate her dinner quickly.
   b. Mary quickly ate her dinner.
   c. Mary has quickly eaten her dinner.
   d. Quickly Mary ate her dinner.

Such an assumption could lead to the production of sentences like (1b), repeated here as (5), where the strict adjacency condition has not been observed:

5. *Mary ate quickly her dinner.

In order to retreat from this position and reset to the value required by English of [+strict adjacency], negative evidence, or information that (5) is ungrammatical, would be required. Such evidence is apparently not reliably available, and not taken into account when it does occur (Brown and Hanlon 1970; Braine 1971). In consequence, the child would have problems in learning that English has an adjacency requirement, since there appears to be no positive evidence that can give the learner this information.

One way to avoid this potential problem is to assume that the learning process is so set up that an English-speaking child will not come up with forms like (5). Given that adjacency violations are possible in some languages, this cannot be achieved by simply banning structures of this type via some restriction within UG. However, it can be achieved by ordering the child's hypotheses, and this is where the Subset Principle is involved.

The Subset Principle is motivated by a consideration of the kind of evidence available in the acquisition process, especially the assumption that negative evidence is not reliably available to first language learners. The Subset Principle "is one of conservative acquisition: the learner should hypothesize languages in such a way that positive evidence can refute an incorrect guess" (Berwick 1985:37).

In particular, this principle addresses the problem raised when language data are compatible with two or more grammars that generate languages in a subset/superset relation to each other, that is, when one of the languages is properly contained within the other. If the learner mistakenly picks the more general grammar, the incorrect guess will result in overgeneralizations that cannot be refuted on the basis of positive evidence. The Subset Principle states that when the learner is faced with input that could be accommodated by either of two grammars, the initial hypothesis is that the less general subset grammar is appropriate. The more general superset option is chosen only if specific positive evidence exists to support this option.

As we have seen, French allows sentences that observe adjacency as well as sentences that violate it, whereas English only allows the former. Data in the form of sentences like (1a) or (2a) are compatible with both values of the adjacency condition, since the [−strict adjacency] value allows a superset of sentences allowed by the [+strict adjacency] value. Thus, the grammar of English is less general than the grammar of French (with respect to this particular property) and is properly contained within it. The Subset Principle, then, says that a child faced with input involving verb-object sequences will assume the narrowest grammar consistent with those data, namely the one observing strict adjacency. As a result, forms like (5) will never be produced by an L1 learner of English. In contrast, a child learning French as the L1 who starts off by adopting the [+strict adjacency] value will encounter disconfirming positive evidence in the form of sentences like (2b). In effect, such sentences indicate that strict adjacency does not apply.[3]

There are two possible ways in which the Subset Principle might interact with UG. One is that UG is so constructed that principles and parameters are ordered within UG via markedness, with the unmarked value generating the subset and the marked value the superset. In this case, the Subset Principle is an instruction to try the unmarked value first. Alternatively, markedness can be removed from UG and parameters within UG can be unordered, leaving the Subset Principle to compute the markedness hierarchies, a position argued by Manzini and Wexler (1987) and Wexler and Manzini (1987). This proposal is attractive as it means that the Subset Principle will be able to deal with any properties of grammar that fall in a subset/superset relation, including language-specific rules and peripheral phenomena that are not part of UG. In addition, it raises the possibility that L2 learners might still be constrained by UG in terms of the types of interlanguage grammars that they come up with, without any longer being constrained in terms of the order in which different hypotheses are tried out.

Implications for L2 acquisition

Let us consider the potential operation of the Subset Principle in L2 acquisition. If the Subset Principle operates in L2 acquisition as it does in L1 acquisition, then L2 learners should be able to apply the principle to the L2 data, adopting a subset grammar unless positive input from the L2 sug-

---

3 I am assuming here that the presence of material intervening between verb and object will provide the necessary triggering data to show that French does not observe strict adjacency. It is, of course, possible that there are other sources of positive triggering data, especially if the [−strict adjacency] value is linked to a further cluster of properties. I will not pursue this issue here.

gests otherwise. I will refer to this as the *subset hypothesis*. According to this view, any learner of English should assume that [+strict adjacency] applies, and, as this happens to be correct, there will be no evidence to cause a change to [−strict adjacency]. In that case, French learners of English should not accept or produce adjacency violations like (1b).

In contrast to this is a position I shall call the *transfer hypothesis*. According to this view, L2 learners can no longer apply the Subset Principle directly to the L2 data; instead, they will be influenced by the situation pertaining in their L1s. Where the L1 has adopted a superset grammar, learners will assume that this superset grammar is also appropriate for the L2 data. In that case, the French learner of English will incorrectly assume that English is [−strict adjacency] like French, and produce and accept sentences like (1b).

The two hypotheses make different predictions as far as French learners of English are concerned: The subset hypothesis predicts that such learners will not allow adjacency violations in the interlanguage, whereas the transfer hypothesis predicts that they will. Both hypotheses make potentially the same predictions as far as English learners of French are concerned, although for different reasons. That is, the subset hypothesis says that these learners will reject adjacency violations in French because they are observing the Subset Principle. The transfer hypothesis also says that these learners will initially reject adjacency violations, due to the situation in the L1. Positive evidence in French in fact motivates the [−strict adjacency] setting, but neither hypothesis specifies when learners will notice this evidence. It is not inconceivable that, where a superset hypothesis is required, the relevant positive evidence is noticed immediately.

Thus, the crucial test between the subset and transfer hypotheses will be French learners of English, rather than English learners of French. However, an investigation of English learners of French allows one to look at the question of whether L2 learners do in fact pay attention to positive L2 evidence that motivates changing from a subset to a superset grammar. In the remainder of this chapter, experimental evidence from French learners of English will be presented which supports the transfer hypothesis. Evidence will also be considered from English learners of French, addressing the question of whether learners notice the positive evidence that motivates change from one value of the parameter to the other.

Experimental evidence

Background

Subjects consisted of two main groups: learners of English as a second language (ESL) and learners of French as a second language (FSL). All the ESL learners were native speakers of French and all the FSL learners were native speakers of English.

The ESL subjects included adults and adolescents. There were 43 adults, most of whom were reported by their teachers as being of intermediate proficiency. Some of the subjects were in the Canadian Armed Forces and were undergoing intensive ESL instruction; others were attending night courses in ESL at a local college in Montreal. Two secondary school groups were also tested, from a city north of Montreal: 29 secondary II students, average age 13, and 23 secondary IV students, average age 15. All the ESL subjects reported little exposure to their second language outside the classroom, particularly the adolescents. There were also 14 adult native speakers of English to serve as controls.

The FSL subjects were children in grades V (average age 11) and VI (average age 12) in various schools near Montreal. At each grade level, there were three experimental groups. One was a group undergoing partial immersion in French. They had started French immersion in grade IV and were taught all academic subjects in French, but had a daily class of English and were taught nonacademic subjects in English. Another group had had early total immersion since kindergarten, with a gradual increase in the use of English for instructional purposes from grade III onward. The third group were undergoing submersion; that is, they were attending French schools and receiving all instruction in French, along with native speakers. In addition, there were native speakers of French in a French school to act as controls. At the grade V level, there were 25 subjects in the partial immersion group, 12 in the early immersion group, 16 in the submersion group, and 17 native-speaker controls. At the grade VI level, there were 24 subjects in the partial immersion group, 25 in the early immersion group, 18 in the submersion group, and 14 controls. Because of the different kinds of exposure to the L2 that the groups were receiving, it was thought that differences in their sensitivity to the adjacency situation in French might be revealed. The submersion groups, in particular, should have had ample positive L2 evidence, both in and out of class, for the adjacency situation in French.

The tests

A number of different tests were devised to try to find out whether or not subjects were aware of the adjacency requirements in the L2. The tests involved three different kinds of grammaticality judgment tasks, described later. Copies of the judgment tasks can be found in the Appendix.

English and French versions of all the tests, except for one, were devised in order to allow comparison of the performance of learners of different languages on the same sentence types. In addition, a passage was translated from English into French, and then checked and rechecked with native speakers of the two languages, and used as a cloze test for both the ESL and FSL learners, as appropriate. Every sixth word was omitted and there was a total of 37 blank spaces in all in both versions of the passage.

THE PACED JUDGMENT TASK

The first task was a paced grammaticality judgment task, where subjects were presented with sentences to be judged in a limited amount of time. The task was paced in the following manner: Subjects read the sentences to be judged, but also heard them, at the same time, on a tape read by a native speaker of Canadian English or French. The tape was paced so that only 3 seconds were allowed for subjects to respond to each sentence. This was to prevent subjects from having time to make conscious comparisons with the L1. Given the limited time available for responding, subjects were not asked to correct sentences they deemed incorrect.

Below each sentence was a 9-cm line. Test participants were instructed to mark a stroke through the left-hand side of this line if they felt a sentence was totally incorrect, a stroke through the right-hand side if they felt it totally correct, and a stroke through the middle if they were not sure. However, they were also encouraged to put a stroke anywhere else through the line if they felt that sentences were not quite grammatical or not quite ungrammatical. In this way, one could get gradations of judgments, which might reveal more than a standard grammaticality judgment task.[4]

The task involved 42 randomized sentences, of which 11 sentences in the English version and 10 sentences in the French version were specifically included to address the adjacency principle.[5] In the English version of the test, 5 of these were grammatical sentences involving direct objects and adverbs/prepositional phrases in normal English word order (Sentences 1, 4, 11, 12, 21); thus the verb and its direct object were adjacent. Six sentences involved adjacency violations (Sentences 5, 16, 26, 35, 40, 42). If the Subset Principle does not operate in L2 acquisition, ESL learners should accept them. In the French version of the test, there were 4 sentences where the verb and object were adjacent (Sentences 1, 4, 11, 36) and 6 where they were nonadjacent (Sentences 5, 12, 26, 35, 40, 42). If FSL learners fail to notice the positive evidence indicating

4 This kind of task has been used in attitudinal testing by the Psychology Department at McGill University, Montreal. As far as I know, it has not been used in a grammaticality judgment task before, though it is, in fact, a variant of other tasks that ask subjects to judge sentences on a scale, with the difference that the points on the scale in this task are imposed afterward.

5 The rest of the sentences were relevant to certain island constraints, which I have reported on elsewhere and which will not be discussed here (see White 1988).

that strict adjacency does not apply in French, native speakers of English should treat these sentences as ungrammatical.

The time for this task, including instructions and practice sentences, was about 10 minutes. Subjects were not allowed to go back and change their answers after the tape ended. The ESL version of this test was taken by the control group and by all subjects except 11 of the adults. The FSL version of the task was taken by the control group and all subjects at the grade V level.

THE MULTIPLE-CHOICE JUDGMENT TASK

Another grammaticality judgment test was an unpaced task, with a multiple-choice format. I shall refer to it as MCGJ. Subjects received a written version of the test in which they were presented with sentences meant to provide a context, followed by three or four more sentences which were to be judged. Wherever possible, the same length and vocabulary were employed in both the grammatical and the ungrammatical versions of a sentence. Subjects were asked to circle any sentences they felt to be incorrect, to put a question mark by any sentence they were not sure of, and to leave untouched any sentences they felt to be correct. The task differed from a true multiple-choice task in that any number of the sentences following a particular context could be correct or incorrect, so that each sentence had to be read and judged. Subjects were provided with a number of examples, which were worked through with the experimenter, and they then worked on the task at their own pace. Most subjects took between 15 and 25 minutes.

There were 80 sentences to be judged in the English version and 77 in the French. Both versions included 24 context sentences. Twenty of the sentences were relevant to adjacency in the English version, and 17 in the French version. In the English version, there were 10 ungrammatical adjacency violations (Sentences 1b, 4a, 6b, 10a, 12c, 12d, 14a, 19a, 24a, 24c) and 10 grammatical sentences observing adjacency (Sentences 1a, 4b, 6a, 10b, 12a, 12b, 14b, 19b, 19c, 24b). In the French version of the test, there were 8 sentences violating adjacency (Sentences 1b, 4a, 6b, 10a, 12c, 14a, 19a, 24a) and 9 sentences observing it (Sentences 1a, 4b, 6a, 10b, 12a, 12b, 14b, 19c, 24b).[6]

Subjects were not asked to correct the sentences they marked as incorrect. This would have been feasible for the adjacency violations, but many of the sentences involved other principles which even native speakers find difficult to correct. It was felt that it would be unreasonable to ask the L2 learners to attempt correction in such circumstances.

6 The English version of the test included slightly more sentences relevant to adjacency because two extra sentences (12d and 24c) were added to the test after the French subjects had been tested. Some of the English subjects took an earlier version of the MCGJ that did not include these sentences either.

TABLE 6.I. ESL CLOZE TEST: MEAN NUMBER OF CORRECT RESPONSES

Group	Exact guesses	Acceptable guesses
Controls (n = 14)	23.92	32.14
Adults (n = 43)	13.59	20.87
Secondary II (n = 29)	—	—
Secondary IV (n = 23)	3.95	5.73

The ESL version was taken by the control group and all of the ESL subjects except for eight of the adults. The FSL version was taken by the control group and all subjects in grade VI.

COMPARISON TASK

The final task involved pairs of sentences that the subjects had to read. They were asked to decide whether the first or second sentence of the pair seemed better, or whether they both seemed the same; they were not asked to make a judgment as to the grammaticality or ungrammaticality of either sentence. Thus, in contrast to the two previous tasks, they were expressing preferences rather than making outright judgments.[7] In this test, which was only prepared for the ESL learners, there were 13 sentence pairs relevant to adjacency out of a total of 30 pairs. Of these, 8 were test pairs where a sentence that violated adjacency was compared with one that did not (Sentences 1, 9, 12, 15, 17, 22, 23, 28), and 5 were control pairs that involved comparing sentences with adverbs or prepositional phrases in different positions in the sentence, neither of them involving an adjacency violation (Sentences 3, 5, 7, 19, 30). In each sentence pair, identical vocabulary and sentence structure were involved, so that the only issue to be judged was the position of the adverb or prepositional phrase. Thirty native speakers of English acted as controls; they were not the same as the controls for the other tests. This test was taken by 25 of the adult ESL subjects.

Results

Cloze tests

The mean scores of the ESL groups on the cloze test, scored by counting exact guesses only and by counting acceptable guesses, are given in Table 6.1. The maximum possible score was 37. The secondary II group reported that they had never had to do a cloze test before and that they found it too difficult; unlike the other ESL groups (who had also not

7 I should like to thank Eric Kellerman for suggesting this kind of task.

TABLE 6.2. FSL CLOZE TEST: MEAN NUMBER OF CORRECT RESPONSES

Group	Exact guesses	Acceptable guesses
Grade V controls ($n = 17$)	12.69	20.94
Grade VI controls ($n = 14$)	13.69	21.08
Grade V partial immersion ($n = 25$)	3.21	5.63
Grade VI partial immersion ($n = 24$)	6.0	10.38
Grade V early immersion ($n = 12$)	6.75	11.75
Grade VI early immersion ($n = 25$)	10.40	16.24
Grade V submersion ($n = 16$)	9.94	17.06
Grade VI submersion ($n = 18$)	12.47	20.65

seen cloze tests before), most of them were not prepared to guess. Their scores are, therefore, excluded from Table 6.1. The FSL cloze scores are given in Table 6.2. Again, the maximum possible score was 37.

The English controls did considerably better than the French controls on the cloze passage. This is probably attributable to the fact that the former are adults; a small group of adult native speakers of French also did the French version of the test and performed very similarly to the English adult control group, so it seems unlikely that the difference in scores is due to anything in the French version of the passage itself.

As far as the subjects are concerned, the ESL adolescent groups are weaker than all the FSL groups except for the grade V partial immersion group. The performance of the adult ESL group is comparable with the grade VI submersion group, but again the fact that the former are adults and the latter children means that strict comparisons will not be possible. The grade VI submersion group scores very similarly to the native-speaker controls of their own age, whereas the ESL adults do not achieve scores close to the adult controls.

The paced GJ task

In this task, subjects were asked to mark a point on a line to indicate their impression of the grammaticality of a sentence. Although instructed that they could use any part of the line to record their responses, the majority of subjects used the two ends (indicating judgments of *correct* or *incorrect*) or the exact middle (indicating *not sure*). A scale was subsequently imposed on this line: A judgment of *incorrect* got a score of 0.5 and a judgment of *correct* got a score of 9. Scores of 4.5 and 5 indicate *not sure*. Scores between 0.5 and 4.5 indicate that subjects were not quite sure but judged the sentences as tending to the ungrammatical, whereas scores between 5 and 9 indicate sentences as tending toward the grammatical. Table 6.3 presents the mean scores for the ESL version of the task. Among the two groups of adolescents, there was a fairly

TABLE 6.3. MEAN SCORES FOR THE ESL PACED GJ TASK

Sentence numbers	− Strict adjacency				Sentence numbers	+ Strict adjacency			
	(C)	(1)	(2)	(3)		(C)	(1)	(2)	(3)
5	0.64	5.57	6.36	5.50	1	8.92	9.00	6.70	8.02
16	2.21	3.85	6.32	7.84	4	9.00	8.73	6.78	8.34
26	2.32	3.97	6.89	6.08	11	9.00	8.73	7.48	7.71
35	0.96	6.32	6.89	5.76	12	8.39	7.84	7.24	6.91
40	0.96	4.81	6.82	3.93	21	9.00	8.85	5.86	6.71
42	1.96	4.91	7.31	5.69					
Totals	1.51	4.91	6.76	5.80		8.86	8.63	6.81	7.54

Note: C = control group ($n = 14$), (1) = adults ($n = 32$), (2) = secondary II group ($n = 29$), (3) = secondary IV group ($n = 23$).

high incidence of responses of *not sure*, but this was not the case for the adult subjects or the control group.

In all the tables, the [−strict adjacency] sentences are those where adjacency is violated; these are ungrammatical in English but grammatical in French, with some exceptions that will be discussed later.

In Table 6.3, scores close to 0.5 indicate accuracy on the ungrammatical [−strict adjacency] sentences, and scores close to 9 indicate accuracy on the grammatical [+strict adjacency] sentences. The adults, in contrast to the adolescents, are very accurate on the grammatical sentences, their performance being similar to the control group. The difference between the group totals is significant, $F (3, 94) = 16.15$, $p<0.001$. A post hoc Scheffé procedure shows that the adult group does not differ significantly from the controls, and the two child groups do not differ from each other.

All experimental groups fail to reject the adjacency violations outright in the ungrammatical sentences.[8] The adults, in particular, seem noticeably less accurate than they were on the [+strict adjacency] sentences. Again, the difference between the group totals is significant, $F (3, 94) = 31.97$, $p<0.001$, with the post hoc analysis showing that the experimental groups do not differ significantly from each other. This result is consistent with the claim that these ESL learners are not observing the Subset Principle in their acquisition of English, since if it were operating, it should cause the subjects to reject the adjacency violations

8 One might argue that this simply shows that none of the subjects are any good at detecting ungrammaticality. However, this same test included many sentences relevant to island constraints, and the adults were very accurate at detecting the ungrammaticality of certain island violations, although the adolescents were not (White 1988). Thus, it cannot be the case that the adults simply cannot detect L2 ungrammaticality at all.

TABLE 6.4. MEAN SCORES FOR THE GRADE V FSL PACED GJ TASK

Sentence numbers	*– Strict adjacency*				Sentence numbers	*+ Strict adjacency*			
	(C)	*(1)*	*(2)*	*(3)*		*(C)*	*(1)*	*(2)*	*(3)*
5	7.24	6.76	4.88	3.53	1	8.41	7.42	7.13	8.28
12	7.97	6.68	6.96	5.50	4	8.06	8.20	8.21	8.22
26	7.35	6.08	4.50	5.16	11	8.47	7.80	8.46	8.97
35	8.50	6.22	5.04	7.53	36	9.00	8.28	8.75	8.91
40	7.65	6.36	5.71	3.94					
42	7.26	5.56	6.46	3.88					
Totals	7.66	6.28	5.59	4.92		8.49	7.93	8.14	8.59

Note: C = control group ($n = 17$), (1) = partial immersion ($n = 25$), (2) = early immersion ($n = 12$), (3) = submersion ($n = 16$)

outright.[9] However, since these are mean scores, reflecting individual responses at both ends of the scale, one must bear in mind that there were not only individual subjects who rated adjacency violations as completely acceptable, but others who rejected them.

The adult results were also analyzed by dividing them into two groups – those who scored above the mean on the cloze test and those who scored below. This was done in order to see whether the most advanced subjects would recognize that adjacency violations are not possible in English. However, the performance of the two adult groups is not significantly different, $t(20) = 1.03$, $p < 0.317$, suggesting that the more advanced adults do not show improvement in attaining the L2 value with increasing L2 ability.

The results from the FSL groups are given in Table 6.4. Scores close to 9 indicate accuracy on both the sentence types, since adjacency violations are admissible in French.

In the case of the sentences that observe strict adjacency, all groups are very accurate, there being no significant difference between them, $F(3, 66) = 1.82$. In contrast, in the case of the sentences violating strict adjacency, the difference between the group totals is significant, $F(3, 66) = 7.88$, $p < 0.001$, the post hoc procedure showing that the control group differs significantly from all experimental groups and partial immersion subjects differ significantly from submersion subjects. These mean scores reflect the fact that only some of the subjects were accepting the adjacency violations. Recall that, of all the FSL groups, it was expected that the submersion group would have the best opportunity to get positive data from the L2 showing that strict adjacency does not

9 For the adolescents, however, the lower performance on both sentence types may simply indicate insufficient mastery to test this issue.

TABLE 6.5. RESPONSES OF "CORRECT" FOR THE ESL MCGJ TASK IN PERCENTAGES

Sentence numbers	− Strict adjacency				Sentence numbers	+ Strict adjacency			
	(C)	(1)	(2)	(3)		(C)	(1)	(2)	(3)
1b	0	16	86	52	1a	100	97	31	55
4a	0	14	52	13	4b	100	97	93	82
6b	25	40	52	18	6a	100	97	62	77
10a	15	54	30	40	10b	100	97	64	90
12c	7	49	65	35	12a	100	94	85	86
12d	25	56	—	—	12b	100	87	71	78
14a	21	54	57	65	14b	100	91	82	83
19a	7	65	83	43	19b	100	60	29	41
24a	0	5	29	17	19c	100	80	71	83
24c	0	90	—	—	24b	100	100	86	96
Totals	10	43	57	36		100	90	65	76

Note: C = control group (*n* = 14), (1) = adults (*n* = 35), (2) = secondary II group (*n* = 29), (3) = secondary IV group (*n* = 23). A blank means no data was obtained.

apply. However, this group appears to be the least inclined to accept adjacency violations.

The MCGJ task

In this task, responses of *correct* will be reported. Such responses are accurate for grammatical sentences and inaccurate for ungrammatical ones. Again, the [−strict adjacency] sentences will be ungrammatical in the English version of the task but not in the French one. Answers of *not sure* have been excluded from the analysis; the incidence of *not sure* responses was very low.

The results from the ESL groups are given in Table 6.5. Among the adults, a number were unable to finish the MCGJ task due to time constraints. Their scores reflect this; the score reported is a percentage of the scores of those actually attempting the questions.

There is a significant difference between the group totals on the [+strict adjacency] sentences, $F(3, 97) = 31.6$, $p < 0.001$. A Scheffé procedure shows that the adult group's mean is not significantly different from the controls, and the adolescents are not significantly different from each other. In fact, the adolescents are accurate on many of the sentences; their total scores are pulled down by their responses to sentences (1a) and (19b), for which I have no explanation.

In contrast, accuracy on the [−strict adjacency] sentences is much lower. All the ESL groups are more likely than the controls to rate adja-

TABLE 6.6. RESPONSES OF "CORRECT" FOR THE GRADE VI FSL MCGJ TASK IN PERCENTAGES

Sentence numbers	− Strict adjacency				Sentence numbers	+ Strict adjacency			
	(C)	(1)	(2)	(3)		(C)	(1)	(2)	(3)
1b	93	79	83	100	1a	36	54	79	83
4a	23	25	32	17	4b	100	100	92	100
6b	50	21	16	24	6a	92	46	44	47
10a	82	29	36	67	10b	100	96	84	94
12c	91	54	46	33	12a	100	08	83	94
14a	82	17	16	28	12b	64	78	46	44
19a	83	73	61	78	14b	100	87	84	89
24a	55	25	08	12	19c	83	73	52	61
					24b	100	89	96	88
Totals	70	40	37	45		86	70	73	78

Note: C = control group ($n = 14$), (1) = partial immersion ($n = 24$), (2) = early immersion ($n = 25$), (3) = submersion ($n = 18$).

cency violations as correct in English. The difference between the group totals is significant, $F (3, 97) = 14.83$, $p < 0.001$, with the experimental groups not significantly different from each other. Once again, this is consistent with the assumption that the Subset Principle is not being applied to the L2 data, so that adjacency violations (permitted in the L1) are accepted in the L2. All experimental groups perform significantly more accurately on the [+strict adjacency] sentences than on the [−strict adjacency] ones, again supporting this assumption.[10] For the adults, $t (34) = -7.21$, $p < 0.001$; for the secondary II group, $t (28) = -4.03$, $p < 0.001$; for the secondary IV group, $t (22) = -2.14$, $p < 0.05$.

The FSL results from the MCGJ task are given in Table 6.6. As before, scores reported are the percentage of responses of *correct* to each sentence. The difference between the group totals on the [+strict adjacency] sentences is significant, $F (3,77) = 3.00$, $p < 0.05$; the post hoc analysis shows that the three experimental groups do not differ significantly from each other.

The FSL learners are significantly less likely than the native speakers of French to accept [−strict adjacency] sentences as grammatical. There is a significant difference between the group totals, $F (3,77) = 8.23$, $p < 0.001$, with the three experimental groups not significantly different from each other. The difference between each experimental group's responses to the two sentence types is also significant. For the partial immersion group, $t (23) = -5.82$, $p < 0.001$; for the early immersion group, $t (24) = -5.42$, $p < 0.001$; for the submersion group, $t (17) = -6.19$, $p < 0.001$. These re-

---

10 For the ESL groups, accuracy on the [−strict adjacency] sentences consists of correctly identifying them as ungrammatical.

sults again suggest that these learners are not fully taking into account the presence of positive data in French indicating the relaxation of the adjacency requirement, and this includes the group with presumably the most exposure to French, namely the submersion group.

There is considerable variation in the responses of the native speakers to the sentences not observing strict adjacency. In one case (4a), the adjacency violation is rejected as ungrammatical, and in two cases (6b) and (24a), the controls seem to be uncertain. This variation may be relevant to the question of the status of the material that intervenes between verb and direct object. As outlined earlier, Stowell (1981) proposes that adjacency violations in French are only possible when a manner or frequency adjunct intervenes between verb and object. The adjacency violations in the tests devised here were not restricted to manner adjuncts (see Table 6.7.) If native speakers of English learning French do reset the adjacency condition to [−strict adjacency], it would be interesting to see whether they unconsciously get the difference between cases when adjacency may be violated and when it may not. Positive evidence from manner and frequency adjuncts between verb and object might lead to overgeneralization, to the assumption that any material may intervene. It seems unlikely that the nature of the permissible intervening material is explicitly taught or that it is directly inducible from the positive data alone. Nothing in the L1 will help them here; indeed, these subjects also judged the adjacency sentences in English, their mother tongue, and judged all violations to be equally bad.

With the exception of (10a) and (14a), the sentences with adjacency violations in the MCGJ task that the native speakers liked least were indeed ones with an intervening temporal adjunct, or locative and dative subcategorized complements. The FSL learners also observe a distinction between intervening manner adjuncts and other intervening material. These results are given in Table 6.7, where it can be seen that subjects and controls are more inclined to accept sentences with intervening frequency or manner adjuncts. The difference between the totals for manner versus nonmanner violations is significant for all groups. For the control group, t $(13) = 5.43$, $p < 0.001$; for the partial immersion group, t $(23) = 5.91$, $p < 0.001$; for the early immersion group, t $(24) = 5.61$, $p < 0.001$; for the submersion group, t $(17) = 5.24$, $p < 0.001$. This suggests that those L2 learners who realize that French does not observe the adjacency condition become aware of rather subtle restrictions on adjacency violations.

Comparison task

The comparison task was only taken by 25 of the adult ESL subjects and by 30 controls, who were different from the controls for the other

TABLE 6.7. FSL MCGJ TASK − RESPONSES OF "CORRECT" TO MANNER AND
NONMANNER ADJACENCY VIOLATIONS IN PERCENTAGES

Sentence numbers	Manner[a]				Sentence numbers	Nonmanner[b]			
	(C)	*(1)*	*(2)*	*(3)*		*(C)*	*(1)*	*(2)*	*(3)*
1b	93	79	81	100	4a	23	25	27	17
12c	91	54	44	33	6b	50	21	12	24
19a	83	73	57	78	10a	82	29	30	67
					14a	82	17	18	28
					24a	55	25	6	12
Totals	89	69	61	70		58	23	19	30

Note: C = control group ($n = 14$), (1) = partial immersion ($n = 24$), (2) = early immersion ($n = 2$), (3) = submersion ($n = 18$).
[a] = manner and frequency adjuncts.
[b] = temporal, locative or dative adjunct.

tests. In this task, subjects did not have to make an outright judgment but instead compare sentences and say whether the first or second sentence of the pair seemed better, or whether they seemed the same. Sentences were randomized so that sometimes the first sentence was the one that was more acceptable, sometimes the second. The results from this task are given in Table 6.8. The first group of sentences, testing adjacency, are ones involving the comparison of a violation with a nonviolation. The results are tabulated according to whether the subjects preferred the sentence that maintained adjacency, (+adj), the one that violated adjacency (−adj), or whether they rated them the same. The second group of sentences involved comparing sentences with adverb or prepositional phrase adjuncts in two different positions, neither of which violated adjacency, and these are tabulated as *early* or *late*, depending on whether the subjects preferred sentences where the position of the adverb was toward the front or toward the end of the sentence, or *same* if they judged them equally acceptable.

The results when subjects were asked to compare a sentence violating adjacency with one where adjacency was not violated show that the controls overwhelmingly prefer the sentence observing strict adjacency. Only 2.5 percent responded that the two sentences seem the same. In contrast, the ESL learners are much more inclined to rate the two sentences as the same: 21 percent responded this way. The difference between the two groups is significant, $t (27) = 4.09$, $p < 0.001$. This is to be expected if the Subset Principle is not being applied to the L2 data; the Subset Principle would result in a preference for the sentences that observe strict adjacency.

The ESL learners do not treat all of the adjacency violations in English in the same way; for Sentences 1, 9, 17, and 28, their judgments are

TABLE 6.8. RESULTS FROM THE ESL COMPARISON TASK IN NUMBER OF RESPONSES

	Controls (n = 30)			ESL (n = 25)		
Sentence numbers	+adj	−adj	same	+adj	−adj	same
Adjacency						
1	29	0	1	24	0	1
9	30	0	0	24	0	1
12	29	0	1	15	0	10
15	28	0	2	15	0	10
17	29	1	0	22	1	2
22	30	0	0	13	0	12
23	28	0	2	20	1	4
28	30	0	0	23	0	2
Totals	233 (97%)	1 (.5%)	6 (2.5%)	156 (78%)	2 (1%)	42 (21%)
	early	*late*	*same*	*early*	*late*	*same*
Other adverb positions						
3	1	21	8	1	15	9
5	0	11	19	0	8	17
7	2	12	16	1	4	20
19	4	15	11	3	9	13
30	15	4	11	4	11	10
Totals	22 (14.6%)	63 (42%)	65 (43.3%)	9 (7.2%)	47 (37.6%)	69 (55.2%)

Note: adj = adjacency.

very similar to the controls. In these sentences, the material intervening between the verb and the direct object is either temporal or locative, suggesting that the manner/nonmanner distinction is carried over from the L1. (However, their treatment of Sentence 15, which has an intervening locative, does not pattern with the other sentences of this type.) When these adult subjects are divided into two groups, those above and below the mean cloze score, there is no significant difference in their responses to the adjacency sentences, again suggesting that level of proficiency does not necessarily increase awareness that English does not violate adjacency.

In the case of the sentence pairs involving the placement of adjuncts not violating adjacency, most of these sentences involved comparing a sentence with an adjunct in initial position with one in final position. For these sentences, the response of *same* received the highest proportion of responses from both controls and subjects, 43 percent and 55 percent respectively, and the difference between them is not significant, $t(51) = 1.4$, $p = 0.168$. Those subjects and controls who do not rate these adjunct positions as the same show a preference for sentences where the adjunct is in final position.

Discussion

In considering whether the Subset Principle operates in L2 acquisition, two possibilities were raised: the subset hypothesis, which says that all language learners will apply the Subset Principle to the L2 data; and the transfer hypothesis, which suggests that L2 learners will treat the L2 like the L1, imposing a superset grammar if that is what the L1 has. The evidence from the ESL learners supports the transfer hypothesis; that is, the results from various tasks suggest that many of the learners assume English to be like French in allowing adjacency violations. These results are not consistent with the subset hypothesis; if the Subset Principle had been applied, subjects should have totally rejected adjacency violations in English, contrary to what was found here.

The results from the FSL learners, on the other hand, suggest that the learners may be only partially aware that French relaxes the adjacency condition; they treat French as if it is more strict than it actually is. This behavior cannot be used to support either of the two hypotheses against the other, since both predict that the initial assumption of the English learner of French is that strict adjacency applies, and both could allow for change on the basis of positive evidence at any point in the acquisition process.

The results reported here suggest that when the L1 and L2 overlap in terms of the structures they permit, parameter resetting is not straightforward; the L2 data will be largely consistent with the L1 setting, regardless of whether that setting results in a subset or a superset language. With those ESL learners who treat English as if the adjacency condition does not apply, one will continue to find errors attributable to the L1, such as *John drank carefully his coffee.* Even the most advanced of the ESL learners, namely the adults who scored above the mean on the cloze test, still had problems in recognizing that English does not allow adjacency violations. Examples of production errors involving adjacency violations from advanced ESL learners are reported in Sheen (1980). It appears that this type of error is likely to be persistent, and a candidate for fossilization. Obvious fossilization, then, would be the result of carrying over a superset grammar from the L1, while failing to apply the Subset Principle to the L2 data.

In contrast, failing to take account of positive evidence that indicates a superset grammar has less obvious effects; the English learner of French who assumes that French is [+strict adjacency] is being overcautious and conservative, assuming a grammar stricter than the L2 data warrant. This conservatism will not result in obvious errors. Instead, there will be a failure to produce as wide a range of sentence types as the target language actually allows. We have seen that many of the FSL learners were conservative in this way, rejecting adjacency violations in French even though they had presumably been exposed to the relevant positive data (for example, the grade V submersion group). However, we have also seen that those learners who realize that French has a different setting for the adjacency condition than English are aware of quite subtle restrictions on the kind of material permitted to violate adjacency.

Other researchers have also recently reported results which suggest that superset hypotheses from the L1 are tried out initially in the L2 (Finer and Broselow 1986; Liceras, 1988; Rutherford, this volume). The question then arises as to the precise nature of the relationship between transfer from the L1 and the failure of the Subset Principle. So far, we have simply seen that these go together. We do not, in fact, know whether a cause-and-effect relationship is involved, and if so, which is cause and which effect. It might be that the Subset Principle does not operate at all in L2 acquisition, with the consequence that superset hypotheses based on the L1 cannot be prevented. Thus, failure of the Subset Principle enables transfer to take place. Alternatively, it might be that the occurrence of transfer causes the failure of the Subset Principle. Suppose that the Subset Principle still operates, but the interlanguage grammar has incorporated overinclusive rules from the L1, or it is influenced by data from the L1 which motivate a superset grammar. In that case, the Subset Principle could only operate unsuccessfully; it would be misled by the interlanguage data. The evidence discussed here cannot determine which of these two alternatives is correct. Support for the view that transfer is a consequence rather than a cause of the failure of the Subset Principle would be provided if L2 learners inappropriately adopt superset grammars in circumstances where the L1 plays no role. A few such cases are discussed in Bley-Vroman (1986), but there is as yet little evidence bearing on this question and it must remain an issue for future research.

Appendix: Test sentences

In all the tasks, a number of structures were tested that are not reported on in this chapter. In this appendix only those sentences are listed that are relevant to adjacency and have been discussed in the chapter. The numbering system from the original tests is retained.

i. Sentences used in the paced GJ task – ESL

1. Mary prepared the dinner quickly.
4. Suzanne explained the problem to her husband.
5. Tony crossed carefully the street.
11. Martin sold his bicycle to his friend.
12. Paul drank the hot coffee slowly.
16. My mother gave to me some advice.
21. Bring your books to the teacher.
26. Peter watched from his window the traffic.
35. John reads often novels.
40. Jane cooked yesterday steaks for supper.
42. Diana put on the table some flowers.

ii. Sentences used in the MCGJ task – ESL

1. Jane loves to eat ice cream.
    a. Jane often eats ice cream
    b. Jane eats often ice cream.
4. Thomas was invited to a party.
    a. He took before the party a shower.
    b. He took a shower before the party.
6. Last week Bill bought a new car. This week he has no money.
    a. Today Bill borrowed 20 dollars from his friend.
    b. Today Bill borrowed from his friend 20 dollars.
10. Robert's birthday was last week.
    a. John sent to Robert a gift.
    b. John sent a gift to Robert.
12. I enjoy reading the newspaper.
    a. Every morning I read the newspaper with interest.
    b. I read the newspaper with interest every morning.
    c. I read every morning the newspaper with interest.
    d. I read with interest the newspaper every morning.
14. Mary moved to Toronto in December.
    a. Peter wrote to Mary a long letter.
    b. Peter wrote a long letter to Mary.

19. Ellen's coffee was hot.
    a. Ellen drank slowly the hot coffee.
    b. Slowly, Ellen drank the hot coffee.
    c. Ellen drank the hot coffee slowly.
24. Peter finished reading his book.
    a. Peter put on the table the book.
    b. Peter put the book on the table.
    c. Peter put carefully the book on the table.

iii. Sentences used in the comparison task – ESL

1. Anne took the letters from the mailbox.
   Anne took from the mailbox the letters.
3. Quickly, Susan finished her homework.
   Susan finished her homework quickly.
5. At noon, the children ate their lunch.
   The children ate their lunch at noon.
7. Sarah will go on vacation tomorrow.
   Tomorrow, Sarah will go on vacation.
9. Yesterday, Jane bought candies for her children.
   Jane bought yesterday candies for her children.
12. John drank his coffee quickly.
    John drank quickly his coffee.
15. Alice put in the freezer some ice cream.
    Alice put some ice cream in the freezer.
17. Peter bought last week some flowers.
    Peter bought some flowers last week.
19. Slowly, the children walked to school.
    The children walked slowly to school.
22. Peter did carefully his homework.
    Peter did his homework carefully.
23. Jessica is watching with interest the television.
    Jessica is watching the television with interest.
28. Fred is reading the newspaper in the kitchen.
    Fred is reading in the kitchen the newspaper.
30. The teacher read the story quietly to the children.
    The teacher read the story to the children quietly.

iv. Sentences used in the paced GJ task – FSL

1. Marie a préparé le repas rapidement.
4. Suzanne a expliqué le problème à son mari.
5. Antoine a traversé prudemment la rue.
11. Martin a vendu son vélo à son ami.
12. Jacques a bu rapidement le café.
26. Pierre a regardé de sa fenêtre les voitures.
35. Normand lit souvent des romans.
36. Diane a envoyé une lettre à sa soeur.
40. Jeanne a fait cuire hier du poulet pour le souper.
42. Diane a placé sur la table des fleurs.

v. Sentences used in the MCGJ task – FSL

1. Jeanne aime manger de la crème glacée.
   a. Jeanne mange de la crème glacée souvent.
   b. Jeanne mange souvent de la crème glacée.
4. Thomas a été invité à une fête.
   a. Il a pris avant la fête une douche.
   b. Il a pris une douche avant la fête.
6. La semaine dernière, Claude a acheté une voiture neuve. Cette semaine il n'a pas d'argent.
   a. Aujourd'hui, Claude a emprunté vingt dollars à son ami.
   b. Aujourd'hui, Claude a emprunté à son ami vingt dollars.
10. La fête de Robert était la semaine dernière.
    a. Jean a envoyé à Robert un cadeau.
    b. Jean a envoyé un cadeau à Robert.
12. J'aime lire les journeaux.
    a. Chaque matin je lis le journal avec intérêt.
    b. Je lis le journal avec intérêt chaque matin.
    c. Je lis chaque matin le journal avec intérêt.
14. Marie a déménagé à Toronto en décembre.
    a. Pierre a écrit à Marie une lettre.
    b. Pierre a écrit une lettre à Marie.
19. Le café de Paul était trop chaud.
    a. Paul a bu lentement le café chaud.
    b. Paul a lentement bu le café chaud.
    c. Paul a bu le café chaud lentement.
24. Pierre a fini de lire son livre.
    a. Pierre a mis sur la table le livre.
    b. Pierre a mis le livre sur la table.

References

Baker, C. L., and J. McCarthy, eds. 1981. *The Logical Problem of Language Acquisition*. Cambridge, Mass.: MIT Press.

Berwick, R. 1985. *The Acquisition of Syntactic Knowledge*. Cambridge, Mass.: MIT Press.

Bley-Vroman, R. 1986. Hypothesis testing in second language acquisition theory. *Language Learning* 36: 353–76.

Braine, M. 1971. On two types of models of the internalization of grammars. In *The Ontogenesis of Grammar: A Theoretical Symposium*, D. Slobin, ed. New York: Academic Press.

Brown, R., and C. Hanlon. 1970. Derivational complexity and the order of acquisition in child speech. In *Cognition and the Development of Language*, J. R. Hayes, ed. New York: Wiley.

Chomsky, N. 1981. *Lectures on Government and Binding*. Dordrecht, The Netherlands: Foris.

  1986. *Knowledge of Language: Its Nature, Origin, and Use*. New York: Praeger.

Clahsen, H., and P. Muysken. 1986. The availability of universal grammar to adult and child learners: a study of the acquisition of German word order. *Second Language Research* 2: 93–119.

Cook, V. 1985. Chomsky's Universal Grammar and second language learning. *Applied Linguistics* 6: 2–18.

Finer, D., and E. Broselow. 1986. Second language acquisition of reflexive-binding. In *Proceedings of NELS 16.* Amherst: University of Massachusetts Graduate Linguistics Students' Association.

Hornstein, N., and D. Lightfoot, eds. 1981. *Explanation in Linguistics: The Logical Problem of Language Acquisition.* London: Longman.

Liceras, J. 1988. L2 learnability: delimiting the domain of core grammar as distinct from the marked periphery. In *Linguistic Theory in Second Language Acquisition*, S. Flynn and W. O'Neil, eds. Dordrecht, The Netherlands: Reidel.

Manzini, R., and K. Wexler. 1987. Parameters, binding theory, and learnability. *Linguistic Inquiry* 18: 413–44.

Schachter, J. 1988. Second language acquisition and its relationship to Universal Grammar. *Applied Linguistics* 9(3). 219–35.

Sheen, R. 1980. The importance of negative transfer in the speech of near-bilinguals. IRAL 18: 105–19.

Stowell, T. 1981. The origins of phrase structure. Ph. D. dissertation, Massachusetts Institute of Technology.

Wexler, K., and R. Manzini. 1987. Parameters and learnability in binding theory. In *Parameter Setting*, T. Roeper and E. Williams, eds. Dordrecht, The Netherlands: Reidel.

White, L. 1985. Is there a logical problem of second language acquisition? *TESL Canada* 2(2): 29–41.

    1988. Island effects in second language acquisition. In *Linguistic Theory in Second Language Acquisition*, S. Flynn and W. O'Neil, eds. Dordrecht, The Netherlands: Reidel.

Zobl, H. 1983. Markedness and the projection problem. *Language Learning* 33: 293–313.

PART III:
SEMANTICS/PRAGMATICS

The chapters in this section are concerned with the multiplicity of factors involved in learning second language word order, particularly the influence of semantics and pragmatics. Languages of the world differ not only in their word order (or more appropriately, constituent order) but also in the strictness of word order. A further differentiating factor among the world's languages is variation among what is known as basic word order, or the predominant order of the primes of subject (S), object (O), and verb (V), if, in fact, a predominant order can even be discerned. Of central relevance to the chapters in this section is what determines interlanguage word order (Rutherford) and what determines the interpretation of word order (Gass).

English is a language with fixed word order: Subject-verb-object (SVO). Sentences such as *Mary loves John* are grammatical, whereas a sentence such as *Mary John loves* is not. On the other hand, there are some languages that have a pragmatically determined word order as opposed to a fixed one. In those languages, word order is determined not by the constraints of the language per se but by the context in which the language is spoken. In Italian, for example, the following sentences are all possible (with variation in intonational and stress patterns):

1. Il lupo ha mangiato il topo.
   The wolf has eaten the mouse.
2. Il topo il lupo (l') ha mangiato.
   the mouse the wolf (it-object) has eaten
3. Il topo ha mangiato il lupo.
   the mouse has eaten the wolf

Not only are these sentences possible given particular contexts, but they all have the same "meaning" – that is, it is the wolf that has done the eating and not the mouse. The interpretation is possible since, in Italian, word order is not the only way of establishing relationships among elements in a sentence; our knowledge of real world facts (in this case that wolves are more likely to eat mice than vice versa) helps Italian speakers sort out the relevant information. Additionally, in languages like Italian, one must also consider not only factors of basic word order (SVO) and pragmatically determined order, as in the examples above, but also grammatically determined devices such as agreement markers. Other languages use grammatical devices such as case markings as a primary means of indicating constituent relationships. For example, in Russian any of the following sentences is possible, all with the meaning *Tanya killed Masha* (taken from Comrie 1981:71–72).

4. Mašu ubila Tanja.
5. Tanja ubila Mašu.
6. Tanja Mašu ubila.
7. Mašu Tanja ubila.
8. Ubila Mašu Tanja.
9. Ubila Tanja Mašu.

The grammatical relations are determined by the -*a* ending on Tanja (nominative) and the -*u* ending on Mašu (accusative). What differentiates these sentences is the pragmatic role each expresses. Thus, Sentence 4 would be appropriate as an answer to Sentence 10:

10. Who killed Masha? or Valja killed Natasha. What about Masha?

whereas Sentence 5 would be an appropriate answer to Sentence 11.

11. Who did Tanya kill? or Valya killed Natasha. What about Tanya?

There are yet other languages in which word order is based on a combination of pragmatically and grammatically determined devices. Japanese is one such language. Word order is strict in the sense that the verb always occurs in final position, yet subject and object order is free to move, depending on pragmatic factors.

It is clear from both studies in this section that the task of learning a second language word order in terms of both production and reception is complex. Learners need to know: (1) if there is a *dominant* word order, (2) if so, what that word order is, (3) how strict that word order is, and (4) if it is not strict, what factors determine the ordering of constituents in a sentence.

Rutherford's chapter considers the bidimensional aspect of the relationship between linguistic theory and second language acquisition, a theme dominant in many chapters in this book. His particular area of inquiry is the relationship between grammatical and pragmatic word order. The data he examines come from English compositions written by native speakers of Spanish, Arabic, and Japanese. The languages in question differed in that the word order of two of them (English and Japanese) is based on grammatical factors, whereas Spanish and Arabic word order is determined by pragmatic factors. Rutherford finds that there is evidence of native language influence in that pragmatic word order is transferred into a learner's interlanguage, even in those instances when canonical English word order (SVO) is violated. Rutherford then discusses possible explanations. In so doing, he considers the strengths and weaknesses of explanations anchored in Universal Grammar, in universal processing procedures, and in discourse constraints. This chapter not only provides us with a basis for examining second language word order acquisition, but also provides insight into the nature of what underlies a pragmatic versus grammatical word order typology for all natural languages.

Gass's chapter is based on the Competition Model of Bates and MacWhinney (1982). She investigates the role of syntax and semantics as determinants of interpretation in a second language. Her data come from two sources, both of which deal with sentence interpretation: The first is from responses by learners of English (of several language backgrounds) to sentences with *tell* or *promise* as the main verb; the second is from responses to all configurations of sentences with two nouns and one verb by Italian speakers learning English and English speakers learning Italian. These latter two languages differ in the degree to which they use such cues as word meaning and word order (the two variables considered in this study) to indicate relationships among major constituents in a sentence.

In her chapter, Gass argues that in acquiring a second language, learners have to learn not only the particulars of syntactic configurations but also the relative strength of syntactic factors vis-à-vis other factors. She uses the Competition Model to account for these facts of second language learning as well as using second language data to expand upon this model. In particular, she argues for the universal prepotency of animacy cues as opposed to syntactic cues in sentence interpretation (whereby learners give preference to animate objects for the assignment of subjecthood as opposed to relying on purely syntactic considerations); she further argues for the important role of second language data in determining the strength of implicational relationships.

References

Bates, E., and B. MacWhinney. 1982. Functionalist approaches to grammar. In *Language Acquisition: The State of the Art*, E. Wanner and L. Gleitman, eds. New York: Cambridge University Press.

Comrie, B. 1981. *Language Universals and Linguistic Typology*. Chicago: University of Chicago Press.

7 Interlanguage and pragmatic word order

William Rutherford

Statements to the effect that the investigation of interlanguage (IL) is a valuable endeavor for any researcher interested in extending our knowledge about what language is and how it comes to be acquired are gradually becoming more common. Interlanguage phenomena in second language acquisition (SLA) have been cited in support of parameterization in Universal Grammar (Flynn and Espinal 1985; Hilles 1986), of a theory of implicational universals (Eckman 1984; Hawkins 1985), of theories of markedness (Zobl 1983a; Ferguson 1984), of accessibility hierarchies (Gass and Ard 1984), and so on.[1] Whether or not the studies in question turn out to have been actual representations of the potential contributions of SLA research to general linguistic theory, they at least have begun to generate a healthy interest in IL as a valuable testing ground for such theory.

Among the language phenomena that have figured in much SLA research of the past four or five years is that of word order,[2] and it is not very difficult to understand why this should be so. Word order constitutes one area of language organization in which a number of separate spheres of linguistic inquiry quite naturally converge. One could identify some of these spheres as Universal Grammar (UG) parameterization, typological work in the spirit of Greenberg, process-oriented approaches such as that of Slobin, theories of language parsing as in the recent research of Frazier, and others. Central to various claims advanced in all these endeavors are: (1) the observed cross-language arrangements of the canonical constituents subject (S), object (O), and verb (V); (2) the other language properties that follow from any given arrangement of these basic constituents; and (3)

The data examined in this paper are taken from Altman and Rutherford (1982). I am therefore indebted to Roann Altman for her earlier contribution to the thesis being further developed here. For useful comments on the earlier version, I wish to thank Lydia White, Helmut Zobl, and Jacquelyn Schachter. My gratitude extends as well to Abdullah Alfaiz for help with the Saudi Arabic data.
1 See Rutherford (1986) for a summary of this research.
2 See Rutherford (1984a, 1986) for a discussion of this.

the effect upon canonical word order (CWO) of other forces impinging on the linguistic event.

A fairly strong functional statement concerning the sources of such impingement is offered by Slobin:

Each language provides conventions for the mapping of communicative intentions onto utterances. These conventions are constrained, for all languages, by: (1) human tendencies to think and image in certain ways; (2) processing demands imposed by a rapidly fading, temporally ordered code (be it auditory speech or visual design); and (3) the nature and goals of human interaction. . . . These three types of constraints limit the range of possible human languages. That is to say, *language has the form it does because of the uses to which it is put* [emphasis added]. (1979:64)

Strong counterarguments to this position, however, are frequently seen in the writings of UG-oriented researchers, especially Chomsky (1975), who effectively demonstrates the futility of assigning any functional explanations to the existence of abstract principles of language organization such as structure dependency, for example. This is not to deny, however, that there may be worthwhile *relationships* of this kind to be observed:

Surely there are significant connections between structure and function; this is not and has never been in doubt. Furthermore, I do not hold that "the essential thing about languages . . . is their structure." I have frequently described what I have called "the creative use of language" as an essential feature, no less than the distinctive structural properties of language. Study of structure, use, and acquisition may be expected to provide insight into essential features of language. (Chomsky 1975:56)

In any discussion of this kind there seem to be at least two things at issue – the nature of the formal constraints that are claimed to be related (or not) to functional exigencies, and the question of possible *explanatory* power to be ascribed to function where claimed form/function relationships are *not* in dispute. (For example, the sorts of constraints talked about in the functional literature [e.g., Searle 1969; Givón 1979; Slobin 1979] and in the UG literature [Chomsky 1981] are in no sense alike.) Frazier (1985) addresses this problem within the context of language processing and, more specifically, parsing, whose operation she would attribute to a mechanism separate from the grammar itself:

What, then, do these considerations [about dependency of successful parsing upon constraints on grammar] suggest about the attempt to provide functional explanations of grammatical facts? Surely they do not suggest that we should abandon the search for correlations between properties of grammars and properties of the language processing mechanism. Rather, they suggest that mere observation of a correlation between grammars and processing will not suffice to explain the relation between grammars and processors. As usual, what is needed is a theory of grammar, a theory of processing, and a theory of the ways they interact. (Frazier 1985:132)

Frazier's stipulation of what is needed for "functional explanations of grammatical facts" is no doubt correct, and certainly there have been in recent years significant advances made in theories of grammar and of language processing. This does not mean, however, nor is Frazier necessarily saying this, that progress in developing one of the two will not bear upon development of the other. Indeed, further discoveries of the *relationship* between form and function would seem to be central to developing any grammar/processing interaction theory. It is the contention of this chapter that a potentially rewarding area of research for gaining insight into this general language relationship is the particular relationship of IL in SLA. What confers upon IL this special significance is the fact that its attainment differs in important ways from acquisition of primary languages, and as such, facilitates the attempted teasing apart of form/function exponents for both IL *and* primary language. This chapter will later return to the matter of substantive differences in primary language/second language acquisition.

It was earlier noted that diverse sectors of linguistic inquiry converge on the phenomenon of word order. This chapter intends to enhance this particular status of word order by extending the investigation of it to IL. (See also Rutherford 1983; Zobl 1983b, 1984b, 1986; Clahsen 1988; White, this volume; and others.) Central to the study here is the report of some empirical research in English IL word order that was originally framed in language-typological terms (Altman and Rutherford 1982). After discussing the research results, this chapter will examine the findings in the light of other approaches to the analysis of linguistic data of this sort – namely Chomskyan UG (in particular, the Subset Principle) and language processing (in particular, parsing routines) – and we will suggest the kind of further research that this points to. Finally, it will be argued that this line of research in SLA is of substantial value to linguistics in general.

Canonical word order in IL

There is now a sizable collection of research findings concerning the influence that the organization of one's native language exerts upon the forms produced in another language that one is attempting to learn. Without recounting in detail the curious history of fluctuating interest in language contact where second language (L2) acquisition is concerned, suffice it to say that there has been a discernible progression from concrete to abstract, and in some cases from attention to product to attention to process. Studies have moved away from straightforward comparisons of a second language learner's IL and native language with respect to some strictly surface feature, and have instead begun investigating the possibility of more subtle influences of the native language (L1) on the shape of the IL (Schachter and Rutherford 1979; Adjemian 1983; Huebner 1983; Rutherford 1983; Zobl 1984b) – influences, for example, of L1 discourse function, of lexical features, of syntactic processes, of abstract organization, and so forth. Such investigations into the less and less obvious instances of L1 transfer have led to the formulation of a claim about L1 transferability that derives from considerations of three language typological parameters – canonical word order (CWO) arrangement, topic- and subject-prominence (Li and Thompson 1976), and grammatical word order versus pragmatic word order (GWO/PWO) (Thompson 1978).[3] Of these three parameters, it has been claimed (Rutherford 1983) that only those two – namely topic- and subject-prominence and GWO/PWO – that are definable in discoursal and not strictly syntactic terms will exert a measurable influence on IL. In other words, L1 (syntactic) CWO does not undergo transfer in the adult L2 learning experience,[4] and it was implied that this apparent correlation between discourse and the transfer-prone typologies is more than mere coincidence.[5]

Although there is no evidence in the literature as yet attesting to L2 transfer of (unmarked) L1 CWO, it needs to be pointed out that from this it must not be concluded that the target language CWO is *immune* to L1 influence. Although LI CWO will not necessarily manifest in the IL a violation of L2 CWO, the converse is not true – it is not *impossible* for violations of L2 CWO to occur in the IL. They can, and do; the following will be a rough attempt to describe the linguistic circumstances in which this will happen for written communication.

The phenomena in question – namely the instances (or not) of IL violations of L2 CWO – were observed with respect to one target language (English) and a wide variety of native languages. These observations led to the formulation of the following hypothesis:

1. The tendency for canonical word order permutation in written ILs will correlate directly with the propensity of the learner's native language to permute its own canonical constituents.

3 Topic-prominence characterizes those languages in which the relationship *topic-comment* is fundamental to the definition of "sentence." For subject-prominent languages the fundamental relationship is that of *subject-predicate*. In pragmatic word order it is discourse factors that at least partially determine the order of canonical constituents in the sentence. In grammatical word order the positioning of canonical constituents obeys primarily syntactic constraints. For helpful discussion and examples of all these distinctions, see the references cited.
4 Clahsen (1988) also makes this claim.
5 See Zobl (1986), however, for another approach. The nontransfer of L1 canonical word order in L2 acquisition has been noted also by Bach (1975) and Ellis (1982). The transfer of topic-prominence is discussed in Fuller and Gundel (1985).

Research

In order to conduct preliminary tests of the hypothesis, IL data were systematically obtained from learners of English whose native languages are typologically diverse vis-à-vis CWO and PWO/GWO. This required scansion of some 600 compositions, part of a battery of tests administered to all matriculating international students at the University of Southern California. The compositions, collected over the course of several semesters, ranged over four different topics and reflected a wide range of proficiency levels. From the compositions scanned (whose authors represented more than 20 native language backgrounds), it was possible to extract a subset of 304 representing three native languages – Spanish (59), Saudi Arabic (149), and Japanese (21) – that was large enough for research purposes.[6]

In terms of the typological parameters previously cited, the research sample thus contained an SOV language with one salient GWO feature – the verb anchored in final position (Japanese)[7] – and two languages leaning strongly toward PWO (Spanish and Arabic).[8] And of course the sample also embraced a target language (English) that is SVO and strongly GWO. It was believed that the rigid constraints governing English SVO word order would render it an ideal candidate for testing the hypothesis.

The hypothesis would therefore be confirmed if:

2a. Speakers of a language manifesting PWO traits and with SVO canonical word order produced English IL that was not SVO, and

---

6 Initially included among the 300 compositions were 75 produced by Mandarin Chinese speakers. However, because Mandarin is principally an SVO language (in the process of becoming SOV, according to Li and Thompson 1981) with its word-order freedom limited to presentative constructions and fronted objects (Sandra Thompson, personal communication), it is relevant to neither of the criteria (2a/b) and therefore did not figure in the testing of the hypothesis.

7 The status of Japanese with regard to PWO/GWO is by no means a matter of precision, and this is touched on again in a later section. Much of what the PWO/GWO typology is designed to capture can be subsumed under "configurationality," where the reflections of grammatical relations via case marking identify a nonconfigurational language. To the extent that Japanese marks case morphologically it is nonconfigurational and thus tends toward PWO. (See Zobl, this volume, for extended discussion.) Rigid verb-finality, however, is a GWO characteristic par excellence.

Another approach to these matters holds that "there are no configurational or non-configurational languages, but simply languages that exhibit a range of adjacency requirements for one or another type of phrase" (Berwick 1985:285).

8 It must be realized, however, that the PWO/GWO feature is a scalar tendency rather than a dichotomy, and, as such, I feel (based upon work with informants) that Spanish leans toward PWO to an even greater extent than does Saudi Arabic.

b. Speakers of a language manifesting GWO traits and with a CWO other than SVO produced English IL that was invariably SVO.

The hypothesis would be *disconfirmed* if:

3. Speakers of a GWO and non-SVO language produced English IL manifesting L1 CWO.

With the written IL data present in the sample, disrupted English SVO word order produced by speakers of Spanish and Arabic (both with PWO tendencies and basic SVO order) would satisfy criterion (2a), and nondisrupted English SVO word order produced by speakers of Japanese (with some PWO tendencies but SOV order and verb anchoring) would satisfy criterion (2b). Obviously, satisfying (2b) would automatically entail satisfying as well the criterion for rejection: (3). Following is a discussion of the data from the standpoint of the usable L1s represented – namely, Spanish, Japanese, and Saudi Arabic.

Spanish

In the set of 59 compositions produced by learners whose native language is Spanish, there were approximately 20 instances where English CWO was violated and 5 instances of these where CWO was simply marked, that is, a permissible order (other than SVO), resulting from application of a root transformation, was used (Emonds 1976). In virtually all cases, the resulting IL word order was XVS, where X stands for an element other than a major constituent.[9] The data in question are listed in Appendix 1, where the section divisions 1 and 2 correspond to main and subordinate clause phenomena, respectively.

Japanese

Japanese, an SOV language, manifests word-order characteristics that embrace both PWO and GWO, as suggested earlier. Thus, although subject and object can be ordered in accord with discoursal requirements, verb is fixed sentence-finally. Rigid verb-finality then is the GWO feature of interest here. The hypothesis predicted that there would be no vio-

---

9 The one exception was the following OSV construction within a relative clause: "The environment in general is like one wonderland in which *everything you can find*."

Zobl (1984a) calls attention to claims that XVS constructions can arise as part of a developmental phenomenon in which only one constituent can occur preverbally. Thus, when the subject competes with another element for sentence-initial position, the result is XVS. Although not taking a stand here on the validity of that analysis, I contend that XVS will not arise in a learner's IL (and in contravention of the L2 target) where the learner's L1 does not manifest PWO tendencies. This is what has been so far observed.

lation of target language CWO – that is, verb-final clause constructions – in the IL written production of these 21 learners, and the prediction was borne out.[10]

Arabic

The largest group of subjects in the study were native speakers of Saudi Arabic (n = 149). Saudi Arabic CWO is generally considered to be SVO (Comrie 1981), with apparent vestiges of an earlier VSO pattern showing up in subordination. Its manifestation of "presentative movement" (Hetzron 1975), or movement of prominent elements to the end of the sentence, is a PWO characteristic.[11]

All instances of CWO violation in the Saudi Arabic data resulted in XVS constructions, just as was seen in the Spanish data. The data in question are listed in Appendix 2, where main and subordinate clause phenomena are again separated.

Discussion

This section will summarize what the data reveal and then state what appear to be their implications. Recall that motivation for the present research derives from previous claims as to the degrees of candidacy for L2 transfer of L1 phenomena identified in terms of the CWO and PWO/GWO typologies. In particular, it had been claimed that the *syntax*-definable construct known as L1 canonical word order would not of itself leave traces in IL syntax, whereas a *discourse*-definable propensity of L1 to permute its canonical constituents *would* leave traces. Another way of stating this is that where IL manifests a CWO that would be disallowed in the L2, that word order will evince transfer not of the L1 CWO but of the extent to which the L1 is *free* to utilize alternate constituent orders. These are the observations that have led to the formulation of hypothesis (1).

10 Again, it is not being claimed here that no canonical word order other than SVO will show up in English IL with Japanese speakers, but rather that it is specifically verb-final constructions that will not show up. Zobl (personal communication) in fact has clear evidence for VSO in some Japanese-English data of his own.

11 As a further check on the movability of canonical constituents in Saudi Arabic, the researchers engaged a native speaker of Saudi Arabic who is fluent in English to render translations in written Arabic of the samples (with some context supplied) from the L1 Arabic data that manifested English CWO departure. An item-by-item English gloss was then requested for each of the translations (with the glosses being read from right to left, as Arabic is read). In all cases the CWO in the IL had a possible corresponding order in Arabic.

The hypothesis is upheld by the data, as can be seen from the findings reported previously, although it will obviously be necessary to continue this kind of inquiry with richer sources of input to the IL — that is, a greater quantity of typologically divergent source languages as L1/L2. In principle, however, this desirable diversity might automatically be limited by factors concerning the nature of language organization itself. For example, it may be the case that PWO (at least if this is defined in terms of verb movement) will be more meaningfully applicable to SVO systems. Schwartz (1975) claims (for L1) that "SVO language-learners do not 'make a decision' about the position of the verb, and so the verb is 'movable'; learners of V-initial and V-final languages view the verb as a fixed point, and so do not 'imagine' it as movable" (p. 457). Certainly the only two L1s represented in the study that manifest significant degrees of PWO are Spanish and Arabic, both identified as having SVO systems. If indeed a significant correlation were found to obtain between PWO and SVO, then the original hypothesis (1) could be similarly constrained.

Some kind of constraint does seem to be in force, at least for the limited data obtained in this study. In the earlier brief discussion of PWO/GWO typological characteristics and their manifestation in IL, nothing was said about the *extent* to which L1 CWO freedom could be reflected in the IL. One might therefore suppose that there would be a direct correspondence between the two, and therefore that whatever PWO is possible in a given L1 is also possible where that L1 is input to some IL. This is not the case, however, as inspection of the data in Appendixes 1 and 2 shows. For the most part the data contain XVS constructions in which the subject is the only noun phrase bearing a semantic argument relation to the verb, and the lexical verbs appearing in these VS constructions are limited to what Perlmutter (1978) identifies (in Relational Grammar terms) as "unaccusatives."[12] In other words, whereas the PWO tendencies of Arabic and Spanish spawn a fairly wide range of possible SVO permutations in L1, what they seem to reflect in English IL is limited to XVS representing a definable class of lexical verbs. Although these facts them-

---

12 I thank Helmut Zobl for bringing this observation to my attention. The unaccusative hypothesis (Perlmutter 1978) was motivated in part by the need to account for the differential syntactic behavior of certain predicates with one argument (or clauses with one term, in the sense of Relational Grammar). For a readable elucidation of this, see Frantz (1981). See also Zobl, this volume. Zobl cites an interesting observation of Burzio (1981) concerning word order with intransitive verbs in Italian. Whereas the discourse-neutral preference for the class of intransitives that includes *telefonare* would be SV (e.g., *Gianni telefona*), the preference for the class including *arrivare* would be VS (e.g., *Arriva Gianni*). The *arrivare* class is identified as ergative (presumably corresponding to Perlmutter's unaccusatives).

selves are in need of some kind of explanation, the matter will remain unresolved for the present (however, see Zobl, this volume, for a proposed solution).

PWO and UG

The phenomenon referred to here as PWO entails related grammatical conditions that have been recognized by researchers working within a UG framework. Languages revealing a significant degree of PWO tend also to be those tolerating null subjects, along with such ancillary properties as the possibility in SVO languages of VS constructions. The properties in question are usually subsumed under "pro-drop" in UG terms, and languages can be assigned a $+/-$ value with respect to this parameter. That is, pro-drop is parameterized. For languages that are pro-drop, pragmatic conditions will determine whether the subject is actually dropped (or possibly whether VS order is appropriate) for any given instance. White (1985a, b, c) has applied the concept of a parameterized UG to the study of language transfer in SLA. Her claim is that certain L1 transfer phenomena can be explained through recourse to a theory of UG wherein languages may differ in their settings of a given UG parameter. Thus, when the L1 and L2 differ with respect to the setting of some parameter P (and when positive evidence for the resetting of P in L2 is lacking), the L1 rather than the L2 setting for P will be manifest in the IL.

How might one go about relating the interpretation of these research findings in typological terms to an interpretation in UG terms? Recall the claim, discussed earlier, that with regard to the three typological frameworks – CWO, PWO/GWO, and topic- and subject-prominence – L1 transfer can be expected in the second and third but not the first case. Recall also that these transferable and nontransferable phenomena are observed as tied to discourse and syntax, respectively. Although the notion of gross discoursal but not gross syntactic transfer may have a certain intuitive appeal, it remains to be explained why transfer should split along these lines. Indeed, with discourse features supposedly having more universality, one might well guess that it should be the other way around – that transfer would be *more* likely with CWO than with PWO/GWO and topic- and subject-prominence.

The particular explanation being looked for is one that might arise through reinterpretation of these transfer phenomena in terms of a parameterized UG. Let us assume, as already proposed in White (1985a, c), that when a certain UG parameter has different settings for a given pair of first and second languages, the L2 learner will apply his or her L1 setting to the IL unless positive evidence from the

L2 is sufficient to trigger the parameter's resetting. Then the previously described transfer situation with respect to the three typological frameworks reduces to a question of the range of availability of positive L2 evidence for the phenomenon in question. Thus, L1 CWO does not transfer under any circumstances, because positive evidence for the L2 CWO is probably available in almost every sample of the L2 from the very first learning experience. However, for the other two typologies – PWO/GWO and topic- and subject-prominence – positive evidence (e.g., where the learner whose L1 is PWO and/or topic-prominent has to notice the *absence* of these features in L2) will be lacking and transfer will occur.[13]

Attempts to recast the IL word-order findings in a UG mold are not without problems of another kind, however – ones having to do with the question of learnability. Consider what has been said about the learnability issue regarding the acquisition of primary languages. There is fairly wide agreement among researchers working within formal theories of L1 acquisition (e.g., Wexler and Culicover 1980; Berwick 1985) that language learning cannot proceed as the result of the successive formulation of hypotheses that can be disconfirmed only by negative evidence, since no such evidence has been convincingly shown to be available to the learner. Disconfirmation can therefore logically come about only through the presence of *positive* exemplars. But in order for disconfirmation on the basis of positive evidence to be possible at all, it is necessary that the learner's hypothesizing be severely constrained – limited in fact to the *narrowest* possible grammar consistent with the data in question. The hypothesized grammar is thus in effect a subset of the other (wider) grammars that otherwise could also be constructed from the same data. This fact of learnability has been raised to the status of a general learning principle – the Subset Principle – and much of what takes place in L1 acquisition has been claimed to be in accord with it.[14]

What light then, if any, does consideration of the Subset Principle shed on the IL word-order acquisition data discussed earlier? Take the case of (PWO) Spanish vis-à-vis (GWO) English, for which we have ample acquisition data for both directions: L1 Spanish→ L2 English and L1 English→ L2 Spanish (arrows indicate *learning*). For both learning situations, application of the Subset Principle requires that the most conservative hypothesis be entertained with respect to word order – namely somewhere near the middle of the PWO/GWO continuum. If this were not the case – if some version of strong PWO (or strong GWO)

---

13 See Zobl (1986) for an explanation of these phenomena based on functional criteria.
14 See Berwick (1985), among others, for an extended discussion of the Subset Principle. See also White, this volume.

were chosen as the default setting – then there would be no way for the hypothesis to be disconfirmed other than through (naturally nonoccurring) negative evidence, for any language located off-center on the continuum (in fact, most languages). The mid-point of the GWO/PWO scale, however, would presumably represent a CWO in which no movement rules have applied at all[15] – neither those of the GWO "move-NP" variety nor those of the PWO "stylistic movement" variety – in other words, a CWO that instantiates maximal surface alignment of syntactic elements and their semantic representation.[16]

Notice then that acquisitional data are in accord with the Subset Principle only with regard to the early IL fixing of target L2 CWO where ample positive evidence is available from the outset. However, the data are in contravention of the principle to the extent that the IL reveals initial learner hypotheses reflecting L1 typological location toward either of the GWO or PWO end points.[17] Since it is obviously unsatisfactory to rest with an ad hoc claim that the Subset Principle is invoked in the one instance but violated in the other, we must look to a principle of another kind in pushing toward an accounting of what is actually occurring. That principle, of course, is none other than language transfer. Thus, while there is evidence to support the existence of the Subset Principle for L1 acquisition, there would seem to be ample *counter*-evidence (at least as revealed by the data under scrutiny)[18] for its application to L2. One might conclude then that

15 Berwick and Weinberg (1984) state that "a language generated by a base component plus no movement rules is narrower than one generated by that same base plus movement rules" (p. 234). Berwick (1985) suggests that the way to represent this constraint is "to assume that all (lexical) categories are bounding nodes. In effect, this would mean that no movement would be possible at all; that is, word order would be fixed as determined by any adjacency constraints" (p. 295).

16 Typological GWO would thus seem to correspond roughly to movement to a theta position in UG terms, PWO to movement to a *non*-theta position. As for surface alignment, Berwick (1985) writes that "a 1–1 syntactic/thematic correspondence follows from the Subset Principle. The most rigid, narrowest possible surface language is one where syntactic and thematic units are strictly aligned; for example, AGENT and Subject Noun Phrase come first; followed by the action; followed by the AFFECTED OBJECT" (p. 23).

17 Given the languages chosen for investigation in this study, it is the IL with traces of L1 PWO that have been looked at. With different choices of L1/L2 reflecting a different balance of PWO/GWO, however, one naturally could have seen IL traces of GWO, for example *il veut moi de dire français à il* (Adjemian 1976).

18 White (this volume) reaches similar conclusions with respect to parameterized adjacency in UG. Another good example of Subset Principle violation in L2 concerns the pro-drop parameter cited earlier. It is well known that where L1 is a pro-drop language, the [+ pro-drop] setting of that parameter will be adopted for the learning of L2, that is, transferred (White 1985a; Hilles 1986). Yet the *default* setting for pro-drop would have to be [− pro-drop], as Berwick (1985) demonstrates, otherwise the Subset Principle is violated. Here again, L2 transfer would appear to supersede the Subset Principle.

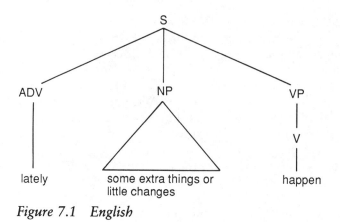

Figure 7.1   English

transfer can, in a sense, override the Subset Principle in second language acquisition.

PWO *and processing*

But again, *why* should L2 transfer countermand the Subset Principle (assuming of course that this conclusion is a correct one)? Although this is not an easy question to answer, it may well be the case that the ways in which languages need to be processed (for production as well as comprehension) can shed some light here. All of the data in Appendixes 1 and 2 display XVS constructions of various kinds. These include a substantial number in which the sentence contains a clausal remnant, the two language groups (L1 Arabic and L1 Spanish) sometimes differing in IL presence or absence, respectively, of the (preverbal) dummy subject placeholder. The material represented in S(ubject) thus ranges from simple noun phrases (e.g., S1.6 – L1 Spanish, first section division, sentence 6) to highly complex ones (e.g., A1.2). Therefore XVS constructions occur when X is exclusively an adverbial element (single adverb or prepositional phrase), V is intransitive or a passivized transitive (more specifically, unaccusative), and S is the sole argument. Notice that the IL structures represented here are *heavily* right-branching, in contrast to the corresponding well-formed equivalents in target English. This can be illustrated in terms of the proposed phrase structure for the relevant portion of example A1.2 together with its target counterpart (see Figures 7.1 and 7.2).

There are several things worth calling attention to here having to do with how sentences like these are processed. Frazier (1985; Frazier and Rayner 1986) has shown that a possible measure of the relative ease or

cross-linguistic distinctions, it may well also represent essentially
nvergence of an assemblage of otherwise separate language ten-
s. This is perhaps what the IL data in this study ultimately point
e IL word-order phenomena discussed here are surely the result
a single monolithic principle of language behavior but rather of
btle interplay among a number of principles educible from the
n which languages are intrinsically organized, from the ways they
ocessed in actual use, and from the ways they are learned – in
words, quite the sort of thing projected at the end of the quote
Chomsky (1975) cited previously. It is investigation of the nature
interplay that holds considerable promise for current research in
language acquisition. Moreover, interlanguage by its very nature
ovide a means for better understanding the forces engaged in that
ay.

ndixes

rs in square brackets following each example indicate written-production
ncy levels in terms of stanines. Stanines are scores that range from a low
bsolute beginners) to 9 (native speakerlike). The examples given were
rimarily from compositions of intermediate-level students (i.e., stanines

ndix 1: Data from L2 English/L1 Spanish

The education in G., are changed so much, because before, in the school
for example, in any class *are* many students, the study are not
good...[3.2]
...but now *are* a many telephones in each department...[3.2]
On this particular place called G.... *happened* a story which now appears
on all Mexican history books...[5.5]
The boy friend has to arrive to the church first and his family after a
few minutes *arrive* the girlfriend with his family too. [3.9]
I have mentioned that in my country *does not appear to exist* any con-
straint on a woman's right to choose a husband. [7.0]
And then at last *comes* the great day. [5.6]
In the town *lived* a small Indian...[5.5]
Then *began* the wars to reconquer the land. [6.3]
In my country *is very easy* to choose a husband or wife because the
fathers of the man or woman not participe in this choose. [2.5]
In my country I often visited the caribean island near to my city, now *is
impossible* for me to go there. [3.0]
Second *is necessary* that all youngs in my country to know very well
others cultures. [3.5]
In the lake of Maracaibo *was discovered* the oil. [4.7]
In this one *was placed* the national school of engineering. [5.7]

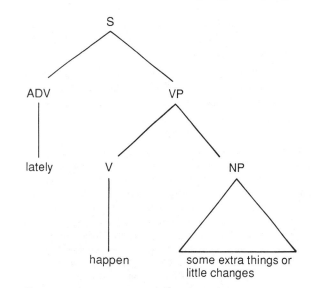

Figure 7.2   Arabic-English IL (A1.2)

difficulty in processing a sentence (more specifically, parsing a string)
will be the extent to which complex constructions occur at positions of
lower depth in the phrase structure configuration. This factor is consistent, for example, with the preference in English for extraposed sentential
subjects.[19] But it also suggests itself as a possible factor contributing to
the prevalence of IL examples like that analyzed in Figure 7.2 and a
number of others with still more complexity involved.[20]

One may also approach the question of PWO and processing, how-

19 Frazier (1985) also cites another contribution to the greater complexity of sentential subjects vis-à-vis their extraposition, namely the number of local nonterminal
   nodes postulated for each. The more such nodes, the more complexity. This measure could obviously apply as well to the IL examples of sentential-subject extraposition, with (in the Spanish examples) or without (in the Arabic examples) the
   dummy placeholder.
      Frazier also shows that creating discontinuity to reduce left-branchingness (e.g.,
   extraposition of relative clauses, as in *Somebody called who needs help*) does not
   result in greater ease of processing (contrary to a claim of Yngve's). It is thus interesting to note that none of these examples, or any others that I can recall, contain instances of discontinuous dependencies.
20 The consignment of complex constructions to phrase structure positions of lower
   depth might also serve as a partial accounting for the Japanese L1/English L2 IL
   examples cited in Schachter and Rutherford (1979) and attributed to the learners'
   attempts to make "generic statements," such as *It is a tendency that such friendly
   restaurants become less in the big city.*

ever, from a discourse perspective and more particularly from that of "rhematicity," "communicative dynamism" (Firbas 1965), or the perceptual salience of a constituent relative to others in the sentence. Frazier (1985) again offers considerable insight here. Although her following claims are made solely on the basis of the behavior of English sentential subjects, one could argue that they are worth considering also as possible motivation for the IL XVS constructions in question:

In general, information may be processed more rapidly when it occurs in a position where the processor expects to allocate considerable resources or attention than when it occurs in some position where less attention is typically required. In the comprehension of speech, it has been argued that more attention is allocated to stressed positions . . . to focused positions than to unfocused positions . . . and it has been shown in both speech and reading that asserted information is verified more quickly than presupposed information . . . In English the predicate of a sentence typically contains the nuclear stress of the sentence and it generally contains new asserted information. It may also be argued to define or correspond to the default focus of the sentence. Hence, if the processor typically devotes more attention to the predicate of the sentence than to its subject, a sentence with an extraposed sentential subject will conform more closely to the processor's expectations about where it should allocate its resources than will a sentence with non-extraposed sentential subject. (1985:14)

In terms of the XVS examples under discussion, the processor's expectations about where it should allocate its resources focus on S(ubject).

But if XVS is to be preferred over XSV by the learners in question for the reasons suggested, why is this not a *general* feature of IL instead of one limited to particular ILs? In other words, if (universal) processing principles can serve to elucidate the special deployment of the canonical constituents under scrutiny here, why doesn't *all* of IL manifest these characteristics? The most plausible answer to this question is, one would suppose, the obvious one: It isn't processing per se that induces the IL emergence of XVS but *processing in conjunction with L1 embodiment of typological PWO* – that is, PWO transfer. Note that it is *not* necessary that nonstandard IL word order be a possible word order in L1; instead the claim here is that nonstandard IL word order will correlate with the degree to which L1 S and V can permute to reflect pragmatic demands.[21]

---

21 This squares, for example, with Zobl's finding of some VS constructions in Japanese-English IL (see Footnote 10) but not VS with French-English IL (Zobl 1984a). I thank him for bringing these observations to my attention and also for alerting me to the existence of some data of Lydia White's to the effect that low-level French-speaking learners of English did produce some VS constructions (in which V is identifiable as ergative).

This then is the real meaning of "propensity" in original hypothesis (1).

Conclusion

Let us now reconsider the phenomenon under has been said about it. Recall that what prompt recognition of an apparent correlation between onical constituents in (English) IL and in L1 inp it was thought that the putative discoursal pr logically identified movability – namely PWO – extragrammatical *monocausal* explanation of t tried to argue, however, is that although the da original hypothesis concerning PWO reflexes i IL-PWO phenomenon is a much more comple:

The attempt to sort out the various forces that to produce violations of CWO in English IL right, for it is a means of exploring what ur typology for natural language in general. The l discussed is what one can infer from the incon tions arising from each of the possible metho stances that can be adopted. Thus, the data o patible with what a parameterized UG has to si of those data to the learner but on the other har Principle.[22] The data on the one hand are w expect from what we know of processing pro computations and default focus but on the ot only representative of ILs whose source L1 is data on the one hand reveal the ostensible in defined PWO but on the other hand are limite verb constructions with only one argument.

Although PWO is certainly a useful typologi

---

22 One should not draw the conclusion from these disc the Subset Principle at all, for this is not necessarily principle, for example, is one of the best known cha development (including IL) – namely, the relatively ceptualization and syntactic realization. Andersen (1 (1973), refers to it as the "one-to-one principle," an strates that it is an instantiation of the Subset Princi yet to be proven, however, that the IL correlation he rather than an accidental one.

S2.1   ...by that time nobody knew *what was* oil. [4.8]
S2.2   They start to think *how is going to be* the woman's dress and the man's suit. [4.1]
S2.3   This historical center was an idea of the national museum of history and it appears *when was found* the "main temple" of the ancient mexico "tenochtitlan." [5.7]
S2.4   ...that's why we don't have subway yet because, *is so slow* the process of execution... [3.3]
S2.4   They knew that inside *were* only 20 boys that had bettwen 14 and 16 years. [5.8]

Appendix 2: Data from L2 English/L1 Arabic

A1.1   In may cuntry no *studay* boy and girle in the same school. [2.2]
A1.2   ...but lately *happen* some extra things or littel changes on this custom because of the civilization, opening on the world and the development idias and movements. [3.0]
A1.3   After that, they'll be lead to their house, and with that *comes* the end of the wedding. [4.0]
A1.4   The first people to come into the church were the closest relatives of the bride and bridegroom and then *came* the rest of the invited people. [6.3]
A1.5   The bride was very attractive, on her face *appeared* those two red cheeks and above them beautiful deep eyes. [5.9]
A1.6   On the walls of this monument *are written* the names of the victories of Napoleon's battles. [6.3]
A1.7   Also it *is important* the right person who want to be one of the staff. [?]
A1.8   Really, it *is terrible* the situation in Lebanon. [5.5]
A1.9   Not only *is* this city *famous* with its history but it also has a good climate. [5.7]
A2.1   From that points we find that not only *are* customs that establish the family arrangements but also *are* the religion rules. [4.9]
A2.2   ...after that they lock for the age, because *must be* the age similer for bowth or neerly. [2.1]
A2.3   Now we are going to the "arc de Triomphe" where *lies* the thumb of the unknown soldier. [6.3]

References

Adjemian, C. 1976. On the nature of interlanguage systems. *Language Learning* 26: 297–320.
  1983. The transferability of lexical properties. In *Language Transfer in Language Learning*, S. Gass and L. Selinker, eds. Rowley, Mass.: Newbury House.
Altman, R., and W. Rutherford. 1982. Canonical word order and L2 acquisition. Paper presented at the Linguistic Society of America annual meeting, December 27–30, San Diego.
Andersen, R. 1984. The one to one principle of interlanguage construction. *Language Learning* 34: 77–95.

Bach, E. 1975. Order in base structures. In *Word Order and Word Order Change*, C. Li, ed. Austin: University of Texas Press.

Berwick, R. 1985. *The Acquisition of Syntactic Knowledge*. Cambridge, Mass.: MIT Press.

Berwick, R., and A. Weinberg. 1984. *The Grammatical Basis of Linguistic Performance*. Cambridge, Mass.: MIT Press.

Burzio, L. 1981. Intransitive verbs and Italian auxiliaries. Ph.D. dissertation, Massachusetts Institute of Technology.

Chomsky, N. 1975. *Reflections on Language*. New York: Pantheon.

1981. *Lectures on Government and Binding*. Dordrecht, The Netherlands: Foris.

Clahsen, H. 1988. Parameterized grammatical theory and language acquisition. In *Linguistic Theory in Second Language Acquisition*, S. Flynn and W. O'Neil, eds. Dordrecht, The Netherlands: Kluwer.

Comrie, B. 1981. *Language Universals and Linguistic Typology*. Chicago: University of Chicago Press.

Eckman, F. 1984. Universals, typologies, and interlanguage. In *Language Universals and Second Language Acquisition*, W. Rutherford, ed. Amsterdam: John Benjamins.

Ellis, R. 1982. The origins of interlanguage. *Applied Linguistics* 3: 207–23.

Emonds, J. 1976. *A Transformational Approach to English Syntax*. New York: Academic Press.

Ferguson, C. 1984. Repertoire universals, markedness, and second language acquisition. In *Language Universals and Second Language Acquisition*, W. Rutherford, ed. Amsterdam: John Benjamins.

Firbas, J. 1965. A note on transition proper in functional sentence perspective. *Philologia Pragensia* 8: 170–76.

Flynn, S., and I. Espinal. 1985. Head-initial/head-final parameter in adult Chinese L2 acquisition of English. *Second Language Research* 1: 93–117.

Frantz, D. 1981. Grammatical relations in universal grammar. Bloomington: Indiana University Linguistics Club.

Frazier, L. 1985. Syntactic complexity. In *Natural Language Parsing*, D. Dowty, L. Karttunen, and A. Zwicky, eds. Cambridge: Cambridge University Press.

Frazier, L., and K. Rayner. 1986. Parameterizing the language processing system: left- vs. right-branching within and across languages. Unpublished manuscript, University of Massachusetts, Amherst.

Fuller, J., and J. Gundel. 1985. Topic-prominence in second language acquisition. Unpublished manuscript, University of Minnesota, Minneapolis.

Gass, S., and J. Ard. 1984. Second language acquisition and the ontology of language universals. In *Language Universals and Second Language Acquisition*, W. Rutherford, ed. Amsterdam: John Benjamins.

Givón, T. 1979. *On Understanding Grammar*. New York: Academic Press.

Hawkins, J. 1985. Language universals in relation to acquisition and change: a tribute to Roman Jakobson. Paper presented at the First International Roman Jakobson Conference, New York.

Hetzron, R. 1975. The presentative movement, or why the ideal word order is V.S.O.P. In *Word Order and Word Order Change*, C. Li, ed. Austin: University of Texas Press.

Hilles, S. 1986. Interlanguage and the pro-drop parameter. *Second Language Research* 2: 33–52.

Huebner, T. 1983. *A Longitudinal Analysis of the Acquisition of English*. Ann Arbor: Karoma Publishers.

Li, C., and S. Thompson. 1976. Subject and topic: a new typology of language. In *Subject and Topic*, C. Li, ed. New York: Academic Press.

Li, C., and S. Thompson. 1981. *Mandarin Chinese: A Functional Reference Grammar*. Berkeley: University of California Press.

Limber, J. 1973. The genesis of complex sentences. In *Cognitive Development and the Acquisition of Language*, T. Moore, ed. New York: Academic Press.

Perlmutter, D. 1978. Impersonal passives and the unaccusative hypothesis. *Proceedings of the Berkeley Linguistics Society* 6: 157–89.

Rutherford, W. 1983. Language typology and language transfer. In *Language Transfer in Language Learning*, S. Gass and L. Selinker, eds. Rowley, Mass.: Newbury House.

1984a. Description and explanation in interlanguage syntax: state of the art. *Language Learning* 34: 127–55.

Rutherford, W., ed. 1984b. *Language Universals and Second Language Acquisition. Typological Studies in Language*, Vol. 5. Amsterdam: John Benjamins.

Rutherford, W. 1986. Grammatical theory and L2 acquisition: a brief overview. *Second Language Research* 2: 1–15.

Schachter, J., and W. Rutherford. 1979. Discourse function and language transfer. *Working Papers in Bilingualism* 19: 1–12.

Schwartz, A. 1975. Verb-anchoring and verb-movement. In *Word Order and Word Order Change*, C. Li, ed. Austin: University of Texas Press.

Searle, J. 1969. *Speech Acts*. London: Cambridge University Press.

Slobin, D. 1979. *Psycholinguistics*. 2nd ed. Glenview, Ill.: Scott Foresman.

Thompson, S. A. 1978. Modern English from a typological point of view: some implications of the function of word order. *Linguistische Berichte* 54: 19–35.

Wexler, K., and P. Culicover. 1980. *Formal Principles of Language Acquisition*. Cambridge, Mass.: MIT Press.

White, L. 1985a. The "pro-drop" parameter in adult second language acquisition. *Language Learning* 35: 47–62.

1985b. The acquisition of parameterized grammars: subjacency in second language acquisition. *Second Language Research* 1: 1–17.

1985c. Universal Grammar as a source of explanation in second language acquisition. Bloomington: Indiana University Linguistics Club.

Zobl, H. 1983a. Markedness and the projection problem. *Language Learning* 33: 293–313.

1983b. L1 acquisition, age of L2 acquisition, and the learning of word order. In *Language Transfer in Language Learning*, S. Gass and L. Selinker, eds. Rowley, Mass.: Newbury House.

1984a. Uniformity and source-language variation across developmental continua. In *Language Universals and Second Language Acquisition*, W. Rutherford, ed. Amsterdam: John Benjamins.

1984b. Typological control in interlanguage. Unpublished manuscript.

1986. A functional approach to the attainability of typological targets in L2 acquisition. *Second Language Research* 2: 16–32.

8 How do learners resolve linguistic conflicts?

Susan M. Gass

This chapter deals with issues of second language performance – in particular, with ways in which learners interpret second language sentences.[1] Current research in second language acquisition is primarily concerned with the acquisition of independent parts of a learner's linguistic system. In fact, most chapters in this volume deal with only one linguistic level. Departing from this tradition, this chapter attempts to consider aspects of learners' performance by focusing on the ways in which syntax, semantics, and pragmatics simultaneously influence learner interpretive behavior. An assumption underlying this is that language development is interactive. In acquiring either a primary or a nonprimary language, one does not learn syntax and then semantics and then pragmatics. Instead, at a single point in time a learner deals with all three as well as with other aspects of the grammar. Thus, a composite picture of the nature of second language acquisition must include studies investigating the simultaneous acquisition of grammatical components.

The influence of the native language in second language acquisition has been a matter of concern for a number of years (for detailed descriptions of recent research, see Gass and Selinker 1983; Kellerman and Sharwood Smith 1986). A central question in second language research is ultimately concerned with the ways in which conflicts in language systems (the native language and the target language, as well as other languages known [see Ringbom 1976]) are resolved. The question then becomes: What kinds of linguistic information assume importance for second language learners and at what stage in their development?

Competition model

The present study takes as its basis the Competition Model proposed by Bates and MacWhinney (1982). Fundamental to their model is the notion of two levels of language to express communicative intentions:

---

1 The work reported on in this chapter has been more extensively discussed in Gass (1984a, 1986, 1987).

form and function. A second major concept is that speakers use cues in determining relationships among elements. Not only do the specific cues vary from language to language but the strength of cues also varies. An assumption underlying the Competition Model is that in order to determine the relationships among elements, there are limited resources which the acoustic-articulatory channel has for dealing with incoming language data. In natural languages there are four means available for determining such relationships: 1) lexical items; 2) morphological markers; 3) word order; and 4) prosody. Because of frequency, ease of interpretation, perception, information value, as well as various other qualities, not all of these possibilities are equally used. Therefore, when the grammar mediates between the form and the function of elements, these possibilities for interpretation come into play and "compete" for dominance during on-line processing. One of the results of research in this area is the finding that different languages rely on different cues for sentence comprehension (Bates and MacWhinney 1982; MacWhinney, Bates, and Kliegl 1984). For example, in a sentence like (1)

1. The girl sees the tables.

native speakers of English use many cues to determine that "the girl" is the subject and "the tables" the object. Word order is a primary cue, since in active declarative sentences the first noun phrase is typically the subject of the sentence. Second, knowledge of the meaning of lexical items contributes to correct interpretation. Third, English speakers will use animacy criteria (i.e., whether or not a noun refers to an animate object – human or nonhuman – or an inanimate object) to establish grammatical relationships. Finally, the morphology (in this case subject-verb agreement) contributes to interpretation, since the singularity of "girl" requires a verb with singular marking. In sum, all elements converge on the interpretation of "girl" as the subject and "tables" as the object. However, there are examples in language where elements do not converge. Consider the sentence in (2)

2. The table sees the girls.

in which there is competition as to which element will fill the subject slot. Using word order as a cue, "the table" is the subject; using semantics and pragmatics as cues, "the girls" would fill the subject slot; using morphology as a cue, it is again "the table" as subject since the verb is marked in the singular. Thus, there is a breakdown in functional coalitions and as a result there is competition as to which member will fill which grammatical slot. Significantly, different languages resolve the conflict in different ways. English uses word order as a primary determinant. Other languages, for example Italian, a language in which word order is more flexible, rely more heavily on morphological agreement as well as on semantics and pragmatics.

The resolution of conflicts which result from the mapping of surface forms onto underlying functions is based on the strength of the cues involved. If in fact there are cross-linguistic differences in cue usage, then a learner of a second language, in order to successfully comprehend utterances of the second language, has to learn not only the appropriate cues of the new language but also the strength of those cues. With regard to second language acquisition, we can ask: To what extent do second language learners use which cues? to what extent do they rely on the cue strengths of their native language? To what extent do they rely on the cue strengths of the second language? To what extent can they be considered to be "in-between" (see Bates and MacWhinney 1981; Kilborn and Cooreman 1987) the native and the second language? This chapter examines how learners interpret second language sentences.

The data on which this chapter is based come from two sources: (1) interpretation of complex sentences with "tell" and "promise" as main verbs (or verbs with the same syntactic frame), and (2) interpretation of sentences with varying word order and animacy conditions.

Word order

One of the differentiating factors of languages of the world is word order, both in terms of the order of canonical elements in a sentence (SVO [subject-verb-noun] vs. SOV vs. VSO, etc.) and the rigidity of those elements. As mentioned earlier, in English word order is necessary for determining relationships between elements in a sentence. In a sentence with a noun-verb-noun sequence (NVN), the first noun is taken as the subject of the sentence and the second as the object. If the order of elements differs, there is a concomitant change in meaning (I am excluding the possibility of intonational contours affecting meaning). Hence, Sentences 3 and 4 differ in meaning.

3. The dog likes the bone.
4. The bone likes the dog.

Not all languages function in this way. In Italian, for example, it is possible to interpret sentences such as (5) and (6) in the same way.

5. Il cane vede l'osso. ('The dog sees the bone.')
6. L'osso vede il cane. ('The bone sees the dog.')

Thus, in acquiring a second language, a learner has to learn not only what possibilities there are for word order, but also how rigid those possibilities are.

Animacy

A second factor to consider in sentence interpretation is animacy. Givón (1976), Duranti (1979), Hawkinson and Hyman (1974), and Morolong and Hyman (1977) have argued on the basis of cross-linguistic evidence that not all elements in a sentence are equally likely to be selected as topics. The universal ordering of elements is given below.

Human > Animate > Inanimate

There is a greater likelihood for a human noun to be selected as a topic than an animate noun which, in turn, is more likely than an inanimate noun to be a topic. This is independent of syntax.

The purpose of this chapter is twofold: (1) to examine this hierarchy in light of second language data; and (2) to investigate the role of animacy as a major determinant in second language interpretation.

Experiment 1

Background

This study deals with the interpretation of sentences with "tell" or "promise" as the main verb (or verbs with the same syntactic and semantic patterning).[2] These verbs have the same surface structure (NP V NP INF ADV) yet differ in their interpretation, as can be seen in (7) and (8) below.

7. The woman told the dog to get the bone.
8. The woman promised the dog to get the bone.

Subjects

Participants in this study were 111 learners of English of varying language backgrounds, ranging in proficiency from Level II to Level V of a 5-level intensive course program.

Method

Each subject was presented with either 14 or 21 sentences[3] followed by a question asking what the subject of the second verb was. The sentences varied in terms of verb type ("promise" versus "tell") and in terms of

---

2 See Gass (1986) for a review of some studies in both first and second language acquisition that deal with these sentence types.
3 Whether a subject responded to 14 or 21 sentences depended on the availability of subjects per proficiency level.

TABLE 8.1. RESULTS OF "TELL" SENTENCES IN WHICH BOTH NPS ARE OF
EQUAL STATUS ON THE TOPICALITY HIERARCHY

Noun phrases	Level II	Level III	Level IV	Level V
Human/Human	2–3	1–9	0–10	1–14
Animate/Animate	1–4	1–8	1–11	1–13
Inanimate/Inanimate	2–3	0–9	6–8	1–15

TABLE 8.2. RESULTS OF "TELL" SENTENCES IN WHICH SYNTACTIC AND
SEMANTIC INFORMATION CONVERGE

Noun phrases	Level II	Level III	Level IV	Level V
Inanimate/Animate	1–5	0–10	2–12	1–15
Inanimate/Human	1–8	3–8	1–7	0–8
Animate/Human	1–4	2–7	1–13	1–15

the two nouns and their place on the topicality hierarchy (see Appendix 1). To place this within the framework of the Competition Model, the sentences differed in that at times semantic (animacy) and syntactic (verb type) information converged (as in Sentence 7) and at times it conflicted (as in Sentence 8).

Results

"TELL" SENTENCES

In Table 8.1 are the results of the sentences in which both NPs have the same status on the topicality hierarchy; in Table 8.2 are the results of those sentences in which the second NP is higher on the animacy hierarchy than the first NP, and in Table 8.3 are the results of those sentences in which the first NP is higher on the hierarchy. In the tables, a response pattern of, for example, 2–3 for a Human/Human sentence such as "The woman told the man to go home" means that two subjects responded that the woman was the subject of the second verb and three responded that it was the man.

As can be seen in Table 8.1, in which semantic factors are neutralized, learners for the most part select the syntactically correct pattern. That is, there were a greater number of responses to the second NP than to the first. In Table 8.2, where syntactic and semantic information converge, there is a strong tendency for the correct semantic and syntactic choice to be made. Finally, in Table 8.3, the semantic and syntactic conflict is evidenced in second language (L2) behavior in that learners do not clearly opt for the second NP as the subject of the second verb.

TABLE 8.3. RESULTS OF "TELL" SENTENCES IN WHICH SYNTACTIC AND
SEMANTIC INFORMATION CONFLICT

Noun phrases	Level II	Level III	Level IV	Level V
Animate/Inanimate	5–4	8–3	4–5	4–4
Human/Inanimate	3–2	5–4	6–8	1–15
Human/Animate	1–5	0–10	2–12	1–15

TABLE 8.4. RESULTS OF "PROMISE" SENTENCES IN WHICH BOTH NPS ARE OF
EQUAL STATUS ON THE TOPICALITY HIERARCHY

Noun phrases	Level II	Level III	Level IV	Level V
Human/Human	8–1	7–4	8–1	8–0
Animate/Animate	6–3	8–3	6–3	8–0
Inanimate/Inanimate	7–2	8–1	9–3	13–0

TABLE 8.5. RESULTS OF "PROMISE" SENTENCES IN WHICH SYNTACTIC AND
SEMANTIC INFORMATION CONVERGE

Noun phrases	Level II	Level III	Level IV	Level V
Animate/Inanimate	3–2	5–4	9–3	12–1
Human/Inanimate	7–2	9–2	8–1	8–0
Human/Animate	5–4	6–5	9–3	13–0

TABLE 8.6. RESULTS OF "PROMISE" SENTENCES IN WHICH SYNTACTIC AND
SEMANTIC INFORMATION CONFLICT

Noun phrases	Level II	Level III	Level IV	Level V
Inanimate/Animate	3–3	4–5	11–3	15–1
Inanimate/Human	2–4	5–5	9–5	14–2
Animate/Human	6–3	8–3	9–0	7–1

"PROMISE" SENTENCES

The presentation of results of the "promise" sentences parallels that of
the "tell" sentences. In Table 8.4 are the results from sentences in which
the two NPs are of equal status vis-à-vis the animacy hierarchy; in Table
8.5 the syntactic and semantic information converge, and in Table 8.6
the information is in conflict.

In the case of neutralized semantic information (Table 8.4) as well as
in the case of converging information (Table 8.5), the results, as with
the "tell" sentences, are in conformity with standard English interpretation (i.e., the first noun is preferred as the topic). In Table 8.6, on the
other hand, the results are less clear, at least at the lower levels of

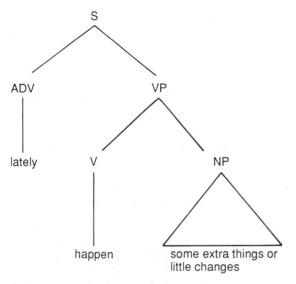

Figure 7.2   Arabic-English IL (A1.2)

difficulty in processing a sentence (more specifically, parsing a string) will be the extent to which complex constructions occur at positions of lower depth in the phrase structure configuration. This factor is consistent, for example, with the preference in English for extraposed sentential subjects.[19] But it also suggests itself as a possible factor contributing to the prevalence of IL examples like that analyzed in Figure 7.2 and a number of others with still more complexity involved.[20]

One may also approach the question of PWO and processing, how-

---

19 Frazier (1985) also cites another contribution to the greater complexity of sentential subjects vis-à-vis their extraposition, namely the number of local nonterminal nodes postulated for each. The more such nodes, the more complexity. This measure could obviously apply as well to the IL examples of sentential-subject extraposition, with (in the Spanish examples) or without (in the Arabic examples) the dummy placeholder.

    Frazier also shows that creating discontinuity to reduce left-branchingness (e.g., extraposition of relative clauses, as in *Somebody called who needs help*) does not result in greater ease of processing (contrary to a claim of Yngve's). It is thus interesting to note that none of these examples, or any others that I can recall, contain instances of discontinuous dependencies.

20 The consignment of complex constructions to phrase structure positions of lower depth might also serve as a partial accounting for the Japanese L1/English L2 IL examples cited in Schachter and Rutherford (1979) and attributed to the learners' attempts to make "generic statements," such as *It is a tendency that such friendly restaurants become less in the big city.*

ever, from a discourse perspective and more particularly from that of
"rhematicity," "communicative dynamism" (Firbas 1965), or the perceptual salience of a constituent relative to others in the sentence. Frazier
(1985) again offers considerable insight here. Although her following
claims are made solely on the basis of the behavior of English sentential
subjects, one could argue that they are worth considering also as possible
motivation for the IL XVS constructions in question:

> In general, information may be processed more rapidly when it occurs in a
> position where the processor expects to allocate considerable resources or at-
> tention than when it occurs in some position where less attention is typically
> required. In the comprehension of speech, it has been argued that more atten-
> tion is allocated to stressed positions... to focused positions than to unfo-
> cused positions... and it has been shown in both speech and reading that
> asserted information is verified more quickly than presupposed information
> ... In English the predicate of a sentence typically contains the nuclear stress
> of the sentence and it generally contains new asserted information. It may
> also be argued to define or correspond to the default focus of the sentence.
> Hence, if the processor typically devotes more attention to the predicate of
> the sentence than to its subject, a sentence with an extraposed sentential sub-
> ject will conform more closely to the processor's expectations about where it
> should allocate its resources than will a sentence with non-extraposed senten-
> tial subject. (1985:14)

In terms of the XVS examples under discussion, the processor's expectations about where it should allocate its resources focus on S(ubject).

But if XVS is to be preferred over XSV by the learners in question
for the reasons suggested, why is this not a *general* feature of IL instead
of one limited to particular ILs? In other words, if (universal) processing
principles can serve to elucidate the special deployment of the canonical
constituents under scrutiny here, why doesn't *all* of IL manifest these
characteristics? The most plausible answer to this question is, one would
suppose, the obvious one: It isn't processing per se that induces the IL
emergence of XVS but *processing in conjunction with L1 embodiment
of typological PWO* – that is, PWO transfer. Note that it is *not* necessary
that nonstandard IL word order be a possible word order in L1; instead
the claim here is that nonstandard IL word order will correlate with the
degree to which L1 S and V can permute to reflect pragmatic demands.[21]

---

21 This squares, for example, with Zobl's finding of some VS constructions in
Japanese-English IL (see Footnote 10) but not VS with French-English IL (Zobl
1984a). I thank him for bringing these observations to my attention and also for
alerting me to the existence of some data of Lydia White's to the effect that low-
level French-speaking learners of English did produce some VS constructions (in
which V is identifiable as ergative).

This then is the real meaning of "propensity" in the formulation of the original hypothesis (1).

Conclusion

Let us now reconsider the phenomenon under investigation and what has been said about it. Recall that what prompted the present study was recognition of an apparent correlation between the movability of canonical constituents in (English) IL and in L1 input to that IL. Moreover, it was thought that the putative discoursal provenance of such typologically identified movability – namely PWO – constituted a tempting extragrammatical *monocausal* explanation of these events. What I have tried to argue, however, is that although the data examined support the original hypothesis concerning PWO reflexes in IL, *explanation* of the IL-PWO phenomenon is a much more complex issue.

The attempt to sort out the various forces that could plausibly conspire to produce violations of CWO in English IL is instructive in its own right, for it is a means of exploring what underlies the PWO/GWO typology for natural language in general. The kind of complexity being discussed is what one can infer from the inconsistencies among predictions arising from each of the possible methodological and theoretical stances that can be adopted. Thus, the data on the one hand are compatible with what a parameterized UG has to say concerning availability of those data to the learner but on the other hand run afoul of the Subset Principle.[22] The data on the one hand are what we might in general expect from what we know of processing procedures based on parsing computations and default focus but on the other hand are apparently only representative of ILs whose source L1 is typologically PWO. The data on the one hand reveal the ostensible influence of L1 discourse-defined PWO but on the other hand are limited to a semantic subset of verb constructions with only one argument.

Although PWO is certainly a useful typological construct for drawing

---

22 One should not draw the conclusion from these discussions that IL does not obey the Subset Principle at all, for this is not necessarily the case. In *accord* with the principle, for example, is one of the best known characteristics of early language development (including IL) – namely, the relatively close fit between semantic conceptualization and syntactic realization. Andersen (1984), drawing on Limber (1973), refers to it as the "one-to-one principle," and Berwick (1985) demonstrates that it is an instantiation of the Subset Principle (see Footnote 16). It has yet to be proven, however, that the IL correlation here is a *causal* connection rather than an accidental one.

broad cross-linguistic distinctions, it may well also represent essentially the convergence of an assemblage of otherwise separate language tendencies. This is perhaps what the IL data in this study ultimately point to. The IL word-order phenomena discussed here are surely the result not of a single monolithic principle of language behavior but rather of the subtle interplay among a number of principles educible from the ways in which languages are intrinsically organized, from the ways they are processed in actual use, and from the ways they are learned — in other words, quite the sort of thing projected at the end of the quote from Chomsky (1975) cited previously. It is investigation of the nature of that interplay that holds considerable promise for current research in second language acquisition. Moreover, interlanguage by its very nature can provide a means for better understanding the forces engaged in that interplay.

Appendixes

Numbers in square brackets following each example indicate written-production proficiency levels in terms of stanines. Stanines are scores that range from a low of 1 (absolute beginners) to 9 (native speakerlike). The examples given were taken primarily from compositions of intermediate-level students (i.e., stanines 3–6).

Appendix 1: Data from L2 English/L1 Spanish

S1.1   The education in G., are changed so much, because before, in the school for example, in any class *are* many students, the study are not good...[3.2]

S1.2   ...but now *are* a many telephones in each department...[3.2]

S1.3   On this particular place called G.... *happened* a story which now appears on all Mexican history books...[5.5]

S1.4   The boy friend has to arrive to the church first and his family after a few minutes *arrive* the girlfriend with his family too. [3.9]

S1.5   I have mentioned that in my country *does not appear to exist* any constraint on a woman's right to choose a husband. [7.0]

S1.6   And then at last *comes* the great day. [5.6]

S1.7   In the town *lived* a small Indian...[5.5]

S1.8   Then *began* the wars to reconquer the land. [6.3]

S1.9   In my country *is very easy* to choose a husband or wife because the fathers of the man or woman not participe in this choose. [2.5]

S1.10   In my country I often visited the caribbean island near to my city, now *is impossible* for me to go there. [3.0]

S1.11   Second *is necessary* that all youngs in my country to know very well others cultures. [3.5]

S1.12   In the lake of Maracaibo *was discovered* the oil. [4.7]

S1.13   In this one *was placed* the national school of engineering. [5.7]

llup Poll conducted in 1967 asked almost 3,800 Americans
erception of the Supreme Court had changed in recent years.
nses varied greatly and ranged across an ideological spectrum.
eading replies, however, give us a clear sense of public opinion

registered general disapproval, indicated a decline in respect,
and believed that the Court was "going downhill."
felt the justices had stifled the police, "made it too easy for the
criminal" and "protects the guilty."
complained that the Court had become too liberal, and saw a
"lean to the left."
disapproved of the rulings that had eliminated prayers from
the public schools.[40]

out the same time a Louis Harris Poll revealed that 52 percent
rican people viewed the Court's performance as "only fair" or
x years later, after Warren Burger had replaced Earl Warren,
t significantly altered the justices' inclinations, a Gallup Poll
her the Court seemed "too liberal or too conservative in its de-
oo liberal was the dominant response (35 percent); too conser-
ved 26 percent; "about right" was the reaction of 17 percent;
t had no opinion.[41]
ugh the Court became less controversial under Burger than it
nder Warren, too few people realize how much residual hostil-
during the 1980s, and how politically advantageous it can be to
justices. In 1982 there were no fewer than thirty proposals
Congress to restrict the Court's powers to interpret constitu-
ers—proposals explicitly designed to by-pass the cumbersome
ocess of amending the Constitution. Busing to achieve school
on, legalizing abortion, and expanding the rights of criminal
were just a few of the provocations that aroused animosity.
eagan and his Attorney General, William French Smith, con-
lividual Supreme Court decisions as well as "judicial activism"
2

differences of opinion may be inevitable as part of the ongoing
onflict within consensus. But in the forms just described they
edifying nor especially educational for the general public. The
role of constitutionalism in American culture are not enhanced
branches of government sharply disagree about the scope of

constitutional principles," advice that Stone repeated to William O.
Douglas in 1946. The title of a widely read essay by Philip B. Kurland
summed up the feelings of many Americans: "The Court Should Decide
Less and Explain More." Kurland called in particular for more carefully
reasoned opinions, greater respect for the proper role of state legislatures
and lower federal courts, and clearer explanations of why judicial precedents needed to be amended or rejected.[31]

In terms of American constitutionalism and its dynamics, three consequences are especially noteworthy: the willingness of governmental
agencies, lower courts, and state legislatures to flout Supreme Court decisions they do not like; the proclivity of disaffected politicians and organizations to attack the Court quite savagely; and the tendency for public
esteem regarding the Court to plummet rather swiftly.

Despite the oath taken by public officials to uphold the Constitution
of the United States, persons in all three branches of the federal government have been known to ignore, misunderstand, or willfully misinterpret
an unwanted Supreme Court decision. Even where good faith is not a
problem, studies have shown that Court rulings can be read and implemented in divergent ways by different parts of the country. *McCollum* v.
Board of Education (1948), for example, invalidated a so-called released
time system of religious education in the public schools of Champaign, Illinois. Classes involving religious instruction had been held in the public
schools during regular hours, and teachers acted under supervision from
the local superintendent. In numerous situations the McCollum decision
led to the termination or extensive modification of weekday programs held
during school hours. In many other locations, however, community leaders
decided that because of some minor variation *McCollum* simply did not
apply to them. In some instances no changes whatever were made in
weekday programs, regardless of their dependence upon public school
time and buildings. In parts of the country compliance began the day after
McCollum was issued. Elsewhere the ruling was flagrantly disregarded.[32]

The most outrageous cases of constitutional disobedience occurred in
response to the school desegregation decisions. State legislatures passed
laws prohibiting desegregation. The Louisiana legislature alone enacted
more than forty unconstitutional laws. Some federal judges in the South
proclaimed that *Brown* v. *Board* was unconstitutional; therefore, to en-
force it would involve a knowing violation of their oath sworn to sustain
the Constitution. Every member of an American school board also takes
an oath to uphold the U.S. Constitution—any provision in the laws or

constitution of his or her own state to the contrary notwithstanding. Needless to say, for many years a large number of school board members petulantly violated their oaths.[33]

In 1957, Representative Clare E. Hoffman of Michigan proposed the impeachment of all nine Supreme Court justices "on the theory that the Court is attempting to overthrow the Government through fallacious reasoning, rendering decisions which make constitutional provisions void." Although Hoffman's initiative may have been extreme, it anticipated recurrent campaigns throughout the 1960s to impeach individuals, notably Chief Justice Warren and Justice William O. Douglas. Between 1961 and 1968 the John Birch Society covered the country with billboards that urged Warren's impeachment. What appeared most alarming to Robert Welch, Jr., and the Birchites, even more than desegregation, were opinions that Warren had written constraining the freedom of congressional committees to investigate suspected Communists. Warren believed that the First Amendment and a "right to privacy" protected persons from unlimited inquiries and from the compulsion to identify other persons who might have been Party members. Warren's removal from office became the Birchites' top priority during the sixties. As Welch explained, "I personally do not think we can save our country unless we can ultimately impeach Warren, nor that the Communist conspiracy can survive if we do." Despite an extensive petition drive designed to mobilize public opinion, and letter-writing campaigns to put pressure on Congress, the John Birch Society was unable to gain support from the *National Review* and other conservative journals.[34]

In 1964, however, when Barry Goldwater's attack upon the Supreme Court became a central feature of his presidential campaign, he received considerable sympathy from conservative journalists and from Americans of both parties who felt that in "coddling" criminals and banishing religion from public schools the Court had gone too far and threatened traditional values as well as national security. Even before Goldwater proclaimed that the Supreme Court "needs to be curbed by constitutional amendment and by legislation where possible," and that it needed to be reconstituted as well, editorials written by the likes of David Lawrence lamented FBI reports that crime rates had increased, and called for a "War Against Crime."[35]

Goldwater launched his candidacy at the Republican Convention in 1964 by pleading that "we revitalize our constitutional principles in all branches of government." Although the Court's directives pertaining to legislative reapportionment (1962–64) troubled him deeply, liberal re-

forms in the administration of criminal jus[...] new emphasis upon an accused person's [...] the manner of obtaining confessions, and [...] an unrepresented defendant by the police[...] campaign, the thrust of Goldwater's mess[...] Supreme Court is the least faithful to the [...] government." He subsequently warned th[...] want men appointed to the Court who w[...] not scoff at it." As the election approache[...] a generalized jeremiad: "Either we conti[...] generation away from constitutional gove[...] away from freedom and away from peace[...] nity. Or we chart a new course of peace, [...] tional order based on the wisdom of our [...]

Not since LaFollette's campaign in [...] criticized the Supreme Court so harshly; [...] assault in 1912 had the judiciary in gener[...] though Goldwater lost to Lyndon Johnso[...] sault—supported by journals of opinion [...] like "Our Vanishing Constitution"—con[...] slide in the Court's reputation.[37] Several [...] the decline. In 1963 and again in 1969 [...] eral, what kind of a rating would you gi[...] sponses ran as follows:[38]

	19[...]
Excellent	1[...]
Good	33
Fair	27
Poor	15
Don't Know	15

In 1965 a series of 405 interviews [...] residents of Seattle, Washington, respon[...] depth than a conventional public opinion [...] resentative responses, an insurance adjus[...] ably because "the outcome as to what is [...] depends too much on one individual." A[...] pany felt that "the Supreme Court has [...] Constitution."[39]

the Court's authority, and when attacks upon the federal judiciary as a whole become both commonplace and vicious. The President and his allies might profitably recall three sage sentences written in 1943 by Thomas Reed Powell: "For years powerful forces have proclaimed constitutional restraints which are of their own conceiving and not those of the compact. It should not be discounted because strident voices today clamor about usurpation and broken bargains when the real issue is only as to the uses to which constitutional power should be put. Constitutional government is neither a free-for-all nor a jointless strait jacket."[43]

IV

Despite the wide range of opinion on matters of constitutional interpretation and authority, Americans have been of two minds, basically, about the desirability of constitutional change. On the one hand, alteration by amendment has been acceptable to both liberals and conservatives for fifty years. That is not a new position for liberals; Progressives had pleaded for it since the turn of the century. Conservatives, on the other hand, once were unenthusiastic about amendments and only turned to that process as a means of deflecting attacks upon the Court by partisans of the New Deal.

Sweeping modifications of the Constitution, on the other hand, not to mention replacing the document with one that more fully reflects contemporary conditions, have been unacceptable though not entirely unthinkable. The Roper Organization presented this question in polls taken seven years apart for *Fortune* (based upon large samples: 5,214 and 3,565):

Which one of the following most nearly represents your opinion of the American form of government?
a.   Our form of government, based on the constitution, is as near perfect as it can be and no important changes should be made in it.
b.   The constitution has served its purpose well, but it has not kept up with the times and should be thoroughly revised to make it fit present day needs.

A strong preference for the first option persisted, which is scarcely surprising.[44]

On occasion, however, starting in the 1930s, increasing in the forties, and accelerating in the sixties, a handful of Americans have risked scorn verging upon contempt by contending that the Constitution of 1787 had become obsolete and did not serve the American people adequately. When William Kay Wallace made such a suggestion in 1932, he was prompted by the imperatives of enhanced economic opportunity and social security for individuals, the need for more efficient government, and a carefully planned national economy. When Henry Hazlitt pleaded for a revised constitution ten years later, he insisted that "we cannot permit ourselves to lose this war, or even to prolong this war, merely because we have become too hidebound to re-examine and to change that document."[45] And in 1951 the retired Senator George Wharton Pepper, a veteran constitutionalist whose vision belied his eighty-four years, discussed the profound changes that had taken place since 1900 and wondered, "am I right in thinking that Americans of today are a new race—and that the changes in our constitutional government are the inevitable result of our changed view of life?"[46]

During the later 1950s, Robert M. Hutchins and his colleagues at the Center for the Study of Democratic Institutions, located in Santa Barbara, California, began to discuss the desirability of far-reaching constitutional changes. In 1964, following a series of seminars modestly entitled "Drafting a New Constitution for the United States and the World," Hutchins invited Rexford G. Tugwell, once a member of FDR's "Brains Trust," to direct a re-assessment of the Constitution. Tugwell accepted and spent two years conferring with hundreds of jurists, politicians, and scholars. In 1966 the Center held a conference called "The Emerging Constitution" and published some of Tugwell's preliminary plans, which responded to problems that had been identified in the operation of the executive branch.[47]

Over the next ten years Tugwell and his staff struggled to improve upon what the founders had accomplished in less than four months. In 1970 the *Center Magazine* (paid circulation in excess of 98,000) printed the thirty-seventh draft of Tugwell's "Model Constitution for a United Republics of America." Two books ensued several years later and amplified the working model that had been issued in 1970 to stimulate nationwide discussion. *The Emerging Constitution,* published in 1974, specified defects in the existing instrument along with remedies proposed by Tugwell. The volume concluded with his fortieth draft of a new constitution. Two years later, during the Bicentennial year, Tugwell brought out *The Compromising of the Constitution,* an attempt to trace historically the growth of distortions and diminished viability of the founders' handiwork ever since 1789.[48]

Tugwell argued that a governmental system designed for an agrarian republic worked much less adequately for an industrial democracy. Moreover, the framers' reluctance to concentrate sufficient power in a central authority resulted in a system of checks, balances, and separated powers that left the national government too vaguely empowered and inefficient to function properly in a world transformed by economic dislocation and potentially disastrous international problems. Tugwell found it "anomalous that a nation whose economic activities are relied upon for that nation's strength and for the well-being of its people, should have a Constitution written before the industrial build-up (and never revised)." He therefore proposed the addition of a regulatory branch of government that would co-ordinate and supervise the nation's economic activities. Private enterprise could continue, but the new branch would charter corporations and prepare codes of conduct for business.[49]

Tugwell wanted to retain a bicameral legislature but alter its composition and function. The lower house would consist of members elected from enlarged constituencies plus "at large" members who represented the nation as a whole. By lengthening their terms and subsidizing their elections, the new scheme would "reduce members' pre-occupation with re-election and . . . free them from binding ties to private financial supporters." The upper house would no longer be an elected body; instead, its members might be appointed for life by the president or chief justice. Tugwell envisioned the senate as "a body dedicated to the national interest and having powers appropriate to guardship. It ought to provide second thoughts, but not to prevent, or even much delay, legislative action; it would advise and assist the president in matters of importance; but most importantly, it would act as watchkeeper for the nation's future and as the expositor of its conscience."[50]

Although Tugwell had strong feelings about the undemocratic consequences of "judicial usurpation," he accepted the need for judicial review. He therefore proposed a radical reorganization of the entire judiciary. A system of tribunals would replace the existing hierarchy of federal, state, and local courts. A supreme court would remain, but with its chief justice to be elected at eleven-year intervals. In addition, Tugwell designated a special court responsible solely for assessing the constitutionality of laws (but subject to concurrence by the house of representatives). A court of administrative appeal would also be created to adjudicate cases involving the rights of citizens and corporations affected by the nexus of administrative regulations undreamed of in 1787.[51]

Tugwell knew from the start that he had undertaken an academic exercise in the most literal sense. Success would be measured in terms of heuristic impact rather than actual adoption. Despite such modest aspirations, the Center's costly and time-consuming project enjoyed only a brief moment in the sun, and can hardly be said to have sparked a nationwide dialogue on constitutionalism. A few major newspapers and weekly news magazines covered it, but with considerable skepticism. *Newsweek* doubted whether the innovative plan would "provoke widespread movement for reform"; and it was correct. Attempts by the Center to sponsor public debates, beginning with a convocation in Philadelphia on November 9, 1970, and another in New York three days later, did little to excite very many intellectuals, never mind the general public. At best, Tugwell had produced a curiosity and a conversation piece.[52]

During the 1970s the Center's primary concerns shifted away from constitutionalism; Tugwell's two major volumes (1974 and 1976) received little attention aside from scholarly journals. When Tugwell died in 1979 at the age of eighty-eight, *The New York Times*'s appreciative editorial did not even mention the revised constitution on which he labored for more than a decade. The *Times* apparently did not regard it as a fitting culmination for a distinguished career in scholarship and public service.[53]

The negligible impact of this seasoned planner's constitutional vision provides a striking contrast with an extremely tradition-oriented interpolation of the U.S. Constitution in science fiction. One popular episode of the television series "Star Trek," written in 1966, received hundreds of reruns during the many years when Tugwell labored over his revision. Millions of Americans watched "The Omega Glory" and recognized its affirmation of the good old Constitution that continued to function even though space, time, and ignorance shrouded its meaning.

Reducing the saga to its ideological essence, Captain Kirk and the starship *Enterprise* land on a planet where the inhabitants are guided by a Prime Directive that must not be violated. Those inhabitants are called Yangs (presumably the descendants of colonizers once known as Yanks), and possess "a worn parchment document" that is "the greatest of holies." Kirk and his crew encounter a bizarre political situation that is not so very different from the one criticized by James Russell Lowell in 1888. The Yangs worship "freedom" but do not understand what it means. Through the ages it has become a ritualized "worship word." The Yangs believe that their ancestors must have been very superior people; they swear an oath to abide by all regulations in the Prime Directive; and they can recite the opening lines of the Prime Directive, but "without meaning."[54]

Following a primitive court scene, complete with jury, it becomes clear that institutions of justice are amazingly resilient—capable of enduring even though their rationale has suffered badly from neglect and amnesia. At the culmination Captain Kirk informs the Yangs that they revere a sacred document without understanding what it is all about. Kirk faces Cloud William, chief of the Yangs, and explains the meaning of the Prime Directive's preamble. Enlightenment then occurs and the great question—is the Prime Directive still operative, and does it apply to this planet?—achieves a satisfactory resolution. To use the language of yesteryear, "constitutional morality" would surely be restored.

Unlike Rexford Tugwell's new constitution, which kept "emerging" for so long that after a while no one cared, "Star Trek" had a constitutional homily with a happy ending. Americans like happy endings. Hence many younger Americans can still narrate "The Omega Glory" (Old Glory? Ultimate Glory?) flawlessly. How much of the homily got through, however, is another matter.

CHAPTER 12

Our Bill of Rights Is Under Subtle and Pervasive Attack

IN 1935, HEYWOOD BROUN BELIEVED HE SAW A BREAK, "a tiny fissure in that great Chinese wall called Property Rights which has been set up to keep us all away from human rights." Six years later Edward S. Corwin anticipated a shift in the Supreme Court's dominant concerns from economic regulation to civil rights; and newly appointed Justice Robert H. Jackson argued that the Court had a special duty to protect those rights guaranteed to individuals by the Constitution. Propertied groups had the capacity to defend themselves quite well, he said, and had enjoyed privileged protection for many years.[1]

Looking back, it seems clear that the years 1939–41 marked a turning point in the history of civil liberties in America. We must add two important qualifications, however. First, the shift occurred in a highly selective rather than a comprehensive manner. It might best be called a symbolic shift in awareness. The substantive follow-up took place gradually and required several decades. Second, this heightened status of civil liberties suffered some major setbacks throughout the 1940s and '50s. World War II provided a stimulus for genuine improvement but also highly regrettable reversals as well. An obsession with internal subversion during the postwar decade caused many Americans to become rather cavalier about their regard for the Bill of Rights. Anxiety about Communist activity made First Amendment freedoms seem less precious than domestic security—a pattern in American attitudes that would recur over the next thirty years. Coddled criminals, "abuses" of free speech, and pornography supplanted communism as threats to society that justified ungenerous interpretations of the first eight amendments.

Consequently we might say that the Bill of Rights was "discovered" in 1939–41 and then "rediscovered" in 1955–56, to mention just two moments of unusually high visibility. In between, and afterwards, civil liberties were menaced, to be sure. Overall, however, a growing number of Americans began to share the sentiments written by Albert Einstein to the National Emergency Civil Liberties Committee in 1954: "The strength of the Constitution lies entirely in the determination of each citizen to defend it. Only if every single citizen feels duty bound to do his share in this defense are the constitutional rights secure."[2]

I

Throughout the quarter century prior to 1939, those who spoke up on behalf of the Bill of Rights and its protections felt rather isolated. Oliver Wendell Holmes is perhaps the most prominent example; but there are others, some of them a bit surprising. H. L. Mencken, for instance, remarked in 1924 that "what disturbs me, of late, is the tendency to abandon the Bill of Rights. The Supreme Court seems to be very careless of it. The Volstead Act drives immense holes through it, and nine-tenths of the Federal judges appear to be unconcerned."[3] As early as 1923 a few naturalization examiners wrote from their regional offices to suggest to the Commissioner in Washington who was responsible for educational materials "that the so-called Bill of Rights in the Constitution should be given prominence and thoroughly explained." Not until 1943, however, did that proposal begin to become a reality in manuals for immigrants who aspired to U.S. citizenship.[4]

One episode enjoyed brief notoriety in 1931 by calling attention to long-standing abuses of civil liberties by the police: an investigation by the U.S. Commission on Law Observance and Enforcement, better known as the Wickersham Commission. Its much-publicized report on "lawlessness in law enforcement," for example, emphasized the widespread use of third-degree tactics in order to obtain confessions from suspects. Austin J. Roche of the Police Department in Buffalo, New York, expressed an attitude widely regarded as typical: "My oath of office as a chief of police requires me to protect this community against crime. If I have to violate my oath of office or violate the Constitution, I'll violate the Constitution. . . .

If, in the process of enforcing the laws, I or my men infringe anyone's Constitutional rights, the law provides a remedy—let him sue."[5]

The attitude of law enforcement officers during the 1930s anticipated laments that would become familiar once again during the 1960s and '70s. "We are at war with crime," and the Bill of Rights is something of a nuisance because "the makers of the Constitution could not have foreseen immigration, could not have foreseen unemployment, slums, prohibition, drug addiction, the automobile, the gangster, or any of the many factors that have created modern crime and made its detection difficult." Abuses of the Fifth Amendment protection against self-incrimination became commonplace as a result of the "self-arrogated police privilege of star-chamber grilling." As an investigator for the Wickersham Commission asserted: "Our devoted law enforcers in most municipalities are in a curiously open state of rebellion against those portions of the Constitution which outline the methods and set forth the principles of the American plan of criminal justice."[6]

The Commission's Report condemned the use of unconstitutional methods by the police, particularly the brutal third degree, and pleaded for public awareness and action. Although that appeal became the most frequently quoted part of the entire Report, the fact remains that the Wickersham Commission had relatively little impact. It received no endorsement from President Hoover and slight support from the public at large.[7]

Seven years later, however, an awakening began to occur, though one that cannot be ascribed to any single stimulus. Following the Supreme Court struggle of 1937, Roosevelt's appointments altered that institution into a body more likely to be interventionist on behalf of civil liberties. In 1938 the veteran Justice Harlan Fiske Stone called special attention to the first ten amendments in his opinion for the Court in *United States* v. *Carolene Products Company.* And in 1938 the American Bar Association established a Committee on the Bill of Rights to investigate "seeming substantial violations of constitutional liberties" in the United States.[8] Also in 1938, members of Roosevelt's cabinet and others began to voice a point of view that had previously been unheard. On June 21, 1938, for example, Sumner Welles spoke at Independence Square in Philadelphia at festivities honoring the 150th anniversary of New Hampshire's clinching ratification. "The greater the importance of safeguarding the community from incitements to the overthrow of our institutions by force and violence," he insisted, "the more imperative is the need to preserve inviolate the constitutional rights of free speech, free press and free assembly in order to maintain the opportunity for free political discussion."[9]

The Reader's Digest had never mentioned the Bill of Rights in any of its first thirty-three volumes. Suddenly, in January and June of 1939 it included two essays on this important yet neglected aspect of American constitutionalism. In January it condensed an article in which James Truslow Adams (a patriotic and popular historian) observed that without the Bill of Rights, either the executive or the legislative branch might threaten the personal freedom of individuals, particularly during a time of war. Adams pointed out that the Bill of Rights protected minorities, among whom new and unpopular ideas were most likely to originate.[10]

Five months later the same mass circulation magazine published an epitome of *Democracy Works,* a new book by Arthur Garfield Hays, national director of the American Civil Liberties Union. Hays compared the condition of liberty and democracy in America with their precarious situation in Europe, argued that the high standard of living in the United States resulted from the fullness of our political freedom, and explained that "when I refer to political freedom I am concerned with those liberties guaranteed by the Bill of Rights."[11]

In 1940 the Bill of Rights Committee of the American Bar Association began to publish a quarterly journal, asserting that the committee had found a strong desire on the part of "informed laymen—publishers and editors, public men, teachers of youth and many others—to learn more concerning the history and nature of our fundamental rights." Also in 1940 the New York State Legislature established a Bill of Rights Week, coinciding with the week of Washington's Birthday, to be observed in public schools throughout the state. Comparable educational programs appeared in Texas, California, and elsewhere. Throughout the week pupils would be taught "the purpose, meaning and importance" of the Bill of Rights. How best to achieve that goal? The bill's sponsor in New York recommended pageants and plays once again. He also hoped that Bill of Rights Week, if successful, would lead to the development of a long-range, nationwide program for "dealing with un-American philosophies." The same people who wanted more attention paid to the document that protected unpopular opinions hoped, as swiftly as possible, to eradicate certain undesirable isms.[12]

By 1941, when the Sesquicentennial of the Bill of Rights was celebrated, organizations began to proliferate: the National Federation for Constitutional Liberties, the Bill of Rights Commemorative Society, and the Society of the National Shrine of the Bill of Rights were among the most active. All of them emphasized (but did not clearly explain) the vital relationship between a strong national defense and the Bill of Rights. During the first annual Bill of Rights Week the Citizenship Educational Service simply declared that the "American people's determination to uphold civil liberties is the 'driving force' behind the defense program." Constant references to dictators, totalitarianism, Nazis, and Communists appeared in newspaper editorials and public programs. As one broadside stated on Bill of Rights Day in 1941: "Today our lives, our fortunes, our stature as free men, all are jeopardized before the shot and shell of fascist guns."[13]

II

World War II turned out to be a mixed blessing for civil liberties in American constitutionalism. What transpired might best be described as a case of three steps forward and three steps backward. On the positive side, American freedoms came to be touted as the very essence of what we were fighting for. On the negative side, an atmosphere in which everyone must either be friend or foe, absolute ally or deadly menace, did not foster tolerance for certain ethnic minorities and unpopular positions. The internment of Japanese-Americans is simply the most infamous and richly documented illustration of America being unfaithful to its civil libertarian ideals.[14]

When we look at other sorts of evidence, doubt arises whether very much of a civil libertarian tradition even existed. Late in 1943 the National Opinion Research Center asked 2,560 Americans: "What do you know about the Bill of Rights? Do you know anything it says? Have you ever heard of it?" The responses are startling.

23%   identified it or stated some part of it correctly.

7%   identified it incorrectly but had some idea "of the spirit of the thing" (e.g., as part of the Declaration of Independence, or including "free enterprise, free to do as you please, etc.").

39%   said that they had heard of it but could not identify it in any way.

4%   identified it utterly incorrectly.

4%   gave a response that was partially right and partially wrong (e.g., freedom of speech, press, fear, and want).

20%   had simply never heard of it.

3%   gave vague responses ("I'm not certain," "Can't say," etc.).

Nearly five months later an editorial in *The New York Times* denounced this national disgrace and urged every American to read the first ten amendments. "We shall learn that with our rights go obligations, one of these being to respect the rights of our fellow-Americans, and that it is only when their rights are respected that our own rights are safe."[15]

Subsequent polls on more specific issues proved to be little more satisfactory. A survey taken in 1944 asked: "In peacetime, do you think newspapers should be allowed to criticize our form of government?" Sixty-six percent answered yes, 30 percent no, and 4 percent couldn't decide. A follow-up inquired: "In peacetime, do you think people in this country should be allowed to say anything they want in a public speech?" This time 63 percent replied yes, 34 percent no, and 3 percent didn't know. Finally, 67 percent believed that members of the Communist Party should be allowed to speak on the radio; 29 percent did not; and 4 percent could not decide.[16]

No single factor can explain this pattern of mild concern mingled with indifference; but some attention to the Supreme Court's history is helpful. We must keep in mind that the Court made relatively few judicial rulings on civil liberties between 1790 and 1917; and the best known holdings after that time tended to go against the advocates of libertarian speech, writing, and activism on behalf of unpopular causes (*Schenck* v. *United States* and *Abrams* v. *United States,* both in 1919, for example). Although the Court began to move tentatively toward "a new civil rights constitutionalism" during the 1940s, its impulse to do so was restrained by several sources of judicial self-doubt. Robert G. McCloskey put it this way: "The Court was sailing uncharted seas, and most of the mariners knew it. Some of them indeed seemed able to develop the self-confidence to drive ahead steadily enough, but no consistently libertarian majority could be marshalled, and the overall effect was a civil rights jurisprudence in which libertarian impulses and misgivings seemed intricately mixed."[17]

Under the circumstances it seems fair to say that during World War II the public did not get very clear signals from the Court on issues involving the Bill of Rights. There are exceptions, to be sure. In *Schneiderman* v. *United States* (1943) the Court ruled that a Communist could not be denaturalized on the ground that he had earlier defrauded the government when obtaining his citizenship by concealing limitations upon his loyalty to the United States. Even that case was decided by a five to three vote, however, with Chief Justice Stone dissenting vigorously.[18]

Yet another source of public confusion about the Bill of Rights may be attributed to a curious phenomenon of the 1940s and '50s that seemed to follow in the wake of the Bill's "discovery" in 1939–41: namely, the creation of new lists of civil rights or (still more general) human rights. In

Roosevelt's 1944 State of the Union message, for example, he defined a "second Bill of Rights under which a new basis of security and prosperity can be established for all."

Among these are:
The right to a useful and remunerative job in the industries or shops or farms or mines of the Nation;
The right to earn enough to provide adequate food and clothing and recreation;
The right of every farmer to raise and sell his products at a return which will give him and his family a decent living;
The right of every businessman, large and small, to trade in an atmosphere of freedom from unfair competition and domination by monopolies at home or abroad;
The right of every family to a decent home;
The right to adequate medical care and the opportunity to achieve and enjoy good health;
The right to adequate protection from the economic fears of old age, sickness, accident, and unemployment;
The right to a good education.[19]

Similarly, in July 1945 Senator Harold H. Burton of Ohio developed a seven-point bill designed to improve labor relations, and called it "The Public's Bill of Rights" or "an industrial bill of rights for the public." Thirteen years later Senator William F. Knowland of California, who opposed compulsory unionism, proposed quite a different sort of "Bill of Rights for Labor," one that required the secret ballot in union elections, reduced the power of national union officials, and audited union funds, ostensibly to protect the members.[20]

In 1941 Robert M. Hutchins, then president of the University of Chicago, made a radio broadcast over NBC in which he questioned the devotion of many Americans to the Bill of Rights. That was not a popular truth to tell; but subsequent polls and critical assessments demonstrated that Hutchins had cause for such an unkind accusation. In 1954, soon after Hutchins assumed leadership at the Fund for the Republic, that foundation committed $100,000 for a national editorial competition that would promote "the best discussion of the Bill of Rights in the United States today."[21] A series of polls taken beween 1947 and 1957 suggested once again that Hutchins the gadfly often stung at suitably sensitive spots.

III

In 1947 a Gallup Poll asked 2,800 Americans a very straightforward question: "What is the bill of rights?" More than 41 percent either did not know or had no answer. Miscellaneous incorrect answers ("the right to vote," "laws governing our country," "the preamble to the Constitution") came from 10 percent. Another 10 percent offered vaguely correct responses ("amendments to the Constitution," "something to do with the Constitution"). Fifteen percent gave replies like "guarantees freedom," "personal freedoms," or "individual rights." Almost 11 percent answered that the Bill protected a variety of specified rights (freedom of speech, press, the right to petition, the right to keep and bear arms, etc.). And 11.6 percent responded with "First Ten Amendments to the U.S. Constitution."[22] Fundamentally, 22 percent gave satisfactory replies, but 78 percent could not.

In 1954, Gallup asked: "What are the first ten amendments to the Constitution called?" Thirty-three percent said the Bill of Rights, 2 percent gave inaccurate answers, and 65 percent did not know. Two years later the National Opinion Research Center asked more than 1,200 people whether they had ever heard of the Bill of Rights. The 91 percent who responded positively were then asked: "What do you know about it? Can you tell me anything it says?" Thirty-six percent drew an absolute blank ("dont know," "don't remember," "can't say"). Eight percent gave a response too vague to be called correct. Ten percent offered totally erroneous answers; and another 18 percent came up with replies that were partly right and partly wrong. Only 28 percent supplied answers that contained nothing incorrect.[23]

Finally, in 1957 a Gallup Poll asked 1,654 Americans this question: "When you hear or read about the Fifth Amendment, what does it mean to you?" Twenty-one percent gave some sort of correct response, though often incomplete; another 21 percent not only answered incorrectly, but for the most part pejoratively (e.g., "a man is guilty if he uses it"). Of the remainder, 11 percent were vague and 47 percent knew nothing about the Fifth Amendment at all.[24]

This persistent pattern of ignorance is all the more alarming because the Bill of Rights in general as well as specific civil rights were very much in the news, at all levels of media communication, throughout the decade

1947–57. The two magazines with the widest national circulation, *Reader's Digest* and *TV Guide,* both printed essays from time to time on the Bill of Rights, on its interpretation in controversial instances by the Supreme Court, and on the networks' demand (based upon the First Amendment) for the right to cover courtroom proceedings.[25]

The Bill of Rights enjoyed unusual visibility during the fall of 1947 because it actually travelled to the people. The Department of Justice, assisted by other government agencies, organized an exhibition of more than 150 documents deemed fundamental to the American political tradition, including the Bill of Rights. Displayed in a red, white, and blue mobile museum called the Freedom Train, these "sacred texts" became accessible to the people amidst considerable fanfare.

Although the 156th anniversary of the Bill of Rights' ratification received special attention in 1947, it is unfortunate that so many speakers made a swift and frequently mindless transition from the liberties enjoyed by Americans to those vast areas behind the iron curtain where truth is suppressed by government censorship. Even in France and Italy, two of our Western allies in the free world, "the Communist conspiracy is using every trick of bribery and terror to warp or conceal the truth." One orator after another pleaded for expanded propaganda facilities, such as the Voice of America, so that benighted souls elsewhere might improve their understanding of the American system of government.[26] To judge by the domestic polls, however, political instruction was needed nowhere more urgently than at home.

The belief that conspiratorial Communists lurked everywhere did more than just diminish attention to the Bill of Rights: it caused many to be watchful lest a subversive take refuge in the Bill, like some scamp seeking sanctuary in a medieval church. The principal speaker on Bill of Rights Day, December 15, 1947, was Attorney General Tom C. Clark, soon to become an associate justice on the High Court. Standing on Wall Street at the site of Federal Hall, where the Bill had been enacted in 1789, Clark warned all Americans (over ABC Radio) "to be ever alert to ferret out those who cloak themselves under the Bill of Rights and who would undermine our form of government."[27]

One of the least attractive ironies in American history persisted throughout the 1940s and '50s: a disparity between rhetorical devotion to our vaunted liberties and pervasive indifference to the very document that legitimized those liberties. In 1940 Congress passed the Alien Registration Act and the Smith Act, a peacetime sedition law; in 1950 the McCarran Internal Security Act; and the Communist Control Act in 1954. Enforcement of these laws, along with inquiries by the House Un-American Activities Committee, only served to tarnish the Bill of Rights by misusing or ignoring it. The right of association was constrained over a significant period of time, and the concept of conspiracy outrageously abused. As Edward R. Murrow declared in a broadcast about HUAC, the Justice Department, and domestic communism: "Nine men in Washington can not hold a nation to ideals which it is determined to betray. Whether justice is done to the particular defendant is important, but in the long run less important than whether a nation does justice to itself."[28]

One of those nine men, Hugo L. Black, felt a particular mission to ensure that his nation would do justice to itself and its citizens. As early as 1944, when his knowledge of the law still seemed suspect to some of his more erudite Brethren, he fearlessly preached to them (by memoranda to "the Conference") about the framers' intentions when they wrote and affirmed the Bill of Rights.[29] Black's famous dissent in 1947 to the Court's opinion in *Adamson* v. *California* can best be described as a bold stroke: without fear and without adequate research. Black insisted that those who wrote the Fourteenth Amendment intended, by means of the due process clause, that the Bill of Rights should apply to the states as well as to the federal government. Frankfurter felt contempt for Black's constitutional fiction; and Professor Charles Fairman devoted 168 pages in the *Stanford Law Review* to a demonstration that Black's knowledge of history left much to be desired. As Fairman concluded, Black "strongly approves of the Bill of Rights and wants to make it applicable to the states (wherein he does not have history on his side although he unsuccessfully attempts to show that he does)."[30]

Black persisted, both on and off the bench, and came to be regarded as the foremost spokesman for the Bill of Rights. Along with William O. Douglas, he dissented in the controversial case of *Dennis* v. *United States*, in which the Court sustained the convictions of eleven leaders of the American Communist Party. The prosecution relied upon the Smith Act, which had made it a crime to advocate or conspire to teach the overthrow of government by force, and also made it illegal to belong to an organization that adhered to such a doctrine. Black and Douglas regarded the convictions as unjustified violations of free speech as guaranteed by the First Amendment.[31]

Early in 1960 Black chose "The Bill of Rights" as his subject for the first James Madison Lecture at the New York University School of Law. (Madison's reputation had risen alongside the rediscovery of the Bill of Rights. When New York University planned its 1951 bicentennial celebration in honor of Madison's birth, the announcement of the conference theme emphasized "the reaffirmation of our faith in the Constitution, in democracy and, in particular, in the Bill of Rights.") Black acknowledged in his Madison Lecture that a sharp difference of opinion existed as to how far provisions in the Bill of Rights "should be held to limit the lawmaking power of Congress." He rejected the position that the Constitution contained no absolute prohibitions, and that all constitutional problems could be reduced to issues of reasonableness and degree. Black reaffirmed the existence of absolutes in the Bill of Rights, and insisted that they constrained the legislation that Congress could enact.[32] He reiterated and expanded upon these themes in a CBS News Special, "Justice Black and the Bill of Rights," that first appeared on December 3, 1968, just when so many Americans were obsessed with "law and order" and believed that the Bill of Rights had become a protective shield for criminals.

Between 1947, when Black's dissent in the Adamson case received ridicule, and the 1960s, when his position prevailed and the entire Bill of Rights became applicable to the states, Black and others watched American attitudes toward civil liberties fluctuate with almost the same capriciousness as women's hemlines (both were erratic phenomena during those decades). The First Amendment's guarantee of a free press took quite a beating in 1948, for example, when the Board of Superintendents of New York City Schools banned *The Nation,* the oldest liberal magazine in the United States, because it had published a series of articles by Paul Blanshard in 1947–48 that criticized the official position of the Catholic Church on such matters as science, medicine, fascism, marriage, and divorce.[33]

Similarly, a movement in support of loyalty oaths became part of a more general tendency to legitimize inquiries into the political values of individuals as a condition of their being hired or of their continued employment. E. B. White's public letter of protest to the *New York Herald Tribune* late in 1947 discussed a fearsome issue to many Americans in a manner that was deft in touch though anything but light-hearted.

I am a member of a party of one, and I live in an age of fear. Nothing lately has unsettled my party and raised my fears so much as your editorial, on Thanksgiving Day, suggesting that employees should be required to state their beliefs in order to hold their jobs. The idea is inconsistent with our Constitutional theory and has been stubbornly opposed by watchful men since the early days of the Republic. It's hard for me to believe that the Herald Tribune is backing away from the fight, and I can only assume that your editorial writer, in a hurry to get home for Thanksgiving, tripped over the First Amendment and thought it was the office cat. . . .

White received many letters in praise (along with some criticism) of his statement. He had expressed the profound concern of millions of Americans.[34]

Finally, as an additional illustration of the flux and ambiguity that characterized the history of civil liberties during the 1940s and '50s, the Godkin Lectures that Justice Robert H. Jackson prepared for Harvard in 1954 revealed the ways in which he had moved from the preferred position he had given in 1941 to human rights over property rights or those of the state. By 1946 Jackson felt uncomfortable with this distinction and no longer regarded it as a sound guideline for the Court. His response to cases involving civil liberties became increasingly pragmatic and selective. When he felt that agencies of the majority, such as Congress or state legislatures, had gone too far in circumscribing the freedom of citizens, he did not hesitate to declare such legislation unconstitutional. But when he believed that government limitations on individual freedom resulted from a reasonable policy choice between the competing imperatives of liberty and order, he would sustain such limitations.[35]

During the 1950s other distinguished jurists (like Learned Hand), constitutional scholars (like Paul Freund), and journalists looked askance at the distinction between property rights and personal rights, and envisioned situations where the two might become indistinguishable for practical purposes. Freund allowed that a bias in favor of civil liberties might be appropriate in certain instances, yet warned against simplistic categories and doubted whether there ought to be a double standard for purposes of judicial review.[36] The history of civil liberties during those years involved a whole series of shifts, some subtle and others sweeping, some regressive and others forward-looking.

IV

The complexity of these developments is well illustrated by a significant coincidence. In October 1947, just when the status of civil liberties in American constitutionalism seemed to be slipping, President Truman's Committee on Civil Rights issued its famous report, *To Secure These Rights*. Its primary target was racial discrimination, and its bold recommendations included abolition of state poll taxes, passage of a national Fair Employment Practices Act, impartiality in health and medical services, as well as equal treatment in public accommodations. Less liberal in other areas, the report suggested that Communists and Fascists should be required by law to register with federal and state agencies so that public authorities could have precise information about their identities.[37]

Although various leaders from the bench and from such organizations as the National Association for the Advancement of Colored People and the American Jewish Congress urged immediate implementation, it will come as no surprise that decades rather than years were required to secure those rights even partially. Nevertheless, a prestigious committee appointed by the federal government had staked out a set of priorities which would not be repudiated, no matter how repugnant some individuals might find the recommendations. For half a dozen years, implementation came slowly; and just as often under private auspices as from executive orders or congressional legislation. By the early 1950s a due regard for civil liberties began to be generally respectable though not consistently implemented with care. The Fund for the Republic undertook a series of exemplary projects. Efforts were made to establish centers with such designations as the Bill of Rights Institute, where research and instruction could be undertaken. And in 1954 a Bill of Rights Fund was created under the chairmanship of Corliss Lamont. It existed to make financial grants to individuals who sought to defend their civil liberties in the courts.[38]

The strongest acceleration of public interest occurred in 1955, however, and not merely on account of the Supreme Court's school desegregation decisions. Earl Warren performed a leadership role as constitutional educator, a role that many of his predecessors as Chief Justice had been unwilling to play. When Warren agreed to write about "The Law and the Future" for *Fortune* magazine, his emphasis fell upon the Bill of Rights. He reminded Americans that they lived at a time "when our Bill of Rights is under subtle and pervasive attack." Lest anyone think that he had Soviet infiltration in mind, he added that "the attack comes not only from without, but from our own indifference and failure of imagination." Warren would return to this theme in 1962 when he declared that "the day-to-day job of upholding the constitution really lies . . . realistically, on the shoulders of every citizen."[39]

On September 17, 1955, the Subcommittee on Constitutional Rights of the Senate Judiciary Committee observed Constitution Day by holding special hearings in response to a Citizens' Petition for the Redress of Grievances. The range of testimony given by leaders of different groups provides some indication of the diversity of American opinion concerning constitutionalism in general and civil liberties in particular. An official of the American Bar Association observed that "this is the age of the slogan. That is no way in which to examine our rights under the Constitution." The president of the League of Women Voters noted that Cold War tensions required constitutional adjustments "without sacrifice of principles and ideals." A past national commander of the American Legion wanted to know whether "that same enemy whom we died to defeat in battle may dress itself in civilian clothes, wrap itself in the Constitution, and by subversion destroy us from within." Eugene Carson Blake, president of the National Council of Churches of Christ, expressed confidence that the Supreme Court would continue to interpret the Constitution in such a way that even the religious liberties of unpopular minorities would be protected. He admitted to an anxiety, however, that in the process "the Court may tend to change this nation from a nation under God to a completely secular state."[40]

A pluralistic society felt the pull of many different constitutional concerns. Roy Wilkins, executive secretary of the NAACP, praised the theoretical freedoms guaranteed by the Bill of Rights, but conveyed the bitter resentment of Afro-Americans because they were not adequately protected by them. Racist interpretations of the Bill of Rights, particularly in the South, "are enforced with the pistol, the shotgun, the blackjack, and, lately, through the state-wide Citizens Councils, with economic sanctions that deprive citizens of employment, credit and homes." The president of the U.S. Chamber of Commerce argued that secondary boycotts were unconstitutional and that compulsory unionism was "inconsistent with the spirit of the Constitution since it compels a person to participate in accomplishing political objectives that may conflict with his personal beliefs." James Russell Wiggins, chairman of the Freedom of Information Committee of the American Society of Newspaper Editors, made an eloquent appeal for full protection of a free press. He noted, as an example, that one third of all congressional committee meetings were held in private. An officer of the AF of L urged repeal of the Taft-Hartley Act and asserted that many states had passed laws which improperly restrained the rights of workers to engage in union activities.[41]

Although this "hearing" of concerns was essentially a symbolic forum, it received the kind of press coverage and transcript distribution that amounted to a compact civics course for anyone who bothered to take notice.[42] Unfortunately, the basic problem remained: too few Americans did. The Supreme Court justices knew it, and felt distressed but helpless.

In 1957 a Gallup Poll asked more than 2,700 Americans: "What is the Bill of Rights?" Fifty-five percent offered responses that were at least partially correct; 45 percent did not know.[43] That same year a representative of the Fund for the Republic inquired of one hundred passers-by in Lincoln, Nebraska, whether they knew about the Bill of Rights and could identify at least one of its provisions. He explained to each person he stopped that the Bill consisted of the first ten amendments to the Constitution. He then offered to pay one dollar if the interviewee could name a single provision. The representative paid out a total of three dollars.[44]

For a fair number of Americans, ignorance remained a convenient form of bliss because three issues about which strong feelings prevailed continued to be barriers against full respect for the Constitution: desegregation, communism, and crime. Senator Sam J. Ervin of North Carolina long enjoyed a popular reputation as a man who revered the Constitution and the law of the land. That did not prevent him from attacking the Supreme Court almost continuously after 1954. It had usurped powers that belonged to Congress and the states, he declared; and he warned that if the justices were permitted to continue on their reckless course, the Constitution would be reduced to "a worthless scrap of paper, the American system of government will perish, and the states and their citizens will become helpless subjects of judicial oligarchy."[45]

Ervin published in *Look* magazine his strongest case for the perpetuation of segregation: blacks accept the system, and many of them prefer it. Pressure from the federal government to integrate only serves to retard rather than improve racial understanding. In July 1967, when the Senate Judiciary Committee reviewed the nomination of Thurgood Marshall to the Supreme Court, Ervin voted against Marshall. He ended an eighty-minute speech by proclaiming that Marshall was "by practice and philosophy a constitutional iconoclast, and his elevation to the Supreme Court at this juncture in our history would make it virtually certain that for years to come, if not forever, the American people will be ruled by the arbitrary notions of Supreme Court Justices rather than by the precepts of the Constitution."[46]

A constitutional iconoclast, I suspect, is a person whose views on constitutional matters are strongly held and diametrically opposed to one's own. Be that as it may, Senator Ervin certainly was not the first American politician, nor will he be the last, to rise from constitutional hypocrite to constitutional hero. Between 1971 and 1973 he emerged as a passionate defender of the right to privacy, an opponent of electronic surveillance devices, and an ardent advocate of freedom of the press.[47] Ervin stated that

Richard M. Nixon abused the Constitution during his presidency; and remarked of John Mitchell and John Ehrlichman, "if either of them ever read the Constitution, he didn't understand it." In 1985, not long before his death at the age of eighty-eight, Ervin sent Ronald Reagan a critique of the President's efforts to circumvent the freedom of religion clause in the First Amendment.

> Despite my admiration for you, I am constrained by my duty to our country to assert that what you say, do and advocate in respect to religion shows that you do not understand the religious clauses of the First Amendment and how obedience to them is essential to the preservation of the religious freedom they are designed to secure to all Americans of all faiths.
>
> You urge Congress to give Federal tax credits to parents who send their children to private schools to be taught the creeds of their churches. Your action in this respect violates the First Amendment, which forbids government to use the taxes of Caesar to finance the things of God.
>
> You named an ambassador to the Vatican—an act in violation of the establishment clause, which in the words of its drafter, James Madison, forbids government to establish an official relationship with any religion.
>
> You urge adoption of a constitutional amendment to authorize prayer in the public schools. The adoption of such an amendment would drastically alter the First Amendment, which commands the government to be strictly neutral in respect to religion and leaves the task of teaching religion to children to the homes and churches of our land.
>
> The government must keep its hands off religion if our people are to enjoy religious freedom—our most precious freedom.[48]

I am reminded of one of Senator Ervin's favorite stories. It's about the commander of a U.S. military unit who had copies of the Constitution stamped with the disclaimer: "This document does not necessarily reflect the views of the commander of this unit."

A Gallup Poll put the following question to 3,800 Americans in 1967: "Do you think the Supreme Court has been impartial in its decisions or do you think it has tended to favor one group more than another?" "Impartial" was the response of 47 percent; "favors one group" the reaction of 31 percent; and 22 percent had no opinion. Those who said "favors one group" were asked a follow-up question: "What group is this?" and their replies are revealing.[49]

Negroes	38%
Whites	4%
Minority groups	12%
Communists	4%
Criminals	12%
Liberals	5%
Rich money groups	3%
Miscellaneous	13%
Don't know/no answer	9%

The follow-up answers might seem to suggest that anxiety about coddling Communists had diminished considerably over a twenty-year period. Although it undoubtedly had, other evidence indicates that anti-Communist hostility ran stronger than American devotion to the Bill of Rights and Supreme Court decisions. Late in 1965 a Gallup Poll asked 3,521 Americans this question: "The Supreme Court has ruled that a law requiring all Communists to register with the government is unconstitutional on the grounds that this law would force a man to testify against himself. Do you approve or disapprove of the Supreme Court's decision in this case?" Only 27 percent approved; 58 percent did not; and 15 percent had no opinion. American intolerance for Communists, and the belief that ordinary protections of the Bill of Rights should not apply to Communists, had barely changed between 1955 and 1965.[50]

In the 1967 poll, those who believed that the Supreme Court showed favoritism to particular groups ranked criminals next after Negroes and minority groups. That ranking reflected a pervasive notion that the Bill of Rights was being interpreted too generously on behalf of those who violated the law (or stood accused of having done so). Many Americans felt scandalized by a long series of decisions that began with *Mallory* v. *United States* (1957), which voided a death sentence for rape in the District of Columbia because "unnecessary delay" had occurred in presenting the confessed rapist before an arraigning magistrate. The title of an acerbic essay in *Reader's Digest* epitomized the national mood: "Let's Have Justice for Non-Criminals, Too!" The essence of Eugene H. Methvin's argument: "By handing down increasingly unreasonable decrees on what constitutes reasonable police procedures, the Supreme Court threatens to make a disgraceful farce of American law enforcement." In 1968 Congress showed its sensitivity to majority opinion and passed a Crime Control Act that restored to federal judges the right to determine the admissibility of confessions on the basis of the "totality of circumstances."[51] The pendulum of public opinion kept on swinging, and with it all three branches of government.

V

Although it would be difficult to define a "normal" year, 1968 surely must have been a peculiar one for civil liberties in American constitutionalism. On the one hand, law and order looked highly problematic to many Americans; and congressional passage of the Crime Control Act did seem to be a slap at the Warren Court's systematic upgrading of the rights to which accused persons were entitled. On the other hand, 1968 also happened to mark the centennial of the Fourteenth Amendment; and a series of Supreme Court decisions had recently used that amendment as a rationale to complete the process of nationalizing the Bill of Rights. The Constitutional Rights Foundation, located in Los Angeles, began to publish a Bill of Rights Newsletter, as well as to sponsor conferences, workshops, and institutes for students, teachers, and law enforcement personnel. The National Emergency Civil Liberties Committee, based in New York, started its annual publication of *The Bill of Rights Journal*. And, on December 3, CBS televised "Justice Black and the Bill of Rights," a one-hour special that was unprecedented, effective, and influential. If 1968 was not the best of years, neither was it the worst.

In one sense its tensions and ambiguities made it a representative year, because Americans have tended to act as though the Bill of Rights was meant to protect the "righteous" rather than all Americans, and have been inclined to cherish the Bill of Rights in an extremely absent-minded way. An episode from the Alfred Hitchcock thriller *Rear Window* is illustrative. About halfway through the film Jimmy Stewart impetuously wants to break into a suspect's apartment in order to search for incriminating evidence. Stewart's friendly rival, a police officer named Doyle, has to remind him that "we have a Constitution" which does not permit searches without a duly authorized warrant. The Fourth Amendment is never mentioned as such. That would be too didactic and heavy-handed for a Hitchcock murder mystery. Nevertheless, a message (if not a reminder) reached millions of viewers that all Americans have a right "to be secure in their persons, houses, papers, and effects. . . ."

Forgetfulness has only been part of the problem, however. For several decades Americans could not agree about the legitimacy of desegregation. When that goal finally gained acceptance (by most people in most places) as the law of the land, Americans then found that they could not agree on the propriety of busing as a means of closing the gap between law and reality.[52] During the 1960s and '70s freedom of the press became highly controversial also; and broadcasters encountered the unanticipated dilemma that a fully free press also had an obligation to be an impartial press. By broadcasting courtroom proceedings, for example, television news programs might prejudice the results of a trial.[53]

Ever since 1973 the American people have been unable to agree whether the Supreme Court was justified in ruling that women possess a constitutional right to abortion. In 1983 an amendment was introduced in the U.S. Senate that contained just ten words: "A right to abortion is not secured by this Constitution." The National Pro-Life Political Action Committee asserts that its "ultimate goal is the right-to-life amendment that even the court would have to obey." Opponents of abortion could not agree among themselves, however, about the proper strategy and solution. Although many favor an amendment, some, like Justice Sandra Day O'Connor and President Reagan, have argued that "the issue of abortion must be resolved by democratic process." To O'Connor and many others that means that legislative bodies rather than courts are the appropriate forum for making determinations about abortion.[54]

Similarly, ever since March 1972 when Congress approved the Equal Rights Amendment (ERA) and passed it along to the states for ratification, there has been a combination of conflict and indifference as to whether women are adequately protected by the Bill of Rights. In 1875 the Supreme Court ruled in *Minor* v. *Happersett* that a woman could be a "citizen" under the Fourteenth Amendment and still not be constitutionally entitled to vote. Although that bizarre inconsistency got rectified by the Nineteenth Amendment in 1920, judicial reluctance (notably in the lower courts) to extend the equal protection clause of the Fourteenth Amendment in cases of sex discrimination convinced many that ERA would not be a superfluous constitutional supplement.[55]

As recently as 1971 the Court seemed reluctant to deal with discrimination based upon gender. When a married female in Alabama challenged a requirement of the State Department of Public Safety that she register for a driver's license using her husband's surname, the Alabama District Court acknowledged the suit as an Equal Protection challenge to the common law rule that a woman assume her husband's family name upon marriage. Nevertheless the Court decided that the rule was acceptable on grounds of long-standing custom, uniformity among the states, and administrative convenience. The U.S. Supreme Court accepted the case on appeal, but sustained the Alabama Court without even rendering an opinion. Not until the case of *Reed* v. *Reed* (1972), which challenged the provision of an Idaho law that preferred men over women as the administrators of estates, did the High Court decide that giving "a mandatory preference to members of either sex over members of the other, merely to accomplish the elimination of hearings on the merits, is to make the very kind of arbitrary legislative choice forbidden by the Equal Protection Clause of the Fourteenth Amendment."[56]

I am reminded of an assertion once made by David Lawrence, the influential columnist and editor of *U.S. News and World Report,* that the Constitution itself was unconstitutional because the Fourteenth Amendment had been ratified by southern state legislatures under duress![57]

Though Lawrence may have lodged tongue in cheek, his vituperative criticism of judicial activism during the later 1950s and '60s was very much in earnest. More recently that role has been carried on by such conservatives in Congress as John Ashbrook, a former member of the House Judiciary Committee who accused a "high-handed" federal judiciary of "overreaching its constitutional powers." Ashbrook informed the more than eighteen million subscribers to *Reader's Digest* that if a judge decides that "there has been a denial of due process or equal protection, he can overrule the President and Congress as well as state and local legislatures. He can seize a school system, prison or mental hospital, appropriate public funds, and set policy." Charges of judicial usurpation are not new, but to imply that the judiciary violates American liberties on a grand scale, using the Fourteenth Amendment as a pretext, is fairly novel. Ashbrook closed with a quotation from Raoul Berger, the careful constitutional scholar: "How long can public respect for the Court survive if people become aware that the tribunal which condemns the acts of others as unconstitutional is itself acting unconstitutionally?"[58]

Shades of David Lawrence! But the pendulum of public opinion never stops moving, and with it (albeit gradually) the Supreme Court. By the mid-1980s the Court began to take a narrower view of the rights of accused criminals than the Warren Court had. In June 1984, for example, the Court created a "public safety exception" to the Miranda rule when it held that a suspect may be questioned without the requisite warnings if "overriding considerations of public safety" were deemed to exist. In March 1985 a six-member majority ruled that initial failure by the police to tell a suspect of his right to remain silent and to have a lawyer present did not necessarily make a later confession inadmissible in court if the suspect had subsequently received the required warning.[59]

Less than twenty years after the landmark case of *Miranda* v. *Arizona* (1966), in which the Court declared that incommunicado police detention is inherently coercive, the Supreme Court started to diminish the meaning of *Miranda*. Law enforcement is apparently being enhanced; but perhaps the Fifth and Sixth amendments are being diminished. Some people might even say that the Bill of Rights is under subtle attack.

CHAPTER 13

The Public Got Strange and Distorted
Views of the Court and Its Rulings

OBSERVERS HAVE REMARKED FROM TIME TO TIME that public opinion plays a particularly important role in American culture. Although the perception certainly applies to constitutionalism, it has been less commonly noticed in that regard.[1] The rhythms of national interest in the Constitution have not yet been charted in any systematic way. Phases of intense controversy over constitutional issues have so often occurred, in part, because balanced analyses or contextual materials were unavailable. Why, at other times, has discussion of constitutional matters been muted despite the existence of considerable press coverage, pamphlets, and books in abundance? Although it is clear that the reality of political conflict elicits more interest in constitutionalism than symbolic commemorative occasions—just compare, for example, the Nullification Crisis of 1831–33 with the Golden Jubilee in 1837–39—the historical problem of sustaining public interest and disseminating pertinent information is more difficult to explain.

A complex relationship between the Supreme Court and the press has been at the core of this conundrum. From the 1790s until the 1960s, both the Court and the news media created barriers to public knowledge of constitutional change: the Court by acts of commission and the press primarily by acts of omission. Although most citizens would accept the assertion (by Professor Louis L. Jaffe of Harvard) that "there will be and there should be popular response to the Supreme Court's decisions," that response has been erratic and unpredictable. While the process of confirming presidential nominations to the Court provides Americans with an opportunity to be informed about the justices and their values, and to a lesser extent about the Court and its place in the governmental system, only in an indirect way does that process make the Constitution itself more visible; and it may not occur for more than four years at a stretch. (Recall that President Carter made no nominations during his term of office.)[2]

Earl Warren insisted in his *Memoirs* that "the judicial process as it functions in the Supreme Court is more open than that of either the legislative or executive branches of the government."[3] Many journalists who have covered the Court, as well as lawyers, scholars, and members of the laity who are interested, find Warren's declaration difficult to accept. For much of American history the relationship between Court and media has too often been one of mutual disdain rather than co-operation. National understanding of constitutional matters has suffered as a consequence. Therefore this strange stand-off between Fourth Estate and Supreme Court deserves examination.

I

Max Freedman, American correspondent of *The Manchester Guardian,* commented in 1956 that "the Supreme Court is the worst reported and worst judged institution in the American system of government." Although he put that observation in the present tense, it is even more valid as an historical assessment. Responsibility for this unfortunate phenomenon must be shared by both sides. For many years after the Court first convened under John Jay, the press paid little attention to the judicial branch and its decisions. On the other hand, the Court could not have been less co-operative. For more than 130 years, printed opinions were not available to the press while decisions were being read orally. Newspapermen were obliged to write about the Court's verdicts without having texts immediately available from which to work.[4]

Not surprisingly, therefore, some members of the press made inaccurate inferences from long and detailed opinions to which they could only listen when their accounts had to be prepared. (Published opinions appeared in the term-by-term series now known as *U.S. Reports.*) In 1921, for example, journalists totally misunderstood a decision by Chief Justice Taft and reported it as being antilabor when in fact he had overruled an earlier precedent and upheld the right to strike and to peaceful picketing.[5] Late in the 1920s columnist David Lawrence persuaded Taft to modify this policy so that reporters could see the texts of judicial decisions more promptly. When yet another serious misinterpretation occurred in 1935, the Court finally adopted the procedure of distributing proofs to newsmen just as the justices began to read their opinions.

Except for a few newspapers, such as *The New York Times* and *Washington Post,* the press gave minimal coverage to most judicial decisions; and, save in moments of unusual crisis (such as 1937), paid scant attention to the Court as an institution. As recently as 1940, Chief Justice Hughes could say quite fairly that the Court "does most of its work without special public attention to particular decisions." Moreover, as late as 1956 the media could gravely misunderstand and misrepresent a decision involving racial segregation on public means of transportation. As Judge Irving R. Kaufman declared in 1965: "The really difficult problem . . . still remains—how to assist hard-pressed news reporters who must explain difficult opinions to the lay public under the pressure of looming deadlines."[6]

What makes the press's selection and interpretation of cases so important is the fact that actual Supreme Court opinions are read by a very small percentage of government officials, including members of Congress. Most of them depend heavily upon the *Post* and *Times* to learn what has been decided, its implications, and to read what a single reporter regards as the most significant extracts. The same is true of lawyers, by the way, which has led some critics to quip that a higher percentage of incarcerated persons read Court decisions in the field of criminal law than do attorneys. The quip is not entirely facetious. Every week the Supreme Court staff mails out several hundred copies of opinions to prisoners who might be affected by a recent Court decision.[7]

It rarely happens that a justice's opinion has been reprinted or discussed outside of *U.S. Reports* and learned journals. Neither masterful prose nor far-reaching significance is sufficient. The case must involve an issue of the highest public interest, and then in some agitating way with ideological implications. That was precisely the situation in 1950 when *The New York Times Magazine* printed lengthy excerpts from Robert H. Jackson's opinion in *American Communications Association, C.I.O., et al.* v. *Douds* under the title, "Justice Jackson on Communism in America." It also happened to be the kind of ambiguous opinion that gave with the left hand but took away with the right. Jackson sustained a 1947 congressional ban against members of the Communist Party serving as officers in labor unions, yet held that a democracy must protect freedom of belief—not exactly a clear signal to the civic culture.[8]

Although having an opinion reprinted may seem uncomplicated and educational, its infrequency does not merely result from the media's skeptical sense of what the public will read. From the very outset the justices developed a strong tradition of shunning publicity. Willis Van Devanter epitomized that tradition by declining to give interviews even after his retirement in 1937. Felix Frankfurter explained part of the rationale behind the tradition when he wrote in 1945 "that judges must leave their opinions to speak for themselves and that, in any event, they should not anticipate adjudication."[9]

Until quite recently the occasions when a justice would speak out on substantive issues were so rare that they attracted considerable attention. One of Brandeis's former clerks remembers vividly that "the Court's business was to become known only through the proper official channels. . . . I learned from the Justice how politely one may withhold even the implication of information from an inquiring news-man by the art of a polite negative." Brandeis startled many people in 1931 when he commented informally and adversely on an opinion upholding government wiretapping that Taft had written in 1928 and from which Brandeis vigorously dissented. On June 23, 1935, Brandeis caused even more surprise by giving an interview to the press in order to defend three major anti–New Deal decisions rendered by the Court.[10]

When Hugo Black made an eleven-minute radio broadcast on October 1, 1937, in order to explain his relationship to the Ku Klux Klan more than a decade before, the event was highly unusual. Many regarded it as unprecedented in Supreme Court history—and indecorous. Subsequently Black became the cause for just the kind of publicity most embarrassing to the justices: breaches of confidentiality among the Brethren themselves. In 1938 one of them apparently supplied a writer for *Harper's Magazine* with information that Black had brought "acute discomfort and embarrassment" to the Court because of his "lack of legal knowledge and experience, deficiencies in background and training that have led him into blunders which have shocked his colleagues." The Washington rumor mill targeted Harlan Fiske Stone as Marquis Childs's chief source; but Stone's secretary adamantly denied the rumor, and Black indicated that he would not initiate a libel action.[11]

In 1945–46, however, a much nastier brouhaha arose between Black and Jackson. The latter, while presiding over the Nuremberg trials in Germany, became convinced that Black had leaked stories to the press in order to maneuver Jackson out of a possible promotion to Chief Justice as Stone's successor. Black, in turn, believed that Jackson had cast aspersions upon his personal and professional honor. The outcome was a 1,500 word cablegram that Jackson sent from Nuremberg, calling Black a "stealthy assassin." The cablegram was intemperate and ill-advised; it created a ten-day sensation in the press that titillated the nation and has been called "the bitterest internecine controversy in the Court's history."[12]

Despite hazy memories of these episodes, and despite the fervor of the Court's commitment to confidentiality and a low profile, the custom has weakened somewhat since 1968 when Black agreed to an hour-long interview on CBS TV. At one point in the program Martin Agronsky asked Black whether the people who demonstrated in Chicago during the Democratic National Convention "were right to assemble the way they did, or the police were right in not permitting them to assemble and charging and breaking up the demonstration?" Black's response managed to be absolutely proper in terms of the Court's self-imposed restraint in not prejudging cases in the media. He nonetheless called attention to the com-plexity of a civil liberties issue very prominent in the public consciousness at that time.

> Well, that gets right on cases that we have. We're liable to have that very case. I don't want to say what my view would be because I don't know what the evidence would show. I don't know what they were doing. I don't know how far they went. Daley says they did so-and-so, and the other side says they're just a group of nice young idealists singing sweet songs of mercy and love, and I don't know. That's what the press seemed to think and the television, that they were just young, budding idealists who should not be noticed.[13]

In 1972, William O. Douglas permitted a candid one-hour interview with CBS in which he declared his respect for the American public and expressed a desire to utilize his role on the Court for a purpose not so dif-ferent from his role as a law professor thirty-five years earlier at Yale. "I'd like to educate them [the public] on what judges are, what judges should be, what civic affairs should be." Earl Warren also granted a television in-terview in 1972, though that occurred after his retirement; and during the Watergate crisis of 1973–74, Warren did make speeches urging that Americans adhere faithfully to the Constitution.[14]

A few of the justices are now, on occasion, outspoken about matters on which they hold strong views, and make revelations or criticisms that would have been inconceivable a generation or two ago. Addressing a convocation at the Northwestern University Law School in 1984, John

Paul Stevens disparaged his conservative colleagues' "enthusiastic attempts to codify the law instead of merely performing the judicial task of deciding the cases that come before them." He specifically criticized three recent Court decisions that limited the use of affirmative action quotas in job discrimination cases, created a "newfangled" good-faith exception to the rule excluding the use of unconstitutionally seized evidence in criminal trials, and limited federal jurisdiction in civil rights cases. Six weeks later, at a nonpublic meeting of the Cosmos Club in Washington, D.C., Justice Blackmun described the Court as "moving to the right, where it wants to go by hook or by crook."[15]

Needless to say, some of Stevens's fellow justices consider him a "loose cannon" and regard Blackmun's candor as well as his shift toward the liberal side of the Court with disdain. Although Chief Justice Burger and the rest tactfully declined to comment on what Stevens and Blackmun had said, Burger, Rehnquist, and others do grant guarded interviews and give speeches that explain or justify their positions in general relating to various matters. On occasion their timing seems purposeful yet oracular. Although it is highly unusual for justices to speak publicly about the Court's relationship to the presidency, Rehnquist chose October 19, 1984, just two weeks before a presidential election, to present the view that any President who tried to use his power of appointment to alter the Supreme Court's ideological composition was likely to fail. Speaking at the University of Minnesota College of Law, Rehnquist remarked that the Supreme Court "is an institution far more dominated by centrifugal forces, pushing towards individuality and independence, than it is by centripetal forces pulling for hierarchical ordering and institutional unity." The press reported Rehnquist's speech with a certain quizzical skepticism, wondering why (in view of the Court's tradition of political discretion), he had chosen that particular moment, when five of the justices were seventy-five or older, to comment on a matter frequently mentioned throughout the campaign.[16]

There has been a recent flurry of interest in the willingness of certain justices to manipulate the media by "planting" ideas that would eventually appear as articles in journals of opinion. The most notorious illustration, which emerged in 1982, involved a long-standing relationship between Brandeis and Frankfurter in which the latter received more that $50,000 between 1916 and 1938 from a special "joint endeavors for the public good" fund created by Brandeis. Ideas and policies that Brandeis wanted to promote, or judicial disagreements that he wished to vet, appeared in

The New Republic or *The Harvard Law Review* through Frankfurter's efforts.[17] Although the determination of these two men to use the press for partisan purposes may be the most unusual illustration of the phenomenon, it certainly is not unique. It dates all the way back to the days of Justice Joseph Story (that moralistic pillar of rectitude) during the 1820s. A century later, during Harlan Fiske Stone's early years on the bench, he too persuaded like-minded friends to write opinion pieces for publication, thereby planting favorable essays or ones that reflected his own point of view.[18]

Although standards of judicial conduct are supposedly clearer and higher in our own time, that remains a risky generalization. In 1981, Warren Burger spoke out for preventive detention laws exactly when several bail test cases were on their way to the Court. On the other hand, Burger frequently talks about matters involving legal reform or administrative aspects of the Court's caseload—both being problems entirely appropriate for the Chief Justice to discuss and bring to national attention.[19]

In the occasional interviews that Burger permits, however, he has been known to make assertions that are either contradicted by the facts or else logically insupportable. In 1973, for example, Burger gave an interview to *Reader's Digest* in which he claimed that "historically it [the Supreme Court] has never in any significant degree retreated before public opinion." He must have forgotten the famous "switch in time that saved nine" back in 1937. Burger was also asked about the growing number of five to four and six to three decisions: "With the membership so evenly balanced between competing viewpoints, how can the Court avoid seeming to leave the law unsettled or dependent on the personalities sitting there at any moment?" Here Burger replied quite reasonably that "such divisions are a source of strength, not weakness." Why and how? "The justices at any given time have come from varying backgrounds. . . .The diversity they bring to the problems tends to ensure that any personal biases are checked and compensated for through our round-table discussions. . . . So people should not worry when the Justices disagree over fundamental Constitutional issues. They should begin to worry if the Justices *cease* to disagree."[20] Even so, John Marshall's shade must be frowning. He knew that a Court which spoke with a single voice would enjoy greater credibility; and he acted accordingly.

Despite some recent and rather impassioned remarks by Stevens, Blackmun, Brennan, and Marshall, we presumably should feel no cause for concern—even though they do.

II

Yet another response that Burger gave in the same interview enables us to look at this matter from a different perspective. When asked whether the Court had been living through a crisis of confidence, Burger explained that "Justices cannot fret about polls. . . . The Founding Fathers did not design the Court to reflect public opinion." That is a reasonable point of view, and represents a line of continuity with most of Burger's predecessors. Looking back from his retirement years, Earl Warren declared that he had made a practice of ignoring incoming mail concerning the Court's cases, either before or after decisions had been announced. Warren worried that he "might be unconsciously influenced, particularly if there was a great predominance of opinion favoring one side." He firmly believed that "the Court's opinion itself is a studied conclusion based on the issues involved and speaks for itself better than any informal discussion of it later."[21]

The Supreme Court does receive spontaneous mail, an impulse that could tell us a fair amount about both the public's constitutional concerns and the Court's customary disdain (not always accompanied by disregard) for public opinion. Within a week after the announcement of their decision in *Engel* v. *Vitale* late in June 1962, in which the Court prohibited use of a prayer composed by the New York State Board of Regents, the Supreme Court received the largest quantity of mail, concerning a single case, in its entire history. (The decision also provoked a great many political cartoons, mostly critical.) Earl Warren once insisted that "people do not write to Supreme Court Justices as they do to their legislators." He may have been right in relative terms; but the letters that come to the Court deserve some notice as an index of public interest in controversial matters.[22]

What is and is not done about this mail seems very curious. If addressed to a particular justice, it is handled and filed by that judge's office staff. The papers of deceased justices commonly include an annual file for "crank letters." If the mail is addressed to the Court as a whole, however, or to the Chief Justice on behalf of the Court, then it is unclear what becomes of it. Warren insisted that he did not read it; and little interest seems to have been taken by anyone else. An inquiry sent to the Public Information Officer of the Supreme Court in 1984 elicited this response: "Neither the Public Information Office nor the Clerk's Office files or otherwise catalogues correspondence by category. Further, no tally of the amount of correspondence received by the Court is maintained. We have no established policy on scholars' access to our correspondence files."[23]

That blank wall brings us back to the central contention of Earl Warren's *Memoirs,*

> that the judicial process as it functions in the Supreme Court is more open than that of either the legislative or executive branches of the government. I would like to repeat that the entire record of any case upon which the Court must make a decision is on file and open to public inspection. The same is true of the briefs upon which it must rely in deciding the issues raised. In addition to the arguments being made in open court, a transcript of them can be inspected in our library five days after their delivery. Thus, the only thing kept from the public until finalized is what the decision is to be and when it is to be made. Furthermore, this does not cause a great delay because normally reaching a decision takes but a few weeks and in troublesome cases a few months.
>
> On the other hand, when a bill is introduced in either house of the Congress, there is nothing to indicate what brought it into being. The hearings are too often conducted secretly; chairmen of the committees have dictatorial powers as to what can reach the floor for action; lobbyists and other pressure groups ply their trade secretly; and bills are reported for action by committees without the right by the main body to improve them through amendments. They must take the bill or leave it as it comes to them from the committee as the result of secret hearings.[24]

Warren's line of argument, serious and thoughtful though it may be, is based upon a naïve perception of the Court's accessibility and potential role in civic affairs. It really does not take into account, for example, public opinion, the news media, and the desirability of achieving the broadest possible understanding of the Court's complex responses to critical cases. The press, many jurists, and legal scholars largely share a belief expressed repeatedly by Linda Greenhouse in 1985 as she neared the end of a seven-year stint covering the Supreme Court for *The New York Times:* "The Court remains, at heart, a mysterious and inaccessible place."[25]

The Supreme Court as an institution, and the judiciary in general, have not been very good at public relations because they have been largely indifferent to public relations. Federal Judge J. Skelly Wright put it very well in 1964: "Perhaps the public image of justice is distorted because we judges have turned our backs to the news media." Two historical illustrations are representative. In 1935, despite the fact that the Court's decision on the National Recovery Act was eagerly awaited as the most momentous of the year, Court staff members made no effort to have extra copies of the ruling available. An hour after the decision had been handed down, the President sent a messenger to the Court to obtain a copy; but the clerk had none available. According to Drew Pearson, "this is not the first time in recent months that attachés of the Court have bungled the handling of an important decision, and caused the suggestion that the august tribunal emulate the rest of the New Deal and hire a publicity man."[26]

A second instance, occurring in 1965, illustrates the problems that arise when too many decisions are announced at the very end of a term. Cases high in human interest get most of the attention, whereas less glamorous cases with long-range importance are likely to be neglected. On June 7, 1965, the Court handed down no less than twenty-one decisions in about two hours, including *Griswold* v. *Connecticut,* which legalized the sale of birth control devices, and *Estes* v. *Texas,* involving the trial of Billie Sol Estes, a flamboyant Texas entrepreneur. *Griswold* and the reversal of Estes's swindling conviction because parts of his trial had been televised got most of the media attention even though some of the other opinions were potentially quite important and, if they had come down on another day, would have received more publicity and explanation.[27]

It seems noteworthy that Article One, Section V, of the Constitution specifies that "each house shall keep a journal of its proceedings, and from time to time publish the same. . . ." Clearly, a presumption of legislative accountability existed from the outset, along with the opportunity for public scrutiny of elected officials. No comparable requirement exists for the Supreme Court, however. Unless an oversight occurred, which is not likely, the framers did not extend their concern for accountability to the Court. Consequently, unlike the House and Senate, the Supreme Court never had an official stenographic transcript made of its sessions. In October 1955 Earl Warren permitted the installation of a tape-recording machine so that the justices could check back on an oral argument. The innovation was not made to serve the press and the public better.[28]

Historically, the Court's opinion of the press has customarily been rather low. In 1944 Chief Justice Stone declared that he was "really shocked" by the "misleading, not to say completely inaccurate statements" made about the Supreme Court in national newspapers. Earl Warren echoed those sentiments in his *Memoirs,* complaining that the media often depicted the Court "as a mysterious body operating behind a veil of secrecy." He then added that the High Court's work is neither well known nor clearly understood because

> the media does not consider the Court's work newsworthy until it makes a decision which stirs emotion on the part of great numbers of people on the losing side. Then the media gives a superficial judgment which is often wide of the mark, and leaves the matter to the public in that unsatisfactory condition. This is largely because news gatherers are not deeply concerned with the proceedings before the Court until decision day; their homework is thus generally inadequate. During the years I was on the Court, I could count on the fingers of one hand those news gatherers who devoted full time to reporting on Supreme Court work, while across the park in the Capitol and down the mall at the White House there were scores of qualified reporters all the time.[29]

Much of Warren's complaint is valid for the period of his tenure (1953–69), and significant portions remain true to this day.

The autobiography of Justice Douglas deemed the press inadequate in other ways.

> The Court, I discovered, got very poor news coverage for several reasons. There were few reporters who made the history of the Court their profession. That is to say, the reporters were bright but uninformed men who were doing the best they could with complicated and technical material. Moreover, the appetite of the news services for spot news put tremendous pressures on the newsmen to write their stories in a few minutes and get them on the wires. The result was usually news stories which the author of the Court opinion would hardly recognize as descriptive of what he had written. That's why the public got strange and distorted views of the Court and its rulings.

Douglas found on the editorial pages of American papers "little insight concerning the substance of the Constitution," with but one exception: the St. Louis *Post-Dispatch* while Irving Dilliard was responsible for its editorials.[30]

Dilliard may well have been the best among a rather small group of journalists who wrote regularly about constitutional matters during the

1930s, '40, and '50s. They had little legal training, but read American political history avidly and cared very much about civil liberties. In 1930, when Dilliard began to write editorials for the *Post-Dispatch,* he chose the Supreme Court and constitutional problems as his special interest, a highly unusual selection at that time. In 1938–39 he spent a year at Harvard among the first class of Nieman Fellows and attended courses given by Thomas Reed Powell, Roscoe Pound, Zechariah Chafee, Jr., and Felix Frankfurter (in his last year before joining the bench). In addition to influential editorials and essays in journals of opinion like *Harper's,* Dilliard edited *Mr. Justice Brandeis: Great American* (1941), *The Spirit of Liberty: Papers and Addresses of Learned Hand* (1952), and *One Man's Stand for Freedom: Mr. Justice Black and the Bill of Rights* (1964).[31]

Others in Dilliard's cohort included Irving Brant, Alan Barth, Dillard Stokes, and Harry S. Ashmore, who handled the editorial page of the *Arkansas Gazette* from 1947 until 1959, headed a study of segregation in education sponsored by the Ford Foundation, and prepared *The Negro and the Schools,* which was published on the eve of *Brown* v. *Board of Education* in 1954 and was consulted by Earl Warren when he prepared the implementation decree in 1955. Ashmore subsequently joined the board of directors at the Fund for the Republic, and wrote *Broadcasting and the First Amendment: The Anatomy of a Constitutional Crisis* (1973). Brant, a bit older than the rest (1885–1976), wrote *Storm Over the Constitution* (1936), a six-volume biography of James Madison (1941–61), and *The Bill of Rights: Its Origin and Meaning* (1965).[32]

Gilbert Cranberg, an editorial writer for the Des Moines *Register and Tribune,* shared Dilliard's enthusiasm and willingness to wade patiently through Supreme Court opinions, and prepared numerous commentaries on constitutional issues. Cranberg's autobiographical candor (in 1967) sheds light on the difficulties involved in analyzing Court opinions as well as some of the reasons for the press's shortcomings cited by Justices Stone, Warren, and Douglas.

I was introduced to the texts of Supreme Court opinions a number of years ago out of the professional necessity to comment on the Court's rulings. The time-honored method of editorializing on a Supreme Court opinion is to study the wire service stories and whatever other newspaper versions of the ruling can be located, then to sit down and write. The variations in the stories, however—the gaps and unanswered questions—made it seem risky business to praise or blame the

Court from these sources alone. Reporters not tied to early deadlines may have several hours to prepare stories on opinion days and are able to spare the time to sit in the Court to hear oral delivery of the opinions, with the sometimes illuminating summaries and signs of inner court conflict this reveals. But the competitive pressure to get the news out quickly requires the wire service reporters—the source of news for most Americans—to prepare stories in advance of the issuance of opinions from briefs and other available information on pending cases. While the Justices perform in the courtroom, the wire service men are in the press room below preparing to make necessary insertions and alterations in the pre-written stories based on texts received from assistants who are hurriedly stuffing opinions into pneumatic tubes in the Court. Should a story manage to leave the Supreme Court building both complete and accurate, even under these conditions, it then is subject to rewriting, trimming, and headline treatment by news people far removed from the Court and from familiarity with the issues in the case.[33]

Cranberg's account helps to explain why the nation was not very well served by its press corps where constitutional matters were concerned. It also indicates that reporters who cover the Court have not operated under optimal conditions, and brings us back to the adversarial relationship that exists, in several respects, between journalists and justices.

Anthony Lewis summarized the feelings of many conscientious reporters who have attempted to cover the Court and its work: "All of official Washington except the Supreme Court is acutely conscious of public relations. The Supreme Court is about as oblivious as it is conceivable to be." After reading through the papers of a fair number of justices, I am not persuaded that they are genuinely oblivious to public opinion. But they certainly do not want their concern to be known; and they are unwilling to elaborate upon the Court's rulings in any way that might make those decisions more accessible to the public. No stenographic record is available of what transpires in the Court. An official but incomplete account is kept in the U.S. Supreme Court *Journal;* and unofficial versions of the Court's proceedings appear in *U.S. Law Week* and *Supreme Court Bulletin.* The justices continue to hold journalists at arm's length. Thurgood Marshall, for example, has his "ten minute rule": if one of his clerks is seen talking to a reporter, the clerk can expect to be "gone" in ten minutes. When rumors about various infirmities began to circulate in 1984, one respected journalist requested interviews with all nine justices in order to ascertain the Court's physical health. Four consented; four declined; and the office of another made some information available. Chief Justice Burger refused without explanation. It has been reported that in 1981 Burger "took a poke" at a television cameraman who had the temerity to follow him into an elevator with his camera rolling.[34]

The question of televising Supreme Court proceedings has been raised, on and off, for more than two decades, but with negative results despite the obvious benefits in terms of civic education. Late in 1964 the president of CBS, Frank Stanton, sought permission to have cameras and microphones record oral arguments concerning the constitutionality of the public accommodations section of the Civil Rights Act. He expressed the belief that the public failed to comprehend "what the role and procedures of the Supreme Court are, how the issues are presented to the Court and how this great institution works in the social and governmental develop-ment of the United States." He concluded that television could enhance understanding of the justices' function by "admitting all Americans at the presence of the Court while its attention was focused on a momentous issue."[35]

Chief Justice Warren responded that "the Court has had an inflexible rule to the effect that it will not permit photographs or broadcasting from the courtroom when it is in session," and he felt certain that the Court had no intention of changing that rule. Exactly twenty years later Chief Justice Burger called television in the courtroom the "most destructive thing in the world," and warned that "there will be no cameras in the Supreme Court of the United States while I sit there." His justification? "Show busi-ness and judicial business just won't mix."[36]

When John Paul Stevens addressed the issue early in 1985, he re-sponded in terms of either/or rather than "mixing"; and he reduced all potential viewers to the lowest common denominator.

> If a randomly selected group of average citizens were asked whether Supreme Court proceedings should be televised, I am sure most would answer "Yes" or perhaps "Why not?" If, however, instead of responding to an abstract question, they were given the opportunity to view four hours of oral argument on live television on a daily basis, I feel sure they would exhibit a rather decided preference for soap operas, grade B movies, or even sumo wrestling. For the most part, what happens in our courtroom is not high drama for the average viewer.[37]

Like Warren and Burger, Stevens follows the curious logic that television should not be permitted at all because much of the Court's work would not hold the attention of most viewers. Then why not permit selective coverage of cases in which interest runs high? Or even comprehensive coverage, with the networks (commercial and public) allowed to make a selection based upon substantive significance, newsworthiness, or educational value?

Various developments and rulings that have occurred in recent years make the High Court's hard line seem especially rigid and even capricious. First, by 1984 forty states permitted live broadcasting of court proceedings. The issue has ceased to be theoretical; empirical evidence exists. Second, the Supreme Court itself ruled unanimously in 1984 that, with rare exceptions, the public and the press must be allowed to attend trial courts, even during jury selection. As Warren Burger explained: "Openness enhances both the basic fairness of the criminal trial and the appearance of fairness so essential to public confidence in the system." And third, when Justices Black and Douglas requested an end to the tradition of reading opinions aloud, on grounds that the custom was too time-consuming, judicial conservatives like Frankfurter insisted that the time-honored practice served to educate the public on constitutional problems and procedures.[38]

Although Frankfurter triumphed at the time, modest concessions to efficiency as well as better conditions for journalists have since been permitted. While the date when any opinion will be released remains a closely guarded secret—making it difficult to prepare adequate contextual coverage—printed opinions are now released at 10:00 a.m. on the day of announcement rather than two or three hours later, after new members have been admitted to the Supreme Court Bar and opinions have been read. That innovation occurred in 1961. Four years later the Court decided to facilitate the work of reporters a bit more by abandoning the Monday tradition and releasing opinions a few at a time throughout the week. In addition, a new service has been available since the later 1960s, a "Preview of United States Supreme Court Cases" that provides brief but clear summaries of the issues and points of law to be covered in pending Court opinions. These summaries, prepared by law professors on a volunteer basis, are written with the layperson in mind and have been helpful to journalists.[39]

On the negative side, however, those judges who set administrative policy for the federal judiciary decided in 1984 that the public benefits of televising trials are "outweighed by the risks to the administration of justice." Therefore the Judicial Conference of the United States, headed by Warren Burger, dismissed a serious proposal for a change in the rules.

Photography remains prohibited in federal courts.[40] For those journalists who cover the Supreme Court, moreover, it remains disappointing that they receive no critical "feedback" whatever from the justices or their clerks. When reporters wonder whether they have explained a decision adequately—with implications for their coverage of subsequent cases—they cannot expect so much as a memo from the justices.

The full-time press corps covering the Court remains shockingly small. The wire services (AP and UPI) maintain two people each. Reuters has a reporter responsible for the Court and the Department of Justice. The Knight-Ridder Bureau and Gannett News Service assign reporters to the Court, but they have other duties as well. *The New York Times, Wall Street Journal, Washington Post, Baltimore Sun, Chicago Tribune,* and *Los Angeles Times* maintain steady coverage—a very short list. The television networks also assign journalists to the Court, and most of them now have law degrees; but they do not spend very much time at the Supreme Court. All have additional "beats" to cover.

For most of its history, reporters who wrote about the Supreme Court lacked any legal training. Felix Frankfurter found that scandalous and launched a campaign to improve the situation. Some justices, like William O. Douglas, had strong reservations, believing that "newsmen who study law usually become advocates of a particular type of jurisprudence that dominates the law school where they went." But Anthony Lewis, who took courses at the Harvard Law School as a Nieman Fellow in 1956–57, did an excellent job, earned Douglas's respect, and set the pattern for journalists assigned to the Court ever since the 1960s. Even the weekly news magazines, like *Time,* began to use part-time legal consultants for their section on Law; and several of the prestigious law schools have developed programs in nonprofessional legal education for journalists.[41]

An ideal equilibrium has not yet been achieved, and doubtless never will. The necessary relationship between judicial confidentiality and public accessibility must vary according to time and circumstance. But the balance has at least improved since the mid-1960s.

III

How—and whether—the news media cover constitutional events really does make a difference. Consider, for example, that the Court issued several important decisions in 1962–63 about prayer and Bible reading in the public schools. The first, *Engel* v. *Vitale,* received extensive press coverage, some of it sensational and misleading in significant ways. The national response ranked exceedingly high on the Richter scale of social anxiety. The next two cases, *School District of Abington Township* v. *Schempp* and *Murray* v. *the Board of School Commissioners of Baltimore City,* were received with comparative calm even though they had much broader implications. The Court apparently received fewer than one hundred letters in response to its decisions in *Schempp* and *Murray.* One contributing factor may be found in the press coverage: fewer provocative wire service leads and skewed headlines ("No Praying in Schools, Court Rules" had been typical in 1962), more carefully chosen language in explaining the decisions, and greater restraint in predicting their consequences.[42]

These illustrations, and others that are comparable, reinforce the central finding of an elaborate survey conducted by the Hearst Corporation in 1982–83: "the media is, by far, the most important conduit of information about our judicial system . . . a much more important source of information about the courts than are lawyers, the public's own personal experience, schools or libraries."[43]

The media must not be regarded as a monolith, however, particularly for purposes of historical analysis. Consequently it is useful to look at what has happened in the schools, at least briefly, and then to consider three forms of communication: (1) scholars reaching out to the general reader; (2) journalism prepared by reporters for popular consumption; and (3) television programs aimed at a mass audience. The outcome, not surprisingly, will be an ascending order of impact—and hence of responsibility.

As we have already seen, teaching the U.S. Constitution in public schools has not been one of the great success stories in the history of American education. To judge by the contents of professional journals prepared for history, political science, and social studies teachers, challenges and opportunities have been invoked far more often than they have been met. The same old exhortations appeared decade after decade: we must incorporate constitutional issues into the teaching of social studies; improve the training of high school teachers in American constitutional history; disabuse students of the notion that "the Constitution is a document of uninteresting and involved subject matter"; utilize primary sources in order to achieve the *"thrill of discovery";* and ask students to rewrite those portions of the Constitution they believe to be in need of revision.[44]

The handling of constitutionalism in secondary education has not been entirely dismal, and some of the brighter moments in recent decades have occurred when educators turned to audio-visual types of materials: a film on John Marshall that *Encyclopaedia Britannica* made in 1950–51; a radio adaptation by the State Department in 1951 of Dorothy Canfield Fisher's book for young adults, *Our Independence and the Constitution;* a co-operative venture in 1954 between the Society of American Historians and Broadcast Music, Inc., to produce a program series covering American history and including educational supplements, available for wide distribution, on such topics as "Establishing a Government: The Articles of Confederation and the Constitution"; or an award-winning network TV movie, as well as an educational film made in the 1960s, *Gideon's Trumpet: The Poor Man and the Law,* both based upon Anthony Lewis's best-seller, *Gideon's Trumpet* (1964).[45]

The frequency with which scholars, even the most eloquent, have reached the general public can be counted on the fingers of two hands. In part this results from pure snobbery. In 1933, when Raymond Moley asked Thomas Reed Powell of Harvard to contribute an essay to *Today: An Independent National Weekly,* a new magazine, Powell responded in a single sentence: "I don't at the moment think of anything to say in the A. Simpleton style." Subsequently the problem also reflected a discipline becoming too obsessed with methodological innovation to be able to communicate effectively with nonspecialist readers. As Robert G. McCloskey complained in 1966: "I think that the current political science writing on 'jurimetrics' is about 90% useless. . . . I believe that a constitutional scholar may sometimes find it valuable to count things, but as far as I can see, simple arithmetic which any eighth grade student can handle is about as sophisticated a tool as is required."[46]

Which scholars, then, and what works have reached a broad audience? Charles Beard's "plea for constitutionalism" (i.e., constitutional understanding), entitled *The Republic,* went through five printings in six months (1943–44), and received rich praise from Hugo L. Black, Edward S. Corwin, and Thomas Reed Powell. Alpheus T. Mason's *Brandeis: A Free Man's Life* stayed on the best-seller list for five months and sold more than 50,000 copies following its publication in 1946. Early the next year Arthur M. Schlesinger, Jr., published a widely noticed assessment of the Supreme Court in which he condemned the lack of historical perspective afflicting laymen and journalists alike: "the current fall in prestige [of the Court] results from widespread popular ignorance of Court history. . . . Newspapers, condemning the present Court on the ground that it has overruled previous decisions and that it is convulsed by internal conflicts, earnestly believe this situation to represent a calamitous descent from Olympus." Schlesinger then showed that the Court had reversed it-self many times in the past, and that personal feuds among justices had equally venerable precedents.[47]

Although it may not be surprising that scholars should have written relatively little for a general audience, the fact remains that journalists have not had much more enthusiasm for constitutional topics. *The Brethren* comes to mind immediately, of course.[48] It sold well—a Book-of-the-Month Club Main Selection, more than 600,000 copies in hardcover, and millions in paperback—because it provided lots of gossip about a contro-versial group of men and conveyed the impression that it had penetrated a sanctum sanctorum. In some respects it had; but if one asks when a compa-rable book last appeared, the answer is 1936: *The Nine Old Men* by Drew Pearson and Robert S. Allen.

Otherwise there hasn't been a whole lot in the mass circulation jour-nals, and what does appear is usually prompted by volatile reactions to Court decisions or else anticipations of a controversial ruling, such as *Re-gents of the University of California* v. *Bakke* (1978). Two magazines with large circulation figures have tended to abuse the Court ever since the 1950s. David Lawrence seems to have added readers rather than losing them with his editorials for *U.S. News and World Report.* A representative example, entitled "Our Vanishing Constitution," insisted that provisions had been "torn to shreds by the autocratic action of a judicial oligarchy." By 1983 *Reader's Digest* appeared in forty-one editions around the world and enjoyed a circulation of 235 million copies printed per issue. Its essays have been less vituperative than Lawrence's, though rarely more positive about the Supreme Court.[49]

The number two magazine in terms of mass circulation, *TV Guide,* has run features related to the Constitution with some frequency. Under-standably, these essays of opinion pertain almost exclusively to one aspect of the First Amendment: whether television and radio should have the right to broadcast courtroom proceedings. Examples might include an edi-torial, "Is Speech on Television Really Free?"; or a dialogue between William F. Buckley, Jr., and Arthur M. Schlesinger, Jr., concerning "The Issue of Free Speech on Television"; and whether the First Amendment provides journalists with the right not to disclose their sources of informa-tion. These have been the dominant variations on a singular theme ever since the later 1950s.[50]

Essays that appear in *TV Guide* take issue with Supreme Court deci-sions on occasion, notably when the Court restricted the possibility of tele-vising criminal cases live (rather than filming re-enactments), or when the

Court decided that journalists did not have an absolute right to protect their informants.[51] The ubiquitous little magazine (available at the checkout counter of every grocery store) is just as likely, however, to voice concern about Congress. In 1971, for example, when CBS president Frank Stanton (claiming First Amendment privilege) refused to turn over to Congress the rejected film footage of "The Selling of the Pentagon," a controversial program, Stanton faced contempt of Congress charges. Those charges were eventually dropped; but *TV Guide* gave the episode maximum visibility.[52]

For the most part, television programs concerned with constitutional issues or with the Supreme Court have been less opinionated and more even-handed than editorials or features in the press. The reason is not because most television reporters and producers hold tepid opinions but because they have felt constrained by the FCC's Fairness Doctrine (which took effect in 1949) as well as its control over licensing. Throughout the 1960s and '70s broadcasters argued that, in terms of freedom of action and expression, its members were treated as "second class citizens." Articles in *TV Guide* and elsewhere pointed out that anyone can publish a newspaper, but only those with licenses are allowed to broadcast. Because the networks are sensitive to close scrutiny and the pressure of regulation, they have complained that their presentations are obliged to be blandly balanced or middle of the road, with more extreme opinions getting much less of a hearing. Consequently the proponents of television coverage complained that they did not enjoy the full freedom of expression assured by the First Amendment. One aspect of that situation began to change in 1968 when the Federal Circuit Court of Appeals in Chicago decided that TV stations were not obliged to provide comprehensive coverage for all points of view. (Television advocates noted that in densely populated areas like Chicago a greater diversity of broadcasts existed than newspapers.)[53]

Curiously enough, the double standard that is applied to TV journalism (particularly since 1969), along with the requirement that broadcasters "operate in the public interest," and the self-imposed caution that results from anxiety about viewer ratings help to account for the fact that television has served the public surprisingly well in terms of highlighting the Constitution in American culture. It might have done better, but it certainly could have done a whole lot worse.[54] The range of television coverage, moreover, has been reasonably varied, and may be considered in no fewer than four categories.

First, we must not ignore the genre known as courtroom dramas, such as "Accused," "Arrest and Trial," "The Defenders," and "They

Stand Accused." Despite melodramatic or nonsensical plots, many of these programs conveyed information and occasionally insights about the Fourth Amendment (security from unwarrantable search and seizure), the Fifth (the rights of accused persons in criminal proceedings), the Sixth (the right to a speedy trial), the Seventh (trial by jury in civil cases), and the Eighth (concerning excessive bail and unusual punishments). Some of these programs, such as "Famous Jury Trials" (1949–52) and "Justice" (1952–55), were developed from historical cases. NBC's "Justice" series, for example, was based upon official files of the Legal Aid Society.[55]

Second, there has been considerably more Constitution-oriented "crisis journalism" on the commercial networks than many of us are likely to recall. Immediately following most major Supreme Court decisions—such as the school prayer rulings or the right to counsel cases like *Gideon* v. *Wainwright* (1963)—thirty-minute or hour-long analyses were aired with remarkably high viewer interest.[56] In addition, important special programs have been prepared in response to the most controversial of these decisions. In 1963, for example, CBS Reports presented a three-part series entitled "Storm Over the Supreme Court." The second broadcast, on March 13, was devoted to "The School Prayer Case" (*Engel* v. *Vitale*) and included footage of Senator James O. Eastland, several congressmen, Bishop James A. Pike, many of the principals in the case (which began in Mineola, Long Island), commentary by such constitutional scholars as Paul Freund and Erwin Griswold of Harvard as well as Eugene V. Rostow of Yale, and schoolteachers shown with their classes.[57]

The third segment of that same series, which aired on June 19, examined "Bible Reading in the Public Schools" right after the landmark decisions of *Abington Township* v. *Schempp* and *Murray* v. *the Board of School Commissioners of Baltimore City* in which Bible reading and recitation of the Lord's Prayer in public schools were held unconstitutional. Once again Eric Sevareid, William Peters, and Fred Friendly teamed up to provide a thorough and dispassionate exploration of a sensitive dispute very much at the core of America's pluralistic value system. Chief Justice Warren's letter to Frank Stanton, written two years later to deny CBS's request to televise oral argument in the Supreme Court, referred to the three-part series, "Storm Over the Supreme Court," as excellent.[58]

The first installment of that trio was designed to provide historical background about the Constitution and the Court. The words of Justices Marshall, Field, Holmes, Brandeis, Jackson, Frankfurter, and Black were quoted extensively, along with the views of Thomas Jefferson, Franklin Roosevelt, Daniel Webster, and various senators, including James F.

Byrnes of South Carolina who served on the Court as well as in the Senate.[59]

This program was characteristic of a third category that has appeared on commercial television with greater frequency since the later 1960s: the in-depth documentary geared to problems and personalities of broad public interest (or else that ought to be). One of the earliest of this type, and one of the most stimulating, was prepared in 1955–56 by the staff of "Omnibus" (a popular television program with diverse presentations—dramatic, documentary, and musical) in collaboration with the historian Richard Hofstadter. Simply called "The Constitution," the three-part series was narrated with dignity, intimacy, and eloquence by Joseph N. Welch, the diminutive lawyer who had won a moral victory over Senator McCarthy in their dramatic, televised confrontation several years earlier. As Hofstadter explained in his introduction to the accompanying book version: "We aimed . . . to produce a script . . . that would enable us to give our audiences an account of as many of the high points in constitutional development as we could include in three programs."[60] With John C. Calhoun played by Walter Matthau, how could they go wrong? In any case, the "Omnibus" program enjoyed considerable impact and intensified the strong surge of interest in the Constitution that occurred in 1956.

Subsequent examples of the genre have not been as frequent as one might wish, but they have been high in quality and just about as significant in terms of success as we can hope to see. "Justice Black and the Bill of Rights" (first shown on December 3, 1968) and "Mr. Justice Douglas" (September 6, 1972) were broadcast by CBS News and broke fresh ground by beginning to legitimize communication between sitting justices and journalists for public edification. Eric Sevareid served as the correspondent and provided an admirable blend of seriousness, informality, and probing candor—candor directed not so much at the justices personally as at the constitutional system and American understanding of it.

More recently there has been a two-hour dramatization of the Scottsboro case (1931–35) on NBC television in 1976, an especially explosive episode because it involved race, class, sex, communism, and deeply felt mores in Alabama's Black Belt. The film resulted in a lawsuit by one of the two white women allegedly raped by the Scottsboro boys—a woman no one knew was still alive in 1976—and the attendant publicity made reruns of the program all the more magnetic. On December 2, 1979, the CBS weekly "60 Minutes" took advantage of recent interest piqued by *The Brethren* and devoted two thirds of a program to segments called "Equal Justice" and "The Brethren." Late in 1984 ABC News offered a close-up documentary called "The Supreme Court of the United States," and speculated whether the Court seemed to be shifting its concern from individual liberty to a more conservative emphasis upon majority and institutional rights. The program explored some serious issues but avoided any clear-cut answers or resolutions.[61]

The fourth type of programming—longer series prepared for public and educational television stations—reaches fewer people initially but may be equally influential in the long run because it is utilized subsequently in secondary schools, particularly senior high schools. A fine example of this sort dates back to 1956–57 when Professor Zechariah Chafee, Jr., developed a sequence of sixteen television lectures for WGBH-TV in Boston and the Lowell Institute Cooperative Broadcasting Council. Called "The Constitution and Human Rights," Chafee's topics included "You Must Have the Body in Court," "Freedom of Debate—In Congress under the Constitution," and "Freedom to Travel." Chafee concluded the sixteenth installment with this homily on the importance of historical perspective: "I have given them in the hope of helping men and women to remember how the human rights in our Constitution grew strong before they gained a place there. These things were not found under a gooseberry bush."[62]

A second example aired on PBS during the fall of 1978. Produced by Jane Hall, WQED-TV in Pittsburgh, and the Judicial Conference of the United States, this series received funding from a congressional grant and had Justice Byron R. White among the consultants. Entitled "Equal Justice Under Law," the programs examined major decisions made by the Court under John Marshall, 1801–35, a period when leading decisions had profound consequences for constitutional interpretation. The format of the programs is particularly notable. They were shown during the day in five installments and at night as two ninety-minute specials. That kind of flexibility maximizes public accessibility and potential use for educational purposes.[63]

One last example brings us to 1984: a thirteen-part program carried on Public Broadcasting called "The Constitution: That Delicate Balance," produced by Fred Friendly and Columbia University's Graduate School of Journalism in conjunction with WNET-TV in New York and WTTW in Chicago. The virtues of this series are many. It draws upon more than two hundred prominent politicians, jurists, journalists, and informed scholars as interactive participants. Retired Justice Potter Stewart supplied the kind of informative (though sometimes bland) commentary that traditionally has been considered off-limits to members of the Court. Each installment demonstrates the diversity of constitutional perspectives in the United States:

all in all, a thirteen-week course on the dynamics of conflict within consensus. As one reviewer concluded following the final segment: "Bless the public-television series for showing viewers that this is how our democracy works."[64]

Getting Americans interested in their Constitution has never been easy, and constitutional education has not been notably successful. When Eric Sevareid interviewed William O. Douglas for CBS in 1972, the aging justice observed, not once but twice, that "the greatness of this country is reflected in the Constitution [which] was designed to take government off the backs of people. Make it difficult for government to do anything to the individual. And the electronic age makes it easy." Douglas shared with Senator Ervin and many others an apprehension that abuses of civil liberties might occur more easily in an electronic age.[65] On the other hand, to judge by the success of programs like "That Delicate Balance" and the splendid conversations with Douglas and Black, the electronic age also offers a bright ray of hope for the future of constitutional education in the United States.

CHAPTER 14

It's What Holds Us All Together

SCANNING THE MOST NOTICEABLE ATTRIBUTES OF constitutionalism in contemporary America brings to mind the familiar French adage: the more things change, the more they remain the same. Indifference and ignorance persist; education continues to be problematic; and human interest stories are more likely to make news than serious but sinewy issues. Ceremonial aspects still weigh equally with substantive ones. Nevertheless, ideological imperatives remain very strong. Consequently they politicize the Constitution, and as a symptom of that keep the Supreme Court politicized too. Thus the well-established pattern of conflict within consensus endures, even though the consensus appears to be a bit precarious at times.

Why should the fundamental character of American constitutionalism change so little when most other aspects of national life have significantly altered? At first glance the problem is peculiarly puzzling. Our literacy rate is high, and the Constitution is taught in various ways at several levels during a young person's progress through the public school system. The role played by the media in providing "constitutional exposure" has improved markedly during recent decades. The constitutional system itself has been extraordinarily stable; and if overt veneration for the document as a governmental blueprint is no longer so common, respect certainly is. As liberal Congressman Maury Maverick wrote in 1939, when he prepared a book aimed at ordinary folks (he wanted to call it *The Grocery Man's Constitution*): "we need some changes in our constitutional practices, but *none in our Constitution*. We have in our written Constitution all the constitutional authority necessary for effective government. We need no amendments; our Constitution is all right."[1]

Maverick may have identified at least part of the explanation. He observed that affluence and privatism had developed so swiftly "that we have forgotten our constitutional heritage." Most Americans seemed content to leave that heritage in the hands of judges and lawyers.[2] Another part of the explanation can be found in the primary attitude that laypersons feel toward history and familiar institutions. Political scientists may like to remodel or revise institutions; and historians may have a fondness for rewriting the past. But the public is more likely to regard revisionism as confusing than as progress toward Truth.

It is difficult to adapt time-honored assumptions to changing realities. Consequently few constitutional issues ever get fully resolved. Most of them are forever being reopened in some mutant form. Scarcely a proposal, concern, or complaint is genuinely new. As we have seen, Roosevelt's "Court-packing" plan in 1937 was not unprecedented. Partly because most Americans believed that it was, however, a constitutional crisis ensued. Similarly, Chief Justice Burger and others have been complaining ever since 1971 that the Supreme Court is overburdened and that a National Court of Appeals needs to be created. Burger has prompted repeated discussions of how best to handle the Court's caseload, and has even provoked a thorough inquiry that indicates he may be incorrect about "the workload crisis." From the perspective of retired Chief Justice Warren, Burger's proposals looked like a fresh form of "Court-packing."[3]

To the historian, Burger's ongoing complaint stimulates a sense of déjà vu. In 1885, for example, the American edition of *Puck* ran a large cartoon with the caption "Our Overworked Supreme Court" (see figure 27); and in September 1887, at the time of the Centennial, Chief Justice Morrison R. Waite chose that occasion to publicize his dominant concern.

What is required is a reduction of the present appellate jurisdiction of the Supreme Court, and if this is insisted upon it will be easy to find very many classes of cases which need not necessarily be taken to that court for final determination, and which can be disposed of with much less expense and quite as satisfactorily by some proper inferior court having the necessary jurisdiction for that purpose, and having sufficient character and dignity to meet the requirements of litigants. Such a court will not be the Supreme Court, but it will be the highest court of the United States which can, under the Constitution, be afforded for the hearing and determination of such causes.[4]

The more things change, the more they indeed remain the same.

I

The reports from those people whose calling it is to take our constitutional pulse are not encouraging. In a 1983 interview, former Senator Sam J. Ervin bemoaned what he considered current assaults on the Constitution, and complained that "the American people aren't paying much attention to the Constitution anymore." In addition, former Secretary of State Dean Rusk observed in 1983 that representatives of foreign governments also found it difficult to understand our governmental system.[5] In 1984 the Center for Judicial Studies, based in Washington, D.C., Cumberland, Virginia, and Irving, Texas, published a thirty-seven-page report entitled *Democracy at Risk: The Rising Tide of Political Illiteracy and Ignorance of the Constitution* that provided ample documentation to support both laments.

Yet another study released in 1983 raised an interesting question. Although the answers do not lead to any clear-cut conclusion, the response of the mass public is depressing, as is the number of "undecided" people polled. The question was: Suppose the President and Congress have to violate a constitutional principle to pass an important law the people wanted. Would you support them in this action? Two possible replies were offered: either No, because protecting the Constitution is more important to the national welfare than any law could possibly be; or Yes, because the Constitution shouldn't be allowed to stand in the way of what the people need and want. The answers were distributed as follows (including a third option, Neither/Undecided).

	Mass Public (N=1993)	Community Leaders (N=1157)	Legal Elite (N=488)	Police Officials (N=224)
No	49%	67%	81%	59%
Yes	22%	14%	7%	21%
Neither/ Undecided	29%	19%	11%	21%

The supervisors of this study, based at the Survey Research Center of the University of California at Berkeley, also found that many Americans fail to understand that under the U.S. Constitution individuals do not lose their claims to such rights as due process or freedom of speech simply because they have committed crimes or violated social norms.[6]

A combination of apathy and ignorance emerges from the various contests promoted by patriotic organizations. The American Legion began to sponsor a national high school oratorical contest in 1938, "developed primarily to instill a keener knowledge and appreciation of the Constitution of the United States." The published speeches given by the finalists in 1957, for example, are uneven in quality, ranging from pedestrian and insipid to a few that are astute and inspired. Many of them assert that the document is "divine" and that the framers were "consecrated men." But 1957 was a comparatively good year.[7]

In 1951 the Hearst newspapers sponsored an oratorical tournament on "the national achievements of James Madison, father of the Constitution." The event went almost unnoticed. Three high school finalists and three college level finalists performed before vast rows of empty seats at the Lyric Theater in Baltimore. The local and national press provided a conspiracy of silence. Only the Baltimore *News-Post* bothered to cover this non-event. Can that be topped for indifference? Yes. Every year since 1957 the Daughters of the American Revolution have sponsored an American History Month Essay Contest. Once and only once in twenty-seven years has the Constitution been selected as the annual topic—in 1970–71. More popular themes have included "How My State Acquired Its Name," "Historic Waterways," and "A Famous American Born in February." The four victorious essays in 1971 are not merely mediocre; they contain errors as well.[8]

If we take into account the innovative conferences held during the 1980s and devoted to such themes as "Teaching About the Constitution in American Secondary Schools," we are likely to feel more sanguine about prospects for improvement. When we observe that agencies such as the Education Branch of the National Archives (active since 1970) prepared a new learning package called "The Constitution: Evolution of a Government," available for sale to teachers since the fall of 1985 (for $30), we are likely to feel even more sanguine.[9] Things are happening. Change is in the air. Yet recent history has also sowed seeds of skepticism. The decade prior to 1973 "marked the dramatic growth of teaching programs and materials dealing with Civil Rights and Liberties." Nevertheless, on the basis of surveys made in 1983–84 of high school seniors' perceptions of the Bill of Rights, authorities found their understanding of it to be "very, very inadequate. The most startling and depressing finding in our polls is that standard civics or government courses don't increase students' sense of the Bill of Rights. The courses are so formal that they don't affect attitudes much." The actual experience of recent years tends to dampen our hopes for the years ahead—despite some encouraging signs.[10]

What, then, *does* engage public interest in the Constitution? The question can be answered, somewhat arbitrarily perhaps, in terms of three categories: ceremonial and symbolic occasions; human interest stories that are people-oriented rather than issue-oriented; and ideological conflict.

As for symbolic occasions, there haven't been many of late, though that situation is certain to change during the years 1987–91. Constitution Day has for some while been a pale shadow of its halcyon period following World War I. It is still observed on September 17, the day the Convention adjourned, when it is observed at all. Not much is done about Constitution Day in the schools, though it lingers on as the occasion for a patriotic naturalization ceremony held annually in the rotunda of the National Archives in Washington, D.C. A distinguished judge, senator, or congressman invariably makes some remarks to the newly sworn group of citizens: Peter Rodino, chairman of the House Judiciary Committee in 1978, Senator Mark O. Hatfield in 1983, and Representative Frank Horton of New York the following year. It may be symptomatic that most Washingtonians now refer to this occasion as Citizenship Day, even though the attractive posters and programs continue to call it Constitution Day. It seems fair to say that Constitution Day isn't what it used to be.

As for human interest, the range of stories is broad but their content tends to be shallow.

- In 1978 fans of former Justice William O. Douglas paid tribute to him by contributing between $10 and $100 apiece to hear the Constitution read and explained at a Broadway theater. The readers and explicators included Lauren Bacall, Henry Fonda, Tammy Grimes, Moses Gunn, and Raul Julia. Helen Gahagan Douglas received the biggest ovation when she read the Fifth Amendment. It sounds scintillating; but why did the show "close" after a single performance?

- In 1981 two of the twenty known copies of the first and second printings of the Constitution sold for more than $500,000 to an unidentified Chicago buyer.

- In 1984 a group called America's Freedom Ride got organized to sponsor national and international bicycle trips that would (somehow) promote the 200th anniversary of the Constitution.

- In 1984 a feature story appeared concerning Johnny H. Killian, who works at the Congressional Research Service, a section of the Library of Congress, where he constantly updates an annotated edition of the Constitution. The photograph of Mr. Killian showed him at the National Archives, peering at the Constitution bathed in its saffron-colored preservative light. The feature's headline read: "Congress's Keeper of the Constitution."[11]

Ultimately, however, for better and for worse, it is ideological conflict that most meaningfully calls attention to the Constitution. We are then reminded that all Americans do not agree about the most appropriate division of authority: federalism tilting toward states' rights or federalism leaning toward national authority? We are then reminded that we still have broad and strict constructionists, followers of Hamilton and followers of Madison. And we are then reminded that we have had two complementary but divergent modes of constitutional interpretation: a tradition of conflict within consensus.[12]

II

The persistence of ideological conflict has kept the Constitution politicized at two levels. One is essentially scholarly; and the populace at large is unaware of it even though they may be affected by it indirectly. (Judges do read law journals as well as treatises concerning the theory and practice of constitutional law.) Conflict at this level, moreover, is currently shaped by several different sorts of concerns: some intriguing but primarily theoretical and academic, others more pragmatic, potentially or even actually applied, and deserving of public attention. The second level is the more visible, evokes intense partisanship, and has a spill-over effect: politicization of the Supreme Court as a governmental institution and of judicial review as a policy-making process. Although we must notice all sources of ideological conflict, the scholarly level is less pertinent to a study of constitutionalism in American culture generally. I will begin with it, but discuss it rather briefly.

One question that has agitated students for most of this century is examined with much more sophistication now than it was seventy-five years ago: How democratic is the Constitution? Ironically, when J. Allen Smith, Charles Beard, and Gustavus Myers answered that question in the negative, they did so in books and journals that were directed at and accessible to a general audience.[13] Their arguments, in fact, comprised a central part of the Progressive critique of American government, considered both historically and contemporaneously. Despite shallow research and (at times) simplistic reasoning, they helped to define the terms of public discourse in the age of Teddy Roosevelt and Woodrow Wilson.

The very same question continues to be bruited about during the 1980s, but no longer in such an accessible way because the uses of theory have become far more sophisticated, and in the process have levitated the debate to a level beyond the public's reach or curiosity. Scholars now discuss "democratic elitism," but are unable to agree whether it is good, bad, or merely inevitable if we hope to avert a crisis of leadership. Scholars now examine political rhetoric with great subtlety and discover that the constraints of an acceptable republican vocabulary caused people who had very different assumptions to sound much closer together than they actually were. Hence an illusion of consensus that made the reality of conflict all the more perplexing. Political parties in the young republic appropriated symbols and word-concepts from one another, thereby creating confusion at the time and considerable disagreement ever since. Modern scholars are also fond of seemingly paradoxical formulations, like "deliberative democracy," which enable them to argue that "the framers embraced an understanding of majority rule that was consistent with the need for certain kinds of restraints on majority desires."[14]

Once upon a time, when we asked, "How democratic is the Constitution?" students of American government answered yea or nay, very or not very. Today they answer, Yes *and* no; or, Yes but . . . ; or, Incompletely so because. . . . Reading a statement by the political scientist Robert A. Dahl, for example, gives us pause in a way that Charles Beard's iconoclasm did not. Readers responded to Beard from their viscera. Dahl, who is eminently readable, nevertheless requires a much more cerebral reaction. Let one example suffice: "To assume that this country has remained democratic because of its Constitution seems to me an obvious reversal of the relation; it is much more plausible to suppose that the Constitution has remained because our society is essentially democratic."[15] You have to chew on it for a while.

Perhaps the general public does not resonate to such matters because they seem too abstract or theoretical. But it is possible that the public has a simpler reason for ignoring imponderables: namely, an impressionistic feeling that however democratic or undemocratic the Constitution may have been at the outset, judicial interpretation, usage, and shifting social values have adapted it to the more egalitarian assumptions of our own time—more egalitarian by comparison with the 1780s. Slavery was constitutionally abolished. Women were constitutionally enfranchised. States were constitutionally prohibited from depriving any person of life, liberty, or property without due process of law. State legislatures were constitutionally told to reapportion their legislative districts so that one person's vote would be worth as much as another's. The Constitution has become, admittedly by fits and starts, more democratic; and that is enough to satisfy most folks who live outside the ivory tower.

Recognition of that reality tends to send some scholars and jurists scurrying in quest of other issues. For example, whether the foremost challenge to modern constitutionalism involves a reconciliation with new technology or a return to the old morality. Or, to take a different example, whether it is really possible to be guided by the framers' intentions. Federal Judge Robert Bork, formerly a professor of law at Yale, insists that "it is necessary to establish the proposition that the framers' intentions with respect to freedoms are the sole legitimate premise from which constitutional analysis may proceed." Professor Arthur Selwyn Miller, on the other hand, argues that "those who wrote the Document of 1787 deserve respect, and possibly even reverence, but they are not to be followed blindly, even when their intentions can be found—which is usually not possible." Bork's reverence for the framers is rooted in his strong sense of tradition. Miller's respect for the framers is modified by his strong sense of modernism. The differences between these two positions are indicative of an important polarization among contemporary scholars.[16]

Another kind of conflict in American constitutionalism bridges the chasm between academe and public affairs. The problem is addressed in different ways, depending upon which side of the chasm one happens to be on; but it is an issue nonetheless now being re-evaluated on both sides. A generation ago, as we saw in chapter 12, the Bill of Rights was "rediscovered" and became fully binding upon the states.[17] That process and the reorientation that it required in American thinking must be considered nothing less than a sea-change in U.S. constitutionalism. During the 1950s, '60s, and '70s, constitutionalism in the minds of many Americans came to be co-extensive with a rigorous application of the Bill of Rights.

For nearly a decade, however, the pendulum has been moving in the opposite direction. When Congressman Bob Eckhardt of Texas and Professor Charles L. Black of the Yale Law School published their dialogue on the American Constitution, they made it clear from the outset where their locus of concern would lie: "Most Americans, when they think of 'constitutional law,' think of the very important protections of the Bill of Rights, and of similar portions of the Constitution—those portions protecting citizens' rights by limiting governmental action. What we have talked about, instead, are the matters which have lately come to be of so much importance and prominence, involving the actually *constitutive* law of the government—the way the government is set up and its powers distributed, without regard to the question of general constitutional limitations on the exercise of power."[18]

This growing desire to redirect attention back to the basic institutions of government has been prompted by diverse motives: partially by a compensatory impulse resulting from the premise that public interest had swung preponderantly toward civil rights; partially by a belief that the core of American liberty is not to be found primarily in the Bill of Rights; and partially from a conviction, as one neoconservative critic of the "rights industry" put it, "that many civil libertarians had become unhinged," i.e., insisted upon too much on the basis of too little constitutional legitimacy.[19]

Although interest (however small in scale) has gradually been swinging back toward the Constitution itself, a parallel concern with some contradictory implications has also been developing. In 1974, the veteran journalist Gerald W. Johnson believed that we had reached a major turning point, possibly even the end of a constitutional era. "The Constitution has been badly battered . . . by the pounding of time and events," he declared, and consequently "some repair work is imperative to prevent collapse of the whole structure." Overstated though it may seem, Johnson's prognosis was actually milder than many. Between 1789 and 1974 there had been no fewer than 356 requests from the states that a new constitutional convention be held—though most of these requests centered upon some specific issue.[20]

Since 1974 the calls have been general as well as particular, and they have occurred with increasing frequency. Although requests come from both ends of the political spectrum, a difference is apparent. Conservatives are more likely to have in mind one or two matters which no branch of government seems disposed to remedy, such as the abolition of abortion or the necessity of a balanced federal budget.[21] Moderates and liberals, on the other hand, are less likely to be single issue-oriented and more inclined to be concerned about the system's functional viability as a whole. That is the broad agenda, for example, of the Committee on the Constitutional System, organized early in the 1980s by C. Douglas Dillon and Lloyd N. Cutler. This group of several hundred citizens, based in Washington, meets regularly for serious study and discussion. When members avail themselves of some public occasion as a "bully pulpit," they are likely to raise subtle questions about the need for constitutional changes that are procedural or structural in nature.[22]

Advocates of a balanced federal budget amendment have been the most determined proponents of constitutional change—and in many respects the most visible—during the 1980s. By 1984 no fewer than thirty-two state legislatures had asked Congress to call a convention that would prepare a balanced-budget amendment. Only two additional requests are needed to force Congress to act. Representative Peter W. Rodino, Jr., chairman of the House Judiciary Committee, has used various political ploys in an effort to stall the movement. How much longer he can resist remains to be seen. If and when two more states require that a convention be called, moreover, it is unclear whether Congress has the authority to regulate a constitutional convention. The American Bar Association says yes; but others say no. If and when thirty-four states demand a convention, therefore, not one but two constitutional issues are likely to agitate the nation: first, whether or not a balanced budget is a policy question better handled by regular legislation; and second, who will control the convention?[23]

Most of us do not realize that such a convention has never been held in all of American history. Because the Constitution is not very explicit about this procedure, no one really knows how it might work. How would the delegates be chosen? Could the federal courts review the convention's methods and proposals? And above all, should such a convention be confined to the single issue of a balanced budget, or could it take advantage of the occasion to prepare amendments on other issues, such as abortion, school prayer, and the death penalty? No one seems to know. It is not inconceivable that the Constitution's Bicentennial will be observed amidst the largest governmental ruckus the nation has seen since 1860–61.

III

Searching for a middle ground in American constitutionalism, former Secretary of State Dean Rusk observed in 1983 that some people "seem to think that the Constitution is what the Supreme Court says it is. That is only partially true. . . . The Court itself understands that there are constitutional questions which are not for it to resolve. It has developed, for example, doctrines with respect to standing and political questions to provide for the abstention of the Court from certain issues."[24] Rusk may be absolutely right; but unfortunately most Americans are unaware of the doctrines to which he referred, and they continue to regard the Court as a highly political institution. Needless to say, the very existence of that perception has the effect of politicizing the Supreme Court even more. Since issues only come before the High Court because of disagreement, it scarcely should surprise us that some Court decisions cause or perpetuate additional controversy.

In 1946 a Gallup Poll presented 3,000 Americans with this problem: "Some people say that the Supreme Court decides many questions largely on the basis of politics. Do you agree or disagree with this?" Forty-three percent agreed, 36 percent did not, and 21 percent had no opinion.[25] There is little reason to believe that public opinion has altered appreciably on that point. If anything, the percentage of those who agree has risen since the mid-1970s. Conservatives were disposed to agree so long as the Burger Court seemed to perpetuate the liberal tendencies of the Warren Court: by sustaining a woman's right to have an abortion, for example, or by banning tax exemptions for educational institutions that practiced racial discrimination.[26] Liberals have been more inclined to agree since the 1983–84 term, when the Court began to shift away from the "wall of separation" tradition in church–state relations and to modify the Miranda-rights rulings for those who are arrested and accused of crimes.[27]

Despite the Court's apparent shift toward more conservative positions during the mid-1980s, particularly on some highly controversial issues, many outspoken conservatives continued to insist that the non-elected judiciary had arrogated to itself too much of a policy-making role, and that it persisted unwisely in making activist decisions simply because elected legislators either could not or would not do so. New life has been breathed into that ongoing debate—nearly a century old now—as to whether the Supreme Court is our least democratic branch of government, and if so, whether the practice of judicial review is fundamentally antidemocratic in character.[28]

By the early 1980s a dedicated band of conservatives, led by Senators Jesse Helms and Orrin Hatch along with Congressmen Philip Crane and John Ashbrook, had begun a campaign to remove or reduce the Court's constitutional authority over certain volatile subjects: prayer in the schools, abortion, school busing, a military draft for males only, and state court rulings. In 1981 alone, twenty-two bills were introduced (many of them repetitive) that would facilitate constitutional change with no more than a majority vote in each house plus the President's signature. Such bills, called "Court-strippers," would effectively reduce the Supreme Court's jurisdiction and give Congress and state courts predominant power to determine how the Constitution should be applied to critical problems. The scheme is not without historical precedents (especially during the 1860s and 1930s); but if the current campaign succeeded, it would not merely eliminate the High Court's jurisdiction over whole classes of cases, but also prevent the Court from enforcing rulings that had already been made in those areas.[29] At stake in all of this is nothing less than a campaign against the system of checks and balances intended by the founders.

The advocates of jurisdiction stripping validate their claims on the basis of Article Three, Section II of the Constitution, which makes the Supreme Court's jurisdiction subject to "such exceptions . . . as the Congress shall make." They contend that the framers selected that language because they envisioned situations where federal courts might "usurp" power or misinterpret the Constitution. Most jurists and constitutional scholars, however, including many conservatives, believe that the provision was included to provide for lesser "housekeeping" or administrative purposes, and they deny that it gives Congress power to prevent the Court from rendering constitutional interpretations on any issue. Former Solicitor General Robert Bork, now a federal judge, feels that the exceptions clause would have been an "odd way for the framers to have provided for congressional revision of court decisions" because it would "create chaos." And in 1982 an angry Barry Goldwater, speaking at a hearing of the Senate Judiciary Committee, argued that Court-stripping "is not a conservative concept. I've spent my whole life railing against those who use any excuse to get around the law or the Constitution." Six months later he warned once again: "I see no limit to the practice. There is no clear and coherent standard to define why we shall control the Court in one area but not another."[30]

Court-strippers also contend that because Congress has the right to create or refuse to create federal courts, it may deprive them of particular areas of jurisdiction. Some extremists even insist that there cannot be proper federal jurisdiction over various categories of issues without an explicit legislative grant, even in the U.S. Supreme Court.

Although conservatives are divided on the best approach to this matter, its ultimate resolution remains unclear: because conservatives and many moderates would prefer and are generally agreed upon the need for greater judicial self-restraint; because Supreme Court justices who share that view, such as William Rehnquist, are becoming more influential on the Court; and because President Reagan consistently appoints to key administrative posts persons ambivalent about Court-stripping. His first Attorney General, William French Smith, frequently made speeches in which he charged the courts with improperly expanding their interpretation of constitutional rights and substituting "judicial judgment for legislative judgment." Early in 1982 Smith warned the American Bar Association that the time had come for judges to terminate the practice of "political policy-making." A year later, when Margaret M. Heckler testified at hearings on her nomination to be Secretary of Health and Human Services, she implied that she might be sympathetic to Court-stripping in order to deprive the Supreme Court of control over such issues as abortion.[31]

Successive presidents of the American Bar Association have spoken out in opposition to Court-stripping, and have insisted that it is imprudent regardless of one's ideological position on the issues that provoked the proposal. David R. Brink warned in 1982 that arch-conservatives "threaten the Constitution as the supreme law of this land. And if we lose that, we lose our system of government." Brink's successor, Morris Harrell, asserted that Court-stripping posed "a possible constitutional crisis that could prove the most serious since the Civil War."[32]

Judicial review has come under attack before. Both the process and the Court have survived intact though not exactly unscathed. The great constitutional issues of the 1980s—calling a new convention and circumscribing the Supreme Court—present a triple threat to the stability of American government. First, because they are largely unprecedented: even the experts cannot predict what will happen if the conservatives succeed. Second, because the public at large has so little notion of what is afoot. And third, because the respectability that these proposals have achieved tends to undermine the legitimacy of traditional constitutionalism in American life. When outrageous proposals receive serious consideration, still others are likely to be spawned.

No matter where one stands on specific issues, it is difficult to deny that the Supreme Court as an institution has become perilously politicized. Not for the first time, and doubtless not for the last. But this time is *our* time, and there are significant variations from earlier conflicts. Quite a gap exists between current realities and the ideal expressed by Chief Justice Hughes in 1940: "By the method of selection, the tenure of office, the removal from the bias of political ambition, the people have sought to obtain as impartial a body as is humanly possible and to safeguard their basic interests from impairment by the partiality and the passions of politics."[33]

IV

Although many Americans take pride in the fundamental stability and longevity of their Constitution, too few realize how unusual our experience with constitutionalism has been. Of the 160 national constitutions existing in 1983, 101 had been established since 1970. In 1983 Salvador adopted its thirty-sixth constitution since 1824. That may be excessive rather than the norm; but neither has the American experience been typical. It has, however, been profoundly influential through structural imitation and borrowing. That is not and has not necessarily been a good thing. At an international conference on constitution writing held at Washington, D.C., in 1983, Professor Albert P. Blaustein (co-editor of the seventeen-volume series *Constitutions of the Countries of the World*) expressed a view now widely shared: "All constitutions have to be autochthonous. That's a key word meaning 'arise from the self.' It must spring from the soil. It must be *the* constitution to represent the needs of these people. We cannot put constitutions together like prefabricated henhouses."[34]

Borrowing per se is neither good nor bad, of course. It all depends upon what is borrowed, how it is utilized, and the culture within which it is expected to function. Latin American nations borrowed extensively from the U.S. Constitution throughout the nineteenth century (especially the concept of federalism), yet they achieved neither political stability nor what we would consider a suitable respect for constitutionalism in the sense of higher law. A case could be made that Latin American constitutions have more nearly resembled U.S. state constitutions: rewritten or replaced from time to time as needed, and incorporating a fair amount of what we would regard as ordinary legislation—hence inappropriate to a national constitution. On the other hand, the influence of the Mexican constitution of 1917 has been quite positive. Its principles and provisions have been borrowed, in varying degrees, by almost every Latin American country. In a very real sense, constitution-making in the southern hemisphere came of age in 1917. The process of maturation owed much to the Mexican model.[35]

Canada did not fully come of age until 1982 when Queen Elizabeth II visited Ottawa, proclaimed the Constitution Act (enhanced by the addition of a comprehensive bill of rights), and formally transferred complete constitutional power from Great Britain to Canada. Although Canada really achieved independence between 1931 and 1949 (when appeals of judicial matters to the Privy Council in London were abolished), the power to make constitutional amendments remained in London because the provinces and the federal government simply could not agree upon a mutually acceptable procedure. The provinces were exceedingly sensitive concerning matters of local prerogative. Canada now has sole power to amend its own constitution.[36]

Needless to say, Quebec was and remains the most problematic province where local autonomy is concerned. Although Quebec officially boycotted the festivities in 1982 (reminiscent of Rhode Island's stubborn recalcitrance in 1787–89), public opinion polls indicated that at least half the population of French-speaking Quebec opposed the boycott. The province remains divided, and the future of Canadian constitutionalism is clouded to that degree. In 1985, for example, the Parti Québécois, which has governed the province since 1976, offered to ratify the 1982 constitution on condition that Quebec retain the right to reject subsequent constitutional changes without forfeiting any financial benefits from the national government. There has been no resolution of the issue.[37]

The problem of Quebec brings to mind the situation of South Carolina in antebellum America. Just as that dispute had its ultimate resolution, Quebec's will too. It will be more difficult, however, because the language and culture of Quebec differ from Canada's to a much greater degree than South Carolina's did from the other states, and because Quebec received a unique right of consent in 1759 when Britain captured it from France. Despite some similarities, most notably federalism, Canadian constitutionalism has had rhythms all its own.

In 1983 South Africa's white Parliament prepared a new constitution that gave nonwhites (or "coloreds") but not blacks limited participation in the national government for the first time. Presented by Prime Minister P. W. Botha as a major reform, it was in fact quite limited—both in the numbers of people added to the polity and in terms of eligibility to participate in the constitutional referendum. Only whites could vote. Nor would coloreds do so in the future, at least not in the same elections as whites. Coloreds can now vote for separate parliamentary seats in a tricameral structure. They still do not enjoy all the rights of citizenship that whites possess; and the ruling Afrikaner party retains a lock on political power by means of a provision that strikes Americans as peculiar indeed. A system of weighted votes in the racially segregated houses of Parliament ensures Afrikaner control of the presidency with the support of as little as 30 percent of the members of Parliament—so long as white Afrikaners maintain a majority in the white chamber.[38]

Although this entire set-up may look like a constitutional sham in American eyes, and justifiably so, it did not come about without intense conflict among the 2.8 million white voters. The Nationalists, who have long been in power, concocted the scheme as a means of co-opting the coloreds and perpetuating white control. The relatively liberal Progressive Federal Party, however, which is the official opposition, contended that the new constitution would only hasten racial confrontation by excluding blacks alone from any part in the political system. The Conservative Party, which split away from the Nationalists in 1982, opposed the new constitution on grounds that "mixed government" would lead eventually to black rule.[39] Thus far the new constitution has not diluted Afrikaner power in any way. The "reforms" are primarily cosmetic—quite literally tokenism. Some South Africans might even be disposed to say: The more things change, the more they remain the same.

China's recent experience highlights with equal drama the distinctiveness of American constitutionalism. In April 1982 a Constitutional Revision Committee unanimously approved a new constitution to replace the 1978 version. Early in December delegates to a National People's Congress approved the text by a vote of 3,037 in favor, three abstentions, and none opposed. The new constitution has 138 articles, more than double the 60 in 1978. Although it abolishes the right to strike which Mao introduced in 1975, it extends the list of civil rights to which Chinese are entitled, guaranteeing them equality before the law, protection from arbitrary arrest, and freedom of speech, assembly, association, and worship. It also *requires* married couples to practice birth control. On the "constitutive" side, it restores the position of state chairman, or president, which Mao abolished after purging the last incumbent; and it hastens the decline of Mao's proudest legacy, the people's commune, by eliminating its political responsibilities. All in all, the new Chinese constitution shortens the length of Mao's political shadow and repudiates practices that became common during the Cultural Revolution. (Hence the prohibition against illegal searches of the homes of citizens, and protection for the privacy of correspondence.)[40] Like all constitutions prepared to stabilize and popularize a particular regime, this one is not likely to outlast that regime for very long.

V

How can these diverse examples help us to understand better our own experience with constitutionalism? Thomas Babington Macaulay, the great Whig historian, liked to contrast the sophistication of constitutional ideas "in a refined and speculative age" with their inevitable crudeness in "rude [primitive] societies." He developed that comparison not to condemn inferior constitutions in his own time, but rather to explain away the inadequacies of England's constitution in ancient times. More meaningful, therefore, is Edmund Burke's explanation of the way that a country's constitution "is made by the peculiar circumstances, occasions, tempers, dispositions, and moral, civil and social habitudes of the people, which disclose themselves only in a long space of time."[41]

Although Burke's emphasis upon an evolving constitution might not seem to suit the American experience especially well, we should recall Maury Maverick's insistence that the Constitution of 1787 "is not the sole constitution of our American liberties. It is not in itself the Living Constitution, but only a part of it."[42] Burke's insistence upon the determinative force of national custom wending its way through time is indeed useful. In fact, his concern for evolution is apropos even if we concentrate upon the U.S. Constitution itself rather than American constitutionalism generally. No one would deny that the former has changed over time. It is the elusive set of attitudes comprising constitutionalism that has been both more resilient yet less malleable, even in times of crisis.

Nevertheless, Macaulay can offer us a lesson every bit as valuable as Burke's memorable definition. When the Reform Bill caused a constitutional crisis in 1831–32, Macaulay (who doted upon historical continuity as an ideal) made a direct appeal to the House of Commons. The progress of society had outgrown the constitution. Therefore it was endangered and ought to be altered sufficiently to bring it back into harmony with the values and circumstances of civic life. Although we tend to think of British constitutionalism as inherently conservative, surely one of its greatest strengths has been flexibility. Flexibility not merely as an institutional fact (it can be changed when necessary), but as an attitude (it *should* be changed when a strong majority feels compelled, morally or administratively, to do so).

In many historical contexts the advocates of constitutionalism have been looked upon as conservatives: people who supported constitutional change in order to reduce the pace of more radical (or even revolutionary) alterations. That formula does not apply very well to the United States, where it has been possible, in fact commonplace, to be both an ardent reformer and a constitutionalist—indeed, to use constitutionalism as a lever of social change. Those members of Congress who drafted the Fourteenth Amendment, or men like Brandeis, Black, and Warren are simply a few of the more obvious examples that spring to mind.[43]

It is instructive to recall that the founders did not expect their instrument of government to achieve utopia: "merely" national cohesion, political stability, economic growth, and individual liberty. Despite abundant setbacks and imperfections, much of that agenda has been fulfilled for a great many Americans. During the past generation social justice got explicitly added to the agenda as a high priority, and the American Constitution, interpreted by the Supreme Court, was adapted accordingly. For a society to progress toward social justice within a constitutional framework, even by trial and error, is a considerable undertaking. To do so in good faith, more often than not, is equally commendable. If from time to time we require the assistance of gadflies, what flourishing political culture does not? Senator Lowell P. Weicker of Connecticut, for example, has played that role rather well on occasion. As he thundered in 1981, during debate over a legislative amendment to endorse organized prayer in public schools: "To my amazement, any time the word constitutionalism comes up it's looked upon as a threat. A threat! It shouldn't be; it's what holds us all together."[44]

That has been true more often than not. Perhaps those who feel threatened by constitutionalism do not fully understand it. People frequently feel threatened by the unfamiliar. Perhaps it has not been fully understood because it has not been adequately explained. Perhaps it has perplexed us because aspects of its meaning have changed over time. Back in 1786 Benjamin Rush believed it "possible to convert men into republican machines. This must be done if we expect them to perform their parts properly in the great machine of the government of the state."[45] His contemporaries not only took Rush at his word, but regarded the conversion of men into republican machines as a national imperative.

More than a century later, Woodrow Wilson presented a piece of wisdom that tacked the other way. Call it constitutional revisionism if you like. He declared that if the real government of the United States "had, in fact, been a machine governed by mechanically automatic balances, it would have had no history; but it was not, and its history has been rich with the influences and personalities of the men who have conducted it and made it a living reality." Walter Lippmann chose to quote that sentence in 1913 when he wrote *A Preface to Politics*. But he promptly added that "only by violating the very spirit of the constitution have we been able to preserve the letter of it." What Lippmann had in mind was the role played by that palpable reality the Progressives called "invisible government": political parties, interest groups, trade unions, and so on.[46]

Lippmann's remark was not meant to be as cynical as it might sound. It reflects the Progressive desire to be realistic and tough-minded. It also reflects the fact that Americans have been profoundly ambivalent in their feelings about government.[47] Then, too, it reflects the discovery by three overlapping generations of Americans—represented by James Russell Lowell, Wilson, and Lippmann—that the U.S. Constitution is not, and was not meant to be, a machine that would go of itself.

Above all, Lippmann wanted to build upon his excerpt from Wilson and establish the point that there has been more to the story of constitutionalism in American culture than the history of the Constitution itself. The latter is a cherished charter of institutions and a declaration of protections. The former, constitutionalism, embodies a set of values, a range of options, and a means of resolving conflicts within a framework of consensus. It has supplied stability and continuity to a degree the framers could barely have imagined.

However complex the history of constitutional development has been in the United States, and however ambiguous its legacy may seem, it is arguable that our tradition of constitutionalism has been remarkably successful in safeguarding the Constitution itself. Although it cannot be denied that many of the most essential liberties guaranteed by the Constitution have been perversely violated or ignored, the "constitutive" document has held up remarkably well and has thereby provided stability for the majority as well as shelter for aggrieved groups and individuals.

The phenomenon that we have described as constitutionalism, in all of its varied manifestations, has buffered the Constitution from our most erratic impulses. It is not tautological to say that the Constitution is scarcely more secure than our underlying tradition of constitutionalism.

The latter remains our best bulwark against those "true believers" who would willingly subvert the Constitution in order to achieve partisan objectives. For constitutionalism to remain viable after two centuries of swift change will require a high degree of political concern as well as critical choices among national options in the years ahead. The process is likely to create a new crucible for American values—an exhilarating prospect.

APPENDIXES
ABBREVIATIONS
NOTES
INDEX

A Note on the Sources

THE ENDNOTES TO THIS BOOK PROVIDE manifold leads to printed sources, both primary and secondary. Citations to unpublished manuscript collections are as complete as their organizational condition will permit. In the paragraphs that follow I comment briefly upon some significant collections that have not previously been used by historians, or are peculiarly difficult to penetrate and have been especially vital in the preparation of this study.

The Historical Society of Pennsylvania (HSP), in Philadelphia, owns the papers of the Constitutional Centennial Commission, 1886–87. Some 2,200 items are contained in nine boxes and a register. These documents do not seem to have been sorted or examined since they were accessioned nearly a century ago. Pertinent material will also be found in the papers of Hampton L. Carson; Colonel A. Loudon Snowden (one of the most active marshals in 1887); and Albert M. Greenfield, who served as chairman of the Pennsylvania Constitution Commemoration Committee in 1937–39. Linda Stanley and Peter J. Parker were particularly helpful and hospitable at the HSP during June 1983.

The National Archives in Washington, D.C., contains extraordinary treasures, but they are not easy to locate. The Legislative and Diplomatic Branch (located on stack level 5 East) has in Record Group 148 the papers of the U.S. Constitution Sesquicentennial Commission, 1935–39, contained in fifteen boxes. Record Group 200 includes an invaluable box of papers generated by David M. Matteson in his role as historian to the Commission and factotum to Sol Bloom, its chairman. The staff member to whom I am indebted for co-operation in using these and related materials is Edward Schamel.

The Judicial, Fiscal, and Social Branch, Civil Archives Division (located on stack level 5 West), has in Record Group 267 a delightful collection of fourteen scrapbooks pertaining to Supreme Court history ca. 1880–1935. The scrapbooks were maintained by the Clerk's Office of the Court, and contain all sorts of fugitive newspaper clippings, primarily dealing with human interest stories (such as the appointments and deaths of justices) rather than issues of constitutional substance.

Unfortunately, many of the clippings are not precisely dated; and for some, the source is not even identified.

The most wonderful treasures in this branch of the National Archives, however—barely used hitherto—are the papers of the Immigration and Naturalization Service in Record Group 85. These include the Americanization and Citizenship Files, which contain citizenship training textbooks, teachers' manuals, educational programs organized by various states, correspondence between regional offices of the Naturalization Service and the Washington Bureau, and countless lists of questions about the Constitution prepared by local examiners for testing applicants. There are more than one hundred boxes, and the material has never been organized or catalogued in any systematic way. The staff member whose guidance in this division was indispensable is Cynthia G. Fox. I am deeply grateful for her swift and imaginative assistance.

The holdings of the Library of Congress Manuscript Division (James Madison Building) are superb, but have been unevenly exploited. The papers of Felix Frankfurter, Harlan Fiske Stone, Willis Van Devanter, Albert J. Beveridge, and William E. Borah, for example, have been used extensively though rather selectively. By contrast, the papers of Cass Gilbert, Charles Warren, John C. Fitzpatrick, and Irving Brant have been little used and comprise a rich lode of source material for this inquiry.

The Harvard Law School Library in Langdell Hall has an unusual number of fine collections, all of them extremely well organized. Mrs. Erika Chadbourn, recently retired as Curator of Manuscripts and Archives, was a thoughtful and intelligent guide to the papers of James B. Thayer, Thomas Reed Powell, Zechariah Chafee, Jr., Henry M. Hart, and Mark DeWolfe Howe, Jr. The Seeley G. Mudd Manuscript Library at Princeton University has three sets of papers that I found notably germane: those of James M. Beck, Edward S. Corwin, and the Fund for the Republic.

The Roper Center's Office of Archival Development at the University of Connecticut in Storrs has a computer-accessible archive of thirty-five polling organizations that have been active since the later 1930s. By punching in such key words as "Constitution," "Bill of Rights," "Supreme Court," etc., it is possible to obtain lists of pertinent polls in each category. The researcher can then request the tabulated results of particular polls that appear most relevant to the inquiry being pursued. The number and variety of polls to be obtained in this way vastly exceed what the researcher will find in *The Gallup Poll: Public Opinion, 1935–1971* (New York, 1972), 3 volumes. The unpublished polls at the Roper Center have been largely neglected by historians, and particularly by constitutional historians.

APPENDIX B

A Supplementary Note on Iconography

ALTHOUGH THE HALFTONE ILLUSTRATIONS IN this book are representative of the Constitution in American iconography and decorative arts, some others deserve mention.

There are several full-length portraits of George Washington (by Gilbert Stuart at the White House and by Jane Stuart at the Corcoran Gallery of Art) in which he is shown standing next to a large table on which there are official documents. Because Washington is wearing his "executive suit," and other presidential trappings are present in these "Lansdowne" portraits, there can be little doubt that the most prominent document on the table is meant to be the U.S. Constitution.

For a likeness of Madison in 1833 when he formulated his ultimate views on the Constitution, see the sensitive portrait by Asher B. Durand at the New-York Historical Society. Durand visited Madison at Montpelier in 1833.

Pertinent paintings will be found in several of the state capitol buildings. A mural by Albert Herter entitled *The Signing of the Constitution* (ca. 1910) is in the Supreme Court Room of the Wisconsin State Capitol in Madison. Thomas Jefferson (who was in Paris at the time) stands on George Washington's left. A mural by Violet Oakley entitled *The Constitutional Convention—Philadelphia in 1787—The Creation of a Strong and True Union* (1917) is located in the Senate Chamber of the Pennsylvania State Capitol in Harrisburg (see figure 16).

The large mural by Barry Faulkner of *The Constitution* (1935–36) is permanently displayed in the rotunda of the National Archives. *The Signing of the Constitution* (1939–40), by Howard Chandler Christy, is located in the House Wing of the U.S. Capitol in Washington, D.C.

An unusually wide mural by Gerald Foster, *Ratifying the Federal Constitution at Poughkeepsie, July 26, 1788* (1938), was commissioned for the sesquicentennial of New York's ratification and will be found on the balcony of the main post office in Poughkeepsie, New York. At the center Alexander Hamilton, a prominent Federalist, shakes hands with Governor George Clinton, a leader of the Anti-Federalists in New York.

Although political cartoons about the Constitution per se have not been common, many have appeared concerning the Supreme Court. For examples involving the Court *and* the Constitution during the New Deal controversy, see the fine ones by Harold M. Talburt in the Washington *Daily News,* June 3, 1935, and by James Berryman in the Washington *Evening Star,* July 20, 1935. Herblock has been responsible for some gems. For a particularly choice example, see "We Were Told They Were 'Strict Constructionists,' " in the *Washington Post,* April 7, 1976.

proficiency, with some subjects opting for one noun and others for the other.

Discussion

In considering these results, one notes an interesting developmental progression in terms of the effects of the animacy hierarchy on the interpretation of L2 sentences. In particular, given the results of the "tell" sentences, where there is no conflict of information, standard English interpretation prevails. On the other hand, where there is conflict, semantic information (as determined by the hierarchical relationships of the nouns) and syntactic information have an equal effect at earlier stages of proficiency, with syntax becoming dominant only at the later stages.

If we consider as an example the relationship of inanimate/human as opposed to human/inanimate sequences of nouns, the pattern of dominance becomes clear. In the first case, represented in a sentence such as (9)

9. The table told the girl to leave.

in which subjects are asked to determine the subject of "leave," it is predicted, on the basis of the animacy hierarchy, that "girl" will be selected as the subject. This prediction is further bolstered by syntactic facts of English. Convergence is reflected in the L2 responses; there is an overwhelming preference at all proficiency levels for the selection of the human noun. However, in a sentence such as (10)

10. The girl told the table to leave.

there is a conflict between semantics on the one hand (on the basis of which it is predicted that "the girl" will be selected) and syntax on the other (on the basis of which it is predicted that "the table" will be selected). In looking at the results, we see that at the early stages of L2 development, there is a slight preference for the selection of the human noun, whereas by Level IV learners begin to opt for the inanimate noun, and finally by Level V the inanimate noun is the overwhelming choice. In Levels II, III, and IV there is an obvious conflict: At Levels II and III semantics is slightly preferred, and at Level IV syntax is slightly preferred, although no single choice clearly dominates. Only the subjects at the most proficient level in this study were able to separate out the dominant role of syntax in English, suggesting that an important part of learning the syntax of a language involves learning the relative importance and strength of syntactic constraints.

The results of the "promise" sentences are more complex than those of the "tell" sentences. In general, syntax appears to dominate at earlier stages of proficiency in the "promise" as opposed to the "tell" sentences.

This may be due to the fact that "promise" is unlike the majority of verbs, thus making it more salient (see Gass 1988) , allowing learners to access and sort out the relevant semantic and syntactic information. If one looks more closely at the data, further complexities emerge. As with the "tell" sentences, where there is equal animacy status of the NPs, syntax dominates. Where there is convergence between syntax and animacy expectations, syntax was found to dominate, but to a lesser degree than with the "tell" sentences. This may be due to the fact that even though there is convergence, there is also conflict with other patterns in the language.

Experiment 2

Background

This study investigates sentence comprehension by speakers of English learning Italian and speakers of Italian learning English. Both Italian and English are SVO languages that overtly mark subject and verb agreement, although the verbal morphology in Italian is richer than it is in English. Furthermore, word order is more flexible in Italian than it is in English and is not a major determining factor in interpretation. In Italian, it appears that pragmatic factors in combination with semantics play a large role in assigning surface structures to utterances. In English, on the other hand, word order overrides other possible factors and is used as the main criterion for surface structure assignment. These differences were illustrated earlier in Sentences 3–7.

Subjects

This study comprised 121 subjects: 72 native speakers of English and 49 native speakers of Italian of varying degrees of second language proficiency. Of the 72 native English-speaking subjects, 41 were studying Italian in a foreign language environment and 31 in a second language environment; within the native Italian group, there was a similar division – 31 were studying English in a foreign language situation and 18 in a second language environment.[4]

Method

Each subject was presented with 27 sentences (in both a written and an oral version) and were asked what the subject of the sentence was (see

4 The results based on learning environment are discussed in Gass (1987).

TABLE 8.7. PERCENTAGE OF FIRST NOUNS SELECTED AS SUBJECT ACCORDING
TO NATIVE LANGUAGE

	NSs of English	NSs of Italian
x̄	61.90	64.77
sd	21.51	14.58

TABLE 8.8. PERCENTAGE OF FIRST NOUNS SELECTED AS SUBJECT AS A
FUNCTION OF WORD ORDER AND NATIVE LANGUAGE

	NSs of English	NSs of Italian	t	p
NVN	83.47	80.39	1.23	ns
VNN	40.45	51.52	4.12	<.0001
NNV	61.77	62.40	.866	ns

Appendix 2). The sentences varied in terms of word order, animacy, and topicality. The format for elicitation and specific lexical items were taken from a study by Bates et al. (1982) in which sentence interpretation of monolingual Italian and English speakers was investigated. Their study provided baseline data for the present study.

The specific sentences included the following three word order types: verb-medial (NVN), verb-final (NNV), and verb-initial (VNN). The animacy relationship of the two nouns was either: (1) animate-inanimate, (2) animate-animate, or (3) inanimate-animate. Additionally, either one of the two nouns was topicalized or neither was, although these results will not be discussed here.

Two tapes for each language were prepared, each tape with different sentence orders. Instructions consisted of telling the subjects that they were about to hear 27 sentences and that they were to respond as to which was the subject of the sentence, or the doer of the action. After each sentence, subjects had a maximum of 20 seconds in which to respond.

Results

The results are presented in terms of the number of learners who selected a given noun as subject of the sentence. In general, there was an approximately equal tendency for both native language groups to select the first noun, as can be seen in Table 8.7. Native speakers of English selected the first noun 61.9 percent of the time, whereas native speakers of Italian selected the first noun 64.77 percent of the time.

In Table 8.8 are the results of the choice of noun based on word order. As can be seen, the choice of noun depends on the word order of the

TABLE 8.9. PERCENTAGE OF FIRST NOUNS SELECTED AS SUBJECT AS A
FUNCTION OF ANIMACY AND NATIVE LANGUAGE

	NSs of English	NSs of Italian	t	p
Animate/Animate	68.30	70.78	1.08	ns
Animate/Inanimate	80.86	91.56	4.31	<.0001
Inanimate/Animate	36.55	31.97	1.21	ns

sentence. Only in the VNN sentences is there a significant difference
between the two native-language groups.

In Table 8.9 are the results for animacy conditions. Italian native
speakers show a greater dependency on animacy than do the English
native speakers. This is predicted on the basis of the native-speaker data
presented by Bates et al.

Discussion

On the basis of data from monolingual English and Italian speakers,
Bates et al. (1982) hypothesized that Italian was more of a "semantic"
language than English in that in determining sentential relations, native
speakers rely heavily on the meaning of lexical items.[5] In English, on
the other hand, word order dominates. To investigate the role of the
native language, I compared the data presented by Bates et al. with those
obtained from this study. In Figure 8.1 is a graph of the word order
results for monolingual speakers and for the two groups of learners in
this study.

As Bates et al. (1982) point out, the English monolingual speakers
have a stronger preference for identifying the first noun in NVN sequences as the subject than Italian monolingual speakers, leading the
authors to suggest that English is more SVO-like than Italian. Further,
English monolinguals show a greater amount of consistency than Italian
monolinguals in their choice of nouns, whether the first noun in NVN
sequences or the second noun in VNN and NNV sequences. Thus, English monolinguals are dependent on word order for interpretation even
in noncanonical word orders. For Italian monolinguals, other variables
assume importance.

The learner data presented here suggest a reliance on native-speaker
interpretation strategies. In the data from Italian native speakers who
are learners of English, one notes a relative lack of importance of word
order. However, interestingly, in all cases the results show that learners
"move" in a direction that exhibits an increased amount of consistency

5 I am excluding agreement, which has also been found to be a major contributing
  factor to sentence interpretation in Italian (Bates et al. 1984).

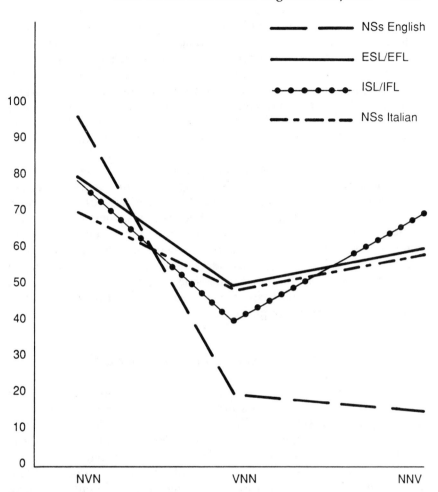

Figure 8.1 Percent choice of first noun as a function of word order

with word order dominance. As is expected, only in the NVN sequence is the change a strong one, and only in that sequence is the change in a direction consistent with native-speaker behavior. While these learners have become aware of the importance of word order in English, they have not yet sorted out the relevant factors that determine which noun to select, since they more consistently opt for the first noun in VNN and NNV sequences, whereas monolingual English speakers opt for the second. Thus, an important aspect of learning the syntax of a language goes beyond the mere ordering of elements within a sentence to include information about the *importance* of syntax within a language. In other words, learners have to learn not only how to order elements, but also the relative importance of ordering versus other possible factors. It is only at later stages of language learning that ordering importance is accurately sorted out. The phenomenon of first noting the importance of an element and then later sorting out the details of the phenomenon is consistent with a view of language learning in which conscious awareness (Schmidt in press) and selective attention (Gass 1988) are necessary conditions. Furthermore, similar phenomena have been noted in other areas of the grammar (cf. Obler 1982; Gass 1984b; Beebe and Takahashi 1989).

In contrast to the data from Italian speakers learning English, in which their performance reflected native-language behavior, the data from English speakers do not reflect native-language behavior but more closely resemble the data of Italian monolingual speakers, suggesting that the English speakers have understood the overriding importance of semantics in Italian. This is further corroborated by the data displayed in Figure 8.2, in which both learner groups more closely resemble the monolingual Italian pattern than the monolingual English pattern. On the basis of these data, one can hypothesize that it is easier to go from a word order language to a semantic language than vice versa.

Linguistic theory and second language acquisition

The data from both experiments bear on a discussion of the ways in which linguistic theory supports and informs the interpretation of second language data. However, the direction of information flow need not be unidirectional. As well as providing a theoretical foundation, linguistic theory can be refined on the basis of the results presented here. As was mentioned in the introduction to this book, the relevance of child language acquisition data for a theory of language is generally accepted. This is not the case for second language data. What I argue here is that second language data can provide unique information, information unavailable from child language acquisition or from monolingual speakers, about the way humans handle conflicting and competing language data and the generalizations which result. This occurs because in second language acquisition we are confronted with the dynamic interplay of two languages.

Placing the results from both experiments within the framework of the Competition Model we see in these data language-neutral conspiring vectors: those of universal language interpretation strategies, with semantics being a stronger one than syntax. Thus, animacy cues may have a universal prepotency in second language learning. Two additional studies (Harrington 1987; Kilborn and Ito 1989) support this view. Both

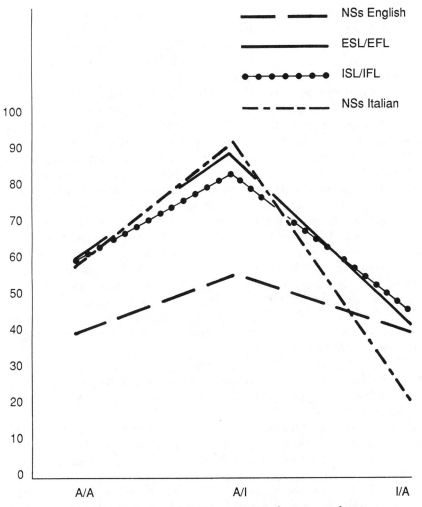

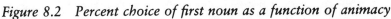

Figure 8.2   Percent choice of first noun as a function of animacy

found that Japanese learners of English were slow to pick up on word order as a cue for interpretation as compared to English speakers learning Japanese, who quickly pick up on animacy cues. Perhaps even stronger evidence for the universal prepotency of animacy cues comes from a study by Kilborn and Cooreman (1987), who investigated sentence interpretation by Dutch speakers learning English. Within their data there were some subjects who favored animacy as an interpretation strategy in both English and Dutch, but none who favored word order.[6] Similarly,

6 There was a subgroup of subjects who opted for agreement, which may in fact turn

Harrington (1987) found a subgroup of monolingual English speakers who did not opt for word order but instead favored animacy cues in interpretation. Importantly, to my knowledge there are no examples of subgroups of speakers whose native languages rely on animacy for interpretation adopting a strong word order cue.

MacWhinney (1987) points out that it might be premature to ascribe a universal built-in prepotency for animacy. In Japanese, an important part of assigning grammatical relations is case-marking, an aspect not considered in Harrington's study. In Italian, subject-verb agreement, a cue not included in my study, cannot be overlooked. With specific regard to second language acquisition, one can ask whether learners, as their initial hypothesis, search for their major native-language cue in the L2. In fact, Hakuta (1976) suggests that morphological features of the native language may form the basis of initial hypotheses. For example, Uguisu, a five-year-old Japanese-speaking child, used "Do you" as an unanalyzed question marker. Hakuta claims that this occurs because Japanese has a question marker. Similarly, Kilborn and Ito (1989) found that English learners of Japanese attempt to make use of rigid word order as a cue (SOV in the case of Japanese) even before they figure out *how* rigid it should be. As did the subjects in both experiments discussed in this chapter, Kilborn and Ito's subjects even used word order more rigidly than native speakers of Japanese.

Thus, it may be that the initial hypothesis in L2 learning is sought in the behavior of the native language. When there is an apparent incongruity between the L1 and the L2, learners resort to fundamental universal properties.

A final point to make with regard to linguistic theory has to do with the strength of hierarchical arrangements. From the study on complex sentences, there are implications for the nature of hierarchical relationships, as frequently put forth in linguistic theory. Mathematical orderings such as $a>b>c$ do not imply equal distancing between a and b and b and c. Within theoretical linguistics as well as within second language acquisition research, there has been little concern with the strength of relationships or with the distancing between hierarchical elements. However, it was seen here that syntax was differentially affected by different hierarchical role relationships. Thus, hierarchies may capture linguistically real relationships, but do not capture psycholinguistically real ones.

The results are only the beginning in our quest to understand the resolution of L1/L2 competition and thus to understand the nature of influencing factors in second language acquisition. Importantly, second language learners provide us with a way to investigate the resolution of

---

out to be a stronger factor than animacy, although the present studies did not include agreement as a variable.

conflicts, which is perhaps more difficult with monolingual speakers at a single point in time since conflicts per se are not readily observable in a static situation. By looking at a synchronic grammar (of either native speakers or second language learners), we never see the process of the resolution of conflicts. At best, all we can see is the result of previous conflict resolutions. It is only in dynamic situations, such as acquisition or diachronic analyses of language, that we have a suitable venue for observing the onset and subsequent resolution of linguistic conflicts.

Appendix 1: Sentences used in experiment 1

1. The women advised the men to go home.
2. The chair told the dog to leave.
3. The chair promised the dog to leave.
4. The boy told the dog to leave.
5. The table promised the boy to leave.
6. The child asked her mother to have a cookie.
7. The girl told the chair to leave.
8. The dog told the chair to leave.
9. The woman allowed her husband to go.
10. The dog asked the chair to have a cookie.
11. The dog promised the cat to leave.
12. The table told the boy to leave.
13. The girl promised the chair to leave.
14. The dog promised the boy to leave.
15. The man warned the woman to leave immediately.
16. The boy promised the girl to leave.
17. The woman asked her child to have a cookie.
18. The woman advised her husband to drive carefully.
19. The boy promised the dog to leave.
20. The chair promised the table to leave.
21. The girl persuaded the boy to study hard.
22. The chair asked the dog to have a cookie.
23. The dog told the cat to leave.
24. The boy told the girl to leave.
25. The man ordered his boss to walk slowly.
26. The dog promised the chair to leave.

Appendix 2: Lexical items used in experiment 2 (translation equivalents were used for the Italian version)

Animate nouns	Inanimate nouns	Verbs
camel	eraser	bite
deer	block	grab
goat	ball	kiss
turtle	rock	pat
bear	stick	look at
fish	pencil	eat
calf	pen	lick
horse	cigarette	greet
lamb		smell
cow		
dog		
sheep		
donkey		
giraffe		
cat		
zebra		
piglet		
monkey		

References

Bates, E., and B. MacWhinney. 1981. Second language acquisition from a functionalist perspective: pragmatic, semantic and perceptual strategies. In *Annals of the New York Academy of Science Conference on Native and Foreign Language Acquisition.* New York: New York Academy of Sciences.
     1982. Functionalist approaches to grammar. In *Language Acquisition: The State of the Art*, E. Wanner and L. Gleitman, eds. New York: Cambridge University Press.
Bates, E., B. MacWhinney, C. Caselli, A. Devescovi, F. Natale, and V. Venza. 1984. A cross-linguistic study of the development of sentence interpretation strategies. *Child Development* 55: 341–54.
Bates, E., S. McNew, B. MacWhinney, A. Devescovi, and S. Smith. 1982. Functional constraints on sentence processing: a cross-linguistic study. *Cognition* 11: 245–99.
Beebe, L., and T. Takahashi. 1989. Do you have a bag?: social status and patterned variation in second language acquisition. In *Variation in Second Language Acquisition: Discourse and Pragmatics*, S. Gass, C. Madden, D. Preston, and L. Selinker, eds. Clevedon, U.K.: Multilingual Matters.
Duranti, A. 1979. Object clitic pronouns in Bantu and the topicality hierarchy. *Studies in African Linguistics* 10: 31–45.

Gass, S. 1984a. Empirical evidence for the universal hypothesis in interlanguage studies. In *Interlanguage*, A. Davies, C. J. Criper, and A. Howatt, eds. Edinburgh: University of Edinburgh Press.

1984b. Development of speech perception and speech production abilities in adult second language learners. *Applied Psycholinguistics* 5(1): 51–74.

1986. An interactionist approach to L2 sentence interpretation. *Studies in Second Language Acquisition* 8(1): 19–37.

1987. The resolution of conflicts among competing systems: a bidirectional perspective. *Applied Psycholinguistics* 8(4): 329–50.

1988. Integrating research areas: a framework for second language studies. *Applied Linguistics* 9(2): 198–217.

Gass, S., and L. Selinker, eds. 1983. *Language Transfer in Language Learning*. Rowley, Mass.: Newbury House.

Givón, T. 1976. Topic, pronoun and grammatical agreement. In *Subject and Topic*, C. Li, ed. New York: Academic Press.

Hakuta, K. 1976. A case study of a Japanese child learning English as a second language. *Language Learning* 26(2): 321–52.

Harrington, M. 1987. Processing transfer: language-specific processing strategies as a source of interlanguage variation. *Applied Psycholinguistics* 8(4): 351–78.

Hawkinson, A., and L. Hyman. 1974. Hierarchies of natural topic in Shona. *Studies in African Linguistics* 5: 147–70.

Kellerman, E., and M. Sharwood Smith, eds. 1986. *Cross-Linguistic Influence in Second Language Acquisition*. Oxford: Pergamon Press.

Kilborn, K., and A. Cooreman. 1987. Sentence interpretation strategies in adult Dutch-English bilinguals. *Applied Psycholinguistics* 8(4): 415–31.

Kilborn, K., and T. Ito. 1989. Sentence processing strategies in adult bilinguals. In *The Cross-Linguistic Study of Sentence Processing*, B. MacWhinney and E. Bates, eds. New York: Cambridge University Press.

MacWhinney, B. 1987. Applying the Competition Model to bilingualism. *Applied Psycholinguistics* 8(4): 315–28.

MacWhinney, B., E. Bates, and R. Kliegl. 1984. Cue validity and sentence interpretation in English, German, and Italian. *Journal of Verbal Learning and Verbal Behavior* 23: 127–50.

Morolong, M., and L. Hyman. 1977. Animacy, objects, and clitics in Sesotho. *Studies in African Linguistics* 8: 199–217.

Obler, L. 1982. The parsimonious bilingual. In *Exceptional Language and Linguistics*, L. Obler and L. Menn, eds. New York: Academic Press.

Ringbom, H. 1976. What differences are there between Finns and Swedish-speaking Finns learning English? In *Errors Made by Finns and Swedish-Speaking Finns in the Learning of English*, H. Ringbom and R. Palmberg, eds. AFTI 1(5). Åbo, Finland: Åbo Akademi.

Schmidt, R. In press. The role of consciousness in second language learning. *Applied Linguistics* 11(2).

PART IV:
LEXICON

Most adult second language learners believe that the most difficult aspect of learning a second language involves the acquisition of a vocabulary sufficient to meet their receptive and productive communicative needs. They recognize that the grammar and the sound system need to be incorporated, of course, but feel that it is the acquisition of vocabulary items that demands the most attention and requires the most time. Intuitively, they are probably right, although perhaps not for the right reasons. A typical learner (especially a classroom learner), for example, will state that what needs to be done in the acquisition of words is to memorize a form (either phonological or graphic) and its associated meaning. But the problem is much more complex than this. Learning a lexical item involves a number of different properties: the sound sequence and the meaning(s) associated with it, to be sure, but also the syntactic category it belongs to, its co-occurrence restrictions, and, if it is a verb, the number of arguments it can take, the thematic roles of the arguments, and how these arguments and their thematic roles may be encoded syntactically.

One would think, therefore, that language researchers would have already put in much time and thought on the question of how the lexicon is learned. But such is not the case, either in the study of first language acquisition or in the study of second language acquisition. And perhaps this is not surprising. There are few if any explicit theories about the acquisition of the lexicon and little knowledge about what kinds of mental mechanisms *or* input information are needed for lexical acquisition to take place.

This section thus contains only two chapters. But they are interesting chapters in that each, in a different sphere, attempts to argue for specific models within which productive work on the acquisition of the lexicon may proceed.

Hudson is concerned about the absence of an explicit model of how *meanings* of lexical items are acquired and argues that such a model is crucially dependent on a formal theory of the lexicon. He first points out the weaknesses in using lexical theories based on formal models of truth in an attempt to account for the lexicon of natural languages. He then proposes that the preference rule system developed by Jackendoff can provide such a theory, which in turn could serve as the core of an acquisition model. Jackendoff's theory is based on two fundamental notions: that there is a level of mental representation at which sensory, motor, and linguistic information are compatible and subject to the same kinds of rules; and that what words refer to are the resulting mental entities projected onto our awareness. The internal structure of a word meaning is determined by the interaction of the three conditions of necessity, centrality, and typicality. Preference rules are the processes by which the interaction of these conditions on lexical meanings results in a preferred weighting of these conditions themselves.

Hudson argues that the three conditions can be used as determinants of cross-linguistic differences in a psychologically insightful way, thus helping to clarify the task of the learner trying to acquire the meanings of lexical items in the target language that are superficially synonymous with words in the native language. Such meanings may well differ in their necessity, centrality, and typicality weightings.

Zobl, on the other hand, is concerned with the acquisition of the subcategorization properties of verbs, and in particular with the question of how linguistic universals play a role in determining the path a learner takes in the process of acquiring certain lexical subcategorization facts in the target language. Evidence for such a role may, he argues, take the form of learner error types not entirely consonant with the input data to which the learner is exposed.

He uses the case of the acquisition of ergative verbs in English to argue that two typological distinctions – one between configurational and nonconfigurational languages, and the other between nominative/accusative and ergative languages – together lead to specific error types in the subcategorization of these ergatives.

9 Canonical typological structures and ergativity in English L2 acquisition

Helmut Zobl

Discussions of the discrepancy between grammatical knowledge and its experiential basis in the primary data of acquisition usually focus on the question of how to account for the attainment of the correct adult grammar. Yet this disparity between knowledge and input data is also apparent in provisional solutions learners arrive at in formulating a grammar. As Lightfoot (1982) points out, of the many logically possible interim solutions that could be derived from the data, only a narrow range is actually attested. Not infrequently these have no obvious model in the target or the first language. It is noncontroversial, by now, that no known inductive learning procedure can satisfactorily account for these salient aspects of acquisition and that innate, specifically linguistic, constraints must mediate the acquisition process. These constraints define the domain for a theory of Universal Grammar.

We can conceive of these constraints as grammatical principles. Universal Grammar will consist of invariant principles which dictate the form grammars can take. Besides these, there are other principles admitting of variation. The manner of their implementation gives rise to the typological variation observable in languages. Since typological variation is sharply circumscribed, and since there is no historical evidence that new linguistic types have evolved (Wode 1981), these principles, too, appear to form part of our biological endowment.

Assume, then, that grammar construction is mediated by principles in such a way that a learner is programmed to search out those data that indicate their manner of implementation. One consequence of this selective data search should be that canonical structures of a linguistic type will have a privileged status as data in the formulation of a grammar (Zobl 1986). We can go one step further. It is quite conceivable that learners arrive at novel solutions for a particular domain in order to satisfy their perception of the design principles of the language type at a certain developmental level. According to this view, the novel solution

I would like to express my gratitude to Jane Power and the teachers of the NICE program at the University of Hawaii, Patsy Lightbown, and Sue Gass for making available to me the L2 data used in this investigation.

should display a higher measure of congruence with the implementation of the principle than the actual acquisition target.

This chapter, in presenting a fairly simple deductive chain involving two typologies in which English participates, exemplifies and supports the preceding remarks. It predicts that constructions such as those in Sentences 1–6 should occur in the acquisition of English as a second language (L2).[1]

1. The most memorable experience of my life was happened 15 years ago. (Arabic native language [L1]; advanced learner)
2. Most of people are fallen in love and marry with somebody. (Japanese L1; high intermediate)
3. My mother was died when I was just a baby. (Thai L1; high intermediate)
4. Sometimes comes a good regular wave. (Japanese L1; low intermediate)
5. I was just patient until dried my clothes.
   "I was just patient until my clothes had dried." (Japanese L1; high intermediate)
6. I think it continue of today condition forever.
   "I think the condition of today/today's condition will continue forever." (Japanese L1; intermediate)

The input data to a learner of English contain no direct model for these examples. In (1)–(3) tense is encoded, nonstandardly, via an auxiliary verb "be." In (4)–(6) the apparent subject occurs postverbally. Although (4) could be rendered grammatical by inserting "there," (5) and (6) resist such a move. In (6) a dummy pronoun "it" acts as a placeholder for the apparent subject noun phrase (NP), "of today condition."

The sentences in (1) through (6) represent different solutions to one and the same problem, namely, the mapping of logical grammatical relations to surface structure in a configurational language (see Chomsky 1981; Hale 1983; Marantz 1984 for discussions of configurationality). The mapping problem originates from a class of verbs that have been termed unaccusative (Perlmutter 1978) and, more recently, ergative (Burzio 1981). These verbs can be characterized semantically as possessing a theta-grid (i.e., argument structure) such that their sole argument bears the theta-role (or thematic role) *theme*.[2] These verbs describe processes in which their subject lacks volitional control (Perlmutter 1978).[3] The claim that all languages recognize, at an abstract level, a distinction between intransitive verbs implying volitional control (e.g., active intransitives like "walk") and those that do not (e.g., intransitives like "fall") is now known as the Unaccusative Hypothesis (Perlmutter 1978).

1 The ESL programs from which the data stem used in-house placement measures. The levels indicated are therefore not based on a common evaluation measure.
2 Anderson (1977:367) defines *theme* as the entity that moves or that undergoes the action described.
3 Admittedly, lack of volitional control only provides a general correlation. Rosen (1982) observes that languages frequently display idiosyncratic variation.

While numerous languages reflect this distinction in syntactic rules and verb affixation, English seems to recognize it only in the lexicon with respect to restrictions on word derivational processes (Keyser and Roeper 1984). These data are rather inaccessible and can safely be excluded from the input available to a learner of English. Yet, as we will show, (1) through (6) can be traced straightforwardly to distinct underlying analyses of active and ergative verbs.

The remainder of this chapter is given over to: (1) an exposition of the deductive chain enabling us to predict the occurrence of constructions like (1) through (6); (2) a presentation of the data supporting the Unaccusative Hypothesis; and (3) a discussion of the relevance of these findings for grammatical theory as well as the contribution, to L2 research, of the linguistic approach developed here.

The deductive chain

Theta-roles and grammatical relations

A fundamental dimension of typological variation concerns the alignments between thematic roles like *theme, agent,* and *goal* (Jackendoff 1972; Anderson 1977) and the grammatical relations *subject* and *object.* The two logical arguments of a transitive verb such as "break" divide into an internal argument, combining with the verb to form a predicate, and an external argument, combining with the predicate to form a proposition (Marantz 1984; Williams 1984). Traditionally, we refer to the former as the logical object and the latter as the logical subject. English belongs to a linguistic type known as nominative-accusative. In this type, the canonical alignment between thematic roles and grammatical relations is subject-*agent* and object-*theme* (Marantz 1984). Anderson (1977) remarks that this correlation is overwhelmingly regular and should therefore form "part of the semantic component of a grammar of English" (p. 367). In the opposite case, the ergative language type, the relevant alignment would appear to be subject-*theme* and object-*agent* (Marantz 1984). The nominative/accusative language type generalizes subject properties (i.e., subject-sensitive rules and coding properties) across the *agent* argument of transitives and the sole argument of intransitives. Hence, a nominative-accusative language such as English makes no grammatical distinction between the subjects in examples (7), (8) and (9), even though we interpret the subjects of (7) and (8) as bearing the thematic role *agent* and that of (9), the thematic role *theme*:

7. Skinny Minnie broke my Louis Quinze chair.
8. Bureaucrats work industriously.
9. Dorian's mirror shattered.

Configurationality

Another major dimension of typological variation arises from the manner in which languages express grammatical relations. Informally, in a configurational language such as English, subject and object are expressed in terms of structural position, specifically dominance and linear order. In nonconfigurational languages such as Japanese, grammatical relations are expressed by means of case-marking. Structural position is not a reliable clue as to the grammatical relation of a noun phrase. As this configurational/nonconfigurational parameter plays a key role in the deductive chain, it will be briefly analyzed vis-à-vis Government-Binding Theory (Chomsky 1981).

Government-Binding Theory recognizes different levels of linguistic representation. At the level of logical form, every language is assumed to be configurational by virtue of the distinction between an internal and external argument; in other words, all languages have logical predicates. Languages differ in how this is translated into syntactic representations. D-structure is a representation of thematic role assignment.[4] In a configurational language like English thematic roles are assigned positionally. The verb assigns the role *theme* to the position of the logical object. Similarly, the predicate assigns the role *agent*, if there is one, to the position of the logical subject. The positional assignment of thematic roles accounts for the fact that in the sentence *John kissed Mary* we interpret "Mary," the logical object, as the person kissed. It also explains why the dative alternation in *John sent Mary a billet-doux* is perceived as somehow "marked." The logical object, "billet-doux," does not occupy its canonical position.

These logical grammatical relations are mapped onto yet another level of representation, surface structure (S-structure).[5] At this level syntactic cases are assigned. Transitive verbs assign the objective case to the postverbal position. Hence, in the dative alternation sentence given earlier, the *goal* argument, "Mary," which is not the logical object, acquires objective case and becomes the grammatical object. Similarly, nominative case is assigned to the position of the grammatical subject by the *inflection* (INFL) node.

As can be seen from the preceding exposition, a configurational language preserves the distinction between an internal and external argu-

---

4 D-structure is a projection level of the thematic and subcategorization properties of lexical entries. In order for a D-structure to be well-formed, X-bar requirements must be satisfied as well. Finally, the extended projection principle requires that the subject position be present, regardless of whether the predicate assigns a thematic role to it or not.

5 S-structure is a projection of D-structure and, if applicable, the transformation "move-alpha," where "alpha" is an arbitrary category.

ment in mapping these into syntactic representations (Hale 1983). This structural isomorphy between logical predicate-argument structure and phrase structure has a number of structural consequences, notably the existence of a "move-NP" rule (Hale 1983).[6] This rule is triggered when a configuration at D-structure cannot be mapped directly onto S-structure without running afoul of conditions on the well-formedness of sentences. A canonical instance of NP-movement in English is the passive. Its productiveness in English (compared with other languages) is an immediate consequence of the extreme configurationality of this language.

Only transitive verbs can passivize in English. Given the configurational mapping principle, the verb will assign the thematic relation *theme* to the position of the logical object. What distinguishes passives from the corresponding actives is that neither the logical subject nor the logical object appear in their canonical positions. Thus, there are good grounds for assuming that the change to a passive participle removes the logical subject and makes the verb syntactically intransitive. This frees up the position of the logical subject and, at the same time, prevents the logical object from appearing in the postverbal position. Now, in order to arrive at a well-formed sentence, there has to be a grammatical subject. In a configurational language like English, an NP can only acquire subject status if it occupies the corresponding position in phrase structure. (This is not required in languages with case-marking nor, apparently, in languages like Spanish and Italian; see Jaeggli 1982.) The logical object moves to the position of the grammatical subject, where it can receive nominative case. The examples (a) and (b) show the derivation from D- to S-structure. Note that the thematic role *theme* is transmitted to the grammatical subject by means of the trace (t) relationship $NP_i \ldots t_i$ (coindexing of antecedent and its copy, marking the position from where it originated).

a. $[e \text{ INFL } [_{VP} \text{ V NP}]]$
b. $[NP_i \text{ INFL } [_{VP} \text{ V } t_i]]$

To summarize, the canonical alignment between thematic roles and (logical) grammatical relations in a nominative-accusative language such as English is object-*theme* and subject-*agent*. In the configurational type of language, the distinction between the internal argument, which combines with the verb to form a predicate, and the external argument, which combines with the predicate to form a proposition, is preserved at the two levels of syntactic representation, D-structure and S-structure. This means that the logical subject and the logical object occupy structural

6 Another structural consequence is that when the position of the logical subject is empty, that position must be phonologically realized by means of dummy pronouns if move-NP does not apply.

positions, as do the grammatical subject and the grammatical object. Because grammatical relations are represented configurationally rather than in terms of morphological case, this linguistic type must have a rule – NP-movement – which permits logical constituents to assume (surface) structural positions when a direct mapping would result in an ill-formed sentence. The passive, then, is a canonical structure of the configurational language type.

Ergativity in current grammatical theory

Although the nominative-accusative type supposedly generalizes subject properties in such a way as to make no distinction between the subject of transitives and the subject of intransitives, research, beginning with Perlmutter (1978), has "made it abundantly clear that all seemingly intransitive verbs are not created equal" (Baker 1983:1). Perlmutter (1978), Burzio (1981), and Harris (1982), to name just a few, have presented convincing evidence that subjects of ergative verbs exhibit interesting differences from active intransitives. While the literature on this topic is too extensive to review here, there are two ergative reflexes that are of direct concern. Perlmutter (1978) and Burzio (1981), using Italian as a reference, and Hoekstra (1984), using Dutch, draw attention to the fact that auxiliary selection for tense/aspect marking is sensitive to the ergative/active distinction. In Italian, for example, active intransitives and transitives select the auxiliary verb "avere" ("have") while ergative verbs select "essere" ("be"). What is especially significant is that the auxiliary "essere" is also selected by the *passive* and the reflexive *si*-construction, which has a passive interpretation. Burzio (1981) also points out that, in Italian, discourse-neutral word order for pure intransitives is subject-verb (SV), while for ergative verbs it is verb-subject (VS).

10. Giovanni telefona
    "Giovanni telephones" (active)
11. Arriva Giovanni
    "Giovanni arrives" (ergative)

Ergativity in nominative-accusative languages has been explored within different grammatical frameworks, all concurring in viewing the sole argument of an ergative verb as its logical object. Consequently, unlike the active class, this group of verbs lacks a logical subject. It was Burzio (1981) who noted that this explains why, in Italian, ergative verbs, the passive, and the reflexive *si*-construction all select the auxiliary "essere": All three lack a logical subject. A more accurate formulation of the Unaccusative Hypothesis would thus state that with ergative verbs, the (surface) grammatical subject originates as the logical object.

The ergative class is comprised of two subgroups (Hoekstra 1984). Verbs like "shatter" in *Dorian's mirror shattered* have a transitive alternation. The other group, which contains verbs like "fall" and "happen," are without transitive counterparts. Generative grammar has long recognized the problem posed by the first group if the subject in *Dorian's mirror shattered* is to receive the same semantic interpretation as the grammatical object in *Dorian shattered his mirror*. Since passive constructions pose the same problem of semantic interpretation, Fiengo (1974) and Bowers (1981) proposed analyses in which a transformation analogous to the NP preposing rule of the passive moved the logical object to the grammatical subject position. This insight has been retained in more recent analysis. For Italian, Burzio (1981) proposes the following D-structure for the ergative class:

$[e \ [_{VP} \ V \ NP]]$

The logical subject position is empty. Move-NP can prepose the logical object; alternatively, since Italian allows the subject position to be filled by an invisible pronoun, the D-structure can be mapped to S-structure and nominative case assigned to the logical object in the postverbal position, resulting in the VS order noted earlier. Thus, the discourse-neutral VS order found with ergative verbs reflects the underlying representation.

Curiously, English has no reflexes of ergativity in its syntax. Keyser and Roeper (1984) have therefore proposed that the D-structure of ergative verbs should be indistinguishable from that of active intransitives. Their analysis situates the movement of the logical object to subject position in the lexicon and not the syntax. (Languages would thus vary on this dimension [see Burzio 1983].) Their ergative rule accomplishes two things. First, it takes as its input the transitive form of "shatter," "break," "sink," and other verbs of this class, depriving the transitive form of the logical subject and thereby making it syntactically intransitive. In this respect, the ergative rule follows the effects of passive morphology. Second, NP-movement preposes the logical object. This changes the subcategorization of the verb so that it is the same as an active intransitive except for the $NP_i \ldots t_i$ trace relationship marking the ergative verb. For the ergative subgroup that does not have a transitive alternation (the "fall"/"happen" group), only the second part of the rule can apply.

Acquisition-relevant assumptions

In predicting that the acquisition of English should give rise to sentences like those in (1)–(6), we made two assumptions. First, learners must be able to determine the canonical alignment between thematic roles and grammatical relations; that is, in English, *theme* goes to the internal argument. Our second assumption involves the Unaccusative Hypothesis. Suppose there exists a core group of verbs cross-linguistically whose predicate-argument structure is [∅ [V NP]], where ∅ refers to the empty category. Knowledge of the semantics of core exemplars is sufficient for a learner to adopt this structure as the initial hypothesis (Baker 1983). From the input data, learners must determine how this representation is mapped to surface structure.

While setting aside, for the moment, Keyser and Roeper's (1984) lexical rule for deriving ergative verbs, their lexical version of move-NP is adopted as Solution 1. It gives rise to intransitive structures conforming to the input data, in which there is no formal distinction between active intransitives and ergative intransitives. Solution 2 is a syntactic solution, and here we can make some fairly precise predictions about possible nonstandard forms.

1. Map [∅ [V NP]] to D-structure and assign *theme* to the internal argument, noting that English requires this to be accomplished positionally because of its configurationality. Map this representation to S-structure, inserting a nonvisible pronoun in the position of the empty logical subject. Let the logical object receive nominative case *in situ* (as is the case in Italian and Spanish). This solution does not differ in its essential aspects from the English presentative construction *there occurred an accident.*[7] Learners producing this surface form have not yet acquired (or fail to apply) the knowledge that the structural subject position must be phonologically realized. This solution leads to sentences such as (4) and (5) given earlier.

2. The next nonstandard mapping is similar to (1) except that learners choosing it have now acquired (or apply) the knowledge that the subject position cannot be empty. A dummy pronoun is inserted, either on the model of the presentative construction or on the model of a passive with a sentential object, for example, *it was claimed that acupuncture speeds up L2 acquisition.* This solution leads to sentences as in (6).

3. The third nonstandard form we can predict derives from the identical aspects of passive verbs and ergative verbs: Both have a logical object, lack a logical subject, and are syntactically intransitive. NP-movement is applied in the D-structure to S-structure derivation. The passive auxiliary "be" is selected on the hypothesis that it marks a change in grammatical relations.[8] This solution makes use of a rule that is a canonical expression of the configurational mapping required by English. Not only does it reveal that thematic relations have been expressed structurally at D-structure but it also takes into account the fact that the logical object can only become the grammatical subject if it appears in the corresponding struc-

---

7 Stowell (1981) has proposed that the postverbal subject in English presentative constructions receives nominative case in that position. The D-structure [e [vp V NP]] can either receive a direct mapping, as in the example, or move-NP applies, resulting in *an accident occurred.*

8 More precisely, it marks the absence of a logical subject (Burzio 1981).

tural position. It results in constructions as in Sentences 1 through 3, given earlier.

Of the three syntactic solutions, both the second and third conform to the configurational requirements of English by virtue of the dummy subject, marking the projected empty logical subject position, and move-NP, a core rule of English. What sets the third solution apart is the identification of ergatives with passives, a move that has cross-linguistic parallels. In numerous languages (e.g., Sanskrit), passives and ergatives have common morphological devices (Rosen 1982).

Predictions

Before presenting the data supporting the Unaccusative Hypothesis, I will state what patterns in the data should count as support for the deductive scheme proposed.

Regarding Solution 3, the proposal will be falsified if the occurrence of "be" as a tense-bearing auxiliary (ideally in conjunction with the past participle form of the main verb) fails to discriminate between verbs with a logical subject (transitives and active intransitives) and the ergative group.[9]

Regarding Solutions 1 and 2, the scheme requires that (Pro)VS only occur with ergative verbs, as this word order is viewed as the result of the preservation, at S-structure, of the position occupied by the *theme* NP.[10] Rutherford and Altman (1985) looked at production data and reported occurrences of VS in L2 English, and suggested that the probability of such word-order permutations is directly correlated with the propensity of the learner's L1 to follow discourse-pragmatic word order. In the following example from a Japanese speaker, it would indeed be difficult to tease apart the discourse-pragmatic and the structural influence. "Everything" in Sentence 12 is nonreferential and consequently unsuited for topic position.

12. It is so changing everything.
    "Everything is really changing."

In order to rule out discourse-pragmatic factors as the sole influence, VS word order will have to occur with subjects that are referential and represent known information. Note, incidentally, that we are also able to control for the possibility that L1 syntactic transfer is responsible for

9 Andersen (1980) has reported nonstandard occurrences of "be" in the English of Spanish speakers. He interprets them as nonstandard markers of aspect. I find no evidence of this in my data.
10 Hilles (1986), in another study that examines production data, found sporadic instances of VS in her Spanish L1 informant's speech. The study did not, however, appear to examine the possible ergative origins of VS. White's (1985) study, which investigated grammaticality judgments on sentences containing VS, will be discussed later.

VS order, since the majority of the informants are Japanese speakers, whose L1 has SOV word order.

The data

Background information

The data come from written productions on a variety of topics assigned as part of regular ESL (English as a Second Language) course work. The majority of the informants are Japanese native speakers (90), but there are also Arabic (10), Spanish (10), Chinese (1), Turkish (1), Thai (1), and Indonesian (1) speakers. The informants are university-age students in ESL programs in Canada and the United States. Eighty-five of the Japanese speakers were enrolled in an intensive English program and had already completed an average of seven years of English instruction (eight hours per week) in Japan. Individuals whose written production provided no clear evidence that they controlled tense-marking were excluded from the population.

As the primary focus of this investigation was not a developmental one, the data provided by the 114 informants was pooled and the total number of verb tokens was tallied. To quantify the kind of tense/auxiliary marking occurring with transitives, active intransitives, and ergatives, all nonfinite verb forms were excluded. In addition, because learners produce morphologically defective continuous verb forms of the pattern *I was go*, it seemed wise to err on the side of safety and to consider any occurrence admitting of a continuous interpretation as an instance of the aspectual auxiliary, "be-ing."

The categorization of verbs as ergative relied on the characteristics given by Rosen (1982), in particular the absence of volitional control. In doubtful cases, the presence of this semantic trait was tested for. Adverbs such as "intentionally" and "willingly" are, as a rule, rejected by ergative verbs:

13. This bureaucrat worked willingly.
14. ?? Rambo trembled willingly.

Finally, cross-linguistic evidence was drawn upon. Rosen (1982), for example, lists verbal meanings that recur with ergative phenomena in a number of languages.

Delimiting the transitive category was by no means easy. The ability of a verb to passivize is not always a reliable indicator. In doubtful cases, the deciding factor was whether the verb and its complement could be interrupted by an adverb.[11] If the verb and complement are sisters and

11 For example, in the sentence *They argued about the plan*, "argue" can be passiv-

TABLE 9.I. VERB TYPES AND TOKENS

Verb type	Types	Tokens
Ergative	43	246
Active		
Intransitive	38	352
Transitive	243	826

TABLE 9.2. AUXILIARY "BE" SELECTION

Ergatives: become (1/26); break (2/4); change-*ed* (2/12); die-*ed* (3/12); fall-*ed* (2/10); gather-*ed* (1/2)[a]; get home (1/4); get through (1/1); go-*ed* asleep (1/4); happen-*ed* (5/20); occur (1/1); separate-*ed* (1/2); stall-*ed* (1/1)[a]; start-*ed* (2/8); suffer (1/3).
Total: 25/110   Number of speakers: 17

Doubtful ergatives: consist of (1/1); enjoy (2/15); pass (a course) (1/1)
Actives
Intransitives: smile (1/4); work (1/31)
Transitives: fight (practice a martial art) (1/4); learn (1/17); like (1/56); look-*ed* at (1/12); mean (1/12); refuse (1/1); send (1/7); study (1/18); visit (1/11)

Total: 11/173   Number of speakers: 10

[a]These verbs take the passive auxiliary "get."

are attached to the same node (i.e., they form a small VP), adverb insertion between them should be ungrammatical.

Yet another problem of categorization was posed by *he is separated his stomach* (as a result of an injury). This seems to be modeled on pseudotransitives such as *he separated his shoulder*. In no way can the grammatical subject be construed as the logical subject. As the part/whole relationship that exists between "he" and "stomach" makes the subject as much an affected entity as the complement, it was decided to include this example in the ergative verb group.

Data analysis

Table 9.1 supplies the total number of verb types and tokens for each of the three verb categories. Table 9.2 lists the verbs of each category that occur with the auxiliary "be." The actual number of occurrences of "be" and the total number of verb tokens are expressed fractionally

ized to obtain *the plan was argued about*. But an adverb can also be inserted: *We argued violently about the plan*. It can be inferred from this that the verb and the prepositional phrase do not make up a small verb phrase. "Argue" is intransitive.

after each verb. Verbs that occurred at least once in past participle form are marked with the suffix *-ed*.

"Be" is attested with roughly one third of the ergative verbs (15/43).[12] These 15 verbs take "be" 25 times in 110 potential contexts. With the active group (intransitive and transitive combined), "be" is found with only 11 verbs (11/281). Of 173 potential contexts, "be" was selected exactly 11 times. The ratio for the occurrence of "be" with ergative versus active verbs is thus, roughly, 1:4.5 to 1:16. Furthermore, of the 17 speakers accounting for the occurrence of "be" with ergative verbs, only 2 are among the 10 who account for "be" with actives, which is important as it indicates that the two types of "be" have distinct origins.

Two other aspects of the data support this interpretation. First, only ergative verbs show repeated use of "be" with the same verb type. For example, *happen* takes "be" 5 times out of 20 possible contexts. Four speakers, representing Japanese, Arabic, and Spanish L1 backgrounds, account for these five occurrences. On the other hand, not a single verb of the transitive group and neither of the active intransitives takes "be" more than once. This, I suggest, shows that only with the ergative group does the occurrence of "be" display a measure of systematicity, an interpretation bolstered by the further finding that nine of the ergative verbs occur in past participle form at least once, exactly what one would expect if ergatives were subsumed under the passive. Taking the transitives and active intransitives together, only one verb, "look," takes the past participle form.

The problem of classification posed by "separate" has been touched on earlier. Three other verbs, "enjoy," "consist of," and "pass" (a course), are listed as doubtful ergatives in Table 9.2. I believe a good case can be made for the ergative status of the latter two. For example, the adverbs "willingly" and "intentionally" are somewhat infelicitous with *I passed the course*. The grammatical subject in that sentence shows up as the object in *Professor Sauerstoff passed me in chemistry*, suggesting that it bears the thematic role *theme*.

The next structure to be discussed is (Pro)VS. The findings contained in Table 9.3 demonstrate conclusively that only ergative verbs give rise to (Pro)VS in our study.[13] The Japanese speakers account for 10 of the

---

12 J. Schachter (personal communication) has provided me with numerous additional examples involving an ergative verb plus "be" culled from productions by ESL learners. I am grateful to her for bringing these supporting examples to my attention.

13 White's (1985) grammaticality judgment data from Spanish and French speakers support the present finding. Of the test sentences containing VS, the one containing the verb "walk" received the lowest acceptability rating by both Spanish and French speakers alike. "Walk" is an active verb. The sentence receiving the highest acceptability rating with both L1 groups contained "escape," an ergative verb taking "essere" in Italian. Unfortunately, it occurs in an adverbial subordinate whose

TABLE 9.3. VERBS OCCURRING IN (PRO)VS

Ergatives: change (1/12); come (5/25)[a]; continue (2/6); dry (1/1); happen (1/20); live (1/7)[a]; occur (1/1); start (1/8)

	Intransitive	none
Active		
	Transitive	none

[a]These do not represent all the tokens of "come" and "live" in the corpus. It was found necessary to distinguish between "live" (as in occupying a dwelling or abode) and "live" (exist). For example, compare *I live on a noisy street* versus *We all live on this planet*. The former accepts *intentionally* but not the latter. Similarly, compare *John came voluntarily* versus *The bus came*.

13 occurrences. For these speakers, L1 transfer can be ruled out, because Japanese has a different word order pattern. Moreover, in four instances the "inverted" subject is definitely not thematic, having been introduced in the prior discourse (e.g., see Sentence 5). Last, four of the informants who produced (Pro)VS are among those who produced "be" with ergative verbs. With these speakers the derivation hypothesized becomes more transparent. The logical object can either be projected to its canonical position and receive nominative case *in situ*, or move-NP can allow it to appear in the position of the subject NP.

Before concluding this section, I would like to discuss briefly two minor phenomena contained in the data, both of which mesh with the ergative analysis. First, assuming that (Pro)VS with ergative verbs derives from an attempt to preserve, at S-structure, the configuration for *theme* assignment, and given the susceptibility of ergative verbs to an analysis identical to that of the passive, we can predict that passive constructions should also surface in the form (Pro)VS. Indeed, that is what is found, albeit in isolated cases only.

15. It was nearly killed all of us. (Chinese L1; high intermediate)
    "All of us were nearly killed."

Analogous passive constructions are reported in Rutherford and Altman (1985).

The second phenomenon involves a form of avoidance. A verb will be used transitively even though this distorts the intended meaning or results in an ungrammatical transitive structure. An ergative construction seems to be required in the following examples.[14]

translation equivalent in French permits inversion. The high acceptability rating for "look" is undoubtedly due to the fact that it was the only sentence employing presentative "there."

14 Eric Kellerman's (1978) findings on the acceptability of the intransitive verb "break" by Dutch learners of English are pertinent here. There was a relatively high degree of rejection by the advanced learners of "the cup broke," even though

16. I hope he's always light up his face.
    "I hope his face will always light up." (when he sees me)
17. Whenever I meet an ill-natured person, I'm break my heart.
    "Whenever...my heart breaks."
18. I changed myself a lot in those years.

In Sentences 16 and 17 a pseudotransitive construction serves to keep the *theme* NP in its canonical position. An interesting point about Sentence 18 is that the discourse context in no way suggests that the personality change was self-instigated. Note that the target form *I changed a lot in those years* can be given either a volitional or nonvolitional reading. But even with the volitional reading, the subject is also interpreted as *theme*. The reflexive construction in (18), despite the intended nonvolitional meaning, helps keep the thematic role *theme* in postverbal position. Although the phenomenon illustrated in Sentences 16 through 18 merits much more detailed investigation, there is a clear tendency with some speakers to avoid a *theme* NP in subject position by resorting to a pseudotransitive construction. Thus, the pseudosubjects of (16) and (17) appear to function much like the dummy pronoun in (Pro)VS.

Discussion

Implications for grammatical theory

We have succeeded in identifying three interlocking phenomena predicted by the typological scheme proposed earlier: "be" V-*ed*, (Pro)VS, and the pseudotransitives. These are nonstandard forms arising from the mapping problem posed by ergative verbs. What bearing does an L2 study of the type presented here have on current grammatical theory?

I think the fact that we are able to predict the nonstandard forms exemplified in Sentences 1 through 6 by employing analyses made available by current grammatical research is persuasive evidence that these analyses are on the right track. (Pro)VS and "be" V-*ed* are difficult to account for unless we assume that English expresses thematic relations configurationally and that NP-movement is a canonical expression of its configurational typology. More generally, these nonstandard forms are wholly compatible with a projectionist model of grammar (Chomsky 1981; Marantz 1984) involving mapping relationships between distinct levels of representations.

The data also allow us to address the trade-off between the syntactic

---

Dutch has the equivalent form. In a translation task, the ergative construction was typically rendered by an agentless passive construction. Overall, about 66 percent of 32 first-year university learners of English avoided a straightforward translation of the Dutch form into English.

component and the lexicon. In the exposition presented here of the Unaccusative Hypothesis, the proposal by Keyser and Roeper (1984) was dealt with, according to which English possesses a lexical ergative rule that takes a transitive verb for its input and removes the logical subject, thereby making the verb syntactically intransitive. The data allow us to question this proposal.

According to Keyser and Roeper, the ergative rule produces the same effects as passive morphology. Now, the data here indicate that on occasion the passive is overgeneralized to ergative verbs. But if the lexical ergative rule and passive morphology both produce the same representation, then there exists another logical possibility – to overgeneralize the lexical ergative rule. This logical possibility is illustrated in Sentences 19 through 21:

19a. The children frazzled her nerves.
  b. ?Her nerves frazzled. (cf. "her senses numbed")
20a. The drought damaged the crops.
  b. *The crops damaged. (cf. "the crops withered")
21a. The government regionalized its departments.
  b. ?The departments regionalized. (cf. Keyser and Roeper 1984 "the department centralized" [Sentence 29d])

The sizable corpus of data collected contains not a single instance of such an overgeneralization. The "passive reading" (Anderson 1977) invited by *the dress tore* and *the mirror shattered* does not induce the subjects in this study to extend the ergative construction. The extreme conservatism displayed by our informants toward this possibility instead tends to support Marantz's (1984) claim that the ergative and the transitive lexical forms are not derived one from the other by a productive rule. The direction of generalization actually found in the data – ergatives being subsumed under the passive – is in accord with the status of the passive as a core rule of English.

There is another good reason for the direction in which the generalization takes place. Not only is the passive a canonical structure of the configurational type of language, it also has the advantage of overtly signaling that a change in underlying grammatical relations has taken place.[15] The perceptual advantages of such an overt signal for sentence processing are obvious.

15 Note that NP-movement, when it occurs in the lexicon, leaves no surface signal that the logical subject is missing. "Be" would represent such a signal. Furthermore, in languages such as French and Italian a reflexive form of the verb occurs with those ergatives that have a transitive counterpart, for example, the French *la porte s'ouvre* ("the door is opened"). Marantz (1984) suggests the reflexive "signals" the missing logical subject.

Implications for L2 acquisition

In conclusion, let us consider the L2 acquisition-relevant contribution of this chapter, both in terms of findings and, more generally, the approach presented.

A long-standing issue in language acquisition research has been the question of the kinds of linguistic representations one can ascribe to learner grammars. The informants in this investigation are no longer at the early stages of L2 acquisition; the discussion is, accordingly, limited to more advanced stages.

It is difficult to account for the patterning of "be" and (Pro)VS unless we assume that active verbs and ergatives have distinct logical predicate-argument structures. This is the substance of the ergative hypothesis and Hoestra's (1984) reformulation of the transitive/intransitive distinction into a category of verbs with a logical subject and a category of verbs without one. Now, in the input a learner of English encounters, the sole argument of ergative verbs *nearly always* occupies the position of the grammatical subject (exceptions being those ergative verbs such as "appear" and "occur," which appear in presentatives with "there"). Tense and auxiliary marking is *always* the same with ergatives as with active verbs. The input data, therefore, only very weakly support the distinct analyses. Thus, the primary motivation must derive from the substantive universal stated in the Unaccusative Hypothesis. While there may be language-specific differences in demarcating the ergative class, we can accept Baker's (1983) argument that there will be a core set cross-linguistically such that once a learner has identified the semantics of a core exemplar, the learner will adopt $[\emptyset \ [V \ NP]]$ as its predicate-argument structure.

This representation cannot by itself explain (Pro)VS and "be" V-*ed* with ergatives like "happen," "fall," and "die" unless learners have also determined that thematic roles are assigned configurationally. If our hypothesis about the extension of the passive rule to ergatives is correct, then that rule must have operated on the configurational representation of thematic roles, specifically $[e \ [V \ NP \ _{theme}]]$. This is the representation that core instances of the passive and ergative verbs share. Of course, the discovery of the passive solution is facilitated if a learner knows, independently of any data, that sentences must have grammatical subjects. Once the structural means whereby subjects are expressed in English are identified, the move-NP rule follows automatically.

If this analysis is at all on the right track, then some very suggestive evidence exists that derivational models of grammar incorporating more than one level of linguistic representation can lay claim to psychological reality. Since the passive solution with verbs like "fall" and "happen" clearly cannot be derived from a surface analysis of the input, the formulation of grammars would appear to follow a mapping procedure from predicate-argument structure to syntax. (Pro)VS is telltale evidence for a configurational mapping at the level of thematic roles, while "be" V-*ed* also takes into account the configurational expression of the (surface) grammatical subject.

The next point has already been touched on in the discussion of the direction of generalization. There it was remarked that the passive reading invited by ergative constructions such as *the mirror shattered* does not incline learners to overgeneralize this construction to other transitive verbs. A cautious interpretation of this finding suggests that the informants in this study do not look upon the lexicon as a source of productive rules and as an appropriate site for trying out hypotheses. Why should this be the case?

Suppose a learner assumes that there exists a productive rule in the lexicon of English that permits the derivation of ergative intransitives from transitive verbs. This learner would then try out such ergative constructions as *crops damaged*. The input data would only supply examples of the adjectival and verbal passive *crops were damaged*. From this sort of evidence, the learner could not conclude that "damage" does not undergo the rule since the transitive counterparts of ergatives can all passivize. Consider, now, the other possibility, as attested in Sentences 1 through 3. Here, tense-marking on intransitive verbs can refute auxiliary "be." More importantly, though, this provisional solution is open to modification with increments of learning. Roughly, syntactically transitive verbs form the input to passive verbal morphology. The passive deprives the verbs of syntactic transitivity by removing the logical subject. If, as Marantz (1984) proposes, ergative verbs are created by analogic generalization, then they are intransitive to begin with. Thus, as soon as a learner redefines the input to passive in terms of the syntactically transitive class, the provisional solution will be abandoned.

The preceding argument avails itself of theoretical considerations guiding work in learnability theory (Baker 1979; White 1986). Since learners are not as a rule instructed on the source of their ungrammatical utterances, they must be able to modify erroneous provisional solutions with the primary data available to them in the input. Of the two logical possibilities discussed, the extension of the passive to ergatives is amendable; the overgeneralization of the ergative derivation from transitive verbs is not. The conservative behavior witnessed with regard to this possibility squares with the prediction learnability theory would make.

In conclusion, let us return to the introductory remarks, where it was suggested that if grammar acquisition is mediated by grammatical principles, novel solutions should display a higher degree of congruence with a principle than the actual L2 target. Ergative structures such as *the mirror shattered* and *Fred and Ginger fell* seem to be removed from the canonical typological structures of English. The *theme* bearing NP, the logical object, is not in its canonical position. There is no verbal morphology to signal the change in grammatical relations as there is with the passive. Set against these considerations, it is almost surprising that the previously mentioned syntactic solutions (2) and (3) to the problem of ergative verbs are not more frequent in the data. But there is a simple explanation for this, I believe. Lexical move-NP must be the developmentally earlier rule, unless we make the assumption – surely untenable – that L2 learners of English cannot deal with ergative verbs until they acquire the passive and dummy pronouns. Seen in this light, solutions (2) and (3) seem to spring from a more sophisticated reanalysis of English.[16] Typically, move-NP either applies in the mapping from D- to S-structure, or the empty logical subject position takes a dummy pronoun. Yet, this reanalysis – made possible by knowledge of the central status of the passive and the structural requirement of dummy pronouns – only succeeds in introducing a measure of indeterminacy and never supplants the earlier, lexical, rule.

References

Andersen, R. 1980. Creolization as the acquisition of a second language as a first language. In *Theoretical Orientations in Creole Studies*, A. Valdman and A. Highfield, eds. New York: Academic Press.

Anderson, S. 1977. Comments on the paper by Wasow. In *Formal Syntax*, P. Culicover, T. Wasow, and A. Akmajian, eds. New York: Academic Press.

Baker, C. L. 1979. Syntactic theory and the projection problem. *Linguistic Inquiry* 10: 533–81.

Baker, M. 1983. Objects, themes and lexical rules in Italian. In *Papers in Lexical-Functional Grammar*, L. Levin, M. Rappaport, and A. Zaenen, eds. Bloomington: Indiana University Linguistics Club.

Bowers, J. 1981. *The Theory of Grammatical Relations*. Ithaca: Cornell University Press.

Burzio, L. 1981. Intransitive verbs and Italian auxiliaries. Ph.D. dissertation, Massachusetts Institute of Technology.

1983. Conditions on representation and Romance syntax. *Linguistic Inquiry* 14: 193–221.

Chomsky, N. 1981. *Lectures on Government and Binding*. Dordrecht, The Netherlands: Foris.

Fiengo, R. 1974. Semantic conditions on surface structure. Ph.D. dissertation, Massachusetts Institute of Technology.

Hale, K. 1983. Walpiri and the grammar of nonconfigurational languages. *Natural Language and Linguistic Theory* 1: 5–47.

16 This phenomenon, U-shaped learning, is discussed in detail with reference to L2 acquisition by Kellerman (1985).

Harris, A. 1982. Georgian and the unaccusative hypothesis. *Language* 58: 290–306.

Hilles, S. 1986. Interlanguage and the pro-drop parameter. *Second Language Research* 2: 33–52.

Hoekstra, T. 1984. *Transitivity: Grammatical Relations in Government-Binding Theory*. Dordrecht, The Netherlands: Foris.

Jackendoff, R. 1972. *Semantic Interpretation in Generative Grammar*. Cambridge, Mass.: MIT Press.

Jaeggli, O. 1982. *Topics in Romance Syntax*. Dordrecht, The Netherlands: Foris.

Kellerman, E. 1978. Giving learners a break: native language intuitions as a source of predictions about transferability. *Working Papers on Bilingualism* 15: 59–92.

1985. If at first you do succeed. In *Input in Second Language Acquisition*, S. Gass and C. Madden, eds. Rowley, Mass.: Newbury House.

Keyser, S., and T. Roeper, 1984. On the middle and ergative constructions in English. *Linguistic Inquiry* 15: 381–416.

Lightfoot, D. 1982. *The Language Lottery: Toward a Biology of Grammars*. Cambridge, Mass.: MIT Press.

Marantz, A. 1984. *On the Nature of Grammatical Relations*. Cambridge, Mass.: MIT Press.

Perlmutter, D. 1978. Impersonal passives and the unaccusative hypothesis. *Proceedings of the 4th Annual Meeting*, Berkeley Linguistics Society, 157–89.

Rosen, C. 1982. The interface between semantic roles and initial grammatical relations. In *Subjects and Other Subjects*, A. Zaenen, ed. Bloomington: Indiana University Linguistic Club

Rutherford, W., and R. Altman. 1985. Discourse competence and L2 acquisition: word order. Unpublished manuscript, University of Southern California and University of California at Los Angeles.

Stowell, T. 1981. Origins of phrase structure. Ph.D. dissertation, Massachusetts Institute of Technology.

White, L. 1985. The "pro-drop" parameter in adult second language acquisition. *Language Learning* 35: 47–62.

1986. Markedness and parameter setting: some implications for a theory of adult second language acquisition. In *Markedness*, E. Eckman, E. Moravcsik, and J. Wirth, eds. New York: Plenum.

Williams, E. 1984. Grammatical relations. *Linguistic Inquiry* 15: 639–73.

Wode, H. 1981. Psycholinguistische Grundlagen sprachlicher Universalien [Psycholinguistic foundations of language universals]. *Working Papers in Language Acquisition* 28, Department of English, University of Kiel, West Germany.

Zobl, H. 1986. Word order typology, lexical government and the prediction of multiple, graded effects on L2 word order. *Language Learning* 36: 159–84.

10 Semantic theory and L2 lexical development

Wesley Hudson

Among the various lines of inquiry in second language research, there are a number of questions that are of central importance. These questions concern: (1) the extent to which learning a second language is a rule-governed process: (2) the nature of the developmental stages involved: and (3) the influence of the first language on the second question raised. The literature on lexical development in a second language (L2) has focused almost exclusively on the last of the above-mentioned issues and usually without reference to a formal theory of the lexicon. To my knowledge, a systematic model of how *meanings* of words are acquired is absent from the field. Most writers on the subject assume L2 lexical development proceeds in the same way as in a first language (L1), without specifying what this is in formal terms. It is the purpose of this chapter to begin to fill this void.

A theory of the acquisition of word meaning relies crucially on the proper characterization of the nature of word meaning. One reason for the state of affairs just described lies in the inapplicability of traditional concepts within the field of lexical semantics to a theory of second langauge word meaning. I will argue that the preference rule system developed by Jackendoff (1983) does provide a characterization of the nature of word meaning, which can serve as a theoretical model for the acquisition of words. After outlining Jackendoff's proposals, I show the relevance of his ideas to the question of cross-linguistic differences in word meaning. Then I explore some consequences of examining the process of acquiring words from the viewpoint of a preference rule system.

Truth-based theories of lexical semantics

Among truth-conditional approaches to semantics, different treatments of word meaning can be seen as falling into one of two camps: theories

I wish to thank Robert Kaplan, D. Poole, and Jacquelyn Schachter for their comments on earlier drafts of this paper.

of meaning and theories of reference. A meaning-based theory (sometimes called an intensional theory) takes the semantic relations of synonymy, entailment, contradiction, and so forth as having to do with the inherent properties of words themselves. A reference-based (or extensional) theory treats semantic relations as determined by relations between the objects to which words refer. Under this view, words do not have meanings per se; meaning is determined by mapping a sentence onto a set of truth values (true or false) as determined by the state of things in the world (or possible worlds).

Many of the points of debate between these two approaches stem from a distinction made in Frege (1892) between the terms *sense* and *reference*. Frege used the term *sense* to designate what distinguishes between two terms referring to the same thing. For instance, the senses of the terms *the evening star* and *the morning star* are different (there being a form of knowledge expressed in the differing modes of designation), but the reference would be the same (the planet Venus). This distinction also helps to explain how we can understand terms that have no referent. For instance, the noun phrase *the first female president of the U.S.* is understandable (even though it has no referent) because it has a sense. A word, therefore, is said to express its sense and to stand for its referent, if it has one.

The question of how to represent lexical meaning (sense/intension) in linguistic terms plays a central role in the work of Katz (1964, 1975), who develops a semantic theory closely related to the goals of transformational grammar. Katz regards word meaning as represented in a word's internal structure; the meaning of a word is built up from a number of semantic primitives, or basic units of meaning. The entry for the word *spinster*, for example, will be analyzed as a complex of the semantic primitives: [FEMALE], [NEVER MARRIED], [ADULT]. These bracketed semantic markers are not meant to be equivalent to the English words they resemble; they are innate concepts drawn from a store of universal substantives (semantic markers whose meanings are not language-specific). This mentalist approach parallels in a semantic domain the transformational grammarians' view of linguistic knowledge as innately represented in the individual's mind.

One specific goal of this treatment of word meaning is to account for the validity of the logical inference of a proposition whose truth is solely dependent on the meaning of the words it contains. For example, the following sentences are true not simply by the form of their logical structures but because of entailments between semantic markers:

1. Cats are animals.
2. Bachelors are unmarried men.

Treating the word *bachelor* as consisting of the semantic markers [UN-MARRIED] and [MALE], or the word *cat* as including [ANIMAL], allows Sentences 1 and 2 to be treated as analytically true (not contingent on facts or beliefs about the world). Under this view, the process involved in acquiring word meaning consists of a rather direct mapping between semantic primitives, drawn from a universal store, and a particular word in a given language.

The premises of Katz's theory have been contested by a number of scholars on both philosophical and linguistic grounds. Many of the objections to an intensionalist approach in general, and to semantic markers in particular, stem from the work of W. V. Quine (1959), who rejects the notion that word meaning enters into the determination of logical inference. For Quine, the truth of Sentence 2 is simply due to our beliefs about bachelors and unmarried men, not because of some inherent property in the words. Two specific examples of the shortcomings of a semantic marker account of semantic relations concern the fuzziness of concepts such as synonymy, and the revisability of word meaning.

As discussed in Pulman (1983), synonymy between the two terms in Sentence 2 should be subject to necessary and sufficient conditions. However, there can be rather fuzzy judgments as to the status of the sentence in (3):

3. A monk is a bachelor.

Not all people agree as to whether this sentence is true or not: It is not clear that a monk is a bachelor even though he is an unmarried man. With respect to the example in (2), it seems that being an unmarried man is a necessary but not sufficient condition for being a bachelor. Therefore, it cannot be said that semantic entailments are exhaustively determined by semantic markers.

The second argument, regarding revisability of word meaning, derives from Putnam (1975). Sentence 1 should be necessarily true if *cat* has as a primitive constituent the semantic marker [ANIMAL]. However, suppose that we discovered that all cats are actually robots controlled from Mars. We would have to revise our knowledge of cats accordingly. But this is not possible if [ANIMAL] is an innate concept that makes up the meaning of "cat" (perhaps considering a "simpler" conception of whales as fish would seem a more plausible example). Putnam's point is that much of our knowledge of what a word means is revisable by future scientific discovery. Therefore, meaning should not be considered an inherent property of words.

This last point is a bit of a problem for a purely extensional account of meaning if only because it goes against intuitions that a word has a meaning that we know in our heads. However, Putnam (1975) presents a treatment of natural kind terms (terms for things that occur in nature, such as *water, gold,* etc.) that avoids this problem by completely bifurcating what we know as users of language and what words refer to.

According to Putnam, words we use refer, willy-nilly, to the objects in the world that are the words' extension. Much like indexicals (such as pronouns), a word like *gold* rigidly designates whatever it is that is gold. We may not know exactly what gold is, but when we use the word *gold,* gold and only gold is being referred to. Although there is no meaning for *gold* in our heads, there are expert members of the society who know the recognition procedures for determining what gold is (by chemical analysis, for instance). We, as comembers of the community, "inherit" the ability of these experts to determine the extensions of words. When we use the word *gold* we refer to its extension as determined by these experts (even if what we say is false, such as when we point to yellow metal that looks like gold and use the word *gold* to refer to it, but it is not gold). This is what Putnam calls the division of linguistic labor, which allows for the revisability of a word's "meaning" as scientific discovery dictates.

The second part of Putnam's account helps to explain how we can use words in communicating with others even when we may have no clear idea about what words refer to (for instance, I may not know what an elm tree looks like, but I can use the term in a sentence). It also explains the intuitions we have that words do have meanings.

For each word we acquire we have a stereotype of it in varying depth and detail. Stereotypes are not linguistic entities, but conventional ideas that constitute our "normal form of description" (Putnam 1975) for the words we acquire. These normal forms of description are not necessary or sufficient conditions for determining the extension of the word. For instance, the normal form of description for a tiger will probably include the idea of orange and black stripes, but an albino tiger is still going to be a tiger. These stereotypes are "part of the cooperative or conformative property of a society." Not only which words we come to acquire but also the depth of information for a stereotype are to a large extent determined by cultural factors. As Putnam puts it: "[T]he nature of the required minimum level of competence depends heavily upon both the culture and the topic." Learning word meaning is thereby subsumed under learning that takes place in sociolinguistic domains. Moreover, determining words' extensions is not a matter of linguistic competence; it does not reside in any one person's mind but is, in a sense, the property of a society.

One of the requirements that a theory of the acquisition of words might be expected to meet is to provide a mechanism that can describe how stages in lexical development progress and how lexical entries are built up from a minimal to a completed entry (as described in Taylor

1978). The theories just outlined do not seem to provide a basis for such a mechanism.

For instance, while a semantic marker theory like Katz's satisfies the intuitive requirement that words are linguistic entities, the fact that markers are claimed to be innate fails to explain not only the revisability of word meaning but also the revisability of hypotheses involved in the process of building an entry. To try to utilize a marker theory without the innateness stipulation simply throws the question of learning back to how particular markers are learned, a question seldom addressed in L2 discussions of, for instance, semantic fields.

For Putnam, on the other hand, words are not themselves meaningful in a psychologically real way. What speakers have in their heads are stereotypes for the objects to which words refer. There are, however, a number of ways in which stereotypes fail to describe lexical competence with sufficient generality. For instance, on a conceptual level the stereotype explanation has nothing to say about how personal experience (as opposed to social cooperation) influences and is reflected in lexical development. There are strong cases of divergence of lexical meaning exactly where one would predict stereotypes to constrain variation in meaning. In an informal study described in Chase (1938), 100 people were asked to describe *fascism*. Not only were 100 different answers obtained, but many answers were at polar extremes in meaning. But there are also problems with extending Putnam's extensional view of natural kind terms as being scientifically determinable to other syntactic classes, particularly verbs and syncategorematic words such as "good."

Jackendoff's theory

The approach to lexical meaning presented in Jackendoff's *Semantics and Cognition* (1983) avoids many of the problems with the theories discussed; it allows for the treatment of the semantic relations between words as involving a relation between their internal structures while at the same time allowing for the fuzziness and revisability of meaning. In addition, his approach provides a theoretical framework for describing the ways in which learning word meaning is a rule-governed process.

The theoretical claim that underlies *Semantics and Cognition* is that there is a level of mental representation at which linguistic, sensory, and motor information are compatible and subject to the same kind of rules: in Jackendoff's terms, conceptual structure. Using the necessity of accepting a visual/motor systems interface in order to explain how we can coordinate information from these two domains in the act of reaching for an object by analogy impels acceptance of a similar interface between sensory and linguistic information in order to explain how we can talk

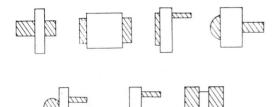

Figure 10.1 (From R. Jackendoff, 1983, "Semantics and Cognition," p. 45. Cambridge, Mass.: MIT Press. Reprinted with permission.)

about what we see. What allows for integration of different modes of information is that information in each mode follows the same rules of organization.

Justification for this claim takes the following lines. Studies of visual perception have shown the large extent to which what we perceive with our eyes is the result of an interaction between environmental input and a complex of active principles in the mind that impose structure on that input. It has also been proposed that there are principles that determine individuation of "things" in the field of vision. It seems that the nature of the interaction of these principles is such that they do not always result in clear-cut distinctions of "thinghood" (i.e., what is or is not a thing) but yield a series of graded judgments that fall along a yes/not sure/no continuum. This is illustrated in Figure 10.1, where judgments are called into play about which of the shaded areas in the figures constitute single "things." Therefore, just as in the general organization of visual input, it is clearly information our minds supply that determines judgments as to what is a thing (and in relation to language, what is a nameable thing). The creativity with which these judgments are made is accounted for by proposing that they are the result of rule-governed processes.

Jackendoff reaches an interesting conclusion from these considerations with respect to a theory of reference; since perception of things is the result of certain information the mind supplies, what linguistic expressions refer to are the resulting mental entities that are projected onto our awareness, not the real world objects themselves. It is simply a fact of nature that we happen to be so constructed as to be unaware of the contribution our minds make to our experience of the outside world. If words refer to our mental constructs, treating extensions of words as outside us is to ignore a basic fact of human makeup. Subsuming the theory of reference to such a mentalist position enables Jackendoff to argue that the meanings of words themselves are organized along principles similar to those operating in the perceptual domain in the determination of thinghood.

As previously mentioned, words are taken to have internal structure. Information contained in a word's entry is built up through experience of examples of the words we perceive or are told about. As it is dependent on our exposure to the world, the nature of this information is qualitatively different from that encoded by Katzian semantic markers. Furthermore, this information is not simply a random list of features or unanalyzable stereotypes but is hierarchically structured into superordinate and subordinate domains, according to a set of principles similar to those at work in organizing visual input. For instance, the lexical entry for the category *dog* will contain internally represented information that distinguishes the concept *dog* from other examples of the category animal: [FOUR LEGS], [HAS FUR], and so on. In addition, the lexical entry for *dog* will be related to subordinate categories such as *poodle* through a set of semantic operators that serve to reduce redundancy of information and permit inferences to be drawn between lexical entries. For example, since *poodle* is an example of *dog* and *dog* has the feature [FOUR LEGS], we can infer that poodles have four legs. The entry for *poodle* will in turn contain information that distinguishes it from other types of the category *dog*. This entry is built up from information about specific examples of poodles, for instance my pet, Spot, which contains information by which to distinguish visually my pet from other pets.

While we may be conscious of the information encoded under a word, the principles that organize this information act subconsciously and are not usually retrievable. These organizing principles make it possible for us to make creative, on-the-spot judgments as to whether some thing we have never seen before should be called a dog or a cat. More specifically, we know something is an example of a dog before we can consciously compute the sum of its parts in order to deduce from this that it is a dog. The immediacy of these judgments is achieved by reference to the rules that organize and relate the information underlying the lexical entry *dog*.

That these judgments fall along the same graded continuum as those in perceptual domains can be seen by considering how an Eskimo with no notion of dogs outside of huskies, might have trouble in correctly judging the "dogness" of a Chihuahua (for example, it might be initially considered a rodent).

This process of judging an object to be an instance of a word (i.e., *x* is a dog) is an example of a process of categorization that is claimed to hold in a strictly parallel manner at further levels of abstraction. Basically, these levels can be broken down into the relation between Tokens and Types. The fact that Tokens and Types are organized along similar lines permits an account of semantic relations without reference to truth conditions.

A Token is an instance of a thing that is "projectable into awareness" in Jackendoff's terms (i.e., we can perceive it), such as the mental entities to which names and definite descriptions refer. A Type is itself a category and so is not directly perceivable. For instance, we can't see the Type *teacher*, which includes all teachers, past, present, and future; we can only see instances of *teacher*, as in Sentence 4b. Information within a Type is built up from information about instances of the Type, which can be either Tokens or other Types. This information is built up in conjunction with principles that organize the information into a stable, related complex.

Examples of the Token/Type distinction are shown in (4a–c):

4a. John is a teacher.
  b. A teacher praised her.
  c. A cat is an animal.

In (4a), a Token, *John*, is claimed to be an instance of the Type *teacher*, which, as a Type, is not an entity that is projectable into awareness. In (4b), the word *teacher* is used as an instance of a Token, in that it refers to an individual. In (4c), both noun phrases are Types; neither is projectable, but the information within each is mutually accessible or extractable according to inference rules that account, in this case, for the semantic entailment. Consider judgments for Sentence 5, taken from *Semantics and Cognition*:

5. An abortion is a murder.

As opposed to (4c), the entailment relation in (5) is open to graded judgments: yes/not sure/no. This fuzziness is attributed to the conflict of certain principles that determine how information in a lexical entry is organized. To see how Jackendoff's account of this phenomenon is superior to proposals framed within semantic theories that rely on necessary and sufficient conditions on word meaning, let us turn to his conception of the preference rules system.

Jackendoff proposes a set of principles called *preference rules* to account for the intractable nature of word meaning. Preference rules are the mechanisms that drive the choices involved in structuring the information internal to a lexical entry. His preference rules system is drawn from the grouping rules of Wertheimer's (1923) study of the perceptual principles that organize collections of shapes into larger units. Consider the following figures:

6. oo   ooo
7. o o   o o o

8. ooooo
9. OOooo
10. OOo oo
11. OOo   oo
12. OO   ooo

In some of the examples, the sets of circles are most naturally grouped together by one of two criteria: proximity, as in (6), and similarity, as in (9). Example (7) shows that the less salient the difference in proximity, the more easily groupings other than the 2-3 grouping in (6) are possible. This demonstrates that the perceptual principle of proximity is a graded condition. Another example, (10), shows how the two principles of proximity and similarity overlap or conflict. In (10), the grouping intuition is not as strong as in either (9), where the principle of similarity is at work, or (11), where the effects of proximity are so strong as to outweigh the effects of similarity, resulting in the 3-2 grouping. The interaction of principles is such that they either reinforce each other, resulting in strong intuitions on grouping, as in (12); are in conflict with, and therefore balance, each other, resulting in fuzzy judgments as in (10); or, as in (8), are not operative in distinguishing between individuals that together form a single group.

The main point of this discussion is that the balancing effect resulting from the conflict between at least two organizing principles gives rise to graded judgments of meaning.

Unlike a set of necessary and sufficient conditions on word meaning, the preference rule account makes very different (and apparently correct) predictions concerning the flexibility of word meaning. In particular, there are three conditions Jackendoff discusses as the minimum set of conditions that interact within a preference rule framework to specify word meaning:

First, we cannot do without *necessary* conditions: e.g., "red" must contain the necessary condition, COLOR, and "tiger" must contain at least, THING. Second, we need graded conditions to designate hue in color concepts and the height—width ratio of cups, for example. These conditions specify a focal or central value for a continuously variable attribute; the most secure positive judgments are for those examples that lie relatively close to the focal value of the attribute in question. I will call such conditions *centrality* conditions. Third, we need conditions that are typical but subject to exceptions – for instance, the element of competition in games or a tiger's stripedness. Bundles of such *typicality* conditions lead to the family resemblance phenomena pointed out by Wittgenstein. Words can differ widely in which kinds of conditions are most prominent. Kinship terms, for example, are among the purest cases involving necessary conditions; in color names, centrality conditions play the most crucial role. (Jackendoff 1983:121)

To illustrate with the cup/bowl example mentioned (from Labov 1978), having a single handle is a typicality condition for cups, not bowls.

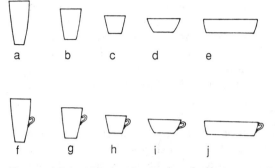

Figure 10.2   (From R. Jackendoff, 1983, "Semantics and Cognition," p. 137. Cambridge, Mass.: MIT Press. Reprinted with permission.)

However, both cups and bowls have centrality conditions based on a height/width ratio. In Figure 10.2, conflict in the height/width centrality condition results in vagueness as to whether (d) can be defined as a cup or a bowl. In (i), the handle typicality condition on cups is capable of overriding the vagueness resulting from the conflict in the centrality condition, but is not strong enough to do so in (e), where the height/width condition is stronger.

The resulting picture of word meaning is that information within a lexical entry will be organized along at least three interacting principles, differing in relative importance, according to the word. With a cup, a necessity condition – the function of containing liquid – will determine the allowable range within which the centrality condition (height/width) can vary to ensure a shape that can indeed contain something. In the cup/bowl example, we can see how the height/width centrality condition that is part of the lexical entry *cup* is conditioned by equivalent information within the entry *bowl*. We can also see that the preference for staking out nonoverlapping territory is only a graded condition.

To summarize, then, lexical information can be seen as structured by the interaction of the three conditions of necessity, centrality, and typicality. The preference rule system is the process by which the interaction of these conditions on lexical meaning results in a preferred weighting (on the grounds, for instance, of structural stability). The particular machinery for storing information in different lexical entries may also provide a description for global structural preferences that can influence the way information for any particular word is structured in relation to others.

The theory outlined in *Semantics and Cognition* seems well-suited to solving some of the stickiest problems in theoretical lexical semantics. Its applicability to second language acquisition (SLA) research, however, needs to be demonstrated.

Certainly one of the requirements that a semantic theory should meet if it is to serve as a model for the acquisition of meaning in an L2 is that it be capable of characterizing cross-linguistic differences in the meaning of words in a psychologically insightful way. I will attempt to demonstrate how the three conditions of necessity, centrality, and typicality can account for a sufficient range of differences, therefore making Jackendoff's theory a prime candidate for use in research into the learning process.

The following examples are intentionally drawn from languages with no direct historic ties to each other – English and Mandarin Chinese. This is essentially for the sake of simplicity, since a number of complicating factors arise when considering languages with extensive cognates.

The first example deals with the centrality condition. Whereas English has two separate focal points – *blue* and *green* – in the color lexicon, Chinese has a word *qing* (blue/green) that overlaps the two English words. For native English speakers, intuitive judgments will be quite strong for clear-cut examples of the two colors, with varyingly graded judgments as a color moves more toward the center of the blue/green dichotomy. For Chinese native speakers, the area of color that would produce varying judgments in English will be a central example of the word *qing*, which will have a different range of judgments along a yes/no/maybe scale. This cross-linguistic difference in centrality conditions reflects a difference in how perceptual·categories are related to language in a given culture.

Examples of words organized by a relatively strong set of necessity conditions are kinship terms. In English, one's uncle is the brother of either of one's parents, and this is necessarily so. Judgments will usually be quite certain as to when to use the word *uncle* and when not to. Chinese has a similar set of necessary conditions on family terms, but they are organized differently. For example, there is one word for one's father's older brother (*bo*) and a word for one's father's younger brother (*shu*). However, the word *shu* in Chinese also has a set of conditions of a more graded quality (which may actually be a culturally influenced centrality condition) in that it can be used as a term for a male of one's parents' generation, even when there is no blood relation. This example shows how a word in one language can have a set of conditions that are absent for the same word in another language – necessity condition for the English word *uncle* versus necessity and centrality conditions for the Chinese *shu*.

Cross-linguistic differences in necessity conditions can also be seen for the verb *persuade* (example from Li 1985). Sentence 13:

13. I persuaded him to go but he didn't go.

would be considered a contradiction by most speakers of English. Normal use of the verb *persuade* "entails" that the action (here, to go) on the part of a persuadee was carried out. In Chinese, however, the verb *chuan*, which in every other respect seems indistinguishable from the English word, does not have this entailment, and this sentence would not be a contradiction. What seems a necessary condition for the English word is not present in the Chinese verb.

Examples of cross-linguistic differences in typicality conditions for word meaning seem so ubiquitous that it is difficult to settle on any one particular example. The reader is invited to consider how much cross-cultural variety there could be, for instance, in superordinate/subordinate relations for typical examples of the following: *fruit, furniture, politician, music, criminal, building, pet.* Taking one example from this list, *pet*, it seems that not only are there societies (or classes within a society) where *pet* is not even a relevant category, but that what in America may constitute one of the most typical pets, *dog*, may serve in another as a source of food.

For the moment, I would like to view these cross-linguistic examples in terms of what they imply about the way a native speaker of either of the two languages attains lexical competence in the L1. One emergent picture is that what is actually learned are the rules determining how the information in a word is structured. As an initial hypothesis for the course of lexical development, then, it seems clear that the process of learning a word is not simply that of matching a word with a referent, but of learning the distinguishing conditions operant in the structuring of information – conditions that make possible the kinds of creative judgments as to how and where to use the words. This process in itself entails knowledge of how words are related to, or differ from, each other through the juxtaposition of, or the relative primacy of, the conditions by which information in each word is organized.

However, there is more involved in the previously given examples than is explicable by positing an abstract set of cognitive rules. These cross-linguistic examples clearly demonstrate another kind of knowledge included in native-speaker competence that must be accounted for – the knowledge resulting from membership in a culture. Looking at the *uncle* example, it could be argued that the Chinese word *shu* used for both a relative and as a respectful/familiar term for an elder actually constitutes two lexical entries. However, more interesting implications for explaining lexical relations can be obtained by looking at *shu* when conditions determining its two uses both reinforce and conflict with each other. It is not surprising in a country with the traditional filial values (and the historic Confucian ideal of nation as an extension of family) that the relative primacy of the necessity condition for the use of the word *shu* for family members should be subsumed by the aspect of respect and hierarchical status typically associated with the notion of elder.

To see this more clearly, consider a culturally neutral example of how extensions of the meaning of words result from a shift in balance of conditions on its makeup:

14. He put the socks in the drawer.

In the most typical uses of the verb *put*, as in this example, there are at least two prominent notions: (a) displacement of an object; and (b) performed by hand. Consider, however, Sentence 15:

15. He put the car in the garage.

Here the necessary meaning of displacement remains but the typicality condition, performed by hand, has been relaxed.

As in the example with *uncle*, we find a word with two uses which share certain criteria, but which in the extended use demonstrate a difference in the relative weight of the conditions. Furthermore, the cultural influence involved in the Chinese *shu* is obviously not restricted to how the word's meaning is extended. It should also be clear that a speaker's decision of when to use the extended meaning of *shu* results from different cultural criteria interacting that are likely to take the form of graded judgments; for example, at what exact age must an elder be addressed by *shu*, and what degree of familiarity is involved.

From this, it seems that lexical development is not most appropriately described as only learning an abstract set of rules for relating lexical information. To a large extent, what native speakers learn are the culture-specific criteria for organizing lexical information. The cultural influence on the three preference conditions will sometimes be quite overt, as for words that are language/culture-specific, and can at times be very subtle, influencing only the relative weight of the conditions that interact in structuring lexical information (e.g., the typicality conditions on *dog*).

While the approach to word meaning adopted here is mentalistic, in that words have internal structures that are built up in a rule-governed process, I think it is important to note the possibility of integrating certain aspects of Putnam's account, presented earlier. In fact, this was one of the points of the previous cross-linguistic discussion: The preference conditions we learn are often learned as an integral part of the process of attaining membership in a social group. The very same forces that work toward conformity within a particular language community are a cause of variation in lexical representation across languages.

Implications for second language research

One of the most common concerns in the L2 literature on the lexicon is that L2 learners initially approach the learning of words as a translation (or transfer) process (see Twaddell 1972; Judd 1978; Schumann 1982). The solution to this dilemma in the more sophisticated treatments of the problem of L2 lexical development (Wilkins 1972; Richards 1980) is that L2 learners must come to employ the same process in learning an L2 as they do in their own L1. This process is usually seen as the gradual progression of more accurate hypotheses of a word's meaning, resulting mainly from massive exposure to language in context.

This characterization of lexical development in the field reveals a host of implicit assumptions that the theory just presented calls into question. One such assumption is that translating and forming hypotheses in the process of acquiring words are actually different mental processes; but consideration is rarely given as to *how* these processes differ or the extent to which they are rule-governed. It is this area I will now discuss in relation to preference rules.

At any one point in the learning process (as well as for the competent native speaker), there are a host of lexical entries that contain minimal or unstable information. Two of the main characteristics of preference rule systems are that: (1) information will be organized along the most stable criteria available, and (2) when sufficient data are not available for a judgment, there are certain default values that allow one to draw inferences based on more global organizational principles that are present in the system. One form of a default value mentioned in *Semantics and Cognition* is the frames of Goffman (1974) where, in the face of insufficient data, reliance is placed on conventionalized expectations in order to structure information. It seems obvious that the ability of a native speaker to make reference to the culturally appropriate default values may not be shared by L2 speakers in the face of what is an incomplete set of facts. In this light, lexical transfer can be seen as the basing of hypotheses about a word not only on the conditions operant in specific L1 equivalents but also on more global L1-based default values.

There are numerous ways in which a lexical entry can be incomplete, and these will have differing effects on learners' strategies. For example, the Chinese word *qing* is incompletely represented for me. I know the pronunciation and orthography, and I have a definition in my mind. The problem is that I have never heard anyone use the word in referring to an example of the color. While I may have enough information from definition alone to make a stab at using the word, what I am really doing is using a set of English-based criteria to deduce its proper use.

Consider another example: An English speaker learning Chinese wants to know how to say "turn on the light," The learner looks up the Chinese terms in a dictionary and uses them quite accurately in asking someone to turn on the light. Does this mean the learner knows the words – is the entry for those words complete?

The theory outlined predicts that there may be many cases where two words in two different languages referring to the same thing can have widely varying mental representations. It may be useful to examine further why this might be so.

In Chinese, the way to say "turn on the light" would literally be translated as "open light." Using a line of argument reminiscent of the earlier discussion of Frege, while both "turn on the light" and "open light" refer to the same action, I argue that considering the terms equivalent misses the fact that there may be definite differences in the internal structures of the two words. Restricting discussion to the Chinese example, the use of the verb *open*, while overlapping with the English word at some points (e.g., "open the door"), differs in other ways. In addition to "open light," there are also the uses of "open (= drive) a car" and "open (= have) a party," among others. If there is, as Frege suggests, different knowledge involved in different modes of designation, this knowledge might be represented as the differences in how the three conditions or organizational principles interact or are weighted in relation to each other. Therefore, just as in Sentence 15 ("He put the car in the garage."), where a difference in the preference conditions accounted for the extended use of *put*, to say that "open the light" and "turn on the light" represent the same knowledge in the mind (while true as far as the extension goes) completely ignores the internal structures of the words. The fact that the verb *open* in Chinese can be used in cases where it cannot be used in English implies that it must have a different (conventionally determined) balance of preference conditions. This suggests that even though one can use the verb *open* for "open the door" in both languages, we should consider them in some ways different verbs.

These observations indicate that an L2 speaker may use many words correctly, but will still have incomplete lexical entries for the word. The importance of this as regards empirical research on lexical competence in an L2 may be easily overlooked, as there may be many words that seem to be used correctly.

One of the more philosophically controversial arguments for a rule-governed system of lexical learning (given in *Semantics and Cognition*) is that only by reference to subconscious criteria in the form of rules is it possible to build a stable complex of information within a lexical entry from a limited number of examples of the thing to which a word refers. In a sense, this inductive process could be what characterizes native-speaker development.

Compare this to an L2 learner who, by building hypotheses for using

L2 words on L1-based definitions (as in the example with *qing*), may be using deductive processes to learn new words. Thus, instead of building up incomplete entries by reference to specific criteria induced from the exemplars of a word, an L2 learner will simply deduce that an L2 word belongs to an already established category based in the L1. While this deductive process may lead to successful use, as in the case where *open* can refer to opening a door, and even though it may play a role in L1 acquisition, it is not the process by which the rule conditions on a word's internal structure are built up.

In summary, it may be that the normal use of the term *hypothesis* in learning theories actually refers to two different phenomena – one inductive, which results in the internalizing of rules, and the other deductive, by which inferences are made based upon a preexisting set of principles as to how a word is to be used. In this view, what has been referred to as a translation process is really a process of deduction.

Conclusion

I have tried to show that viewing the organization of the lexicon as based on a preference rule system can shed new light on our understanding of many aspects of the nature of lexical development. Further inquiry along the lines of the Type/Token distinction (or how a learner comes to represent a Type after exposure to instances of that Type) and especially the way that culture-specific criteria influence the conditions that organize lexical information (on a global as well as a discrete level) would doubtless yield new insights on L2 lexical acquisition. The greatest advantage of the theory presented by Jackendoff may be the way in which principles at work in both perceptual and linguistic/cognitive domains can be integrated with a theory of mind to provide a deeper understanding of meaning across culture.

References

Chase, S. 1938. *The Tyranny of Words*. New York: Harcourt, Brace and World.
Frege, G. 1892. On sense and reference. Reprinted in *The Logic of Grammar* (1975), D. Davidson and G. Harman, eds. Encino, Calif.: Dickenson.
Goffman, E. 1974. *Frame Analysis*. Cambridge, Mass.: Harvard University Press.
Jackendoff, R. 1983. *Semantics and Cognition*. Cambridge, Mass.: MIT Press.
Judd, E. L. 1978. Teaching and TESOL: a need for reevaluation of existing assumptions. *TESOL Quarterly* 12(1): 71–76.
Katz, J. J. 1964. Analyticity and contradiction in natural language. In *The Struc-*

ture of Language: Readings in the Philosophy of Language, J. A. Fodor and J. J. Katz, eds. Englewood Cliffs, N.J.: Prentice-Hall.

———. 1975. Logic and language: an examination of recent criticisms of intensionalism. In *Language, Mind, and Knowledge,* K. Gunderson, ed. Minnesota Studies in the Philosophy of Science, Vol. 7. Minneapolis: University of Minnesota Press.

Labov, W. 1978. Denotational structure. In *Papers from the Parasession on the Lexicon,* D. Farkas, W. M. Jacobsen, and K. W. Todrys, eds. Chicago: Chicago Linguistic Society.

Li, Y. A. 1985. Abstract case in Chinese. Ph.D. dissertation. University of Southern California, Los Angeles.

Pulman, S. G. 1983. *Word Meaning and Belief.* Norwood, N.J.: Ablex.

Putnam, H. 1975. The meaning of "meaning." In *Language, Mind, and Knowledge,* K. Gunderson, ed. Minnesota Studies in the Philosophy of Science, Vol. 7. Minneapolis: University of Minnesota Press.

Quine, W. V. 1959. Meaning and translation. In *On Translation,* R. A. Brower, ed. Cambridge, Mass.: Harvard University Press.

Richards, J. 1980. The role of vocabulary teaching. In *Readings on English as a Second Language,* K. Croft, ed. Boston: Little, Brown.

Schumann, J. H. 1982. Simplification, transfer and relexification as aspects of pidginization and early second language learning. *Language Learning* 32(2): 337–66.

Taylor, S. H. 1978. On the acquisition and completion of lexical entries. In *Papers from the Parasession on the Lexicon,* D. Farkas, W. M. Jacobsen, and K. W. Todrys, eds. Chicago: Chicago Linguistic Society.

Twaddell, W. F. 1972. Linguists and language teachers. In *Readings on English as a Second Language,* K. Croft, ed. Cambridge, Mass.: Winthrop.

Wertheimer, M. 1923. Laws of organization in perceptual forms. Reprinted in *A Source Book of Gestalt Psychology* (1938), W. Ellis, ed. London: Routledge & Kegan Paul.

Wilkins, D. A. 1972. *Linguistics in Language Teaching.* Cambridge, Mass.: MIT Press.

PART V:
PHONOLOGY

It is common knowledge that a foreign accent is typical of postpubescent language learners. Comedians who mimic speakers of foreign languages always select the foreign accent as an object of their humor; they less frequently target syntax or the lexicon. With so much attention paid to phonology in everyday treatments of foreign language speakers, it is surprising how little attention has been paid to this area of the grammar within the second language acquisition literature.

Learning a second language phonology is more complex than generally thought. Much pedagogical material focuses on the learning of segments; most learners, as a result, are concerned with the accurate production and reception of segments. However, it is clear that learning a second language (L2) phonology embraces considerably more than achieving accurate segment production: One must also gain knowledge of allowable and disallowable sequences, phonetic detail of segment combinations, meaning-bearing and nonmeaning-bearing prosodic elements, and so forth.

The chapters in this section approach phonology from different perspectives. Ard takes a global view of L2 phonology, presenting a model for L2 phonological development. Mairs, on the other hand, provides an in-depth investigation of one aspect of L2 phonological acquisition – stress assignment.

Ard's chapter points out that there is no existing model of L2 phonology. He claims that the problem is not with the output side of phonology; many studies have addressed and systematized the actual pronunciations and perceptions of second language learners. Instead, the problem is with the input side of phonology; not enough attention has been paid to the representations on which the posited phonological rules and processes are assumed to operate. As he notes, phonological representations are not given a priori, even in the most extreme innatist theory. They must be constructed.

Ard's chapter presents a model for the development of second language phonology. He provides principled explanations for phenomena that have until now gone unaccounted for. He further argues that any proposed phonological process is only as plausible as the input on which

239

it operates. If the phonological representations have not been justified, then the process itself is without justification.

His chapter suggests that second language learners must construct phonological representations because there is no such representation that is automatically available to them. In particular, they do not have access to the information assumed available to ideal speaker-hearers, as assumed in generative phonological work. Nor do they have automatic access to phonemes. On the other hand, second language learners utilize information other than what is allowed in deriving phonemes and underlying representations. As a result, learners may construct representations different from those assumed for ideal native speakers.

Mairs's chapter contains a metrical analysis of the patterns of stress assignment found in the interlanguage of Spanish speakers learning English. Her goal is to identify the interlanguage rules that generate these patterns and to determine the factors that play a role in the formulation of these rules. The subjects in her study show a strong tendency to produce the same correct and incorrect patterns of stress assignment in their interlanguage speech.

Mairs takes as the theoretical basis of her study the metrical analysis of English stress provided by Hayes (1981) and the metrical analysis of Spanish stress proposed by Harris (1983). Three different aspects of the Spanish speakers' shared linguistic competence are considered as possible sources of influence on their interlanguage stress system: (1) their knowledge of the stress rules of their native language; (2) their knowledge of universal tendencies in stress assignment; and (3) the learners' acquired knowledge of the target language stress assignment. Her analysis reveals that only one of these three components of the Spanish speakers' linguistic competence – their acquired knowledge of the target language stress system – can be used to derive a set of rules that successfully accounts for the interlanguage data. Transfer of the native language stress system is not pervasive. She provides evidence to suggest, however, that the transfer of constraints on native language syllable structure plays a role in the formulation of learners' interlanguage stress rules, a finding consistent with the conclusions in other recent studies of transfer in interlanguage phonology.

As we pointed out in Chapter 1, there are two major ways of viewing the relationship between linguistic theory and second language acquisition. Mairs's chapter shows the importance of both these perspectives. Her interlanguage analysis is based on a well-established linguistic analysis. While she does not make the strong argument that second language data can serve to differentiate between linguistic theories, she does argue that standard generative phonology cannot account for her data, whereas a metrical analysis can.

References

Harris, J. 1983. *Syllable Structure and Stress in Spanish: A Nonlinear Analysis.* Cambridge, Mass.: MIT Press.

Hayes, B. 1981. A metrical theory of stress rules. Ph.D. dissertation, Yale University. Reproduced by Indiana University Linguistics Club, Bloomington.

11 *A constructivist perspective on non-native phonology*

Josh Ard

The purpose of this chapter is to argue for a constructivist model of how second language learners acquire phonological competence in a second language. The term *constructivist* is borrowed from the philosophy of mathematics (see Barker 1964; Bishop 1972; Davis and Hersh 1981). In classical mathematics, functions and other mathematical objects can be defined implicitly. That is, these objects are said to exist if certain conditions have been established even if there are no known procedures involving a finite number of steps through which the objects can be determined. A constructivist approach to mathematics only allows mathematical objects that can be constructed by finite means.

Current accounts of second language phonology cannot be considered constructivist. Instead, they proceed much as does classical mathematics. Once certain facts are established about the native language, the target language, and the actual performance of a learner, then it is simply postulated that a particular phonological representation is justified for the learner. No attempt is made to justify how the learner managed to construct that representation; it is simply assumed to be automatically available and accessible to the learner.

This chapter argues that this point of view is mistaken. There is no phonological representation of a second language that is automatically available to a learner. The learner must construct one. Furthermore, the one he or she constructs may be different from the one constructed by a native speaker of the language.

Phonological representations are crucial in any phonological model or theory, since the entire phonological analysis is grounded on the representations. If the representations are incorrect, then the rules cannot be correct. Representations are thereby an essential part of phonology, or perhaps prephonology. This latter term reflects the fact that most models of phonology assume that the correct representations are already known. If that is true, then the questions addressed herein precede phonology. The matter is purely terminological. The point remains that: (1) representations are crucial; (2) they have been largely ignored in previous discussions of second language phonology; and (3) they have to be constructed by the learner. Thus, any acceptable model or theory of second language phonology rests upon the foundation of representations constructed by learners.

The importance of representations in theory

About a decade ago, Tarone (1978) was largely justified in making the following remarks about second language phonology:

The phonology of interlanguage is an area which was largely neglected by second language acquisition research until very recently. There seemed to be little interest in the pronunciation patterns of the speech of second language learners. When Schumann summarized existing second language acquisition research in 1976, he found absolutely no studies on the phonology of inter-language. Even now, we have only a small amount of phonological data collected from second language learners in reasonably natural speech situations. (Tarone 1978)

Even though studies such as that by Moulton (1962) are worthy of note, little was written about the phonology of second language learners until recently. The very existence of the anthology (Ioup and Weinberger 1987) in which Tarone's article was reprinted is proof that this situation has changed. By now a great deal has been written about the phonology of second language learners. Nevertheless, there is still no extant model or theory of second language phonology vis-à-vis interlanguage phonology.

This is doubtless a controversial claim, but the point is not to decry previous efforts. It is not that nothing has been done regarding second language phonology, but that what has been accomplished is not sufficient to establish a true phonological model or theory.

First, we should examine major models and theories of phonology and determine if research on second language acquisition suffices to justify that model or theory as a framework for investigation of the activities of second language learners. An obvious candidate is generative phonology. However, it is generally accepted that no model or theory of second language phonology has met the requirements for generative phonology as spelled out in Chomsky and Halle (1968), and it is highly unusual to find studies of second language phonology utilizing the vocabulary and descriptive techniques of classical generative phonology. The fundamental reason for this is that the prerequisites for generative phonological analysis are not met in the second language acquisition situation.

Chomsky and Halle (1968) state that "the phonological component is a system of rules ... that relates surface structures ... to phonetic representations" (p. 14). Surface structures are the output of the syntactic component. Chomsky and Halle make clear that surface structure contains lexical representations that are rather abstract, that is, they diverge from actual pronunciation, in large part because the lexical representations only contain "those phonological properties that are not determined by a general rule" (p. 44). General rules are determined primarily by linguistically significant generalizations, including those relating words that enter into alternations. For instance, a uniform vowel is posited for the three different sounds spelled by *o* in *harmony, harmonic,* and *harmonious.* Since the Chomsky-Halle model is based on the competence of an ideal speaker-hearer who knows the entire lexicon of English, there is no need to determine which words are known by the speaker-hearer. On the other hand, accounts of the competence of real speaker-hearers, including children, should be based on what the individuals in question actually know. No researcher in second language phonology has undertaken the enormous burden of determining what lexical representations would be required for a particular generative phonological analysis of second language learners.

This, of course, does not preclude the existence of a satisfactory second language phonological model or theory. It only means that any existing one cannot satisfy the strict requirements of classical generative phonology. Hence, we need to look elsewhere.

A reasonable first step would seem to be to consider the nature of phonology in general and examine definitions of phonology. This step is not particularly enlightening, though, because the major purpose of defining phonology seems to be to distinguish it from other components of linguistics that also deal with sound patterns (Ducrot and Todorov 1979). Even in Chomsky and Halle's discussion of generative phonology (p. 54), a major point of their criticism is that the phonological component subsumes all of what Martinet (1964) assigned to phonetics, phonology, and morphology. Trubetzkoy (1969) is likewise concerned primarily with separating phonology from other areas of linguistic description, namely phonetics and phonostylistics. This is all quite useful in determining the boundaries of phonology, but is not particularly informative about the nature of the domain within the boundaries. In other words, definitions tell us what phonology studies and what it does not study, but they tell us little about how phonology studies its domain.

It is therefore necessary to read between the lines of treatises on phonological theory to see what is presupposed about its nature. An important clue comes from Trubetzkoy's insistence that phonology deals with the system or norms of the language. A significant facet of this notion is that phonology must be an immanent account of the sound facts of a language. This does not mean that an analysis must always be done in ignorance of what goes on outside the language, which is presumably what happens when children learn their first language; on the contrary, in practice if not always in theory phonologists use what they know of other languages in positing a phonological description. The requirement of an immanent analysis does not necessarily preclude the inclusion of phonological universals in a description either. It simply requires that the analysis be justifiable solely with data available to speakers of the language being described.

Let us now return to descriptions of sound patterns used by second language learners. In the quotation previously cited, Tarone speaks of the pronunciation patterns of second language learners. Concern with these patterns is certainly necessary to construct a phonology, but it is not sufficient. Actual pronunciation patterns, or an idealization thereof, such as "potential [pronunciations] by an idealized speaker-hearer who is unaffected by... grammatically irrelevant factors" (Chomsky and Halle 1968:3), are relevant in determining phonetic representations, which are crucial in all phonological approaches. In any approach, however, these representations are related to another kind of representation, variously known as phonological, phonemic, morphophonemic, and so forth. Within the phonological component rules (and/or processes) relate the phonetic and phonological representations. Even though rules are perhaps more obvious in some phonological approaches, such as generative phonology, than in others, such as American structuralism, Anderson (1985) argues that the two notions of *rule* and *representation* are crucial for all major phonological approaches from the time of Baudouin de Courtenay (1877) and Kruszewski (1881) a century ago. Both notions are required for a successful phonology. In particular, the success of a phonological description depends on the correctness of the non-phonetic representation. One cannot decide the correctness of a posited rule unless the representations are correct.

Consider what phonological descriptions could be like if there were no conditions placed on representations. Let us imagine a scenario in which phonological representations could be developed from facts of one language and used in the description of another language. Note that this is a worst-case scenario. No practicing phonologists have proceeded in this fashion. This scenario is not presented to criticize existing work, but rather to indicate what would be possible if there were no requirements for immanent analyses.

For two closely related languages, such as Czech and Slovak, it is possible to construct rules deriving pronunciations of words in one language from words in the other. Czech and Slovak are particularly closely related, but the same argument can be made for more distantly related languages such as Russian and Ukrainian, which are clearly distinct. Now it is impossible to have a single set of simple rules that will derive all Slovak words from words in Czech (or Ukrainian and Russian, respectively). There are several mechanisms that will destroy a simple relationship between all items in the lexicon. In some instances, one of the languages lost an item in a cognate set. In some instances, a word developed in one language without a cognate pair developing in the other. Nevertheless, one could construct a reasonably successful mapping from one language to the other by incorporating either exceptions or complex rules or both. Although such a description would be reasonably accurate, it could not be considered a phonological description of Slovak (or Ukrainian). All of the components in the description must be justified within the language being described (or be a universal for certain approaches, including generative phonology). Within the system of Slovak (and Ukrainian) alone there is no justification of the Czech (or Russian) forms, so there is no rationale for their use in a phonological description of Slovak (or Ukrainian).

The moral of this fable is that we are not justified in using forms from one language in phonological analyses of another, even if it were mechanically possible to be successful in doing so. Similarly, we cannot use forms justified for an ideal speaker-hearer in analyzing a learner, even if it were mechanically possible to be successful in doing so. These forms are only valid if they can be justified for the learner.

Given this discussion, the claim made earlier can be amplified: There is no extant model or theory of second language phonology because there is no model or theory for determining the correct representations for second language learners. Moreover, discussions concerned with second language phonological issues have been much more concerned with rules than with representations. This is evidenced by the introductory remarks in Ioup and Weinberger (1984:xi):

Within the past few years there has been a resurgence of interest in the phonological aspects of second language acquisition research. This is due primarily to the fact that phonological theory is currently undergoing revolutionary changes unprecedented in generative phonology. Not only are there new approaches to a characterization of the rule systems, but there are innovative non-linear models, such as metrical and autosegmental phonology, which provide a principled account of phenomena that were previously resistant to an adequate analysis.

Note that the discussion does not address the content of representations. Nonlinear models have the same content in their representations, but the information is coded differently. This would not be a major difficulty if representations could be automatically determined, but this cannot be done, even in the most innatist models. Kiparsky and Menn (1977) note that in generative phonological treatments of child language acquisition, the child must learn the correct underlying forms, that is, the lexical representations. These forms are neither innately available nor immediately obvious to a child hearing the language.

It may seem that phonological representations could be easily, if not automatically, determined by second language learners within a phonemic model of phonology. This hope, engendered in part by oversimplistic views of phonemic theory by many generative phonologists, is also futile. For example, it is commonly assumed that there is an unambiguous, universally accepted phonemic analysis of a language, especially one so well studied as American English. The falsity of this assumption is amply demonstrated by the collection of articles in Joos (1957). These articles, written by proponents of phonemic theory, attest to the significant controversy existing over the correct phonemic descriptions of languages, including American English.

Strict adherence to the methodological principles of phonemic analysis sometimes led to controversial and counterintuitive descriptions. Anderson (1985) provides an excellent summary of some of the problems that arose in consistently carrying out the methodological requirements of phonemic analysis – one is that theoretical discussions of phonemics could not agree as to what was the correct phonemic analysis of a language such as American English. Thus, determining the reference of the phrase *the phonemic representation of a word* is difficult, if not impossible. In consequence, it is hard to imagine how a learner could have access to this elusive unique representation.

One possibility, of course, is that a phonemic presentation is necessary to proper performance in a language. If we utilize phonemes in perception and a learner does perceive a word correctly, then by inference the learner must have discovered the correct phonemes in that word. Similarly, if we utilize phonemes in pronunciation and a learner pronounces a word correctly, then by inference the learner must have discovered the correct phonemes in that word. If either of these claims were true, then phonemes would automatically be learned in learning correct perception and/or pronunciation. If so, then there would be no ontological problem in using phonemes as a phonological representation, because there would be sufficient evidence that the learner is aware of them.

At various times phonemic analyses have been justified on the basis that phonemes are just the units necessary to account for production or perception. As we shall see, neither a simple phonemic representation nor phonemes augmented with distinctive features is sufficient for describing perception, the original impetus of the phoneme concept. The latter is an important point often overlooked. Let us consider the evidence in detail.

First, native speakers are often capable of hearing more differences than there are phonemes in their language. For example, five or six vowel phonemes have been posited for Russian, yet Russians are capable of accurately perceiving more than a dozen different vowels in their language (Bondarko et al. 1966; Verbickaja 1970). In other words, they can hear differences linguists have claimed to be redundant as well as those that have been described as distinctive. Second, the features that are salient in identifying and distinguishing words are not necessarily those that linguists have marked as distinctive (Kohler 1981). Distinctiveness in linguistics codes distributional relations. But perceptual discrimination is a different task. For example, there are many different salient characteristics that English listeners use in discriminating among words that allegedly differ only in the voicing of one segment (Kornfeld 1978). Third, the locus of the salient parameter may be different from the distinctive feature (Delattre, Liberman, and Cooper 1955; Liberman, Delattre, and Cooper 1958). For example, perceptual cues for discriminating between words that supposedly end in voiced versus voiceless consonants reside in the preceding vowel (Wang 1959). In essence, phonemes alone do not account for the perception of native speakers. Likewise, there is no reason to assume that a learner bases his or her perceptions on phonemes alone. Thus, there is no reason for non-natives to learn to automatically perceive in terms of phonemes. On the basis of perceptual tasks alone, there is no reason for non-native speakers to infer phonemes at all. Hence, perceptual facts cannot be used to support the automatic availability of phonemes as a representation.

Another factor to consider is that "foreign accents" are often characterized primarily by subphonemic differences. If we only heard phonemic differences and differences in distinctive features, we would not be nearly so proficient at detecting and identifying foreign accents.

Phonemes are also not adequate for modeling production (cf. Ladefoged 1967). Several years ago, it was widely believed that something like phonemes could be used in programming production. The belief went like this: There are certain extrinsic allophones, generally the ones marked in a relatively broad phonetic transcription, that have to be predicted within the description of a particular language, such as aspirated versus unaspirated voiceless stops in English. However, other allophones, the extrinsic ones (the majority) could be accounted for universally through coarticulation rules. Thus, the commands could be given in terms of extrinsic allophones. It is now clear that even coarticulation has a language-internal basis (Daniloff and Hammarberg 1973; Hammarberg 1976, 1981; Kent and Minifie 1977). But as the amount of fronting of velars before front vowels varies from language to language, there can be no universal accommodation made by the articulatory mechanism. Second, there are other differences in detail. For example, the exact nature of vowels and exact places of articulation vary from language to language (Ladefoged 1980). Third, articulatory commands and gestures do not appear to be segmentally based at all (Koževnikov and Čistovič 1965; Fowler et al. 1981; Linell 1982). Thus, neither native speakers nor learners can be said to pronounce strings of phonemes or even extrinsic phonemes when they speak. Another difficulty with the idea of accounting for production in terms of phonemes is that learners often create sounds that are different from canonical forms for phonemes in either their native or target languages (cf. Beebe 1984), but this phenomenon is often overlooked due to the tradition of reporting learner production in terms of which phoneme in the target language it resembles.

Given all of this, there is no reason to believe that the task of the learner is to aim for the "phonemes" of a language, or to derive what he or she does from strings of phonemes. Teachers sometimes try to teach phonemes. Researchers often report what they hear in terms of phonemes, but this does not necessarily characterize learner behavior. There is simply no reason to assume that learners are inferring phonemes at all, much less basing their phonological representations on them.

In summary, there is no reason to assume that a phonological representation will be automatically available to second language learners. They cannot be expected to have the underlying forms of classical generative phonology available to them. Neither can they be expected to have the phonemes of a classical phonemic analysis available to them.

Following the insight of Kiparsky and Menn (1977), we need to recognize that phonological representations need to be constructed by learners. Although the remarks of these researchers were directed to the problems of child language acquisition, they are also relevant to the problems of second language acquisition. They propose the following framework to account for the acquisition of phonology, suggesting that three levels of representations are relevant for acquisition: A – underlying representations hypothesized by the child; B – phonetic representations perceived by the child; and C – the child's pronunciation. Kiparsky and Menn call the rules that relate A and B learned rules and those that relate B and C invented rules.

In the early stages of language acquisition, A and B coincide, while B and C are maximally distinct. As the child masters more of the phonetics, after the initial period of rule invention, C approaches B and the system of rules (B→C) shrinks. The process normally terminates when C becomes identical with B. Independently, and surely concurrently in part, though continuing well into adolescence, a second learning process goes on. As the child keeps discovering the phonological relationships of his language, A becomes increasingly different from B and the system of rules (A→B) becomes increasingly elaborate. This process terminates when A and A→B develop into the adult lexicon and rule system. (Kiparsky and Menn 1977 [p. 37 of the 1987 reprint])

The importance of representations in acquisition

At this point, a careful reader might object that abstract phonological representations are not really necessary. So what if learners cannot have automatic access to an abstract representation! There is no need for any representation except actual pronunciations, an objection may continue. This line of reasoning is mistaken, however.

Every phonological theory utilizes an abstract phonological representation, though of course the degree of abstraction varies, as does the status of the representation. There are different purposes a phonological representation is designed to serve (cf. Linell 1982 for a thorough discussion), depending in part on the degree of abstractness from actual pronunciations. Since no word is ever pronounced in exactly the same fashion twice, the target pronunciation that learners aim for cannot be equivalent to actual phonetic pronunciations. A more abstract representation is required.

The status of representations in phonological theories and models of second language learning

Discussions of phonological issues concerned with second language acquisition have not been able to dispense with representations. Quite the contrary, representations are usually clearly given. What is missing in general, however, is overt discussion of the nature of the posited representation and its justification. One exception to this is Eckman (1981), who made a careful attempt to justify particular facts of the phonological representation he posited for Spanish learners of English. While other studies have consistently posited phonological representations for learners, rarely are representations proposed by someone else criticized. Representations seem to pass without controversy.

Following the terminology of Bourdieu (1977), we cannot say that there is an orthodox position on phonological representations in second language acquisition. By definition, an orthodox position is one adopted by the field as a whole in reaction to an attack. When there has been no overt controversy or dispute, the term *orthodox* is inapplicable. Rather, a position that is assumed without considering alternatives or even recognizing that there might be alternatives is, in Bourdieu's terminology, a *doxic* position. Thus, a doxic position exists for phonological representations in discussions of second language phonology. The next step is to discover what that position is.

Data for determining this must be taken from actual discussions of second language phonology. We need to discover what the authors must have assumed phonological representations to be like in order for them to have discussed phonology in the way they did. Inevitably, an analysis of this sort will be *prima facie* unfair to the authors. As previously discussed, the nature of phonological representations has rarely been thematized in debates about second language phonology. Thus, there is little reason to believe that authors gave the matter much thought. Perhaps they even repeated rather formulaically the conventional positions on representations, but did not voice any disagreement with these positions because to do so would have required more discussion than they wished to devote to the issue and would have deflected attention from the primary knowledge-claims they wished to raise. It is often strategically useful to gloss over a point you may disagree with to get to the main points, if expressing your disagreements with a standard assumption would run the risk of either confusing readings or detracting from your major point(s).

Typically, discussions of phonological representations in the literature on second language phonology have been in terms of phonemes. Rarely is there any direct relationship to another particular theory or model of phonemics or phonology in general. Thus, little is said explicitly of whether generative phonology is rejected *in toto* in favor of an older approach or whether some unspecified (and perhaps undeveloped) hybrid of generative phonology and phonemics is assumed. Let us review some of the research and attempt to discover the assumptions made about phonological representations.

First, consider Tarone (1978), who refers to phonemes and uses the traditional slashed brackets [/ /] to enclose them. She consistently refers to phonemes as *sounds* as in the following passages:

[B]oth the native language and the target language have the *phoneme* /t/, so we would expect that the learner will have no difficulty with this *sound* in the target language. (p. 71)

[W]here there are two *phonemes* /f/ and /v/ in the native language, these two *sounds* are considered variants in the target language of a single *phoneme* /f/. (p. 71)

/x/ [is] very different from any American English *sound*. (p. 72) [emphases added in all citations]

Taken literally, this cannot be related to any commonly accepted theory or model of phonology. First of all, /x/ is a systematic phoneme in Chomsky and Halle (1968) serving several functions. It is the typical systematic phoneme which surfaces as initial [h]; it is in the underlying representation of *right* and *righteous* (the underlying representation of the former is /rixt/; and it is found in words like *dinghy* and *hangar*, which have underlying representations of /dinxi/ and /xænxr/, respectively. Thus, Tarone, in referring to the absence of /x/ in American English, is clearly not discussing the Chomsky-Halle model.

Second, there are no commonly accepted theories in which phonemes are simply sounds (cf. Jones 1973; Anderson 1985). Sometimes, the word *sound* has been used, but clearly a more abstract notion is meant. Consider Jones's analysis of Baudouin de Courtenay's usage:

Viewed "psychologically" a phoneme is a speech-sound (a "linear" or "seg-mental" element of speech) pictured in one's mind and "aimed at" in the process of talking. The concrete sound (phone) employed in any particular speech-utterance may be the pictured sound or it may be another sound hav-ing some affinity to it, its use being conditioned by some feature or features of the phonetic context. (Jones 1973:22)

Clearly, Baudouin de Courtenay was referring to an image of a sound and not just a physical sound.

Even though the idea of a phoneme as a sound cannot be related to an established theory of phonology, Tarone is not unusual in her usage. Wode (1981) consistently talks of phones substituting for phonemes. For example:

he should fairly frequently substitute [s] for /θ/ (p. 218)
The only substitutes to occur for /w/ are [v] and [f] (p. 219)
The [f] substitute for /sw/ (p. 219)

Major (1987) presents a more complicated pattern. In general he speaks of one phone substituting for another, for example, [w] for [l] (p. 105), but there are nonetheless instances that indicate that phonemes directly represent sounds. In one case he states (p. 104), "In L2 phonology, learners' substitutions typically take the form of phoneme substitutions (e.g., [R] for [r])." Note that substitution of phones is correlated with substitution of phonemes. There are other remarks, such as "substitution of [w] for English /r/" (p. 112). These remarks indicate that phonemes are the kinds of things that sounds can substitute for, the obvious in-ference being that phonemes themselves must directly represent sounds.

Unlike traditional phonemics, distinctive features and phonological rules are discussed in several studies of second language phonology. These characteristics do not arouse criticism, so it appears that they occur in the standard accounts of second language phonology. Since the focus of this chapter is on representations rather than rules, rules will only be discussed when they directly affect representations.

The rules that are allowed generally do not lead to much abstractness, since another inference that can be gained from the common usage in discussions of second language phonology is that the representations are viewed as relatively concrete. All of the discussions implicitly assume that there is a close connection between a phoneme and a basic variant. This is evident by the symbolism; generally the same symbol is used for a phoneme and a basic variant. Thus, Major (1987:105) discussed the common development sequence [a] > [aˆ] > [æˆ] > [æ] by Spanish learners of English as a second language. Notice that the same symbol is used for the correct phone [æ] and the target phoneme /æ/. Presum-ably, the assumption is that this primary variant is the "elsewhere" variant, the one that is least changed by the phonological rules. We have to say presumably because the actual rules deriving the surface phones, the variants, are rarely given.

In summary, the doxic (normal, noncontroversial) account of second language phonology assumes that there are representations that are relatively directly related to actual pronunciations, especially toward certain basic pronunciations of the segment being represented.

The objections raised in this chapter are not that representations with these properties are wrong. Instead, the problem is that there is no theoretical basis for determining exactly which representations will be chosen nor is there a theoretical justification for how second language learners are able to construct the representation.

This chapter could legitimately end here. My aim was to establish that representations are important, that representations apparently assumed in the literature are not automatically available to learners, and that learners must therefore construct them. These hypotheses have been supported. Nevertheless, it would be better to go beyond these essentially negative conclusions.

A glimpse of a constructivist model

A theoretical model of phonology that appears particularly promising as a model for the construction of representations by second language learners is that developed by Linell (1982). He views the phonological representation as an abstraction based on careful pronunciations:

I propose to define phonology as the study of language-specific aspects in the phonetic behavior (pertaining to different languages) or, alternately, as (the study of) the rules for the conventional use of phonetic mechanisms in specific languages. The phonological form [i.e., representation] of a certain linguistic item in a given language may be seen as a plan (disposition) to produce a certain phonetic event meeting those phonetic conditions that define the linguistic identity of the item (make it different from other possible items). (Linell 1982:43)

The types of abstractions involved in the creation of a phonological form are essentially suppressions of certain information that is redundant or predictable in careful pronunciations. In other words, the phonological form contains only some of the phonetic specifications needed to describe the actual pronunciations, but enough information to predict all of the phonetic specifications that are left out.

Within this model, the representations must be reasonably close to actual pronunciations. Moreover, since they are based only on the careful pronunciations, there is no problem of availability of data. All of the information in the representation is found in the pronunciation.

Nevertheless, the model cannot be applied directly to the second language situation. Linell assumes that speakers will automatically be able to decide which information in the careful pronunciations is redundant, and so all speakers will construct the same representations. As I will argue later, different speakers may construct different representations and may utilize information found in sources other than careful pronunciations. The important insight of Linell's model is that representations must be constructed. Hence, in accounting for how pronunciations of second language learners differ from those of competent native speakers, there are two possible sources of error. Either the wrong representation may be constructed or the implementation of the pronunciation of the representation may be in error.

In some cases it is difficult to determine which type of error is more predominant. Recent careful analyses (e.g., Port and Mitleb 1983; Beebe 1984) have found several instances in which learners of English as a second language make real distinctions between sounds that are not identical to the distinctions made by native English speakers nor to distinctions in their native language. In the past, such phenomena have typically been described as phoneme substitutions, because native speakers of English *heard a different phoneme in the learners' pronunciations*, but this actually describes the perception of native speakers more than the pronunciation of learners. The explanation for the learners' pronunciation may be either that they constructed the correct representations but failed to implement them in the nativelike manner (the explanation adopted by Port and Mitleb [1983] in their analysis of Arabic learners of English) or they constructed a representation close to the correct one but not close enough.

For some errors, the most parsimonious explanation is that learners have constructed an incorrect representation. For example, phonetic differences between the native and target languages may lead learners to construct an incorrect representation.

The phonetic detail of English /r/ and /l/ is fairly unusual in the world's languages. Not surprisingly, the phonological representations of second language learners often diverge from canonical English norms. Wode (1981) has noted that English prevocalic *r*'s are generally replaced by [w] at early stages, but *r*-sounds in other target languages generally lead to different substitution patterns, indicating that there is something special about English *r*'s. One possible explanation is that *r*'s in English are often labialized, that is, accompanied by secondary lip rounding, while *r*-sounds in most other languages are not. Interestingly, Wode found that *r* in *thr* clusters is not generally replaced by [w]. In this environment, *r* is generally different: often a flap without lip rounding (cf. Bloch 1941). Hence, there is a reasonable phonetic explanation for the distribution of substitutions for *r* in English and other languages. The learners appear to utilize the secondary lip rounding in constructing a representation for *r*.

In English, *l* is often velarized, or retracted, especially postvocalically. Also, in postvocalic position, there is often no tongue contact at all, so that a vowel + *l* sequence is really more of a back and down-gliding diphthong. This helps explain certain facts of the second language acquisition of English phonology that would otherwise remain inexplicable. First, backer and lower vowels are often found before *l*'s. For example, Wode (1981:222) reported the following errors among German learners of English:

Incorrect vowel	Target word
[ʊ]	milk
[ɔ]	help
[ɔ]	twelve

Second, learners sometimes produce diphthongs for *v* + *l* that are not the same as canonical English pronunciations. For example, Eckman (1987:136) transcribes the "interlanguage phonetic form" of *filled* as [fiud] or [fiudə] for Mandarin Chinese learners of English. Presumably the reason for this transcription is that the diphthong they produced was appreciably different from that found in canonical standard English. Note also that a motivating factor for these learners' pronunciation may be the typical pronunciation of Chinese, which has complex diphthongs but no postvocalic *l*'s. Third, Moulton (1962:105) found that English speakers who did not know German and who were not exposed to the orthography of German imitated the German word *wird* as [vilt]. This can best be accounted for by considering the phonetics of German postvocalic *r*, which is uvular, and English postvocalic *l*. Both consonants are relatively retracted and cause a retraction of the preceding vowel. Thus, it is not surprising that English learners may misanalyze German and construct an incorrect representation.

Learners may utilize other information not contained in careful pronunciations when constructing representations. A clear instance of extrapronunciation evidence comes from spelling. Major (1987:105) reports that

an American speaker's acquisition of syllable final Portuguese /r/ (phonetically [x]) may change from [r] (interference) to deletion (an L1 developmental process) to [x] (TL [target language – ed.] pronunciation), e.g., [pɔrta] > [pɔta] > [pɔxta].

The question is why an American speaker would construct *r* in the first stage. The most likely explanation is the spelling. There are numerous errors made by second language learners in which they pronounce words as might seem reasonable from the spelling, but which cannot reasonably be viewed as derived from actual pronunciations. Spelling pronunciations have long been mentioned for second language learners (cf. Altenberg and Vago 1983). What has not always been mentioned is that spelling pronunciation is more likely to affect the representation constructed for a word than affect the rules that derive the pronunciation from the representation.

Conclusion

A truly explanatory theory or model of the phonological competence of second language learners must provide an explanation of how learners could construct the phonological representation used in their pronunciations. Neither of the two most popular theories of phonology, generative phonology and classical phonemics, provide any basis for why second language learners construct phonological representations. In particular, the types of representations posited for competent native speakers could not be assumed to be available to second language learners.

Nevertheless, the general nature of phonological representations assumed implicitly in the literature on second language acquisition seems to be reasonable. The major problem is to discover how learners construct suitable representations. It was suggested that a potential answer could be based on the model proposed by Linell (1982). Not only is this model capable of providing for the construction of phonological representations, but, when suitably augmented, it can also explain why learners may sometimes construct representations that diverge from those that native speakers construct.

References

Altenberg, E., and R. Vago. 1983. Theoretical implications of an error analysis of second language phonology production. *Language Learning* 33: 427–48. [Reprinted in Ioup and Weinberger, pp. 148–64]

Anderson, S. 1985. *Phonology in the Twentieth Century.* Chicago: University of Chicago Press.

Barker, S. 1964. *Philosophy of Mathematics.* Englewood Cliffs, N.J.: Prentice-Hall.

Baudouin de Courtenay, J. 1877. *Podrobnaja programma lekcij I. A. Boduèna-de-Kurtene (J. Baudouin de Courtenay) v 1876–1877 učebnom godu.* Kazan': Izvestie Kazan'skogo Universiteta.

Beebe, L. 1984. Myths about interlanguage phonology. In *Theoretical Issues in Contrastive Phonology,* S. Eliasson, ed. *Studies in Descriptive Linguistics,* Vol. 13. Heidelberg: Julius Groos Verlag. [Reprinted in Ioup and Weinberger, pp. 165–75]

Bishop, E. 1972. *Aspects of Constructivism*. Las Cruces: New Mexico State University Press.

Bloch, B. 1941. Phonemic overlapping. *American Speech* 16: 278–84.

Bondarko, L. V., L. A. Verbickaja, L. A. Zinder, and L. P. Pavlova. 1966. Različaemye zvokovye edinicy russkoj reči. In *Mexanizmy rečeobrazovanija i vosprijatija složnyx zvukov*. Moscow: Nauka.

Bourdieu, P. 1977. *Outline of a Theory of Practice*. Cambridge: Cambridge University Press.

Chomsky, N. and M. Halle. 1968. *The Sound Pattern of English*. New York: Harper & Row.

Daniloff, R., and R. Hammarberg. 1973. On defining coarticulation. *Journal of Phonetics* 1: 239–48.

Davis, P., and R. Hersh. 1981. *The Mathematical Experience*. Boston: Houghton Mifflin.

Delattre, P. C., A. M. Liberman, and F. S. Cooper. 1955. Acoustic loci and transitional cues for consonants. *Journal of the Acoustical Society of America* 27: 769–73.

Ducrot, O., and T. Todorov. 1979. *Encyclopedic Dictionary of the Sciences of Language*. Baltimore: Johns Hopkins University Press.

Eckman, F. 1981. On the naturalness of interlanguage phonological rules. *Language Learning* 31: 195–216. [Reprinted in Ioup and Weinberger, pp. 125–44]

Fowler, C., P. Rubin, R. E. Remez, and M. T. Turvey. 1981. Implications for speech production of a general theory of action. In *Language Production* B. Butterworth, ed. Vol. 1. *Speech and Talk*. London: Academic Press.

Hammarberg, R. 1976. The metaphysics of coarticulation. *Journal of Phonetics* 4: 353–63.

1981. On redefining coarticulation. *Journal of Phonetics* 9: 123–37.

Ioup, G., and S. H. Weinberger, eds. 1987. *Interlanguage Phonology: The Acquisition of a Second Language Sound System*. Cambridge, Mass.: Newbury House.

Jones, D. 1973. The history and meaning of the term "phoneme." In *Phonology*, Erik C. Fudge, ed. Harmondsworth, U.K.: Penguin, pp. 17–34. [Originally in *Le Maître Phonétique* 1957]

Joos, M. 1957. *Readings in Linguistics*. Vol. I. Chicago: University of Chicago Press.

Kent, R. D., and F. D. Minifie. 1977. Coarticulation in recent speech production models. *Journal of Phonetics* 5: 115–33.

Kiparsky, P., and L. Menn. 1977. On the acquisition of phonology. In *Language Learning and Thought*, J. MacNamara, ed. New York: Academic Press. [reprinted in Ioup and Weinberger, pp. 23–52]

Kohler, K. J. 1981. Contrastive phonology and the acquisition of phonetic skills. *Phonetica* 38: 213–26.

Kornfeld, J. 1978. Implications of studying reduced consonant clusters in normal and abnormal child speech. In *Recent Advances in the Psychology of Language. Part A. Language Development and Mother-Child Interaction*, R. Campbell and P. Smith, eds. New York: Plenum.

Koževnikov, V., and L. A. Čistovič. 1965. *Reč', artikuljacija i vosprijatie*. Moscow: Nauka.

Kruszewski, Mikolai. 1881. Über die Lautabwechslung. Kazan'. [A thorough discussion is found in Roman Jakobson. 1971. *The Kazan School of Polish Linguistics and Its Place in the International Development of Phonology. Selected Writings II.* The Hague: Mouton.]

Ladefoged, P. 1967. *Three Areas of Experimental Phonetics.* London: Oxford University Press.

1980. What are linguistic sounds made of? *Language* 56(3): 485–502.

Liberman, A. M., P. Delattre, and F. S. Cooper. 1958. Distinction between voiced and voiceless stops. *Language and Speech* 1: 153–67.

Linell, P. 1982. The concept of phonological form and the activities of speech production and speech perception. *Journal of Phonetics* 10: 37–72.

Major, R. C. 1987. A model for interlanguage phonology. In *Interlanguage Phonology*, G. Ioup and S. Weinberger, eds. Cambridge, Mass.: Newbury House.

Martinet, André. 1964. *Elements of General Linguistics.* Chicago: University of Chicago Press.

Moulton, W. 1962. Towards a classification of pronunciation errors. *MLA Journal* 46: 101–09.

Port, R., and F. Mitleb. 1983. Segmental features and implementation in acquisition of English by Arabic speakers. *Journal of Phonetics* 11: 219–29.

Tarone, E. 1978. The phonology of interlanguage. In *Understanding Second and Foreign Language Learning*, J. Richards, ed. Rowley, Mass.: Newbury House. [Reprinted in Ioup and Weinberger, pp. 70–85]

Trubetzkoy, N. S. 1969. *Principles of Phonology.* Berkeley: University of California Press.

Verbickaja, L. A. 1970. Akustičeskaja xarakteristika vosprinimaemyx zvukovyx edinic russkoj reči. *Proceedings of the Sixth International Congress of Phonetic Sciences.* Prague: Academica.

Wang, W. 1959. Transition and release as perceptual cues for final plosives. *Journal of Speech and Hearing Research* 31: 1490–99.

Wode, H. 1981. *Learning a Second Language.* Tübingen: Gunter Narr.

12 Stress assignment in interlanguage phonology: an analysis of the stress system of Spanish speakers learning English

Jane Lowenstein Mairs

The primary objective of this study is to conduct an analysis of the stress patterns found in the interlanguage of native speakers of Spanish learning English as a second language. These stress patterns are largely identical to those of native speakers of English, but they include a body of systematic errors. Using the theoretical framework of metrical phonology, an attempt will be made to formulate a set of rules to account for the system of stress assignment of these language learners, based on other components of the learners' linguistic knowledge and experience. The stress system of Spanish will be considered as a possible source for interlanguage rules, as will the learners' acquired knowledge of the target language system and universal tendencies of stress assignment.

The results of this analysis will be used to provide tentative answers to broader questions in the field of second language acquisition, questions concerning the role of transfer in the acquisition of phonology in general and in the acquisition of stress in particular.

Description of methods and data

The empirical data for this research was gathered in interviews with 23 native speakers of Spanish studying English in the United States. Seven of these informants were interviewed twice, yielding a total of 30 interviews. During the interviews, informants were engaged in casual conversation and then asked to read sentences, paragraphs, and short stories containing "test words" that had been selected to provide data about Spanish speakers' stress assignment in English. Since preliminary research seemed to indicate that Spanish speakers make stress errors only in words of more than two syllables, the test words all contained at least three syllables. All interviews were taped.

I would like to express my gratitude to Georgette Ioup, Ellen Broselow, and the editors of this volume for their suggestions regarding earlier versions of this paper; and to extend special thanks to Robert Bley-Vroman for his unending aid and support, without which this study might never have been possible. I would also like to thank the University of Texas Linguistics Department for its financial support.

Over the course of the study, four different versions of the test materials were used to collect data. Some of the test words and some of the embedded material was changed. Some parts of the test materials remained the same from one version to the next. (Subjects who were interviewed twice were asked to read different versions of the test materials at each sitting.) Many of the test words that were introduced into later versions were chosen because they had been stressed incorrectly by informants in the conversational portion of earlier interviews. This means that the errors found in the Spanish speakers' interlanguage stress assignment were not restricted to their "reading aloud" style.

For 69 out of the 80 test words, or in 86 percent of the cases, the informants showed a strong tendency to make the same predictions about target language stress assignment.[1] Each of these 69 words occurred at least five times in the data with the same stress pattern, and this pattern occurred at least twice as often as any other. In fact, for at least half of these 69 words, only one stress pattern occurred in the data.

A list of these words with their predominant interlanguage stress patterns is given in Table 12.1. The list includes polysyllabic nouns, verbs, and adjectives of a variety of structural types. They are divided into two categories: (1) words with the same stress pattern in both the interlanguage and target language, that is, words the Spanish speakers stressed correctly; and (2) words the Spanish speakers stressed differently from native speakers of English, that is, words they stressed incorrectly. It will henceforth be assumed that the data on stress presented in Table 12.1 are representative of the interlanguage stress assignment of Spanish speakers in general once they have passed the initial stages of learning English.[2]

The phonetic transcription listed next to each word in Table 12.1 represents its interlanguage pronunciation, including stress assignment. Since there was some variation among individual speakers with respect to vowel quality and treatment of syllable-final consonant clusters, the transcriptions of these elements should be considered approximations.

As can be seen from the data presented in Table 12.1, the words

1 For 11 of the 80 test words, the informants showed no obvious preference for a particular stress pattern. While no definitive explanation for this lack of consistency can be offered at this time, it is the opinion of the author that in all 11 cases it is attributable to one of two factors: Either the informants were not familiar with these words and had difficulty pronouncing them, or they were confused by the strong resemblance between these words and their Spanish cognates.

2 No formal evaluation of the proficiency of the informants who participated in this study was undertaken. All of them had, however, reached a level of competence at which they were able to read the test material in a relatively fluent manner. Thus, in this context Spanish speakers who have "passed the initial stages of learning English" will be defined as those able to read simple passages in English with relative fluency.

TABLE 12.1. INTERLANGUAGE STRESS ASSIGNMENT

Correct

apartment	[əpártmɪnt]	literature	[lítəračur]
argument	[árgumɪnt]	Madison	[mǽdɪson]
article	[ártɪkəl]	magazine	[mǽgəzin]
attitude	[ǽtɪtud]	necessary	[nésəsɛri]
avenue	[ávɪnyu]	offices	[ɔ́fɪsɪz]
barbecue	[bárbɪkyu]	Olympic (a.)	[olímpɪk]
bilingual	[bɪlíŋgwəl]	Olympics (n.)	[olímpɪks]
biology	[biáloǰi]	Paramount	[páramawn]
company	[kómpani]	passengers	[pǽsɪnǰərs]
computers	[kompyútərz]	publishing	[públɪšiŋ]
difficulty	[dífɪkulti]	qualify	[kwálifay]
disconnect	[dɪskonɛ́kt]	remember	[rimémbər]
Emerson	[ᵢémərson]	remembered	[rimémbərd]
employees	[ɛmplóyis]	ridiculous	[ridíkyulɪs]
executive	[ɛksékyutlv]	Saturday	[sǽtərdey]
expensive	[ɛkspénslv]	solitude	[sólitud]
February	[fébruɛri]	telephone	[téləfon]
finally	[fáynəli]	temperature	[témpəračur]
gigantic	[ǰigántɪk]	temporary	[témporari]
government	[góvərmɪnt]	understand	[əndərstán]
hamburger	[hǽmbərgər]	Washington	[wášiŋton]
holiday	[hólidey]	yesterday	[yéstərdey]
library	[láybrɛri]		

Incorrect

advertisement	[ǽdvərtáyzmɪnt]	interview (n.)	[ɪntərvyú]
advertising	[ǽdvərtáysiŋ]	interview (v.)	[ɪntərvyú]
Budweiser	[bədwáyzər]	irritates	[ɪrɪtéyts]
calculator	[kælkuléytər]	operator	[apəréytər]
complicated	[komplikéytld]	organize (v.)	[organáyz]
demonstrate	[dɛmonstréyt]	organized (a.)	[organáyzd]
elevator	[ɛləvéytər]	realize	[riəláyz]
exercise (n.)	[ɛksərsáys]	recognized	[rɛkonáyz]
frustrated	[frustréytld]	refrigerator	[rəfrlǰəréytər]
helicopter	[ɛlikóptər]	supervisor	[supərváysər]
illustrator	[ilustréytər]	televisions	[tɛləvíšəns]
interesting	[ɪntəréstiŋ]	translator	[transléytər]

Spanish speakers stress incorrectly are almost entirely limited to words of two structural types: (1) those ending in the rime³ configuration VOWEL + GLIDE + CONSONANT# (−VGC#); and (2) those ending in −VGC followed by a stress-neutral suffix. Apart from five exceptions, which will be accounted for later on, all of the words stressed

---

3 A rime is a syllabic unit of metrical phonology which includes the vowel and any segments that follow it within the syllable.

incorrectly fall into one of these two categories. Some examples are given.

− VGC#		*− VGC + stress-neutral suffix*	
demonstrate	dɛmonstréyt	advertising	ædvərtáysiŋ
organize	organáyz	complicated	komplikéytld
realize	riəláyz	operator	apərétyər

The analysis

When second language learners from a common first language background produce the same approximations of target language forms, it may be assumed that they are using the same rules to generate these forms, and that these rules are based upon linguistic knowledge (conscious or otherwise) available to all of them. Furthermore, according to current second language acquisition theory, both correct and incorrect forms are generated by the same set of rules – the interlanguage grammar.

For these learners, there are three apparent bodies of linguistic knowledge from which the rules of their interlanguage grammar may conceivably be drawn: (1) the learners' prior linguistic experience (i.e., their native language grammar); (2) rules the learners have already mastered from the target language; and (3) the learners' knowledge (presumably innate) of universal tendencies in language.

In the present study, it has been observed that native speakers of Spanish show a strong tendency to produce the same set of correct and incorrect patterns of stress assignment in English. It may reasonably be assumed, therefore, that these language learners have a common set of rules for assigning stress in English words, and that these rules are largely based on one or more of the following factors: (1) transfer from their native language stress rules; (2) knowledge acquired of the English stress system; or (3) universal tendencies of stress assignment.

We will begin by considering the first possibility, that the learners' system of stress assignment in the target language is largely based on stress rules transferred from their native language.

The native language stress system

The basic generalization for assigning stress in Spanish pronunciation is that consonant-final words have primary stress on the final syllable (*mujér* – "woman, wife"), and vowel-final words have primary stress on the penultimate syllable (*distínto* – "distinct") (Harris 1983:85). Clearly, this generalization cannot account for many of the stress patterns found in the data presented in the list of test words ([ekspénslv], [télǝfon], [kómpani], and [láybreri], for example).

However, even in Spanish, there is a sizable class of words whose stress patterns cannot be predicted according to this generalization. And it is possible that the rules that generate these marked forms in Spanish could be used to generate the problematic forms found in the interlanguage data. In order to explore this possibility, a more comprehensive understanding of the Spanish stress system is required.

The following description of Spanish stress rules is based entirely on the account given by Harris (1983), which, in turn, is formulated within the framework of the metrical theory of stress as developed by Liberman and Prince (1977), Kiparsky (1979), Hayes (1981), and others. This description is restricted to the stress patterns found in nouns, adjectives, and adverbs – the syntactic categories in which stress is phonologically determined. Verbal stress patterns are determined by morphology in Spanish, and Harris makes no attempt to account for them (Harris 1983:84). Fortunately, stress patterns that are linked to particular inflections are unlikely candidates for transfer between languages that are not closely related (Broselow 1984b:266; Gass, personal communication), and thus the rules for verbal stress assignment in Spanish can be overlooked in the present context.

According to Harris, the process of stress assignment in Spanish begins at the level of the syllable rime (see Footnote 3). Rimes are gathered into binary-branching metrical feet, constructed from right to left. The right branch of each foot is labeled "weak" or "w," and the left branch is labeled "strong" or "s."

The first (or rightmost) foot is quantity-sensitive,[4] that is, the weak branch of this foot cannot be assigned to a branching rime, or one that contains more than one segment. Therefore, in words with final syllables containing branching rimes, the first foot will necessarily be nonbranching and labeled "s." Nonbranching feet elsewhere in the word are not labeled at the foot level. Examples are given in Examples 12.1a and 12.1b (R and F stand for rime and foot).

Feet are gathered into a third level of metrical structure, known as the *word tree*. In Spanish, the word tree is constructed by joining feet together in binary-branching units labeled beginning at the right edge of the word. Some examples are given in Example 12.2 (W in the vertical column stands for word).

The system described so far can account for the unmarked pattern of stress assignment in Spanish words: vowel-final words with primary stress on the penultimate syllable (Example 12.2a), and consonant-final words that have primary stress on the final syllable (Example 12.2b).

---

4 It is actually a minor simplification of the facts to say that only the rightmost foot is quantity-sensitive, but it will have no impact on the issues being explored here (cf. Harris 1983: 111, 122).

Example 12.1

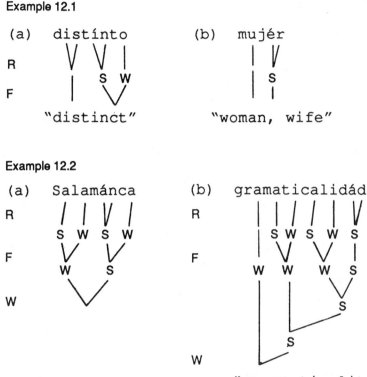

(a) distínto

R

F

"distinct"

(b) mujér

"woman, wife"

Example 12.2

(a) Salamánca

R

F

W

(b) gramaticalidád

R

F

W

"grammaticality"

However, as mentioned earlier, there are a considerable number of words whose stress markings do not follow the unmarked pattern. These include vowel-final words with antepenultimate stress (*métrico, naúfrago*) and final stress (*Panamá, dominó*) and consonant-final words with penultimate stress (*útil, jóven*). In order to account for these patterns, Harris introduces two additional concepts: (1) extrametricality, which is an aspect of metrical theory; and (2) the morphological distinction between derivational stems and terminal elements.

Extrametricality is a feature that characterizes elements left out of the prosodic structure at certain stages in the derivation of a word. It is represented orthographically by crossing out extrametrical elements with a slash mark. In Spanish, extrametricality may apply to elements within rimes, and these are generally recorded in the lexicon. Elements marked as extrametrical are invisible to foot-building rules and thus remain outside of the prosodic structure until the final stage in the derivation of a word, when they are incorporated by the universal convention of Stray Rime Adjunction (Harris 1983:98):

Example 12.3 Extrametricality

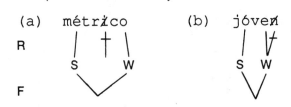

(a) métrico   (b) jóven

Example 12.4 Stray Rime Adjunction and other rules

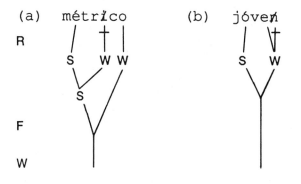

(a) métrico   (b) jóven

Adjoin a stray rime as a weak node of an adjoining foot, in a structure-preserving manner (one that preserves the labeling... of branching of the relevant metrical structures).

The effect of extrametricality and Stray Rime Adjunction on metrical structure is illustrated in Examples 12.3 and 12.4, in which it is apparent that in words with extrametrical elements, stress may be shifted further to the left.

Extrametricality in Spanish is constrained by another universal convention, the Peripherality Condition, which dictates that all extrametrical rime elements be peripheral, "that is, not separated from the edges of their morphological domains by any other element on the same level of representation" (Harris 1983:98). Here, "level of representation" refers to the level of syllable rimes, the level on which extrametrical elements occur in Spanish. The Peripherality Condition may be represented as follows:

á → a / [X ___Y b Z]

The distribution of extrametrical elements is also governed by the morphological distinction between the derivational stem and the terminal element. The derivational stem consists of the root of a word, plus any derivational affixes. Terminal elements are inflectional elements that lie outside the derivational stem, but inside the domain of the word. In all but a few cases, the terminal elements are vowels: *a, e,* or *o.* In formal notation, the derivational stem of a word is set in parentheses, as shown in the following examples.

[(bonít) o]   [(métric) o]
"pretty, handsome"   "metric"

Extrametricality normally occurs only in derivational stems, not terminal elements. There is one exception to this generalization: Terminal elements rarely contain consonants, but when they do, these are extrametrical. This can be expressed in a phonological rule (where C stands for consonant, WD for word, and Z for anything in the terminal element which might precede the consonant) which Harris (1983:115) calls "Predictable Extrametricality":

$$C \rightarrow \mathcal{C} / [\,(\ldots)\, Z \underline{}]_{wd}$$

The Peripherality Condition and the rule of Predictable Extrametricality apply to lexical representations before any metrical structure has been created. The effect of these rules can be seen in the following examples:

[(núm*é*r) o]   →   n.a.
  number
[(num*é*r + ós) o]   →   [(numer + ós) o]
  numerous
[(bícep̸) s]   →   [(bícep̸) s̸]
  biceps

With the addition of extrametricality, governed by the Peripherality Condition and the rule of Predictable Extrametricality, the rule system described here can account for the stress markings of the vast majority of Spanish words (see Harris 1983). It is now possible to examine how well these rules account for the patterns of stress assignment observed in the interlanguage of Spanish speakers learning English.

The Spanish stress rules correctly predict the two major classes of words that Spanish speakers stress incorrectly: words ending in −VGC#, and words ending in −VGC + stress-neutral suffix. According to the interlanguage data (see list of test words), Spanish speakers assign primary stress to the syllable containing the −VGC rime in words of these two types. Since words ending in −VGC# (without a suffix) end in a branching rime, which must be assigned a strong foot, applying the Spanish stress rules in a straightforward manner, without introducing any extrametrical elements, will produce the stress patterns in Example 12.5.

These rules will also generate the interlanguage stress pattern seen in words ending in −VGC + stress-neutral suffix, if one follows the ad-

Example 12.5

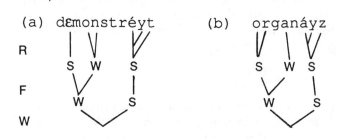

(a) dɛmonstréyt   (b) organáyz

ditional rules laid out by Harris for assigning stress in words with suffixes added. According to Harris's analysis (see Harris 1983:122ff), stress rules apply cyclically at the level of the word in Spanish. This means that when a suffix is added to a word, it is not incorporated into the prosodic structure of that word until a later cycle. Furthermore, this process of incorporation takes place "with the minimal alternation in existing structure that yields a well-formed tree" (Harris 1983:124). Thus, in words ending in − VGC + stress-neutral suffix, primary stress will be assigned to the syllable containing the − VGC rime on the first cycle, and will remain on this syllable when the suffix is incorporated into the prosodic structure on the next cycle.

One assumption must be made in order to derive the correct prosodic structure for words like [apəréytər] and [ædvərtáysɪŋ]: The final segments in the stress-neutral suffixes added to these words must be marked extrametrical in the lexicon, thus allowing the remaining elements of these suffixes to be adjoined to the existing structure as the weak node of the rightmost foot.[5] This is illustrated in Example 12.6.

As explained earlier, however, a successful analysis of the interlanguage data must satisfactorily account not only for the learners' errors but for those aspects of the target language they reproduce correctly, which means the Spanish stress rules must also account for the words that Spanish speakers get right. In fact, they cannot. When these rules are applied to words in several of the structural categories the language learners stress correctly, the rules predict that the learners will get them wrong. Representative examples of these categories are given in Examples 12.7–12.9.

---

5 It must also be assumed that in the stress-neutral suffixes added to words like [ædvərtáysmɪnt], which have rimes containing a vowel followed by more than a single consonant, the final element in the rime − which was rarely pronounced by the informants − is not present in the phonemic representation. Otherwise, because of the effects of the Peripherality Condition, at least two nonextrametrical elements will be present in these suffixes, and it will not be possible to adjoin them as the weak node of a metrical foot.

Example 12.6

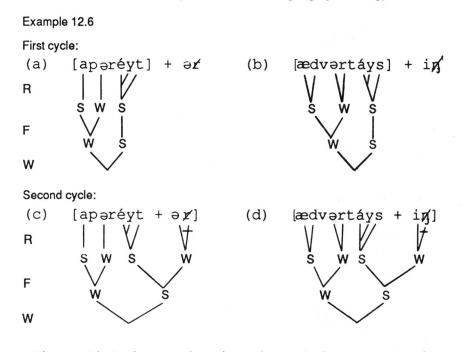

First cycle:

(a) [apəréyt] + əɾ   (b) [ædvərtáys] + iŋ

(c) [apəréyt + əɾ]   (d) [ædvərtáys + iŋ]

Second cycle:

The asterisks in the examples refer to the metrical structure given for each word. It indicates that this structure is incorrect, since it assigns primary stress to the wrong rime. The rime supposed to receive primary stress is indicated by a stress mark. The strong foot at the right edge of the words in Example 12.8 was assigned by the Strong Foot Rule, according to which all word-final vowels and glides in words with no terminal elements are assigned a nonbranching strong foot (Harris 1983:118).

The metrical structure in these examples was derived according to the stress rules of Spanish. In each case, the derived structure assigns stress to the last syllable, while according to the data gathered in this study, Spanish speakers correctly assign stress to the antepenultimate or initial syllable, as indicated by the stress marks placed above the words.

Examples 12.7–12.9 represent a considerable body of data which the Spanish stress rules cannot account for, clearly indicating that the interlanguage stress system of Spanish speakers acquiring English is not based on a direct transfer of these rules from their native language. This does not necessarily mean that the Spanish speakers' interlanguage stress system is not strongly influenced by the stress rules of their native language, however, for it could be that when language learners transfer native language stress rules to an interlanguage grammar, they alter these rules in ways they believe necessary to capture important generalizations about stress in the target language.

Example 12.7
(a) with open penult   (b) with closed penult

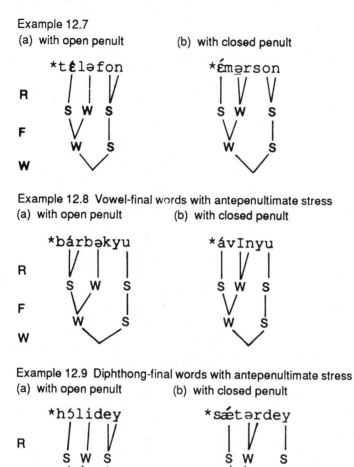

Example 12.8 Vowel-final words with antepenultimate stress
(a) with open penult   (b) with closed penult

Example 12.9 Diphthong-final words with antepenultimate stress
(a) with open penult   (b) with closed penult

If this is the case, then it should be possible to identify revisions which could be made in the Spanish stress system that would account for virtually all of the interlanguage data, including the words that the learners stress correctly. The revisions would need to be relatively conservative, preserving the core aspects of the Spanish system so that it would be reasonable to claim that the "revised" stress system had been derived from it. Also, the revisions should be ones likely to be made by Spanish speakers, in that they are motivated either by differences all Spanish speakers might perceive between their native language and English, or by principles of markedness.

Careful consideration of the facts reveals, however, that there is no such reasonable and well-motivated set of revisions that could be made in the Spanish stress system to resolve the inconsistencies found between the interlanguage data and the patterns of stress assignment predicted by the rules of the Spanish speakers' native language system. Two possible solutions were considered in Mairs (1985), but both of these not only failed to satisfy the criteria just outlined but were deficient in other respects as well.

In short, neither a direct transfer of stress rules from the learners' native language nor a stress system derived from the native language by means of some reasonable and motivated changes in the native language stress rules accounts for the interlanguage data. Thus, the source of Spanish speakers' interlanguage stress rules must be sought in some other component of their linguistic competence.

Universal tendencies and the acquired target language stress system

In this section, two other hypotheses will be considered. One is that the rules that produce the observed interlanguage stress patterns are based on universal tendencies of stress assignment; the second is that the rules are based on the Spanish speakers' acquired knowledge of the target language stress system.

"Universal tendencies of stress assignment" refers to two concepts that might play a role in a language learner's selection of rules for stress. The first is the simplicity metric, which may well govern the second langauge learner's choices between otherwise equivalent rules (or rule sets). The other is the principle of markedness, which is used to account for the fact that certain kinds of rules appear to be much more uncommon, or "marked," than others. According to the theory of markedness, this disparity reflects some as yet unspecified aspects of human cognitive structures or innate linguistic competence (Chomsky 1981).

Theoretically, second language learners' attempts to formulate rules for stress could be completely governed by considerations of simplicity and markedness. That is, the learners could ignore much of the target language data and devise a stress system that was as simple and unmarked as possible. However, that is clearly not the case here. The data presented earlier demonstrate that the interlanguage stress system of Spanish speakers learning English cannot be described using simple and unmarked rules. (See Hayes 1981: chapter 3 for examples of simple and unmarked rules.) The stress patterns produced by these language learners are varied and complex. Furthermore, the stress patterns are quite similar to those of native speakers of English, which are known to be the product of an unusually complicated stress system. It is still possible, however, that the concepts of simplicity and markedness play a secondary role in the Spanish speakers' formulation of rules for stress. This possibility will be considered later.

The second hypothesis is that the stress system of these learners is based primarily on acquired knowledge of the target language system. To test this hypothesis, it is necessary to identify the changes that would have to be made in the target language system in order for it to account for the interlanguage data. Then it would be necessary to determine whether or not these changes can be independently motivated.

The model used here to represent the English stress system is the metrical analysis proposed by Hayes (1981). Because this model already offers a satisfactory account of stress assignment in words Spanish speakers stress correctly, modifications are needed only to account for those words Spanish speakers stress incorrectly. Therefore, our consideration of the Hayes's model will be limited to those aspects of the system which apply to words in this latter group.

As in Harris's metrical analysis of Spanish stress, the rules in Hayes's system apply on the rime projection. The first rule of foot construction, Long Vowel Stressing, assigns a nonbranching foot to word-final rimes containing long vowels. Hayes categorizes English vowels as long and short (Hayes 1981:147), after Halle (1977).

Long		*Short*	
divine	pounce	pit	put
obscene	moon	pet	putt
vane	vote	pat	pot
Bermuda		impudent	
point			
Catawba			
Chicago			

In order to demonstrate this rule more concretely, Long Vowel Stressing has been applied to representative examples of the two word types Spanish speakers stress incorrectly: [organáyz] and [ɛksərsáys] (noun), which end in – VGC#; and [kælkuléytər], which ends in – VGC + stress-neutral suffix. Since in English as in Spanish, stress assignment is cyclic at the level of the word (Hayes 1981:162), the [- r] suffix in [kælkuléytər] will not be incorporated until the second cycle.

Long Vowel Stressing – first cycle

```
    organáyz      ɛksərsáys (n.)     [ kælkuléyt ] + ər
R   or a ayź      ɛk ər ayś          æl u eyt
F        |             |                  |
```

After Long Vowel Stressing, two rules apply which cause the final elements of words to become extrametrical. The first is Consonant Extrametricality, according to which all consonants at the end of a word are marked extrametrical. The second is Noun Extrametricality, which causes the entire final rime of nouns to be marked extrametrical. The Consonant Extrametricality Rule, according to Hayes (1981:150), is as follows:

$[+\text{cons}] \rightarrow [+\text{ex}] / \underline{\hspace{1cm}}]_{wd}$

Some examples are:

(a) organáyz   (b) ɛksərsáys   (c) [kælkuléyt] + ər
R   or a ay\z̷   ɛk ər ay\s̷   [æl u ey\t̷
F | | |

The Noun Extrametricality Rule (Hayes 1981:152) can be expressed as:

$\text{Rime} \rightarrow [+\text{ex}] / \underline{\hspace{1cm}}]_{noun}$

The following example illustrates it.

(a) NA   (b) ɛksərsáys (n.)   (c) NA
R   ɛk ər á\y̷\s̷
F |

Following the extrametricality rules, the English Stress Rule applies. This rule has the marked characteristic of being able to delete a structure that has been assigned earlier in a derivation (Hayes 1981:165). Any foot constructed at the right edge of a word by a previous rule, such as Long Vowel Stressing, will be removed, and the English Stress Rule will construct another in its place. However, if all the segments contained in a pre-existing foot have been marked extrametrical, this foot is "invisible" and cannot be deleted. The English Stress Rule will then construct a foot immediately to the left of the extrametrical foot. As Hayes (1981:150) expressed it: "At the right edge of the word, form a [quantity-sensitive] binary foot on the rime projection, with the left node dominant."

In such words as [organayz] and [kælkuleyt + ər], the foot constructed by Long Vowel Stressing will be deleted and replaced by the English Stress Rule. Because the foot assigned to the word [ɛksərsays] is now extrametrical as a result of Noun Extrametricality, it is not subject to deletion by the English Stress Rule. A second foot will be constructed to the left of the existing one in this word, as shown below.

(a) organáyz   (b)ɛksərsáys   (c) [kælkuléyt] + ər
R   or a ay\z̷   ɛk ər á\y̷\s̷   æl u ey\t̷
F | | ✝ |

Note that in all three examples a nonbranching foot has been constructed, since the feet assigned by the English Stress Rule are quantity-

Example 12.10 Strong Retraction

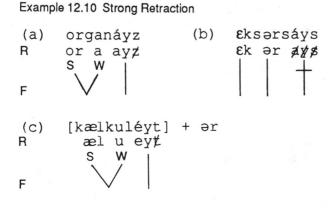

(a)   organáyz   (b)   ɛksərsáys

Example 12.11 Sonorant Destressing

(a)   ɛksərsáys

sensitive, and in all three examples the rightmost available syllable contained a branching rime.

The final rule of foot construction is Strong Retraction, which assigns left-dominant, binary branching feet, going from right to left, to all the remaining syllable rimes in a word (Hayes 1981). If there is an odd number of syllables remaining, the leftmost rime will be assigned a nonbranching foot. The application of this rule is shown in Example 12.10.

Following the assignment of metrical feet to all the available rimes, one last extrametricality rule, Trisyllabic Extrametricality, applies. But first, words such as [ɛksərsays], which contain two adjacent nonbranching feet, with the second ending in a sonorant, undergo the rule of Sonorant Destressing (Hayes 1981:174). This collapses the two nonbranching feet into a single, binary foot, as shown in Example 12.11.

According to Trisyllabic Extrametricality, the final rime in any word of three or more syllables must be marked extrametrical. This applies to the representations of Strong Retraction and Sonorant Destressing, so that the final rimes of these words are marked extrametrical. With respect to [ɛksərsáys], the application of this rule is vacuous.

All feet that are not extrametrical are then gathered into binary-branching word trees. Trees are labeled according to the rule: "Make right nodes strong" (Hayes 1981:197). In the representations in Example

Example 12.12 Initial word-tree construction and labeling

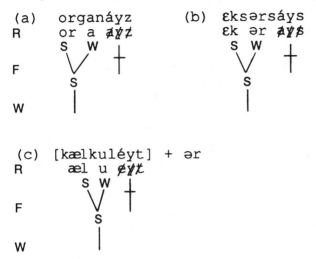

12.12, the only existing word tree nodes have been labeled strong. After the initial word tree construction and labeling, any remaining feet not already incorporated into the tree are incorporated into the existing structure through the process of Stray Foot Adjunction (Hayes 1981:197). This process, patterned after the universal convention of Stray Rime Adjunction, adjoins unincorporated feet as weak members of the word tree, just as Stray Rime Adjunction incorporates stray units on a lower level of prosodic structure. This is illustrated in Example 12.13.

For words such as [organayz] and [ɛksərsayz], which have no suffixes, the process of stress assignment is now complete. But for [kælkuleyt + ər], which has the stress-neutral suffix [− ər], an additional step is required to incorporate this suffix into the prosodic structure. Stress-neutral suffixes are joined up as weak members of existing word trees on a second cycle through a process like Stray Foot Adjunction. Note that the extrametricality markings imposed on the first cycle are erased on the next cycle as a result of the Peripherality Condition.

As can be seen from the final representations in Examples 12.13 and 12.14, the English stress system assigns primary stress to the left of the syllable containing the − VGC rime in words ending in − VGC# and − VGC + stress-neutral suffix. Primary stress is two syllables to the left if the preceding syllable is open or contains only a vowel followed by a sonorant; otherwise one syllable to the left, as in *kaopéctate*. However, native speakers of Spanish assign stress to the syllable containing the − VGC rime in words of these two types: [organáyz] and [kælkuléytər]. Therefore, the set of rules just described cannot be used to account for

Example 12.13 Stray Foot Adjunction

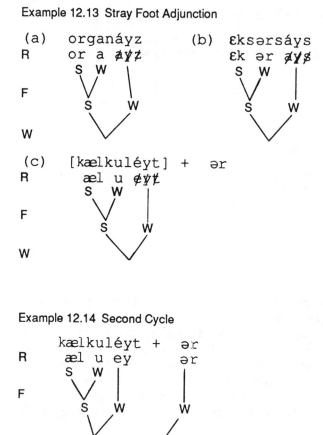

(a)   organáyz   (b)   ɛksərsáys

(c)   [kælkuléyt]   +   ər

Example 12.14 Second Cycle

these speakers' interlanguage stress assignment in these cases. It remains to be seen whether these rules can be altered in some relatively simple way so that they generate the stress patterns seen in the Spanish speakers' interlanguage, and if so, whether the changes can be independently motivated.

If some means can be found to alter the English stress system so that it assigns stress to the syllable containing the −VGC rime in words ending in −VGC# (without a suffix), the same changes will enable it to assign stress to this syllable in words with stress-neutral suffixes. As illustrated in Example 12.14, adding a stress-neutral suffix to a word does not effect its prosodic structure; the suffix is merely adjoined as a weak branch of the existing word tree. Therefore, once primary stress

Example 12.15 Without Noun Extrametricality and Trisyllabic Extrametricality

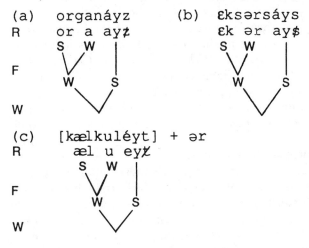

(a)   organáyz   (b)   ɛksərsáys
R   or a ayz̷   ɛk ər ay$

(c)   [kælkuléyt] + ər
R   æl u eyz̷

is assigned to the final syllable of a word ending in − VGC on the first cycle, it will remain on this syllable even if a stress-neutral suffix is added.

One means of altering the English Stress System to produce the desired results would be to discard the two rules that cause the final rime of a word to become extrametrical: Noun Extrametricality and Trisyllable Extrametricality. In words ending in − VGC# or − VGC + stress-neutral suffix, the foot containing the − VGC rime would then be incorporated into the word tree and labeled *s* during word tree construction and labeling on the first cycle, as shown in Example 12.15. However, if Noun Extrametricality and Trisyllabic Extrametricality were discarded, the stress system would make the wrong predictions about stress assignment elsewhere in the interlanguage data. Without the rules imposing extrametricality on word-final rimes, it would be impossible to derive antepenultimate stress within a single cycle, since neither of the two rules which construct feet at the right edge of a word (Long Vowel Stressing and the English Stress Rule) can construct anything larger than a binary foot. And a substantial portion of the words Spanish speakers stress correctly are assigned antepenultimate stress on the first cycle (e.g., ǽtltud, kómpani, dífɪkulti).

Finding a solution

Evidently, suppressing the rules of rime extrametricality will not produce a stress system capable of generating the interlangauge data. However, if these rules could be prevented from applying in words that end in − VGC on the first cycle, yet still play a role in the derivation of words of other structural types, then this revised version of the English stress system would make the correct predictions about stress assignment in all of the interlanguage data. Words that end in − VGC# would be assigned primary stress on the syllable containing the − VGC configuration, and stress would remain on that syllable in words that have a stress-neutral suffix added. Stress assignment in all other word types, which were already well accounted for under the original system, would remain unchanged.

This small adjustment in the English stress system would enable it to account for all of the stress patterns found in the interlanguage of Spanish speakers learning English. But in order to establish that this is a reasonable change for Spanish speakers to make in adapting the English stress rules to their interlanguage stress system, some independent motivation − based on the speakers' previous linguistic experience − must be found for restricting the application of the extrametricality rules.

Now is the time to consider the possibility that universal tendencies of stress assignment are playing a secondary role in the Spanish speakers' formulation of interlanguage stress rules for English. It is worth asking, for example, whether a stress system in which the rules of rime extrametricality do not apply to words ending in − VGC on the first cycle could be considered more simple and/or less marked than the English stress system. However, because such a system would require an additional distinction to be made between rime configurations before certain rule applications, it would be more complicated, not less.

Fortunately, motivation for this restriction on extrametricality can be found in the fact that the rime − VGC appears to be highly marked for Spanish speakers. In fact, this configuration occurs only once in Spanish, in *auxilio* ([awksilio]). Because of native speakers' strong negative reactions to nonsense words containing − VGC rimes, Harris concludes that these rimes are ungrammatical in Spanish and that the existence of *auxilio* is an "extrasystematic oddity" (Harris 1983:16). If these rimes are ungrammatical in their mother tongue, then it is reasonable to assume that Spanish speakers consider them marked.

If − VGC is a marked configuration for a syllable rime, Spanish speakers might have trouble constructing rimes with these elements, causing the rimes to remain divided into separate units, such as − VG and − C. The Peripherality Condition, which prohibits extrametrical elements anywhere but at the edge of the relevant domain, would then prevent extrametricality rules from applying to any but the rightmost unit. In short, the proposed failure of Noun Extrametricality and Trisyllabic Extrametricality to apply to − VGC rimes in the Spanish speakers' interlanguage can be seen as a natural consequence of markedness and the Peripherality Condition.

This restriction on rule application in the Spanish speakers' interlanguage can be formulated as a general condition on rule application in interlanguage grammars, known as the Marked Rime Hypothesis: Rules of rime extrametricality fail to apply to entire rimes which are marked for second language learners.

Governed by this condition, English stress rules in second language acquisition will now generate the correct interlanguage stress patterns for words ending in −VGC# and −VGC + stress-neutral suffix. But in order to demonstrate the applicability of this approach to the full set of interlanguage data, the other rimes in the data must be considered. For in addition to −VGC, there are other rime configurations that appear to be ungrammatical for Spanish speakers and that should be as difficult for them to accept as well-formed rimes. The configuration of −VCC does not occur at all in Spanish rimes, and −VGN occurs only rarely and is not accepted by native speakers in nonsense words (Harris 1983:15). According to the condition in the Marked Rime Hypothesis, one would expect that words ending in these rimes also fail to undergo the rules of rime extrametricality and are assigned primary stress on the final syllable.

Of the three test words in the data ending in −VCC# on the first cycle, two are assigned stress on the syllable containing the −VCC rime ([dIskonékt], [Intəréstiŋ]), as the Marked Rime Hypothesis predicts. And while the third ([dÍfIkulti]) is stressed on the pre-antepenultimate syllable, suggesting that Spanish speakers are able to apply the rules of rime extrametricality to the −VCC rime of this word on the first cycle, it seems likely that the stress pattern of this word is more reflective of the learners' familiarity with the lexical item (particularly the root word *difficult*, which subjects used often in casual conversation with antepenultimate stress) than of any fault with the condition proposed in the hypothesis.

Only one word in the data ends in −VGN − *paramount*, which is consistently pronounced by the informants without the final *t* ([paramawn]). As with *difficulty*, the antepenultimate stress pattern assigned to *paramount* ([páramawn]) suggests that Spanish speakers are able to apply rime extrametricality rules to the final syllable of this word. If further empirical research were to prove the stress pattern of [páramawn] to be representative of words ending in −VGN,[6] it would be necessary

---

6 This is unlikely, due to methodological obstacles. No other English words could be found ending in this rime configuration that Spanish speakers in the intermediate stages of acquiring English could pronounce with relative fluency.

to allow for the possibility that Spanish speakers can apply rime extrametricality rules to words ending in this configuration. Fortunately, the Marked Rime Hypothesis can easily be made consistent with this possibility.

Although −VGN is a marked rime in Spanish, it does not appear to be quite as marginal as −VGC or −VCC (Harris 1983:16). Because −VGN is more familiar than the other rimes to Spanish speakers, it is reasonable to suppose that they can construct well-formed rimes of this phonological shape even if unable to do so with −VGC or −VCC. Thus, one can still claim that Spanish speakers cannot apply rules of rime extrametricality to words ending in marked rimes, even in the face of data which indicate that words ending in −VGN are subject to these rules.

In sum, the Marked Rime Hypothesis appears to be consistent with all of the available data on interlanguage words ending in marked rimes. And given this constraint on the application of rules of rime extrametricality in the interlanguage grammar of Spanish speakers learning English, the English stress rules can account for virtually all of the interlanguage data.

There is one small segment of the data that remains to be accounted for. It was mentioned earlier that in addition to words ending in −VGC# and −VGC + stress-neutral suffix, there were five other words the informants stressed incorrectly. In order to claim that the target language stress system, by invoking the Marked Rime Hypothesis, accounts for the interlanguage data, it is necessary to show that the interlanguage stress patterns of these five words can be derived using this system. The five words are:

interesting [Intəréstiŋ]
Budweiser   [bədwáyzər]
helicopter   [ɛlikóptər]
interview   [Intərvyú]
televisions [tɛləvíšəns]

Interesting ends in a marked rime on the first cycle ([- ɛst]), so its penultimate stress pattern is consistent with the revised version of the English stress system, as governed by the Marked Rime Hypothesis. The interlanguage stress patterns of *Budweiser* and *helicopter* can also be derived under this system, even without the Marked Rime Hypothesis. Both these words are apparently treated somewhat exceptionally by native speakers of English, for a regular application of Hayes's stress rules would result in the penultimate stress patterns assigned to these words by speakers of Spanish.

In order to account for the interlanguage stress patterns of *interview* and *televisions*, one need only consider the interlanguage treatment of compound words. In a pilot study of compound stress conducted with the first nine informants, it was found that native speakers of Spanish show a strong tendency to assign primary stress to the second element in a compound phrase. Since this is the correct rule for compound stress in their native language, it is likely that this pattern is due to transfer.

Accounting for the stress patterns of these five words demonstrates that the English stress system, as described by Hayes, can be used to generate the stress patterns found in the Spanish speakers' interlanguage. No changes in this system itself are required. It is only necessary to assume that some kind of ill-formed internal structure exists for these rime configurations, which are marked for Spanish speakers learning English. This would account for the failure of Noun Extrametricality and Trisyllabic Extrametricality to apply fully to words ending in these rimes.

Summary and conclusion

Early in this chapter, it was suggested that there are three components of a second language learner's linguistic knowledge and experience that might contribute to the development of his or her interlanguage stress system: (1) the learner's native language stress system, (2) knowledge of universal tendencies of stress assignment, and (3) acquired knowledge of the target language system. An effort was then made to determine whether any of these components could be used to derive a satisfactory account of data collected on stress in the interlanguage of Spanish speakers learning English.

While stress systems based on universal tendencies or on the Spanish speakers' native language stress rules did not appear to account for the interlanguage data, it was determined that all of the stress patterns that did occur in the data can be generated by the target language stress system, given the independently motivated condition on rule application formulated in the Marked Rime Hypothesis. This hypothesis, which states that second language learners fail to apply rules of rime extra-metricality fully to rimes that are highly marked in their native language, assumes that if a series of segments does not constitute a well-formed rime in a speaker's native language, the speaker will have difficulty constructing a well-formed rime of these segments in his or her inter-language speech – an assumption upheld by recent research in inter-language phonology (Tarone 1980; Broselow 1984a, b). Given this difficulty, it is furthermore assumed that at least one of the segments of these ill-formed rimes will remain disassociated from the others and will then fail to undergo rime extrametricality rules because of the Peripherality Condition, a universal convention which limits extrametricality to the edge of the domain of rule application.

On the basis of the findings in this study, one may tentatively conclude that during the intermediate stages of Spanish speakers' acquisition of a stress system for English, the role of transfer is limited to the influence of the learner's native-language syllable structure constraints on the learner's ability to apply target language stress rules. The stress rules of the native language do not appear to play a role in this process, except perhaps at the level of phrases or compound words.

These findings on the role of native-language syllable structure rules are consistent with the conclusions reached by Broselow (1984a, b) and Tarone (1980), who also found interlanguage errors attributable to transfer of these rules. However, unlike the errors described by Broselow and Tarone, the effects of the transfer reported in this study are not directly observable in the restructuring of target language syllables in accordance with native language rules. Instead, they are observable in the indirect effect they have on the learners' application of phonological rules to syllables that violate the syllable structure constraints of their native language.

The results of this analysis further suggest that while transfer of constraints on native-language syllable structure may be important in developing interlanguage grammars and influencing a number of different levels of grammatical structure, the tendency to transfer stress rules from the learner's native language may be less pervasive.

Further empirical research on stress assignment in interlanguage phonology is needed to test the predictive value as well as the explanatory adequacy of these tentative conclusions. In addition to exploring other cases of systematic errors in interlanguage stress assignment, it is important to conduct further research on markedness in rimes in order to determine whether the $-VGC$ and $-VCC$ rimes, categorized as marked for Spanish speakers, are universally marked as well. If so, this would suggest that the apparent failure of rules of rime extrametricality to apply to $-VGC$ and $-VCC$ in the Spanish speakers' interlanguage is a consequence of universal tendencies of syllable structure instead of the syllable structure constraints of the speakers' native language. Such results might lead to a different conclusion not only about the derivation of the Spanish speakers' interlanguage stress rules but about the relative importance of transfer and language universals in second language acquisition in general.

Finally, if one had not understood the internal structure of the syllable captured in the metrical theory of stress, it would have been difficult to come to any principled understanding of the role of transfer in the Spanish speakers' interlanguage stress rules. A standard generative approach to stress assignment would have enabled one to make the generalization that the Spanish speakers' stress errors occur in words ending in segmental configurations (such as −VGC) not permissible word-finally in their native language, but it would have made it difficult to identify a causal connection between these problematic configurations and the stress errors associated with them. The Peripherality Condition, which restricts the application of the rules of rime extrametricality, helps account for the difficulty Spanish speakers have in applying English stress rules to words ending in −VGC#, −VCC#, and perhaps −VGN#. This condition can be understood only within the framework of a theory of stress that recognizes the importance of the internal structure of the syllable. The contribution that metrical theory has therefore made to this analysis recommends further use of this approach in analyses of interlanguage phonology.

References

Broselow, E. 1984a. Nonobvious transfer: on predicting epenthesis errors. In *Language Transfer in Language Learning*, S. Gass and L. Selinker, eds. Rowley, Mass.: Newbury House.
  1984b. An investigation of transfer in second language phonology. *International Review of Applied Linguistics* 22: 253–70.
Chomsky, N. 1981. *Lectures on Government and Binding: The Pisa Lectures.* Dordrecht, The Netherlands: Foris.
Halle, M. 1977. Tenseness, vowel shift, and the phonology of the back vowels in modern English. *Linguistic Inquiry* 8: 611–25.
Harris, J. W. 1983. *Syllable Structure and Stress in Spanish: A Nonlinear Analysis.* Cambridge, Mass.: MIT Press.
Hayes, B. P. 1981. *A Metrical Theory of Stress Rules.* Ph.D. dissertation, Yale University. Reproduced by Indiana University Linguistics Club.
Kiparsky, P. 1979. Metrical structure assignment is cyclic. *Linguistic Inquiry* 10: 421–41.
Liberman, M., and A. Prince. 1977. On stress and linguistic rhythm. *Linguistic Inquiry* 8: 249–336.
Mairs, J. L. 1985. Stress assignment in interlanguage phonology: an analysis of the stress system of Spanish-speakers learning English. M.A. thesis, University of Texas at Austin.
Tarone, E. 1980. Some influences on the syllable structure of interlanguage phonology. *International Review of Applied Linguistics* 18: 139–52.

Index